OXFORD EARLY CHRISTIAN STUDIES

General Editors

Gillian Clark   Andrew Louth

THE OXFORD EARLY CHRISTIAN STUDIES series includes scholarly volumes on the thought and history of the early Christian centuries. Covering a wide range of Greek, Latin, and Oriental sources, the books are of interest to theologians, ancient historians, and specialists in the classical and Jewish worlds.

Titles in the series include:

Pelagius' Commentary on St Paul's Epistle to the Romans
Translated with introduction and commentary
T. S. de Bruyn (1993)

The Desert Fathers on Monastic Community
Graham Gould (1993)

Arator on the Acts of the Apostles
A Baptismal Commentary
Richard Hillier (1993)

Origen and the Life of the Stars
A History of an Idea
Alan Scott (1991) paperback (1994)

Athanasius and the Politics of Asceticism
David Brakke (1995)

Jerome's *Hebrew Questions on Genesis*
Translated with an introduction and commentary by
C. T. R. Hayward (1995)

Ambrose of Milan and the
End of the Nicene-Arian Conflicts
Daniel H. Williams (1995)

Arnobius of Sicca
Religious Conflict and Competition in the Age of Diocletian
Michael Bland Simmons (1995)

Gregory of Nyssa's Treatise
on the Inscriptions of the Psalms
Ronald E. Heine (1995)

Ascetics and Ambassadors of Christ
The Monasteries of Palestine 314–631
John Binns (1994) paperback (1996)

John of Scythopolis and the Dionysian Corpus
Annotating the Areopagite
Paul Rorem and John Lamoreaux (1998)

Ascetic Eucharists

Food and Drink in Early Christian Ritual Meals

ANDREW McGOWAN

CLARENDON PRESS · OXFORD

1999

Oxford University Press, Great Clarendon Street, Oxford OX2 6DP
Oxford New York
Athens Auckland Bangkok Bogotá Buenos Aires Calcutta
Cape Town Chennai Dar es Salaam Delhi Florence Hong Kong Istanbul
Karachi Kuala Lumpur Madrid Melbourne Mexico City Mumbai
Nairobi Paris São Paulo Singapore Taipei Tokyo Toronto Warsaw
and associated companies in
Berlin Ibadan

Oxford is a registered trade mark of Oxford University Press

Published in the United States
by Oxford University Press Inc., New York

© Andrew McGowan 1999

British Library Cataloguing in Publication Data
Data available

Library of Congress Cataloging in Publication Data
Ascetic Eucharists: food and drink in early Christian
ritual meals / Andrew McGowan.
(Oxford early Christian studies)
Includes bibliographical references and indexes.
1. Lord's Supper—History—Early church, ca. 30–600. 2. Food—
Religious aspects—Christianity—History of doctrines—Early
church, ca. 30–600. 3. Asceticism—History—Early church, ca.
30–600. I. Title. II. Series.
BV823.M39   1999   264'.36'09015–dc21   98–42962

ISBN 0-19-826972-2

1 3 5 7 9 10 8 6 4 2

Typeset by Joshua Associates Ltd., Oxford
Printed in Great Britain on acid-free paper by
Bookcraft (Bath) Ltd., Midsomer Norton

To my grandparents
in memoriam

Preface

The spate of recent publications examining meals, fasting, and asceticism in the New Testament and early Christianity means that the importance of food in these areas no longer needs to be demonstrated, even if the subject has yet to be exhausted. Of course in one sense it has never needed to be demonstrated, given the prominence of the eucharistic meal in so much of Christian history, and the great modern tradition of research on the history of the liturgy. One of the things this book tries to do is draw these two scholarly strands, of liturgical and social history, closer together for their mutual benefit. By examining what is a very specific phenomenon (and, some will still conclude no doubt, a marginal one), I hope at least to have raised much broader questions that will be fruitful both to those interested in the wider social history of early Christianity and to those concerned, whether historically or theologically, with the eucharist and its significance.

It may be all too obvious that this book began life as a doctoral dissertation. Most of its merits and flaws are those which I was willing to defend at the University of Notre Dame in 1996. I am happy to have the opportunity to thank again those whose support and help made its initial production possible: the University of Notre Dame for the award of a Presidential Fellowship and similarly the Anglican Diocese of Perth for a Sambell Scholarship; my Director, Harold W. Attridge, and Paul F. Bradshaw, Blake Leyerle, and Jerome Neyrey who served as my advisory committee, for their advice then and since and for their examples in similar fields of research; my wife and daughter, Nicole and Madeleine, for their support and encouragement.

I am most grateful to the series editors for their inclusion of this work in Oxford Early Christian Studies, and to them and an anonymous reader for the acuity and the modesty of their suggestions for revision. Hilary O'Shea and Elizabeth Alsop have offered very significant 'virtual' help to a far-flung author. There are others whose advice on specific issues, practical assistance with materials, or conversation during my initial research and since, has been invaluable: John Cavadini, Nancy Dallavalle, Laura Holt, Mary Gerhart, Lawrence Hoffman, Robert Kugler, Lester Ruth, and William Tabbernee must represent a list which would be far longer if exhaustive. This version has appeared in the midst of two enjoyable years teaching at the University of Notre Dame Australia in Fremantle. My thanks go to Michael Jackson, Dean of the College of Theology, and to the academic staff here for their collegial and congenial support.

There have been waggish suggestions that my interest in ancient food is not unrelated to my interest in its modern manifestations. However, the fact that this study is concerned with rather ascetic meals, distinguished by community rather than luxury, is a reminder of my most important culinary lesson, learnt at the simple (but not sparse) tables of my grandparents, to whom this book is dedicated; as they would have put it, 'better is a dinner of herbs where love is . . .' (Prov. 15: 17).

A. B. McG.

Fremantle
June 1998

Contents

Abbreviations   xi

1. Liturgy, Meal, and Society   1

   Food and Society   1
   Meal and Eucharist in Early Christianity   10
   Liturgy and History   18
   Interpreting Diversity   27
   Conclusion   32

2. Ordering Food in Graeco-Roman Antiquity   33

   Introduction   33
   Food and Drink   35
   The Banquet   45
   The Cuisine of Sacrifice   60
   Asceticism   67
   Conclusions   87

3. Food and Drink in Early Christian Ritual Meals   89

   Introduction   89
   Bread and Wine   91
   Cheese   95
   Milk and Honey   107
   Oil   115
   Salt   118
   Fruits and Vegetables   125
   Fish   127
   Summary   140

4. Bread and Water in Early Asian and Syrian Christianity   143

   Introduction   143
   Jewish–Christian Eucharistic Meals   144
   Justin Martyr   151
   Tatian and Friends   155
   Encratites, *Hydroparastatai*, and Apostolics   160
   Valentinian Bread and Water: Theodotus   162
   Marcion, Tertullian, and Montanism   164

Vienne and Lyons   169
Elkesaites and Manichees   170
Conclusions   173

5. Bread and Water in Radical Pseudepigrapha   175

Introduction   175
The Pseudo-Clementine Literature   176
The Apocryphal *Acts*   183
Conclusions   195

6. Orthodox Use of Bread and Water   199

Introduction   199
Pionius of Smyrna   199
Cyprian   204
Aquarians   211
Afterword: Later Ascetic Movements and the
Bread-and-Water Tradition   213

7. Bread and Water and the New Testament   218

Introduction   218
Bread and Water in the New Testament   219
The New Testament in the Bread-and-Water Tradition   239
Conclusion: Many Tables   249

8. To Gather the Fragments   251

Introduction   251
Describing the Bread-and-Water Tradition   252
Interpreting the Bread-and-Water Tradition   256
Asceticism and the Cuisine of Sacrifice   270
Conclusion   276

Select Bibliography   279

Index Locorum   295

Subject Index   307

Abbreviations

Other abbreviations for Biblical, ancient Jewish and Christian literature, and for reference works, are those of the *Journal of Biblical Literature* where applicable.

ABRL	Anchor Bible Reference Library
Act. Vercell.	*Acta Vercellenses* (Latin *Acts of Peter*)
Adv. Haer.	Irenaeus, *Adversus Haereses*
Adv. Jov.	Jerome, *Adversus Jovinianum*
Adv. Luc.	Jerome, *Adversus Luciferianos*
Adv. Marc.	Tertullian, *Adversus Marcionem*
Agr.	Cato the Elder, *De Agri Cultura*
Ann.	Tacitus, *Annales*
1 Apol., 2 Apol.	Justin Martyr, *First Apology* and *Second Apology*
Apol.	*Apologia*
Ap. Trad.	(Hippolytus), *Apostolic Tradition*
Brev. Hipp.	*Breviarium Hipponense*
Can(n).	Canon(s)
CCL	Corpus Christianorum Series Latina
CCSA	Corpus Christianorum Series Apocrypha
CMC	*Cologne Mani Codex*
Comm. in Amos	Jerome, *Commentariorum in Amos*
Comm. in Ep. ad Gal.	Jerome, *Commentariorum in Epistulam ad Galatas*
Comm. in Ep. ad Tit.	Jerome, *Commentariorum in Epistulam ad Titum*
Comm. in Is. Proph.	Jerome, *Commentarii in Isaiam Prophetam*
Comm. in Joh.	Origen, *Commentarius in Evangelium Johannis*
Comm. in Matt.	Origen, *Commentarii in Matthaeum*
Conc. Carth.	*Concilium Carthaginense*
Conf.	Augustine, *Confessions*
Cont.	Pseudo-Clementine *Homilies, Contestatio*
Contempl.	Philo, *De Vita Contemplativa*
Cyn.	Ps.-Lucian, *Cynicus*
Cyr.	Xenophon, *Cyropaedia*
De Abst.	Porphyry, *De Abstinentia*

De Antro Nymph.	Porphyry, *De Antro Nympharum*
De Bapt. contra Don.	Augustine, *De Baptismo contra Donatistos*
De Cat. Rud.	Augustine, *De Catechizandis Rudibus*
De Err. Prof. Rel.	Firmicus Maternus, *De Errore Profanarum Religionum*
De Haer.	Augustine, *De Haeresibus*
De Ieiun.	Tertullian, *De Ieiunio contra Psychicos*
Deip.	Athenaeus, *Deipnosophistae*
Dem.	Lucian, *Demonax*
De Medic. Antiq.	Hippocrates, *De Medicina Antiqua*
De Morte Pereg.	Lucian, *De Morte Peregrini*
De Myst.	Iamblichus, *De Mysteriis Aegyptorum*
De San. Praec.	Plutarch, *De Tuenda Sanitate Praecepta*
De Vita Pyth.	Iamblichus, *De Vita Pythagorica*
Dial.	Justin Martyr, *Dialogue with Trypho*
Div. Haer. Lib.	Filastrius, *Diversarum Haeresium Liber*
Dys.	Menander, *Dyskolos*
Ep.	*Epistulae* (*Letters*)
Ep. Clem.	Pseudo-Clementine *Homilies*, *Epistula Clementis*
Epig.	Martial, *Epigrammata*
Ep. Pet.	Pseudo-Clementine *Homilies*, *Epistula Petri*
Fam.	Cicero, *Epistulae ad Familiares*
fr.	fragment
Fug.	Lucian, *Fugitivi*
Haer. Fab.	Theodoret, *Haereticorum Fabularum Compendium*
HE	*Historia Ecclesiastica*
Hom.	Pseudo-Clementine *Homilies*
Hom. in Jer.	Origen, *Homiliae in Jeremiam*
Hom. in Matt.	John Chrysostom, *Homilia in Matthaeum*
Hymn. contra Haer.	Ephraem Syrus, *Hymni Contra Haereses*
Hypoth.	Philo, *Hypothetica* (*Apologia Pro Judaeos*)
IG	*Inscriptiones Graecae* (Berlin: G. de Gruyter, 1913–)
In Matt. Comm. Ser.	Origen, *In Matthaeum Commentariorum Series*
JECS	*Journal of Early Christian Studies*
JW	Josephus, *Jewish Wars*
Liber	Gregory of Tours, *Liber de Miraculis Beati Andreae Apostoli*

Lives	Diogenes Laertius, *Lives of the Famous Philosophers*
Mart. Perp.	*Martyrdom of Perpetua and Felicitas*
Mart. Pion.	*Martyrium Pionii*
Mart. Pol.	*Martyrium Polycarpi*
MGH	*Monumenta Germaniae Historica*
Mor.	Plutarch, *Moralia*
Most.	Plautus, *Mostellaria*
Nat.	Pliny the Elder, *Naturalis Historia*
NA	Aulus Gellius, *Noctes Atticae* (*Attic Nights*)
ND	Cicero, *De Natura Deorum*
Off.	Cicero, *De Officiis*
Oneir.	Artemidorus, *Oneirocriticon*
Orat.	Tatian, *Oratio ad Graecos*
Paed.	Clement of Alexandria, *Paedagogus*
Pan.	Epiphanius, *Panarion*
Phil.	Cicero, *Philippicae*
PO	Patrologia orientalis
Pol.	Aristotle, *Politics*
Praed. Haer.	'Praedestinatus', *Praedestinatorum Haeresis*
Prob.	Philo, *Quod Omnis Probus Liber Sit*
Quaest. Conv.	Plutarch, *Quaestiones Conviviales* (in *Moralia*)
Recog.	Pseudo-Clementine, *Recognitions*
Ref.	Hippolytus, *Refutatio Omnium Haeresium*
Rep.	Plato, *Republic*
Sat.	Horace, *Satirae*
Sept. Sap. Conv.	Plutarch, *Septem Sapientium Convivium*
Strom.	Clement of Alexandria, *Stromateis*
Symp.	*Symposium*
Tract.	Priscillian, *Tractatus*
Tract. in Io. Ev.	Augustine, *Tractatus in Iohannis Evangelium*
Vita Ant.	Athanasius, *Vita Antonii*
Vita Apoll.	Philostratus, *Vita Apollonii*
Vita Pyth.	Porphyry, *Vita Pythagorae*

I

Liturgy, Meal, and Society

FOOD AND SOCIETY

Introduction

There was a time, it seems, when history could be written as though people did not eat.[1] Not only has it often appeared that there were more interesting or worthy things about which to write, but as a leading theorist of food and meals has put it, 'food is a blinding fetish in our culture . . . It is more convenient for us to take a veterinary surgeon's view of food as animal feed, to think of it as mere bodily input, than to recognize its great symbolic force'.[2]

The force of food as a 'blinding fetish', as a means of sociability sometimes too obvious to attract attention, may lie in its mediation of nature and culture. As a realm of practice in which social relations are linked to a biological base, its use as a creator and symbol of various forms of sociability is almost inevitable, but bears with it significant potential for ideological use.[3] Since eating does involve biology, it is difficult and all the more necessary to explore the ways in which food is not really just the stuff of natural processes, as it may appear, but the stuff of society itself in various forms. As not merely plant or animal but bread or meat, food is always a matter of production, distribution, and exchange and hence of power. As plant or animal nevertheless, food provides a powerful medium for the expression of power relations, and one which invokes the legitimacy which the natural order so often brings with it. Those who control food, who distribute and sell it, who order its consumption by law and custom, control not merely the obvious fact of life but the forms of life as well. It is convenient that we consider food as

---

[1] Adalbert Hamman attributes this observation to Fernand Braudel, without further reference: 'Pour une lecture concrète des textes', in F. Paschke (ed.), *Überlieferungs-geschichtliche Untersuchungen*, TU 125 (Berlin: Akademie-Verlag, 1981), 285.

[2] Mary Douglas, 'Food as a System of Communication', *In the Active Voice* (London: Routledge & Kegan Paul, 1982), 123.

[3] As is the case with gender relations also. See Karen Fields's foreword to Nancy Jay, *Throughout Your Generations Forever: Sacrifice, Religion and Paternity* (Chicago: University of Chicago Press, 1992), p. xv.

fodder not merely because of the difficulty but also because of the threat involved in doing otherwise.

At the other extreme, however, lies an equal and opposite problem: the tendency to discuss, even at great length, particular acts of eating without considering the food involved as 'food' at all. This is particularly the case for discussion of the food of the Christian eucharist, whose history is at issue here. Not only have those theologically interested in the history of the eucharist as a source of authority for contemporary liturgy tended to regard the food of the eucharist in entirely divinized or sacramental terms, but also general theorists of religion have been inclined to keep secular food and religious sacraments far apart. As a result, in both ancient practice and modern discourse we see the character of the eucharist as meal and as food effaced, to the point that it becomes first token, merely ritualized food (but food none the less), and then in some cases not food at all. While this may be an accurate reflection of the development of eucharistic piety and practice,[4] it is not necessarily a complete or adequate account of just what the uses of food in eucharistic meals may have signified. That is to say, there may indeed have been a tendency for eucharistic meals gradually to become attenuated and purely token; this does not mean that accounts which assume that their significance was always purely that of tokens are historically adequate. If the eucharist is not only sacrament but also food, then the consideration of the ritual meals of early Christians as food and as acts of eating may be a useful contribution, not only from the point of view of those historians who have an interest in culture and social practice, but even for theologians and historians of liturgy.

In particular, this book will argue that serious consideration of the food and drink of the eucharistic meals of early Christianity in social and cultural perspective helps create the possibility of a new and somewhat different historical picture of the diversity of eucharistic practice in the first few centuries, as well as offering potential insight into the meanings of food in these various meals. In sum, this picture is one in which the well-known use of bread and wine is more than just a liturgical statement of the obvious, a continuation of the practice of Jesus at the Last Supper; it is, while the most common pattern of using food in eucharistic meals, not the only such pattern. While there are certain instances of foods such as cheese, milk, honey, oil, and salt being put to ritual use in communal Christian meals, the most important and most common alternative to

---

[4] See e.g. J. W. Riggs, 'From Gracious Table to Sacramental Elements: The Tradition History of Didache 9 and 10', *SecCent* 4 (1984), 83–101.

bread and wine was, it seems, the use of bread and water, or the omission of the cup altogether. This ascetic version of the eucharist was, I will argue, early and quite widespread, although certainly more common in some geographical areas and in communities whose self-understanding was, to risk anachronism, more counter-cultural or sectarian. The case for these conclusions will be made in the chapters ahead; first, some further attention needs to be paid to the method and rationale of this enquiry.

Food and Social Theory

It is a good thing that the rather mundane processes of eating have now become of interest not only to the social historian but also to anthropologists and other students of society and culture. In fact the ability of the historian to investigate this aspect of life owes much to anthropological and sociological investigations, from which it is possible to assert that there are some generalized aspects of meal practice, and of the relation of meal to society, that have significance for other aspects of social organization and action.[5] Cultural anthropology, in particular, provides some useful models for understanding food and meals in relation to other aspects of society and practice, suggesting first of all that food is indeed something worthy of study, not only because of its economic importance but because of its place in symbol and ritual. Since Durkheim at least, ritual action has been something to be studied in its own right as meaningful and useful, rather than as simply to be explained away or reduced to material or economic causes. From Durkheim through Lévi-Strauss to Mary Douglas there has been a continued discussion of the way in which food and meals can be understood largely by analogy with language, as a code or metaphor whose structure somehow patterns the structures of the universe of the participants.[6]

The suggestion, for instance, that the body of the individual may serve

[5] While there are various theories and studies which have contributed to this suggestion, the work of Mary Douglas stands out; see esp. 'Deciphering a Meal', *Implicit Meanings* (London: Routledge & Kegan Paul, 1975), 249–75.

[6] Lévi-Strauss's contributions such as *The Raw and the Cooked* (New York: Harper & Row, 1969) and 'The Culinary Triangle', (*Partisan Review*, 33 (1965), 586–95) remain of great theoretical interest; see also Roland Barthes's foray into this realm, 'Towards a Psychosociology of Contemporary Food Consumption', in R. Forster and O. Ranum (eds.), *Food and Drink in History* (Baltimore: Johns Hopkins University Press, 1979), 166–73). The summary of these and other theories from a qualified structuralist perspective by Roy C. Wood, *The Sociology of the Meal* (Edinburgh: Edinburgh University Press, 1995), is very helpful.

as a model on which the concerns of the social body may be acted out has received some attention in discussion of sexual asceticism in early Christianity, and for food and meals in New Testament texts.[7] Practices with regard to food, as indeed to sexuality and other aspects of bodily culture, may be understood as part of a system where levels of anxiety or openness might be reflected in terms of issues such as fasting and food prohibitions. More generally, Douglas also argues for an analogous relationship between meal practice and social organization, suggesting (for instance) with regard to a survey of modern British households, that 'with an entirely monophagous and unstructured diet we would have been surprised to find a structured family life'.[8] However unaware we may be of eating and meals as ritual action, they are highly significant even in a very secular society.

These interpretations tend to work by regarding food as code or metaphor, and that suggestion is fundamental for this study. The eucharistic meals of the early Church can be considered as revealing, to the careful observer, of the attitudes of Christians not only to food but to other important aspects of life and practice also. Nevertheless this suggestion is itself metaphorical and cannot be taken uncritically; food is *like* a metaphor, and in what follows it will be considered as such to the extent that is heuristically useful.[9] The process of deciphering a meal is not simply one of reducing the phenomenon of a meal or meal-tradition to another aspect of thought or practice. Rather, what seems most useful is some combination of reduction or of interpretation in terms related to

[7] Mary Douglas, *Natural Symbols: Explorations in Cosmology* (New York: Pantheon Books, 1982). This idea has been widely used, e.g. by Peter Brown, *The Body and Society: Men, Women, and Sexual Renunciation in Early Christianity* (New York: Columbia University Press, 1988), and by Jerome Neyrey, *Paul, in Other Words: A Cultural Reading of his Letters* (Louisville, Ky.: Westminster/John Knox, 1990). Douglas's use of the body in this sense has been criticized, e.g. by Michael Jackson, 'Knowledge of the Body', *Man*, NS 18 (1983), 327–45; Jackson prefers the concepts of Merleau-Ponty ('lived body') and Bourdieu ('habitus') as less abstract. This is an important corrective, but the extent of correction may depend on the degree to which one concept or another used in analysis, including 'metaphor', is itself to be regarded as metaphorical. Presumably Douglas understands 'symbol', and 'metaphor' or 'code' for that matter, as illuminating but not exhaustive ways of talking.

[8] Douglas, 'Food as a System of Communication', 86.

[9] See Jack Goody, *Cooking, Cuisine and Class: A Study in Comparative Sociology* (Cambridge: Cambridge University Press, 1982), 29–33. Goody comments critically on Douglas that culture must be related to society (particularly to economy) and history. Goody's contrast between the differentiated cuisines of Asia and Europe and the undifferentiated cuisines of pre-colonial Africa may mean that the patterns that Douglas's work encourages us to pursue are not universals, but related to the specific histories and culture involved.

other spheres of practice on the one hand, and of identifying the relationships between foods as 'signs' on the other. As Lévi-Strauss put it:

Science has only two ways of proceeding; it is either reductionist or structuralist. It is reductionist when it is possible to find out that complex phenomena on one level can be reduced to simple phenomena on another level . . . And when we are confronted by phenomena too complex to be reduced to phenomena of a lower order, then we can only approach them by looking to their relationships, that is, by trying to understand what kind of original system they make up.[10]

I will argue that meals and food, or at least the meals and food of early Christianity, are best understood by relating them to the world of culinary signification, itself part of a wider world of social signification. The foods of the ancient Christian eucharist are therefore to be set in the context of the patterns of eating in Graeco-Roman antiquity, which themselves need to be understood as part of systems of power.

Yet eating is not merely a sign of something else, but is among the most fundamental forms of social action there is; meals do not merely encode society, they are society, or a part of it. Jack Goody's suggestion that the relationship between meal and society is one of metonymy, rather than merely of metaphor, seems apt.[11] This means that, rather than imagining that we can ultimately decode meals and hence reduce them to other social structures, we ought to consider them as one aspect of social life which even has a certain autonomy and does not merely mask some other form of activity which itself determines and explains the uses of food.[12] Yet if it is not always entirely adequate to speak of a meal as an act of communication, it seems reasonable to say that a meal both creates, expresses, and reaffirms sociability in various ways. Food ought, then, to be related to the whole of the social system.

Another important contribution from social analysis is the kind of descriptive method involved in ethnography, in which the observer asks questions of participants and (so to speak) of observed data itself within a discrete society and culture, about just who does what, when, where, and why.[13] These rather simple concerns have at times been ignored by historians whose theoretical interests have led them to dismiss much of what might not have seemed immediately to be of interest with regard to

[10] Claude Lévi-Strauss, *Myth and Meaning* (New York: Schocken, 1979), 10.
[11] Goody, *Cooking, Cuisine and Class*, 30–1.
[12] Ibid. 150–3.
[13] Clifford Geertz, 'Thick Description: Toward an Interpretive Theory of Culture', *The Interpretation of Cultures: Selected Essays* (New York: Basic Books, 1973), 3–30.

meals, but which in the long term has the capacity to enrich (or to disqualify) results. Lévi-Strauss's distinction between the scientific or 'engineering' approach that starts with a theory or construct and seeks the events that correspond with it, and the process of *bricolage* which works unsystematically to relate one piece of evidence to another, expresses this helpfully.[14] While perhaps not ultimately a sustainable opposition,[15] the difference between these models offers some opportunity to consider the relatedness of the evidence in less ambitious ways, somewhere between the philological and archaeological tasks of actually establishing the existence of texts and artefacts, and those of grand theory which seeks to relate the pieces to some envisaged whole.

A further insight may be drawn from social-scientific discourse with particular relevance to the question of ritual meals, including those which no longer have a substantial nutritive content, in relation to other meals. To speak of food as a code, or even to acknowledge that meals are a system or subsystem of the symbolic universe of a given society, it would seem necessary that quite different meals are capable of being understood both as similar to, and as different from, one another. Douglas emphasizes the similarity:

The smallest, meanest meal metonymically figures the structure of the grandest, and each unit of the grand meal figures again the whole meal—or the meanest meal. The perspective created by these repetitive analogies invests the individual meal with additional meaning . . . A meal stays in the category of meal only in so far as it carries this structure which allows the part to recall the whole.[16]

This general suggestion, drawn with particular reference to the English bourgeoisie, will be taken up with reference to Christian meals, and provides an important part of the rationale for use of the terminology of 'meal' even for the eucharistic rituals which are often understood to be meals only in a most attenuated sense. While I will be suggesting that some eucharists were meals in terms of scale as well as symbol, it is important to acknowledge that no symbolic meal can quite escape comparison with the day-to-day meals of the community which celebrates it.[17] The historical difficulties involved in deciding e.g.

---

[14] See Lévi-Strauss, *The Savage Mind* (Chicago: University of Chicago Press, 1962), 16–36.

[15] Note the critique by Jacques Derrida, 'Structure, Sign and Play in the Discourse of the Human Sciences', *Writing and Difference* (Chicago: University of Chicago Press, 1978), 278–93.   [16] Douglas, 'Deciphering a Meal', 257.

[17] Perhaps, in the most high sacramental practices of the eucharist, the use of food and drink which are in fact quite unlike any other eaten, or even the removal of one or both

whether amounts of food are token or substantial, are not absolute obstacles to consideration of any eucharistic celebration as 'meal'. Neither is the question of whether or not a particular meal is sacral or eucharistic in a particular sense one which always and everywhere serves to divide certain meals from others absolutely. Even when the character of a particular meal has an importance that is denied to other meals, or seems to involve stress on some aspect of religious belief and/or social relations, this does not free it from being considered as 'meal'. Thus the choice of foods in a particular meal must be considered in the light of other choices made at other meals, and of the general value or significance these foods may have for a particular group or society. This study is therefore an attempt to establish something of the symbolic force that food had in these early communities for whom it was arguably rather more than fodder and rather less than fetish.

History and Social Theory

So far these are a number of ways in which social enquiry suggests helpful methods and approaches to the matter at hand. Yet the interests of the anthropologist at least tend to be rather different from those of the historian, whether this difference is a purely disciplinary or aesthetic matter or something deeper. The apparent preference for the isolated 'simple society', or tendency towards the conceptual isolation of a section of a complex society, exemplifies the fact that the anthropologist seeks repeatable patterns at some level, as do physical sciences; i.e. laws or at least testable theories which should achieve the same results when repeated. An isolated or closed system of some sort makes this exercise more likely to be achieved.

It is interesting and cautionary that although theorists such as Douglas and Goody have made perceptive suggestions as to the meaning and purpose of meals in contemporary industrial society, the model of anthropological observation of the 'simple society' is never far away. While there are good and perhaps incidental reasons for that, having to do with the history of the social sciences, the fact that food and meals are often pursued by analogy with the observation of a far distant and far different society is a further reminder that considering meals in one's own tradition and society is rather difficult. This is part of the problem of

elements from the actual eating and drinking process, are indicative of the force that eating and meals have, and of a consequent desire to make the eucharist seem something entirely *sui generis*.

food as 'fetish', as Douglas put it. The social-scientific approaches are heuristically useful partly because they enable us to take a certain distance in considering our own society, or another for which fresh insight is necessary.

For history however, the discernment of the common is an important but preliminary step in the discussion of the uncommon, and the naming of repeated patterns and structures may also be a part of the process of recognizing and naming uniqueness and difference. However valuable it may be to consider a group or culture as self-contained, there must ultimately be not only a comparison of cultures but an account of the concrete connections between them that are likely to have existed before one studied the other, and hence a qualification of any claims based on the isolation of one community by another for the purposes of analysis.[18]

To take foods as elements of a system of cuisine and of social relations does generally mean that it is important, in the first instance, to place them within a set of signs particular to the society and situation in question. Here history and social science need have no quarrel. Structuralist approaches, at least, will acknowledge this particularity freely, and seek the repeatable not in the signs themselves but in the relations between the signs. While not intending necessarily to endorse the claimed universality of binary oppositions fundamental to structuralism, this study will in fact make significant use of the possibility that signs and foods in particular may be comprehensible in terms of structured opposites. There is possible difficulty, however, in the structuralists' positing of the arbitrariness of the sign, the suggestion that its only meaning comes from the system in which it is placed. As discussions of gender symbolism have resisted this conclusion of arbitrariness, so too must a discussion of food;[19] not because food does not function symbolically or because its meaning is not specific to a particular system of signs or culture, but because the signs must be understood as historically formed by processes and relations including those of power. To view meals in terms of symbolism but not of power may serve to render invisible, or simply to legitimate, processes and structures responsible for the surfeit of some and the poverty of others.[20]

---

[18] The failure to proceed in this way has led to accusations of anthropology imitating or facilitating colonialism in its objectification of 'simple societies'.

[19] See Nancy Jay's important book, *Throughout Your Generations Forever*, which attempts to discuss sacrifice and patriarchy cross-culturally.

[20] Douglas's recent article 'The Gender of the Beloved', *Heythrop Journal*, 36 (1995), 397–408 expresses this dilemma but fails to overcome it, I think, dealing with the realms of power and symbolism as though separate.

The meaning of food is therefore, while contingent, not arbitrary but rather highly purposeful.

While it may seem futile to take up a moral cudgel against the inequities of the past, recognition of social processes as conflictual, rather than simply as the normal or natural by-products of social function, has some interpretative value. Actions with regard to food or anything else cannot always be properly understood in terms of established custom and shared values. There may be struggles in which the status of one person or group is pitted against the starvation of another, and there we are dealing with conflicting systems and values rather than simply identifying different *paroles* spoken in the same *langue*. There may still be the possibility of positing a common social or political backdrop for such forms of social action, but in terms of participation in the same economic and social processes rather than in terms of culture or shared assumptions and symbols alone.

While the usefulness of considering foods as an element of social history and as a form of symbolic action may be obvious, the consideration of the food of Christian ritual meals is a special case. Liturgists have considered the history of the eucharist with care and erudition, and the legitimacy of interpreting eucharistic meals and the uses of food therein largely on the basis of models drawn from comparison with other food and other cultures may seem to be dubious or reductionist, both historically and theologically. Certainly a claim that social science can explain the food of the eucharist would be presumptuous. The claim here will not, however, be that explanation can proceed from the identification of the repetition of patterns or by ignoring stated religious meanings, but rather that previous accounts of eucharistic practice have often been insufficiently historical in their imposition of constructs less beholden to historical accuracy (or perhaps even to Christian theology) than to claims to institutional power, and have not been able fully to consider the 'implicit meanings' in the aspects of meal practice including, but not limited to, food.

Thus, to the acknowledged usefulness of seeking repeated patterns in both liturgical and anthropological terms, we may add a concern for difference, and for change. The evidence for what have tended, in the quest for normative eucharistic procedures, to be dismissed as oddities of eucharistic practice, will lead us to consider certain forms of eucharistic eating as acts of resistance against dominant religious and social forces.

MEAL AND EUCHARIST IN EARLY CHRISTIANITY

Introduction

The period between the New Testament on the one hand, and the emergence of fuller texts and other evidence for liturgy after the recognition of Christianity by the Roman Empire on the other, is an especially important and difficult one for the historian, not least in terms of the form and development of eucharistic meals. On the one hand, the questions of the New Testament evidence of meals, while far from having been neatly resolved, have at least received copious attention and will continue to do so. On the other there seems to be no lack of interest, whether from the liturgists or other historians, in the evidence associated with the clearer picture of the fourth century and beyond.

This study will sometimes consider evidence from those two more fully examined categories of time and of literature in so far as they impinge on the practices of the second and third centuries, but by and large the period between the writing of the canonical documents and the emergence of the great Church recognized by the Roman Empire will be the subject of discussion. In setting up these particular boundaries of time we are also acknowledging that what is at issue is more than the illumination of difficulties concerning just what happened at certain meals themselves, but also the question of how the life of Christian communities changed in that same period from that of Jewish sect to that of Graeco-Roman religion, with all that entailed. The history of eating has the capacity to contribute to an understanding of more than the liturgical changes in that period.

'Eucharist' and Meal

While study of the history of early Christianity has recently seen an upsurge of interest in various aspects of social life and practice, and particularly in asceticism, only very limited attention has yet been given to the place of food and of meals therein.[21] There have been important

---

[21] Insights from social theory have been taken up and applied to NT texts in particular, but usually not far beyond. See esp. Gillian Feeley-Harnik, *The Lord's Table: Eucharist and Passover in Early Christianity* (Philadelphia: University of Pennsylvania Press, 1981), 1–23; Philip Esler, *Community and Gospel in Luke–Acts* (Cambridge: Cambridge University Press, 1987), 71–109; Halvor Moxnes, 'Meals and the New Community in Luke', *SEÅ* 51 (1987), 158–67; Jerome H. Neyrey, *Paul, in Other Words*, 75–146 and 'Ceremonies in Luke–Acts: The Case of Meals and Table Fellowship', in Neyrey (ed.), *The Social World of Luke–Acts: Models for Interpretation* (Peabody, Mass.: Hendrickson, 1991), 361–87.

studies of New Testament materials, from the historical Jesus through to Paul and the life of the communities revealed to some extent in the canonical documents, but scholarly interest in the social aspect of meals seems to wane as explicit talk of 'meal' and 'table-fellowship' fades somewhat in the sources and talk of 'eucharist' becomes more prominent.[22] This is an indication of the disappearance of the eucharist as food, both historically and for the historian, and these disappearances need to be distinguished, re-examined, and even challenged. The fact that the eucharist was eventually not a substantial meal but token in nature does not mean that it was always so. Liturgical historians have often tended to see the earliest eucharists as specific acts involving token foods within a meal, perhaps in part because of squeamishness about the possibility that the eucharistic bread and wine might have been eaten in substantial quantities. There also seems to be some difficulty in imagining even that bread and wine or water were in fact the typical, central, or only food and drink of a meal, at least for the majority of people; hence their use is taken to be odd, and necessarily sacramental in a somewhat anachronistic sense.[23]

I have already used terms such as 'eucharistic meal' and 'Christian ritual meal', referring to texts and practices generally called 'eucharist' as well as to the problematic *agape*, intending by this shift of phraseology not only to focus attention on these events as meals and not merely as liturgies, but also to suggest a somewhat open-ended approach to definition and inclusion.[24] The significance of a eucharistic meal is not limited to its apparent genetic connections with the Last Supper or any other model; nor is it determined solely by the use of the term 'eucharist'. Whatever the origins and antecedents of the various forms

[22] Fasting (not eating!) may seem to be something of an exception in that a number of recent discussions of asceticism give it some prominence; in Peter Brown's *The Body and Society* it makes brief but suggestive appearances (220–2). There is not yet an equivalent for early Christianity of Caroline Walker Bynum's *Holy Feast and Holy Fast: The Religious Significance of Food to Medieval Women* (Berkeley: University of California Press, 1987), despite Veronika Grimm, *From Feasting to Fasting, the Evolution of a Sin: Attitudes to Food in Late Antiquity* (London: Routledge, 1996).

[23] J. C. O'Neill's discussion has the merit of seeing that there is little or no evidence for the 'distinct act of worship . . . being disentangled from something embedded in a full-scale meal' ('Bread and Wine', *SJT* 48 (1995), 179) but resolves the problem in the wrong direction, I think, simply asserting that the elements of the eucharistic meal were always token and (even more remarkably) extending this quantitative assertion to other meals such as those described or prescribed in the Qumran library.

[24] One of the more suggestive studies is that of Bo Reicke, *Diakonie, Festfreude und Zelos in Verbindung mit der altchristlichen Agapenfeier*, Uppsala Universitets Årsskrift, 5 (1951) (Uppsala: Lundequistska, 1951), 9–15, who argues for consideration of the different meal traditions together, but under the title *agape*, which seems to me a problematic choice.

of meals attested in early Christian communities, they have value for the purposes of this exercise precisely as communal meals which, in the social-scientific terms discussed, can be seen as meaningful in relation to other aspects of thought and practice.

One thing Christian ritual meals in the early centuries virtually all seem to have in common is the giving of thanks (*eucharistia*) or of blessing (*eulogia*), commonly accepted as synonymous in at least some texts and communities as terminology of prayer. By 'eucharistic meals', therefore, I mean the communal meals of early Christians, in which these processes of giving thanks tended to play a central part. This rather inclusive definition is not intended as a denial of the value of attention to differences of terminology, procedure, or even origins, but rather as an assertion that the common elements even of rather different Christian ritual meals make them comprehensible as a whole, within which diversity must then be acknowledged. The creative imprecision involved in this move may not be the only way in which the relations between different meals in Christian tradition need to be explored, but it provides an opportunity to consider meals in their relatedness as well as in their difference.

I have already taken up Mary Douglas's suggestion that the analogies between different meals may be a sufficient basis on which to attempt some consideration of the Christian meal as 'meal' rather than purely as 'eucharist'. Two further sets of reasons may be added for taking this step, one narrowly historical and the other more theoretically informed. The first is that, as I have indicated, there were probably some instances, and perhaps many, where the eucharist was a meal (and not merely part of a meal) in the most literal sense of the word. Since, as will become evident, I do not understand early Christian meal practice as unitary in form, it is not my primary concern to suggest that this was always the case; but a number of instances will be considered further in which it is difficult or impossible to say that the eucharistic meal does not consist of a real or substantial meal. In these cases, at least, it will therefore be quite evident that the category of 'meal' can and should be employed in analysis of the texts and practices.

A second reason for the use of the categories of meal and food in discussion of the early eucharist has to do with the problem of the distinction between sacral or sacramental meals and secular or ordinary eating. These categories are widely employed and implied, and have even been argued as universal in human experience in terms of generalized theories of religion, but there is increasing doubt about the value or legitimacy of such a division of eating or of other experience, at least in the ancient Graeco-Roman world, including for early Christian communities. Discussions of other religious meals in antiquity by classicists and others have exposed the extent to which even earlier anthropological studies of mystery cults and sacrifice were informed, often unwittingly, by a set of assumptions that were the product of specifically Christian (and much later) categories. Under the influence of theories of the sacred and of sacrifice from such as Frazer, Durkheim, and Mauss, both Mithraic and Dionysiac cult-meals were often characterized as sacramental and thought to involve the eating of the god; these approaches seem now to have been dependent on the abstraction of sacramental theory from medieval and later Christian reflection on the eucharist. Rather than being keys to a generalized theory of the sacred, these earlier theories turn out to have been anachronistic. Theory of the sacral has often, in fact, been ideology of the sacral.[25]

A certain openness of mind is therefore necessary when considering the sacral quality of a given Christian meal. Not only must we be careful to avoid reading back full-blown theories of the presence of Christ in the elements, we must also be wary even of assuming the existence of well-defined realms of sacred and secular for ancient Christians and pagans alike. This is not by any means to say that there was no ordering of the sacred in antiquity, which there obviously was; but the ways in which persons, places, and objects took on and kept the sort of significance we call sacred was not necessarily the same as that of later Christian practice.[26] In the discussion of food and meals in Graeco-Roman antiquity in the next chapter I will take up and develop some suggestions about how the sacred or numinous might extend from obvious places of religious practice, such as temples, to the dining tables of what might otherwise be assumed to be 'secular' meals. For the moment I simply

---

[25] See the discussion and critique by Nancy Jay, *Throughout Your Generations Forever*, esp. 1–16 and 128–46. On the classical world, Marcel Detienne, 'Culinary Practices and the Spirit of Sacrifice', *The Cuisine of Sacrifice Among the Greeks* (Chicago: University of Chicago Press, 1989), 1–20; on the specific cases mentioned, J. P. Kane, 'The Mithraic Cult Meal in its Greek and Roman Environment', in John R. Hinnells (ed.), *Mithraic Studies: Proceedings of the First International Congress of Mithraic Studies* (2 vols.; Manchester: Manchester University Press, 1975), ii. 313–51, and Dirk Obbink, 'Dionysus Poured Out: Ancient and Modern Theories of Sacrifice and Cultural Formation', in Thomas H. Carpenter and Christopher A. Farraone (eds.), *Masks of Dionysus* (Ithaca, NY: Cornell University Press, 1993), 65–86.

[26] It may seem that to speak of 'the sacred' in this absolute sense risks the same sort of anachronism already mentioned; but the point here is not to construct or avoid general theories, but to deal with the ordering of space, time, food, etc. in a given society.

suggest that the distinctions between different foods and meals in the ancient world are not the same as those of 'sacred' and 'secular' or of 'sacrament' and 'meal' in common contemporary terminology. What distinctions did apply, and how they were of significance for the eucharistic meals of early Christianity, remains to be seen.

The Promise of Enquiring into 'Meals'

At its simplest, the neglect of eating and meals in the study of Christianity is therefore probably due to a certain difficulty in acknowledging that the ritual meals of Christians do, or at least in the earliest centuries did, qualify to be considered as meals *per se*. Instead they have been treated largely as specifically sacral acts whose nature belongs to the realm of worship and prayer, and hence have been interpreted together with actions less clearly related to the day-to-day. While in one sense this might seem more historical, at least in the sense of being more obviously related to the inner-Christian understanding of the practices in question, in fact it may also be understood simply as assimilation to a different set of cross-cultural categories, i.e. those of religion.

If it would be wrong to protest altogether the understanding that they are liturgical or sacral, the characterization of the eucharistic meals of early Christianity as acts that are only comprehensible in these terms tends to lead to further historical problems of two kinds. One is fairly conventional, to do with the question of what happened, where, and when; the other is to do with the related questions of meaning that follow on from our assumptions or conclusions about what happened.

While the discussion of Christian meals by the liturgical historians has led to great achievements and advances, it has also tended to place constraints on the interpretation of texts that have led to a less than adequate historical picture of just what people did. Since the evidence for the period between the New Testament writings and the fourth century is so fragmentary,[27] the imposition of a model more appropriate to a later stage has tended to be the way to resolve the questions of uncertainty of practice in the time between. This model has at times been not only anachronistic but simplistic or reductionist, in the sense that it has

---

[27] 'The early evidence on the eucharist is both fragmented and complicated. Not only its interpretation but its discovery is often a matter needing a very delicate discernment,' Gregory Dix, *The Shape of the Liturgy* (New York: Seabury, 1982), 209. 'The nearer we get to the earliest period the more bewildering, and apparently contradictory, the evidence becomes,' R. D. Richardson, 'A Further Enquiry into Eucharistic Origins', in Hans Lietzmann, *Mass and Lord's Supper* (Leiden: E. J. Brill, 1979), 266.

excluded practices which do not fit within the pattern; the strategies of exclusion will be discussed further below. This problem may also be understood as one of power, in the sense that the reading-back of later patterns functions as an ideology of legitimation for ecclesial order and practice.

The second problem is one of meaning, and concerns the neglect of the wider range of possibilities for interpretation that recent research and theoretical discussions such as those mentioned above have suggested may be applied to questions of eating and meals in general: that what people eat, where, when, how, and with whom, deserves discussion and analysis and can fruitfully be related to other questions of belief and practice. Lawrence A. Hoffman's work in Jewish liturgy exemplifies the fact that such interpretation can be done even within the framework of liturgical studies, but this is partly because his concern is focused on ritual as revealing Jewish community life as a 'discrete cultural system'; here I am concerned to set the particular evidence for early Christianity in the somewhat wider and more complex system of Graeco-Roman society, a choice which has much to do with the fact that Christian ritual was meal-based and drew heavily on other conventions.[28] This neglect, too, can be related to the questions of ideology and power in the history of scholarship. As the possibility of a diversity of practice is removed in the model that seeks uniformity, the possibility of a diversity of meanings is also removed.

It should be obvious that these issues are related, in the sense that a different reconstructive picture of Christian ritual meals in the second and third centuries will lead to a different basis on which interpretative discussion will seek to build. Yet the nature of the problem may already suggest how methods of interpretation in anthropology and social theory themselves have the capacity to contribute to the more specifically historical reconstructive project. Different questions might be asked from the perspective of one who seeks to describe the use of food in meals as part of the life of a given community, and to observe particular phenomena with a descriptive task related to the whole of social life and not merely to one aspect defined as religious, liturgical, or sacramental.

---

[28] See Lawrence A. Hoffman, *Beyond the Text: A Holistic Approach to Liturgy* (Bloomington, Ind.: Indiana University Press, 1987), 1–19, and 'Reconstructing Ritual as Identity and Culture', in Paul F. Bradshaw and Lawrence A. Hoffman (eds.), *The Making of Jewish and Christian Worship* (Notre Dame, Ind.: University of Notre Dame Press, 1991), 22–41.

History and Imagination

The evidence for early eucharistic meals is very sparse and difficult to interpret, and in order to make sense of it one must do more than merely establish the nature of the data with sufficient rigour to allow necessary conclusions to fall into place, as though naturally. Rather, we must engage in something more like a creative or imaginative process, just as students even of empirical sciences have been increasingly willing to do, in order to relate texts which often do not possess 'joins' with each other as though they were pieces of a larger puzzle.[29]

To pursue this puzzle metaphor for a moment, we may adapt it to something a little closer in time and space to the actual data to be discussed; it is as though we were archaeologists who have discovered a few fragments of a mosaic at a dig which has been disturbed; there is no longer a clear sense, for most practical purposes, of just how large the picture was, what it represented, or whether there might even have been more than multiple subjects or multiple pavements.[30] Our assumptions make a great deal of difference in determining the results. There can be no absolute answers, but only more or less adequate ones; and it is important to make explicit what historical adequacy means in this case.

A quest for historical adequacy of explanation and analysis of such a scattering of fragments should involve an emphasis on two things in particular: plausibility and inclusion. Criteria of plausibility can probably be arrived at without too much difficulty; to borrow from science again, hypotheses used to explain the evidence ought to be relatively simple. This principle is important but does not tell us where to start; it only provides a basis on which to reject a particular hypothesis or model. As for inclusion, there is little value in a solution which takes only a few of the fragments to construct a picture, however attractive, and leaves out much or even most of the evidence. This has probably been the most important deficiency in the bulk of attempts to reconstruct the eucharistic practice of early Christian communities. A new model or approach

---

[29] This process is discussed with explicit reference to Kuhn and Lakatos by Hoffman, 'Reconstructing Ritual as Identity and Culture', 22–41.

[30] Paul Bradshaw uses the imagery of a graph or connect-the-dots puzzle: 'All [the pieces of evidence] are, in effect, little more than a series of dots of varying sizes and density on a large sheet of plain paper . . . Because, however, the dots on this sheet of paper are not pre-numbered, and so the connections which should be made between them are by no means obvious, the assumptions and presuppositions with which one begins such an operation are vitally important in determining its outcome,' *The Search for the Origins of Christian Worship* (New York: Oxford University Press, 1992), 56.

must involve a conscious effort to account not merely for the fragments most like the kind of art pleasing to the observer, or even for the largest and otherwise most significant, but ought as far as possible to consider the implications of all the parts for the whole. The failure to consider diversity has not simply been the result of aesthetic preference for a simpler or more coherent picture, it has also been guided by the persistence in some quarters of inner-Christian polemics about authority and about liturgy. Very often the scholarly agenda is all too easy to relate to an ecclesiastical will-to-power.

The creative pictures that have dominated the investigation of early Christian meal practice have been provided by liturgical history, a close ally in this century and the last with liturgical theology. Liturgical historians have used great care in establishing the nature of the evidence with all the philological and historical tools available through critical study. Yet they have also used an interpretative model of a particular type, specifically a set of assumptions about the possible shape of early Christian meals which, while sometimes presented in terms of 'scientific' historical study, has actually also been very theological in nature.[31] It is not my purpose to pit science or history and theology against one another here; theologians and historians all make use of creative and imaginative faculties, as well as those of careful examination of evidence, in reaching their conclusions.[32] The difficulties that ought to be acknowledged in the liturgical historians' picture of early Christian meals are not so much to do with the inevitable exercise of creativity and imagination, as with the adequacy of the model constructed by the imagination to deal with the evidence at hand. But some fuller sense of this picture constructed by traditional scholarship is necessary before proceeding.

---

[31] Admittedly this is less true of Dix than of others. But note Josef Jungmann in *The Early Liturgy to the Time of Gregory the Great* (Notre Dame, Ind.: University of Notre Dame Press, 1959), 3–4: 'Liturgical history today has become a science . . . A scientific history of liturgy has existed since the sixteenth century'. See also the discussion by Bradshaw, *The Search for the Origins of Christian Worship*, 57–63, of the use of scientific paradigms by Baumstark, Bishop, and Cabrol; and further Fritz West, *The Comparative Liturgy of Anton Baumstark*, Alcuin/GROW Joint Liturgical Studies, 31 (Nottingham: Grove, 1995). Hoffman discusses the 'scientific' position of another major figure, Edward J. Kilmartin, in 'Reconstructing Ritual as Identity and Culture', 28–34.

[32] The imaginative voice at work here is not without its theological aspect either; ultimately, it seems to me, the historian also has to answer to value commitments which may be termed theological. Yet such a commitment is not an excuse for constructing the past we might like to have had in disregard of the evidence we do have.

LITURGY AND HISTORY

The Search for Uniformity

Before the rise of what we think of as modern critical method, it would seem that Christians of most centuries in most places understood the eucharistic meal practice of the early Church as rather like their own. Catholics and Orthodox understood their traditions to preserve the primitive forms of worship practised by Jesus and taught to the apostles. This conflation of first-century and later practice is made explicit by some examples of the so-called Church Order literature, which use a dialogue between the Saviour and the apostles as the literary frame for the prescription of order in worship.[33] Protestants did not regard maintenance of tradition as a guarantee of conformity to biblical models, but made explicit attempts to restore order, as well as faith, as they perceived it to be described and prescribed in the Bible. In either case there was what we might regard as a collapse of history upon itself, with an understanding that ancient and contemporary ritual were, or at least ought to be, exactly alike.

In the nineteenth century, wedges were driven between the ancient and later elements by the rise of historical-critical method. The renewed study of ancient texts enabled the recognition that there were important differences between various ancient, as well as between ancient and modern, liturgies. Attention focused for some time on a 'quest for the historical eucharistic prayer', a supposed archetype for all later forms. In this phase of research, scholars acknowledged that the prayers used at ritual meals were somewhat diverse, but nevertheless remained committed, for the most part, to the idea of an original form which could still be harmonized with the dogmatic assertion that the Christian eucharist was dominically instituted, i.e. that Jesus himself had founded it and prescribed its form and content.[34] Traditionalists seem to have tried to address the historical problems by swinging a rope from the Gospel accounts of the Last Supper (or the eucharistic meal-catechesis of Paul to the Corinthians on the same story) across centuries to the forms of liturgy attested in the later Church Order documents, attempting to arrange the intervening evidence along the line established.

---

[33] See Bradshaw, *The Search for the Origins of Christian Worship*, 80–110. More sophisticated versions of this theory were being pursued in the 17th–19th cents. based on the 'discovery' (in the West) of the *Apostolic Constitutions*: Bradshaw, ibid. 131–2.

[34] Ibid. 131–7. See further Louis Duchesne, *Origines du culte chrétien: Étude sur la liturgie latine avant Charlemagne*, 5th edn. (Paris: E. de Boccard, 1925).

Perhaps the single most important and influential shift since that time was the recasting by Dom Gregory Dix of this search for an archetype. Dix rejected the notion of a 'primitive standard type or model of eucharistic prayer' and what seemed inappropriate assumptions about original uniformity in liturgy.[35] He attempted to reconstruct the earliest history of eucharistic meals in terms that were at least somewhat radical, hinting that the 'institution narrative' of Jesus' Last Supper might not have been essential to the earliest eucharistic meal prayers.[36] Yet Dix dealt with the problem of variety in eucharistic prayers by positing a different kind of original uniformity: 'What was fixed and immutable everywhere in the second century was the outline or Shape of the Liturgy, what was *done*.'[37] Dix claimed to be able to abstract from the diversity of prayer texts and descriptions of eucharistic meals a core of *praxis* that was just as solid as the earlier scholars had thought the prayer itself must be. This consisted of the offertory or taking of bread and wine; the prayer of thanksgiving; the fraction or breaking of the bread; and the distribution and reception of the elements of bread and wine. 'In that form and in that order these four actions constituted the absolutely invariable nucleus of every eucharistic rite known to us throughout antiquity from the Euphrates to Gaul.'[38] In this emphasis on form, Dix's work exemplifies what became and continues to be a dominant theme in liturgical history and theology.[39]

The idea of *The Shape of the Liturgy* has continued to be very influential to the present day, and this influence is not undeserved. But how does this treatment stand up to the sort of analysis suggested earlier, the criteria of plausibility and of inclusion? Dix himself takes some pride in the way his thesis measures up to the former:

[35] Dix, *The Shape of the Liturgy*, 208–14.

[36] Ibid. 225–37. Here the difference between the way liturgists and New Testament scholars have dealt with these questions becomes obvious and indeed striking, since the uniformity assumed by the biblical scholars is based on the liturgical use of the institution narratives. Formally, however, the problems are very similar. Bruce Chilton engages in a critique not unlike my own, but directed against the influence of Joachim Jeremias's paschal identification of the Last Supper and the centrality of the institution narratives: *A Feast of Meanings: Eucharistic Theologies from Jesus through Johannine Circles*, NovTSup 72 (Leiden: E. J. Brill, 1994), 1–7.

[37] Dix, *The Shape of the Liturgy*, 214.

[38] Ibid. 48.

[39] See Gordon Lathrop, *Holy Things: A Liturgical Theology* (Minneapolis: Fortress, 1993), 15–83. In Lathrop's work the presence of structure (*ordo*) is itself seen as the key element, and a retreat from the insistence on a *particular* structure (whether Dix's position or that of Alexander Schmemann from whom the *ordo* concept is drawn) has thus taken place: the *ordo* for Sunday is no more specific than 'word and table'.

To me personally the most satisfying thing about the results at which we seem to have arrived is that at no stage of the argument does it require us to go beyond the known facts and the evidence as it stands. We require no silent revolutions accomplished by Antiochene gentile converts, no liturgical innovations by S. Paul, no pagan infiltrations from the mysteries, no inventions or misunderstandings of what happened at the last supper, to account for anything in eucharistic history. And there are no subsequent improbabilities or gaps in the evolution.[40]

Dix alludes here to some of the theories that seemed less than probable to him compared to his own picture. Yet not all of these were offered simply because of the exotic content of the materials their proponents used. There were (and are) others for whom a theory of single origin seems less than adequate, not so much for what it does not posit to explain the evidence, but simply because of the evidence which it does not include. Here is where Dix's theory, and any which bases itself on assumptions about uniformity, is at its weakest. To produce a comprehensive theory of 'the absolutely invariable nucleus of every eucharistic rite known to us throughout antiquity', whether formal or verbal, it is necessary to exclude some important evidence related to meals, and even to explicitly eucharistic meals, in ancient Christianity. Dix's theory is neat but not comprehensive.

In suggesting that the dominant approach to early Christian meals has not been adequate to encompass the apparent diversity of the evidence, I do not wish to suggest that there is no substance whatsoever to the picture of an emerging 'normative' tradition in Christian eucharistic worship,[41] but rather that attempts to portray all liturgical traditions other than those upon which the fourth-century pattern was based as eccentric, heretical, or simply trivial are exaggerated and unhelpful. By the late second or early third century there is a sense of agreement among most writers who would be termed 'orthodox' about certain key issues of the characteristic ritual meal of early Christianity. But the very significance of this picture depends on the context in which it emerges, in terms

---

[40] Dix, *The Shape of the Liturgy*, 232.

[41] This language comes not so much from liturgical discussions as those concerning doctrinal, and to some extent ethical, unity and diversity in early Christianity (and Judaism): see Arland J. Hultgren, *The Rise of Normative Christianity* (Minneapolis: Fortress, 1994). I will sometimes use the term 'normative tradition' in a somewhat modified way, to describe practices directly antecedent to the liturgies of the 4th and following centuries, and especially to the use of bread and wine (in that order) in imitation of the Last Supper of Jesus. It should not be assumed that the liturgical antecedents of the normative eucharist and the theological antecedents of orthodox Christianity are exactly the same.

of both the general background of the religions and society of the Graeco-Roman world, and also the evidence for forms of Christian practice that do not fit so well into this paradigm. Further, the same writers, Irenaeus, Tertullian, Justin, and Clement, are all important witnesses to odd practices, even in their own communities or traditions. No blueprint approach can really do justice to the criteria of inclusion adopted here.[42]

Since much of the rest of this study will be taken up with presenting some of that evidence and trying to relate it to the wider picture, two examples will have to suffice to illustrate the problems of inclusiveness in the Dixian model and the need to pass it by. The first is to do with the question of order which was the linchpin of Dix's quest for a fundamental unity; this further illustrates the value of an inclusive construct such as that of 'eucharistic meals' for present purposes. The second will serve to introduce the issue with which this study is most directly concerned, the use of food in eucharistic meals and particularly the tradition in which the elements of the eucharist were bread and water, not wine.

First Case: the Didache

The ancient text which may be the litmus test for the presuppositions of any modern theory of order in early Christian meals is the *Didache* or *Teaching of the Twelve Apostles*. This may be described as an early example of the Church Order literature, dating from sometime between the mid-first and mid-second centuries and consisting of instructions for ministry, baptism, moral exhortation, and a ritual meal. It includes what is apparently the earliest formulary or actual set of instructions for a eucharistic meal.[43]

The text of chapters 9 and 10 describes a meal called *eucharistia*, which uses bread and wine; yet there is no reference whatsoever to the Last Supper or to Jesus' death. This was not so much of a problem for Dix as were questions of order; the elements of the meal are dealt with in the 'wrong' order, with the cup first. On the basis of this question of order, Dix consigned the meal of the *Didache* to the obscure category of the

---

[42] Even a more explicitly theologically committed approach that acknowledges a quest for orthodoxy, and is willing to choose what fits a preconceived picture, cannot really understand what that picture means without considering the exceptions and contrasts.

[43] It may be objected that Paul provides something like that in 1 Cor. 11: 23–7, but I share the view of (e.g.) C. K. Barrett, that this is more like a model for behaviour than words to be recited: *A Commentary on the First Epistle to the Corinthians*, 2nd edn. (London: A. & C. Black, 1971), 264.

agape, understood to be another form of ritual meal whose very vagueness has often made it a convenient dumping ground for the unwanted meal evidence of the first few centuries.[44] Yet not only does the meal of the *Didache* use the term we might otherwise translate 'eucharist', it does not use the term *agape*. Not content with conceptually marginalizing the *Didache* evidence, Dix trivialized it as well, apparently intending to diminish the work by calling it 'a guide for the laity' and quite clearly intending to do so when speaking of 'these little *agape* prayers', when length was not the question at hand.[45]

This sort of strategy of marginalization is far from being unique to Dix. In other liturgical approaches to the *Didache*, some scholars have argued that the absence of 'body and blood' talk or of reference to the death of Jesus is a more serious objection than it was for Dix.[46] Others take the terminology of 'eucharist' more seriously, but argue that the same essential elements are simply hidden, assumed, or left out because of a *disciplina arcani*.[47] Either of these positions may also involve identifying the meal in the text as an *agape*; in this and other problematic cases, it is sometimes thought that there were two meals in the early church, one real (*agape*) and the other sacral (eucharist), which might in some cases be combined, but without essential confusion. Thus only the non-eucharistic meal is subject to analysis as 'meal' in any broader sense. Each commentary or study seems to provide its own variation on these themes. In all such cases there seems to be an a priori refusal to deal with evidence for eucharistic meals in terms other than the search for a previously defined norm.

Second Case: Bread and Water

The limitations of the Dixian model are more evident again when the specific questions of the use of food and drink, which are at the centre of

[44] Dix, *The Shape of the Liturgy*, 90–3. On the cup–bread eucharist, see further my note, ' "First Regarding the Cup": Papias and the Diversity of Early Eucharistic Practice', *JTS* NS 46 (1995), 551–5.

[45] Dix, *The Shape of the Liturgy*, 93.

[46] So (e.g.) Jungmann, *The Early Liturgy*, 35–6.

[47] See e.g. Willy Rordorf (ed.), *L'Eucharistie des premiers Chrétiens* (Paris: Éditions Beauchesne, 1976), 38 n. 3, 39, and 41, and now 'Die Mahlgebete in *Didache* Kap. 9–10: Ein neuer *status quaestionis*', *VC* 51 (1997), 229–46. Of course there are exceptions. For further examples relevant to this and the following discussion, see the opinions on *Didache* 9 and 10, essentially divided between eucharist and *agape*, collected in Kurt Niederwimmer's commentary: *Die Didache*, Kommentar zu den Apostolischen Vätern 1 (Göttingen: Vandenhoeck & Ruprecht, 1989), 173–80.

this study, are asked of the evidence. At the risk of blaming Dix for the omissions of a whole discipline, his insistence on a uniformity even of shape did not allow serious consideration to be given to questions either of the actual diversity of foodstuffs used in eucharistic meals, or of the significance of those foods used.

Dix's rhetorical strategy in dealing with the most significant exception to the tradition of using bread and wine, i.e. the eucharists involving water in the cup or no cup at all, was much the same as that of marginalization and trivialization already seen with reference to the meal of the *Didache*. These practices are 'abnormal' and 'peculiar', and their participants characterized by 'fanaticism', while the arguments used by some other scholars to suggest more careful consideration of these eucharists are 'childish' and 'staggering in their arbitrariness'.[48] Dix's judgements on the dates between which these practices can be confined verge on the tendentious: no earlier than 150 and no later than Cyprian's *Letter*, 63, i.e. 100 years later. As we shall see, while the lack of any adequate summary and discussion of the bread-and-water eucharists may have been a problem for Dix, even the evidence known to him suggests that the practice was much earlier and more widespread than he allows.

The End of Unity

These examples can only serve as an invitation to consider the question further; they do not do much more than problematize the position of Dix and the consensus of liturgical theologians and historians on the question of order. In what follows many more texts must be discussed to provide a sense of how often the traditional paradigms of uniformity cannot really account for what we find, at least in terms of the food and drink of eucharistic meals. For now I merely suggest that in the second and third centuries there may be as many instances where a text does not fit well within that 'nucleus of invariable order', or within other constructs related to the maintenance of a tradition concerned with the Last Supper of Jesus or the emergence of later liturgical practices, as there are exemplars of what came to be the dominant tradition.

This means that a different imaginative picture or paradigm is necessary. There may still be good reasons why it is important to distinguish, say, the meal of the *Didache* from other Christian ritual meals; the desirability of classification and analysis of specific traits is not at issue here. What is at issue is the refusal to deal seriously with texts

---

[48] Dix, *The Shape of the Liturgy*, 61–3.

which present evidence that simply falls outside the paradigm. Theological reasons may perhaps be adduced to favour one set of practices, but this is not to say that such reasons are adequate, either as theology or as history. For different scholars the paradigm varies somewhat, but in many cases there is some notion of an 'essential' eucharist which lurks above as archetype, while the evidence is sorted through for the exemplars that bear the stamp of authenticity. As more and more scholarship is examined, a common shape may be discerned for these transcendent forms of the eucharist: they are the abstractions of later liturgical practices, being read back into the problematic texts such as the *Didache*. It has already been suggested of late, with more and more force, that liturgical historians have tended to read into the scanty and diffuse evidence of the second and third centuries the later and clearer pictures of the fourth, and that this is historically problematic.[49] A metaphor used by another great liturgical scholar of this century, Josef Jungmann, makes for interesting comparison with the mosaic one I have suggested: 'The liturgy of the Catholic Church is an edifice in which we are still living today, and in essentials it is the same building in which Christians were already living ten or fifteen or even eighteen centuries ago . . . Hence we must look up the old building plans, for these will tell us what the architects of old really wanted . . .'[50]

The claim has thus tended to be that objective historical scholarship provides a picture of uniformity of practice, which then becomes the basis for liturgical theology. In fact the theological quest for order, or more specifically for uniformity, informs a historical quest that sorts evidence according to its ability to bolster that initial theological commitment.[51] The traditional picture is best understood as a theologically committed one, in which assumptions about the life of the high patristic period as a golden age for faith and order are manifest both in reconstruction of earlier evidence and in critique of later. If that picture or similar ones produced from the ecumenical convergence on liturgical questions in recent times have continued value for the interpretation of early evidence, it must be on a more explicitly theological basis.

---

[49] Bradshaw, *The Search for the Origins of Christian Worship*, 35–55.
[50] Jungmann, *The Early Liturgy*, 2.
[51] A point also made by Gordon Lathrop without the same negative connotations: *Holy Things*, 33–84, esp. 33–4.

Dual Origins

Not all students of early liturgies have followed the line of uniformity. The key figure in the most significant alternative tradition of interpretation of early eucharistic meals is Hans Lietzmann, whose key work *Messe und Herrenmahl* actually preceded Dix's and did have some influence on it.[52] Lietzmann developed most fully suggestions that there was a twofold, rather than a unitary, pattern among early eucharistic meals.[53] By considering differences between early eucharistic prayer forms in particular, but also making use of the arguments then still in circulation about deep distinctions between Pauline and Petrine or Jerusalem forms of earliest Christianity, Lietzmann sought to reconstruct two trajectories through the first 200 years or so. One led from Paul's interpretation of the Lord's Supper, focusing on the remembrance of the death of Jesus, seen as linked symbolically to pagan sacrificial meals, through to rites emphasizing this anamnesis such as the episcopal and baptismal eucharists of the '*Apostolic Tradition*' attributed to Hippolytus of Rome; this is the Pauline or Roman form. The other begins with other New Testament meals such as those of the resurrection appearances and the witness of the Acts of the Apostles to an ongoing practice of 'the breaking of the bread', understood as a sort of Jewish *ḥaburah* meal, and continues through the *Didache* to later eucharistic prayers which do not include the command to 'do this in memory' of Jesus such as the Liturgy of Sarapion; this is the Egyptian type. In the primitive form of this second type the bread was originally the sole element and remained the more significant one. Thus as far as general theories of eucharistic origins go, Lietzmann's has been the most important as far as recognizing the possible importance of departures from the expected pattern of using bread and wine, always and alone.

Lietzmann's argument has also been influential, but significantly less so than that of Dix (especially in the English-speaking world); some

---

[52] Hans Lietzmann, *Mass and Lord's Supper: A Study in the History of the Liturgy* (Leiden: E. J. Brill, 1979).

[53] Most fully prior to Lietzmann by Friedrich Spitta, *Zur Geschichte und Litteratur des Urchristentums* (3 vols.; Göttingen: Vandenhoeck & Ruprecht, 1893–1907), i. 207–337. Not all dichotomies suggested were as radical: a sort of distinction is made by Paul Drews between two forms of eucharistic meal within the *Didache* itself: 'Untersuchungen zur Didache', *ZNW* 5 (1904), 74–9. Edmund Bishop also makes a modest suggestion of two types in 'Observations on the Liturgy of Narsai', in R. H. Connolly, *The Liturgical Homilies of Narsai*, TextsS 8/1 (Cambridge: Cambridge University Press, 1909), 145, apparently meaning only tendencies in East and West in the use of institution narratives derived from different Synoptic Gospel accounts.

disciplinary boundaries may be at work here, in that the work of Lietzmann the New Testament scholar and historian has perhaps been better received in those fields, and that of Dix better received by liturgists and ecclesiastics. Lietzmann's proposals have a number of merits, not least that they answer some of the complaints already made against Dix with regard to the brushing aside of evidence. The *Didache* is not consigned to oblivion in Lietzmann's work but rather becomes the centrepiece of the envisaged development of one type of eucharistic meal.[54] So too, other instances of what are called *agape* meals are treated with more interest, not as second-class meals but as examples of a different type of some significance to the whole picture.[55] The bread-and-water tradition, with which much of this book is concerned, is given some prominence also, if not analysed entirely adequately.

But few have been able to undertake all the twists and turns necessary to follow Lietzmann to the end of the trail.[56] It seems likely that the inspiration or creative paradigm operative in this aspect of Lietzmann's work was the sort of dichotomy in early Christianity suggested especially by F. C. Baur, who argued that there were two types of theology and of church order in the earliest period, later fused into 'early catholicism'.[57] The merits of this theory are now acknowledged to be limited at best, and not surprisingly the evidence seems at times to be dealt with in a somewhat fast-and-loose manner to make it conform to the trajectories suggested. Neither the fully developed forms of the two models, nor the intermediate evidence for one or the other, really exhibit the characteristics they ought according to Lietzmann's hypotheses.[58] We may add that his interpretation of the odd uses of food, such as cheese and of the bread-and-water eucharists, as indicative of indifference to the food of the meals may owe as much or more to turn-of-the-century polemics on questions of order and freedom in worship than to the understandings native to the witnesses to the bread-and-water meals.[59] Too much special

[54] Lietzmann, *Mass and Lord's Supper*, 188–94.   [55] Ibid. 161–71, 195–203.

[56] Bradshaw, *The Search for the Origins of Christian Worship*, 51–5. Dix's criticism of the extent to which his opponents had to invoke complex and speculative elements does apply here to some extent.

[57] Dix describes the dual origin theory as 'only one more of those visitations by the ghost of F. C. Baur to which theological scholarship is still occasionally liable': *The Shape of the Liturgy*, 236.

[58] A cup is highlighted in the *Didache*, which supposedly exemplifies the model that should use bread only; the other example of this 'Jerusalem' form, the Lord's Supper of the *Apostolic Tradition*, is in the wrong (geographical) place, and so on.

[59] On those polemics and their effects on historical reconstruction of a related issue, see James Burtchaell, *From Synagogue to Church: Public Services and Offices in the Earliest Christian Communities* (Cambridge: Cambridge University Press, 1992).

pleading is required to preserve the dichotomy in the form in which it stands.

Yet just as Dix's move from preoccupation with prayer texts to questions of form will have lasting influence even if and when his overall model can no longer hold its ground, Lietzmann's willingness to acknowledge some fundamental diversity deserves to be considered further as a positive step in the historical reconstruction of early Christian meals. To anticipate the argument of this study somewhat, it may be fair to say that while his critics tended to argue that Lietzmann had exaggerated diversity of practice regarding the food and drink of eucharistic meals, he had in fact underestimated it.

INTERPRETING DIVERSITY

Models of Diversity

The question just posed has been that of the adequacy of traditional liturgical approaches to provide a reconstruction of early Christian meals that is historically plausible and takes sufficient account of the evidence available. Since the question is not simply one of technical skill or objectivity in dealing with evidence, but also one of dominant creative images or paradigms, it should be clear that something more than a call for greater accuracy or clarity must be involved in a positive proposal.[60] An acceptance of diversity, and hence a certain retreat from claims to unitary or even dichotomous eucharistic origins, is a necessary step before further progress can be made.[61]

Both Dix's and Lietzmann's proposals for reconstruction owed something to political models, or at least to understandings of the social organization and hierarchy of early Christian communities. For Dix, the unitary model of eucharistic worship presupposes a similar picture of Church authority; and in fact the relation of various texts to this authority is one of the bases on which he seeks to legitimate his decisions for inclusion or marginalization.[62] So too, Lietzmann's dual origin

---

[60] Hoffman, 'Reconstructing Ritual as Identity and Culture', 21–8.

[61] Thus Bradshaw's work represents the necessary step away from accepted models and assumptions, characterized by him as that of a 'splitter' of the data who works analytically rather than of the 'lumper' who seeks to bring it together (*The Search for the Origins of Christian Worship*, p. ix).

[62] See his discussion of the traditions using bread and water, *The Shape of the Liturgy*, 60–1.

theory, while less obviously beholden to a particular contemporary ecclesiastical agenda, has already been related to F. C. Baur's theory of Jewish–Gentile divisions and the emergence of *Frühkatholizismus*.

In the contemporary scholarly picture of the early development of Christian communities, significant consideration has to be given to the likelihood that local traditions of organization, as much as of theology, may have been diverse at the earliest accessible stages of Christianity, and even that 'heresy' may have preceded 'orthodoxy' in some cases at least; this theory of early diversity owes much to Walter Bauer.[63] Although there will continue to be qualms about the particular form of the Bauer hypothesis, there are also many indications that even the canonical documents which define 'orthodox' developments in the first and early second centuries arise from somewhat diverse settings, and that they are at times substantially different in theology.[64] The impact of this recognition of diversity in other fields of study related to early Christianity is sufficient to suggest that its application to the question of early Christian meals is overdue. To remedy this would mean, among other things, giving greater attention to the evidence that can be associated with particular communities where that is possible, with the expectation of more or less diverse results.[65]

The inadequacy of the traditional model to encompass the bulk of the evidence is not the only problem with which its defenders need to grapple. There have also been specific challenges to the historical value, or at least precise significance, of some key elements in the usual picture of an early and continuous normative tradition of eucharistic celebrations. Most obvious are the doubts increasingly being entertained about the date and authorship of the '*Apostolic Tradition*' attributed to

[63] W. Bauer, *Rechtgläubigkeit und Ketzerei im ältesten Christentum*, 2nd edn. (Tübingen: J. C. B. Mohr (Paul Siebeck), 1964); trans. as *Orthodoxy and Heresy in Earliest Christianity* (Philadelphia: Fortress, 1971).

[64] Other NT scholars have been quite adamant on the question of diversity even in the canonical books: compare the different versions and uses of this insight made by Ernst Käsemann, 'The Canon of the New Testament and the Unity of the Church', *Essays on New Testament Themes* (London: SCM, 1964), 95–107, and by Raymond Brown and John Meier, *Antioch and Rome: New Testament Cradles of Catholic Christianity* (New York: Paulist, 1983). The work of James M. Robinson and Helmut Koester represents the inheritance of Bauer more directly; see *Trajectories through Early Christianity* (Philadelphia: Fortress, 1971).

[65] The possibility or desirability of doing this may owe something to contemporary understandings of pluralism in Christianity and in society generally, but at least at the level of 'principles of falsification', I intend my own investigations to be governed more directly by the criteria specified, rather than by the attractiveness or usefulness of the picture of early Christianity thus assembled.

Hippolytus of Rome, regarded by Dix and his followers, but also by most scholars of this century, as the earliest known collection of liturgical materials, including prayers and other instructions for the conduct of eucharistic meals. The studies which call into doubt the date or authenticity of the texts, and hence their place in the reconstructed picture, also question the picture itself. It is in fact difficult to argue that a further revolution in paradigms is necessary in this case simply because of actual new data, which is really very limited; yet willingness to include or pay serious attention to data hitherto neglected or insufficiently carefully read may amount to a change not much less radical.[66] The work of scholars such as Paul F. Bradshaw has turned these specific doubts into what amounts to a challenge to the whole paradigm, although the shape of a new constructive approach to early Christian meals and early liturgy in general remains to be seen.

Genealogy and Structure

I have already suggested that the questions of social analysis and description on the one hand and those of historical reconstruction on the other are at least potentially linked; new methods of considering texts open up the possibility of a different reconstructive picture. The same is true of the potential for social description to contribute to the more interpretative questions of meaning.

The issue of origins has often dominated the consideration of the meaning of early Christian meals. While this is a reasonable field of enquiry in itself, the question of eucharistic origins has, at times, been so far pursued as to subvert other questions of eucharistic meaning. We have already seen the blueprint approach, which assumes a coherence and unity not merely between different eucharistic meals celebrated at one time in the past, but between those of different times, sufficient to extend the significance of the supposed archetype to all the subsequent manifestations. While Jungmann's statement about the 'intention of the architects' might imply a search for the creative will of an emergent corporate ecclesial authority in patristic times, there are Protestant versions of the same idea which differ only in the stress placed on the intention of Jesus, rather than on that of apostles or bishops. The same sort of concern would often seem to operate when New Testament scholars of whatever stripe debate the identification of the Last Supper of

[66] See further Bradshaw's 'Ten Principles for Interpreting Early Christian Liturgical Evidence', *The Search for the Origins of Christian Worship*, 56–79.

Jesus and a Passover meal; what is at stake seems to be not merely the reconstruction of that one event, but the nature of what is mediated historically through the ongoing tradition of eucharistic meals.[67] In either case the significance of the tradition of Christian meals is assumed to be exhausted by the origins of that tradition and particularly by the intention of the tradition's author(s).[68]

While more subtle than many in their development of the arguments, as in their reconstructions of the tradition, Dix's and Lietzmann's discussions share an assumption that the significance of the eucharistic meals they identify and discuss is to be sought largely in the alleged type of meal from which any later example is said to proceed. These are therefore similarly 'genetic' approaches at heart, in which the formal issues of shape or order which are more of interest to these scholars have taken the place of the problematic question of the actions or intentions of the historical Jesus or of the exalted role of the successors to the apostles.

Whether or not there is seen to be some ongoing theological significance, or even a controlling significance, in the origins of eucharistic meals (and whether these consist of the actions of Jesus or those of the earliest communities, of a Last Supper or of a meal-tradition among the first followers of Jesus during or after his lifetime, etc.) it is simply not adequate to reduce the meaning of those meals in later times to their origins. Whatever theological judgements may be made about what could be or should be normative, it is obvious that (e.g.) the Corinthian Christians and Paul had different understandings of the eucharist, and that the author of Jude had differences with some members of the audience of that letter over conduct at the *agape*.

Those who came to participate in the ritual meals of early Christianity did not do so in a vacuum, but rather with significant cultural expectations about foods, and especially about meals held by religious societies, whether Jewish or pagan. For them the eucharistic meal took on meaning not only as a result of the catechesis of a distant apostle or even the words of a present leader, but from the place all these words, actions, and foods took on in terms of the system of which they were a

---

[67] This sort of assumption is manifest to an extraordinary extent in O'Neill ('Bread and Wine', 169–78) for whom a carefully executed discussion of the chronology of Jesus' death and the paschal identification of the historical Last Supper (not that of the Gospels or Paul etc.) is deemed to be the most important step in resolving the nature of the early eucharist.

[68] Granted that origins are the explicit concern, this wider correlation of origins and meaning seems to be implicit in works as different in other respects as Jeremias's *The Eucharistic Words of Jesus* (New York: Scribner, 1966) and Burton Mack's *A Myth of Innocence: Mark and Christian Origins* (Philadelphia: Fortress, 1988).

part. What Wayne Meeks says about the practice of baptism in the Pauline communities is quite applicable to the significance of eucharistic meals also:

These passages have often been analyzed for their ideational content and for their parallels, connections, and possible antecedents in the history of religions. Our purpose is different; we are trying to see what baptism did for ordinary Christians, disregarding the question of where its elements may have come from and even the profounder theological beliefs that Paul and some of the other leaders associated with it, unless we can be sure those were integral to the common understanding.[69]

Some real attempts have been made to approach the New Testament texts regarding meals with these concerns in mind; it remains for such a task to be pursued beyond the first century or so.

This project would amount not to a reduction of particular phenomena to supposed origins, nor to the analysis of liturgical structures outside of the broader social and historical context, but to an account of the changing manifestations, structures, and meanings of a given practice. Each instance of a eucharistic meal, each text, prayer, indication of participation, and other aspect of practice ought to be examined not merely in the light of an assumed origin but in its own terms and in the terms of the participants, to the extent that we can reconstruct them. The same, most importantly for present purposes, is true of foods. The meaning of particular food and drink in a given instance cannot be reduced to the meaning these held at an earlier point; nor can the actual use of food and drink at one point in an acknowledged tradition of meals be seen as a guarantee of the same use at another point.

This study is not an attempt to write a new history of the eucharist and its development, but to take up one aspect of what will be necessary for such a history; the use and meaning of the most obvious elements of meals, foods themselves. It will also be limited in its focus not on the better-known tradition and its use of bread and wine but rather on the different patterns of use of foods, such as the 'addition' of 'odd' foods to the eucharistic meal, and particularly the important and neglected tradition based on use of bread and water. Fuller consideration of these will enable a more complete picture of early eucharistic diversity, as well as help shed light on the 'normative' tradition as rather more than the repetition of a command or maintenance of a custom, but as one profound possibility among others.

[69] W. Meeks, *The First Urban Christians: The Social World of the Apostle Paul* (New Haven: Yale University Press, 1983), 154.

CONCLUSION

The preceding discussion has argued the need for new approaches to early Christian meals. Despite their undoubted contributions to establishment of the actual evidence and to its interpretation, traditional liturgical approaches have not always provided adequate pictures of the whole, even in fairly straightforward historical terms. The tendency to exclude or marginalize important evidence, such as that for what will be termed a bread-and-water tradition of eucharistic meals, is the most obvious deficiency of such reconstructions in purely historical terms.

Further, the consideration of the Christian meal as a specifically liturgical act has had limiting consequences as well as positive ones. The recent development of new approaches from liturgical scholars does pave the way for a more adequate understanding of eucharistic meals, but necessitates moving beyond what might usually be called 'liturgical' texts and concerns. Recent approaches to food and meals offer some important possibilities for a fuller account taking into consideration implicit meanings. These possibilities now need to be considered in terms of the foods and meals known to the ancient Graeco-Roman world, before considering the specific evidence for the variety of uses of food and drink in early Christian ritual meals. Further questions must thus be asked of the texts to consider the history of early Christianity as though people did indeed eat.

2

Ordering Food in
Graeco-Roman Antiquity

INTRODUCTION

If the place of food and drink in the ritual meals of early Christianity is to be reconstructed and interpreted in the terms suggested in the previous chapter, a number of tasks must be undertaken. We need to deal not only with particular foods as specific to Christian ritual use, but with food in Graeco-Roman society, in the hope of seeing how the understandings and practices of specific Christian communities were related to those of the wider world. The uses of food must be described in a reasonably comprehensive way, and foods must be related to one another, in so far as we are considering them as symbols or signs whose meaning is not merely determined by nature, but is part of the general system of signification in the society under discussion. This means that we must deal not only with various foods as separate items or commodities, but with their uses and in particular therefore with meals and with the other ways, such as non-consumption, in which order can be established over food. We need also to avoid the assumption that this system of signs is entirely arbitrary, and hence the fallacy of regarding foods merely as code, representing something else such as power or sex, however much it is connected with other fundamental concerns and practices. Where some eat and others do not, food does more than merely *symbolize* power.

In this chapter the aim is therefore to begin to assemble a picture of foods and their uses in the wider world of which early Christianity was a part, starting with the relatively narrow expectations of the poor and moving to the highly complex and differentiated world of banquets, sacrifice, and matters for dispute regarding eating and meals, and particularly the edibility, desirability, or appropriateness of certain foods. Not all the foods or patterns of consumption discussed here will be of direct relevance to Christian ritual meals, although perhaps more of them will be than would otherwise be expected. The purpose in going further in discussion of foods themselves than simply to the common elements of eucharistic meals is to get some sense of the system as a whole, and of the desirable and even the fearsome foods which various members of society might eat, seek, or otherwise encounter. Similarly the discussion of the banquet and its forms serves the purpose of setting the scene before the narrower focus of the following chapters, and gives the opportunity to engage in critical discussion of theories of eucharistic origins in which the meaning of the foods employed is seen largely in terms of the meal models from which the eucharistic meal is supposed to be derived.

More difficult than simply obtaining the evidence are the interpretative questions of presenting it. Here I will begin by consciously accepting the somewhat artificial, but perhaps useful, process of categorization which might characterize ancient and modern 'scientific' studies alike, attempting merely to list foods that might have been widely available or highly prized, and in either case of some importance to ancient eaters. In the first section I will also give some passing attention to what is arguably the most fundamental aspect of order imposed upon food and revealed in diet, the economic and social power by which distribution is determined. Although quantity and nutrition are not the main subjects under discussion, these issues must always be kept in mind when considering the importance of particular foods and of food in general. After this I will deal with the relations between these 'signs', discussing further consumption and non-consumption under headings which may draw together the further issues of order of most concern to Christian and other eaters. These are: the Graeco-Roman banquet, the 'cuisine of sacrifice', and aspects of asceticism. These categories are not parallel or mutually exclusive, but overlap considerably. They do not represent schools of thought or discrete sets of issues as such, but ways in which ancient eaters and writers on the one hand, and modern scholars on the other, may have grouped various concerns about the form and content of meals. In each case some specific attention will be given to the ways in which these issues were reflected in Jewish meal practice, both because of the obvious importance of Jewish custom for the earliest Christian eating, but also in an effort to examine critically some of the operative assumptions (which have been especially prominent in discussion of the ascetic bread-and-water tradition of eucharistic meals) about just how Jewish and Christian meals ought to be regarded in relation to one another.

FOOD AND DRINK[1]

There is a reasonable amount of evidence about the diets and other aspects of meal practice of the peoples of the ancient Greek and Roman worlds. Apart from direct archaeological materials such as agricultural and hunting implements and actual remains of foods, utensils, and buildings where meals took place, there is a good deal of literary evidence as well as depictions of foods and their preparation in art.[2] Despite important variations from time to time and place to place, we can identify some prevalent patterns concerning food and drink which might reasonably be expected to apply to areas as distant from one another as Africa, Rome, and Syria throughout the period in question.[3] Since this study of Christian meals involves evidence taken from many regions from a period of more than two centuries, what follows is a rather general survey. We should also acknowledge, however, that through classical and late antiquity there were changes in eating patterns related to the increasing domestication of animal and plant species, and to other developments in economy and society. Commodity prices and incomes varied with changes in the wider world; so too did other influences and expectations. Nevertheless it seems reasonable to assert that the main elements of food and cuisine can be subject to generalization.

If we can, with due care, move back and forth across provincial boundaries and the space of a few centuries to gather evidence about foods, we cannot afford not to exercise discrimination as to what was available to people of different classes.[4] Although the literary evidence

[1] The solid/liquid division seems a well-recognized one for foods in antiquity, despite there having been some preparations or mixtures of a semi-solid nature; see Artemidorus, *Oneirocriticon*, 1. 65. It would perhaps be more accurate again to speak in terms of three somewhat different categories: staple, relish, and drink (cf. Thucydides, 1. 138. 5).

[2] It will be obvious that I have concentrated on literary evidence, partly in the interests of constructing a picture of the perceptions of foods and not of mere fodder issues; but see the brief example and discussion of Peter Garnsey, 'Mass Diet and Nutrition in the City of Rome', *Nourir la plèbe: Actes du colloque tenu a Genève les 28 et 29 IX 1989 en hommage à Denis van Berchem*, Schweizerische Beiträge zur Altertumswissenschaft, 22 (Basle: F. Reinhardt, 1991), 67–99, esp. 86–8.

[3] The apparent conflation of Greek and African evidence in the works of Latin authors, bemoaned by J. André, *L'Alimentation et la cuisine à Rome* (Paris: C. Klincksieck, 1961), 15, whose interest was specifically Roman, is perhaps an advantage for this study. On the other hand Andrew Dalby's gastronomically oriented history of Greek food acknowledges a certain homogenization because of increased trade from Hellenistic times on: *Siren Feasts: A History of Food and Gastronomy in Greece* (London: Routledge, 1996), 133–6.

[4] See also Garnsey, 'Mass Diet and Nutrition', 67–70, who emphasizes Greek and Roman differences as well as urban and rural ones.

is that which provides most detail, it must be treated with care or even suspicion. The interests of ancient authors on agriculture, natural history, and medicine, as well as those concerned more directly with food, tend both to reflect the lives of the élite and to follow systems either drawn from élite experience or simply of their own making, which taken uncritically could suggest a greater variety and quality of foods than most people were likely to have often or ever eaten. The treatise of 'Apicius' on cooking, *De Re Coquinaria*, is concerned with a range of dishes and ingredients largely reflecting what we might call the sumptuary cuisine of Rome. Pliny's *Natural History* displays the schematic interests of a would-be scientific observer. Galen's opinions are of course concerned with optimizing health, but need to be related more closely to evidence for the available resources before a real benefit to the many, rather than only the few, can be assumed. All these treatments reflect lives in which significant varieties of foods were available, but also where the configurations of those foods were highly differentiated and specialized, both in actual dishes and in discourse, too. The detailed recipes of Apicius, the definitive (for us, at least) Roman cookbook, and the highly structured banquet conversation of Athenaeus' *Deipnosophistae*, which manages to raise the art of cooking at least to the pretensions of philosophy by taking over the form of the Platonic dialogue, suggest complex uses of food and specialized interest in its properties.[5]

The food of the poorer sections of society, even artisans and labourers, let alone the destitute, was less differentiated and hardly likely to be described by them in literary terms. Menus, recipes, and the like were neither used nor usable; these imply not only a level of literacy, but a variety of foods and a complexity of use. Lists, relatively undifferentiated structures, are the form in which evidence of humble cuisine, itself rather meagre in quantity and variety, often comes to us. Of course 'lists' would likewise be misleading if we imagined long catalogues; often food for the poor was simply a few things, or even one or two, such as bread and water. We start then, with two lists of food for people who were not destitute, but were without any appreciable choices in the forms of their meals or in other aspects of life.

Of the lists to be discussed here, the first, from the Mishna, gives one week's ration prescribed for a separated wife in Palestine. The second, from Cato the Elder's *De Agri Cultura*, provides advice on

---

[5] On 'Apicius' and Athenaeus, see the discussion by Dalby, *Siren Feasts*, 168–83.

foods for farm workers. Both are suggestions from people with significant power, for the needs of the poor. They come from rather different contexts, but they are not atypical of the evidence and may not be at all unrepresentative.

If a husband maintained his wife at the hands of a third person, he may not grant her less than two *qabs* of wheat or four *qabs* of barley. R. Jose said: Only R. Ishmael provided her with barley because he lived near Edom. He must also give her half a *qab* of pulse and half a *log* of oil and a *qab* of dried figs or a *mina* of fig-cake; and if he has none of these, he must provide her with other produce in their stead. (*m. Ketub.* 5: 8–9)[6]

Rations for the hands: Four *modii* of wheat in winter, and in summer four and a half for the field hands. The overseer, the housekeeper, the foreman, and the shepherd should receive three. The chain-gang should have a ration of four pounds of bread through the winter, increasing to five when they begin to work the vines, and dropping back to four when the figs ripen. Wine ration for the hands: For three months following the vintage let them drink afterwine. In the fourth month issue a *hemina* a day, that is $2\frac{1}{2}$ *congii* a month; in the fifth, sixth, seventh and eighth months a *sextarius* a day, that is, 5 *congii* a month; in the ninth, tenth, eleventh and twelfth months 3 *heminae* a day, that is, an amphora a month. In addition, issue $3\frac{1}{2}$ *congii* per person for the Saturnalia and the Compitalia . . . and an additional amount for the chain gang proportioned to their work . . . Relish for the hands: Store all the windfall olives you can, and later the mature olives which will yield very little oil. Issue them sparingly and make them last as long as possible. When they are used up, issue fish pickle and vinegar, and a pint of oil a month per person. A *modius* of salt a year per person is sufficient.

(Cato, *Agr.* 56–8)[7]

These give us the beginnings of a general picture of the humble person's diet, granted the prescriptive (and hence perhaps optimistic, from the recipients' view) nature of these sources; granted also that we could be more specific if we were to consider the passage from classical to late antiquity, the differences between urban and rural eaters, and the

---

[6] As cited in translation by Gildas Hamel, *Poverty and Charity in Roman Palestine, First Three Centuries C.E.* (Berkeley: University of California Press, 1990), 40. The *qab* was a measure of volume, approximately 2 litres; the *log*, a quarter *qab*; the *mina*, a Roman measure, was 341 grams. On the *qab* and related measures, see Hamel, *Poverty and Charity*, 39–41 and 243–6, and Magen Broshi, 'The Diet of Roman Palestine in the Roman Period: Introductory Notes', *Israel Museum Journal*, 5 (1986), 41–2.

[7] The *modius* was about 9 litres; for liquid measures the *sextarius* (0.54 litres) was divided into 2 *heminae*; there were six *sextarii* to the *congius* and eight *congii* to the amphora, which was therefore about 25 litres.

different parts of the Mediterranean world. We can be reasonably certain in saying that for most people, food was bread or cereal in other forms, with smaller amounts of vegetables and fruits, oil and salt according to circumstance.[8] Meat is not mentioned in either of these descriptions, and from this and much other evidence it seems that it was at least not a day-to-day item for many people.

Most of the nutritional needs of most inhabitants of the ancient Roman world seem to have been met by cereal grains, usually in the form of bread, but also in pastes and porridges.[9] The Mishna suggests, as we saw, that a separated wife in Roman Palestine was owed two *qabs* of wheat (about 4 litres) or 4 of barley per week, along with smaller amounts of lentils, oil, and dried figs (*m. Ketub.* 5: 8).[10] These amounts may have been more than many such women, or others, were likely to get in reality.[11] Cato prescribed something more like a litre of wheat per farm worker per day. In all these cases the amounts specified may have been intended to feed dependants also. The urban males who were the beneficiaries of the grain dole in the city of Rome itself are estimated to have used about 200 kg. of grain each per year, presumably on their dependants as well as themselves.[12] The political furore that was prone to erupt over threats to the supply is an eloquent indicator of the importance of this practice and the centrality of bread.

The quality of these breads and other products varied greatly, and different types of bread were normal for those of different means (Artemidorus, *Oneir.* 1. 69). Although there were certainly many bakers in the towns and cities, bread-making was still often a domestic task undertaken by women (see Pliny, *Nat.* 18. 27), with considerable regional variety. Pliny the Elder discusses the merits of various kinds of grain or bread in terms of taste and digestibility (*Nat.* 18. 27–8). Not all of what is described as 'bread' can be assumed to have been leavened (and indeed Latin *panis*, Greek ἄρτος, and Hebrew לחם all mean simply

---

[8] See also Dalby, *Siren Feasts*, 24–9.

[9] The cost of milling, as well as of baking, was significant: Pliny, *Nat.* 18. 90.

[10] Hamel estimates the amount of wheat specified would have yielded six 600 g. loaves: *Poverty and Charity*, 40–1.

[11] Broshi, 'The Diet of Roman Palestine', 42, suggests that the wife's list represents a calorie intake comparable to that presently recommended by the United Nations' Food and Agriculture Organization.

[12] These are the estimates of Don R. Brothwell, 'Foodstuffs, Cooking and Drugs', in M. Grant and R. Kitzinger (eds.), *Civilization of the Ancient Mediterranean: Greece and Rome* (4 vols.; New York: Scribner, 1988), i. 248. Garnsey suggests a more generous 1 kg. per day, based on calculating the weight of the ration of 5 *modii* per month as about 33 kg.: 'Mass Diet and Nutrition', 70–2.

'food' at times).[13] Rather it may often, especially for the poor, have been something more like a biscuit, wafer, or damper.[14]

The exact varieties and quantities of fruits and vegetables available to common people must have depended on just where they lived and worked. In general these were seen as a valued addition to the usual bread diet.[15] We may presume that even poorer agricultural workers had some access to the crops they actually harvested,[16] yet not every meal of the poor is likely to have included them.

It is no surprise to find plentiful references to the use of figs, dates, and grapes in the Palestinian evidence, from the Gospels to the rabbinic literature.[17] Figs were widely cultivated in the West also, but Roman demand necessitated imports.[18] Dates were known fresh only in the East and in Africa, and were accordingly expensive, the preserve of the rich except on special occasions.[19] Grapes were of real importance, often in the form of wine, on which more will be said below. All of these would have been more familiar in dried and other preserved forms. Apples, pears, plums, quinces, and pomegranates feature prominently in sources dealing with Roman diet.[20]

Olives were a more widespread addition to the bread staples, fresh for some but also pickled and, of course, pressed as oil. These were widely cultivated and accessible to very many in one form or another. Cato's

[13] The *Moretum* attributed to Virgil describes the making of such an unleavened bread (40–51) and calls it *panis* (119).

[14] For more information on Palestine and some comparative material, see Hamel, *Poverty and Charity*, 39–42, and Broshi, 'The Diet of Palestine', 41–4; on bread in Rome and the Greek world, see André, *L'Alimentation*, 52–74, and now the material in J. Wilkins, D. Harvey, and M. Dobson (eds.), *Food in Antiquity* (Exeter: University of Exeter Press, 1995), 25–100, and Dalby, *Siren Feasts*, 89–92.

[15] Hamel tends to downplay the importance of vegetables, going so far as to call them 'despised' at one point (*Poverty and Charity*, 9), but the evidence points to the contrary conclusion; see *t. 'Arak.* 4. 27. 548, where to have vegetables daily is clearly desirable, if not the greatest luxury.

[16] *m. Ma'aś*, 3. 1–3. Hamel discusses this and the further rabbinic comment (*Poverty and Charity*, 38) in terms of the command not to 'muzzle the ox', but the issue seems to arise from circumstances not peculiar to Palestine or Judaism. Cato decreases slaves' rations when figs come into season: *Agr.* 56.

[17] On fruits in Palestine see Hamel, *Poverty and Charity*, 9–10, and Broshi, 'The Diet of Palestine', 45–6.

[18] Columella's comments on the different forms in which figs were dried in different provinces indicate that these were found right around the Mediterranean (*De Re Rustica*, 12. 15. 5). Pliny indicates that some were cultivated in Italy (*Nat.* 15. 83) but more seem to have been imported.

[19] See Pliny, *Nat.* 13. 45.

[20] André, *L'Alimentation*, 75–93, goes into detail on the fruits available in Rome, including their production and preparation.

farm workers are given a ration of olives, apparently as the most basic element after bread itself (*Agr.* 58). It was the form of olive preparation, rather than the presence of olives in the diet, that seems to have differed between richer and poorer diners.[21] Olive oil was used not only as a cooking medium but also a sauce, as a glance at Apicius indicates, and seems to have been regarded as quite basic rather than as a luxury item.[22] It is present in the lists pertaining both to the Italian farm labourer and to the Palestinian wife.[23] Radish and other seed-oils seem to have been more popular in Egypt and the East (Pliny, *Nat.* 15. 24–32, 19. 79).

Regular use of other vegetables generally seems to have indicated at least moderate wealth, although some, such as onions and garlic (as dishes rather than merely as flavourings), were apparently available to the poor,[24] and capers were proverbially associated with frugality (Plutarch, *Quaest. Conv.* 668 A; Philemon, fr. 98). If the discussions in ancient authors are a reasonable indication, brassicas (cabbages and the precursors of cauliflower and similar species), root vegetables such as carrots, cucurbits such as gourds, and leafy vegetables related to modern lettuce were among those most commonly featured.[25]

Legumes were an important food source, and from ancient perspectives might have been seen more as grains than as vegetables; beans (lentils, chick peas, and fava or broad beans) could be dried and cooked as gruel, and were sometimes ground to make flour (Pliny, *Nat.* 18. 30). Although well-regarded for the most part, beans are often spoken of as a food available for artisans and others who were relatively poorly off (Horace, *Sat.* 2. 6. 63–4; Martial, 10. 48. 16).[26]

Salt should be regarded as a food second in importance only to bread for the ancients. Obviously salt did not feature at meals in the sort of quantity that some other additions to bread might have, but it was highly significant: the addition of salt, the most basic form of flavouring, as a

---

[21] These are discussed by Cato, *Agr.* 117–19, Columella, 12. 49, and Pliny, *Nat.* 15. 16. See Don and Patricia Brothwell, *Food in Antiquity: A Survey of the Diet of Early Peoples* (New York: Frederick A. Praeger, 1969), 153–7.

[22] Garnsey, 'Mass Diet and Nutrition', 84.

[23] On the basic nature of olives and oil see further A. S. Pease, 'Ölbaum', PW xvii. 1998–2022.

[24] In both Plutarch (*Quaest. Conv.* 669B) and Plautus (*Most.* 48) the use of these rather than meat is a sign of poverty and vulgarity.

[25] On vegetables, see further Brothwell, 'Food, Cooking and Drugs', 250–1; André, *L'Alimentation*, 15–51; Broshi, 'The Diet of Palestine', 46–7; and Hamel, *Poverty and Charity*, 17–18, 33, 43.

[26] See further Garnsey, 'Mass Diet and Nutrition', 84–5; André, *L'Alimentation*, 35–42; Brothwell, 'Food, Cooking and Drugs', 249; and Hamel, *Poverty and Charity*, 15–17.

relish (ὀψάριον), turned the mere eating of bread into the conduct of a meal. According to Pliny, Varro had reported that earlier Romans saw salt as a dish in its own right (*Nat.* 31. 89), and Horace seemed still to think it so (Horace, *Sat.* 2. 2. 17–18). Plutarch reports the proverbial expression of friendship, 'people of salt and a bean'; the point being that some friends are good enough to enjoy dining together even on a meal as frugal as this, the most basic imaginable (*Quaest. Conv.* 684 E–F).[27] Use of more elaborate pickles and sauces based on olives, oil, or fish seem to echo this most basic meal structure of bread plus salt.

The preservative quality of salt was also very important. Despite its association with frugality and its availability even to the likes of Cato's workers (cf. Lucian on the pseudo-Cynics, *Fug.* 14), salt was not always cheap, especially for those who were far from the sea. Even some on the coast cooked in sea water rather than using salt separately (Pliny, *Nat.* 18. 68).[28] The flavouring given by salt was seen not only as an adjunct to sound food but as a remedy for what otherwise tasted bad (see Job 6: 6). Thus Plutarch also reports and comments on the Homeric designation of salt as 'divine' (see *Iliad*, 9. 214), comparing this to the common views of such basic things as earth and air (*Quaest. Conv.* 684 F–685 D). His diners also call salt an aid to digestion, a tenderizer, and a medicine (668 E– 669 E).

Both fish and meat are included here for the sake of completeness and ease of reference, but will be discussed further in connection with the practice of sacrifice and of banquets, where they were more likely to be found. The access of most poor people to them will have been limited.[29]

Meat deserves careful consideration as an element of the ancient diet even though it does not appear in the lists of provisions for the poor, and will not figure prominently (except negatively) in evidence concerning Christian ritual. The fact that meat is often a missing element will prove to be significant in itself. Meat was the most desirable and also usually the least obtainable element of meals. Few had no access to it at all, since public festivals and sacrifices, as well as dubious 'cook-shops', gave the relatively poor in cities at least some opportunities to indulge what comes across in the sources as nothing less than a craving; yet only a very few

---

[27] For a wider variety of Graeco-Roman and Near Eastern references on salt as symbol of commensality and friendship, see further J. E. Latham, *The Religious Significance of Salt*, Théologie Historique, 64 (Paris: Éditions Beauchesne, 1982), 50–63.

[28] André, *L'Alimentation*, 193–5; Hamel, *Poverty and Charity*, 14, 10–12; Broshi, 'The Diet of Palestine', 52.

[29] The chapters on meat and (in particular) fish in Wilkins, Harvey, and Dobson (eds.), *Food in Antiquity*, 102–70, are useful surveys.

can have made the sort of use of meat implied in the work of Apicius.[30] For the wealthy, the regular use of meat was a sign of exalted status; for the poor its consumption indicated the exalted status of particular times and events. The more numinous aspect of meat will be discussed further below in conjunction with issues of sacrifice.

Pork was the traditional favourite for Romans; Varro describes the pig as a gift from nature for celebrations (*De Re Rustica*, 2. 4. 10; cf. Artemidorus, *Oneir.* 1. 70). Apart from its status as a delicacy, pork gives rise to no conflict over the use of the animal for agriculture, milk products, or transport, a factor which sometimes prevented greater use of cattle, sheep, and goats.[31] Despite the Jewish prohibition on pork, pigs are attested in Palestine also (Mark 5: 11–14), and seem to have been present in other parts of the East and in North Africa.[32] Wool and milk products were more important to the farmer than the meat from sheep (Columella, 4. 2) and cattle were more likely to be slaughtered when old or ailing (Menander, *Dys.* 430–9; Tertullian, *Apol.* 14. 1).

The availability of fish varied more than that of meat because of the difficulty of transporting it once caught. In Palestine, those who lived closer to the coast and to the Sea of Galilee would seem to have had more opportunities to eat fish than did others. Yet there were various preparations more widely obtainable than the raw product: fish could be dried, salted, and transformed into sauces.

Many city-dwellers might rarely have eaten fresh fish. In both the second century BCE and the fourth CE, there is evidence that fish was more expensive than meat.[33] Plutarch has his diners discuss the relative

---

[30] Meat was added to food doles under Aurelian in 270 CE; granted some indications of a gradual 'secularizing' of meat in later antiquity, I think it is hardly daring to see scarcity and religious overtones as persisting into the second and third centuries. See further below on the cuisine of sacrifice.

[31] Brothwell, 'Food, Cooking and Drugs', 257–8, discusses recent archaeological evidence on proportions of bone remains. Jerome, *Contra Iovinianum*, 2.7, notes that in his time the use of veal was frowned upon as an irresponsible use of resources needed for cultivation.

[32] André, *L'Alimentation*, 139.

[33] Cato is quoted by Plutarch (*Quaest. Conv.* 668B) as decrying the fact that a fish was more expensive than a cow, along with a related complaint about Roman excess and the cost of imported smoked fish which is also recorded by Athenaeus, *Deipnosophistae*, 6. 274–5, and attributed to Bk. 31 of Polybius' now fragmentary *Histories*. It thus seems reasonable to say that Plutarch's quote from Cato may also have been in Polybius and therefore a contemporary report. In 301 CE, the edict of Diocletian on maximum prices (*CIL* iii. 801–41 etc.; trans. in *TAPA* 71 (1940), 157–74) makes sea-fish twice as expensive, weight for weight, as pork.

merits of fish and meat, and seems to indicate that despite the general desire for meat, the true gourmet was likely to prize fish as highly as meat, or perhaps more so (*Quaest. Conv.* 667 C–669 E). On the other hand, forgoing fish voluntarily, as it seemed the Homeric heroes had, was a sign of highest frugality or self-control (Plato, *Rep.* 404 B–C). Apuleius makes the fishmonger sound like a financial drain upon society (*Apol.* 32) and provision of fish inland seem like magic (*Apol.* 41). Fish did not have the same connection with sacrifice, a fact which may be connected with the somewhat different attitude towards it; to this factor we shall return.

Salted preserved fish was more common, and was produced for export all over the Mediterranean; Sicily, Spain, and the regions surrounding the Black Sea are prominent.[34] Diocletian's price-limiting edict makes salt fish one-quarter the cost of the best fresh, and even Apicius' elaborate cuisine is far more concerned with using preserved fish-products than with fresh fish. Especially popular was a sort of fermented fish sauce known as *garum* or *liquamen*. This made use of the changes in taste and (further) ability for preservation involved when fish was allowed to decompose with herbs and salt.[35] The solid remnant or perhaps intermediate stage of this process is the fish-pickle (*hallec*) mentioned by Cato, from whose testimony it seems clear that these preparations were within the reach of all but the poorest. Lucian also indicates fish-pickle was food for the poor in comparing the diet of dissipated Cynics (meat and wine) with what it should have been (salt fish and thyme) (*Fug.* 14).[36]

Only two drinks really need feature here in any detail, i.e. water and wine. Beer was not generally favoured by those who understood themselves to belong to the Empire and to Greek culture generally; it was associated with barbarians.[37] Although milk was available to some, it was largely either a rural or a rare food; most milk was consumed by kids, lambs, and calves, and that used for human food was for the most part turned into cheeses.[38] Its direct culinary use would probably have been

---

[34] Strabo, 3. 4. 2 (Spain); Athenaeus, *Deip.* 5. 209 (Sicily) and 6. 275 (Pontus); Tacitus, *Ann.* 12. 63 (Byzantium).

[35] André suggests, plausibly, that preparation (and presumably result) would have been similar to the fish sauce (*nuoc mâm*) popular in South-East Asian cuisine.

[36] On fish, see André, *L'Alimentation*, 97–116, and on *garum* in particular, 198–200. Broshi, 'The Diet of Palestine', 49–50, stresses both the desirability of fish as a Sabbath meal and the limited availability of the food.

[37] D. and P. Brothwell, *Food in Antiquity: A Survey of the Diet of Early Peoples*, 166–8.

[38] See André, *L'Alimentation*, 153–60.

extraordinary, and deserves special attention when attested in ritual contexts.

It seems obvious that water was the normal drink for many, although this is something rather difficult to ascertain. The place of water as the drink of choice for those who followed an ascetic regimen or accepted voluntary poverty is perhaps the clearest indicator of what choosing to drink water indicated in the ancient Mediterranean; except for those somewhat 'odd cases' where choice meant refusal of opportunities, wine was preferred. Lucian's castigation of so-called Cynics for drinking wine (*Fug.* 14) and Cato's practice of refusing to drink anything but water when on campaign (Plutarch, *Cato the Elder*, 1. 13) are examples of this.

The commonly found statement that wine was a luxury item is at least an overstatement; more careful recent studies suggest that its consumption was 'more or less ubiquitous', at least in large cities.[39] While the poorest might have had to make do with water, wine was not reserved for the wealthy, although the best wine undoubtedly was. Cato's workers receive a wine ration varying with the weather between about 250 ml. and 750 ml., which at its peak was probably a significant contribution to their caloric intake, as much as one-quarter.[40] This *lora*, or 'afterwine', was produced by mixing water with the pulp remaining after the first pressing of the grapes. Cato gives a recipe elsewhere in the *De Agri Cultura* (25); he prescribes it for only three months after the harvest, because the wine would last no longer (or perhaps the servants would not!), after which they were to be given an even more forbidding mixture also described in the treatise (*Agr.* 104), involving vinegar and sea water added to the grape pulp as preservatives. These 'wines' were themselves close to vinegars by contemporary standards. Diocletian's edict of 301 sets the price of the cheapest wine at one-third that of second-rate oil;[41] but perhaps the type that Cato describes might not even have been sold. More expensive wines could require quite elaborate preparation, with various stages of manufacture and the addition of herbs and other flavourings such as honey.[42] The separated wife's 'food basket' does not include wine, and this could be an indicator of different expectations about men's and women's diets in Palestine.[43] Roman mores were also

[39] Garnsey, 'Mass Diet and Nutrition', 84.
[40] Broshi, 'The Diet of Palestine', 46.
[41] A *sextarius* (0.54 l.) of wine cost 8 denarii, oil cost 24 denarii.
[42] André, *L'Alimentation*, 164–70. Artemidorus, *Oneir.* 1. 66, indicates that such flavoured wines were exclusively for the wealthy.
[43] Broshi, 'The Diet of Palestine', 46.

opposed to women's consumption of wine, but this was not a universal rule by any means.[44]

Thus far we have considered all the foods mentioned in the two ancient lists, with free reference to other ancient authors. Despite variations of time and place, it seems quite clear that most people ate bread, and added to it 'relishes'—oil, salt, pulses, and other vegetables—in whatever quantity or variety they were able.[45] They drank water or cheap wine. The list was thus a short one at best. Meat and fish were special-occasion dishes for all but the rich, and meat carried overtones of sacrifice as well as of luxury or even of dissipation. This weight of meat-meaning might have been less burdensome for the wealthy élite, whose practices were atypical but not insignificant for our understanding of ancient attitudes to food. These questions, then, already begin to take us past mere 'food' to 'meal'. It is worth noting, before passing on, that a meal of bread and wine or water would not have been remarkable in itself, unless chosen by those who could have eaten better.

THE BANQUET

Introduction

Plutarch quotes a popular saying: ' "I have eaten, but not dined today," ' implying that a dinner always requires friendly sociability for a seasoning' (*Quaest. Conv.* 697 C). In specific models of ancient meal practice we see highly structured uses of food and concern about issues such as the presence of specific diners in a particular place, the postures they adopt, the order of proceedings, and of course the desirability or appropriateness of the actual foods eaten.[46] If these

[44] See Pliny, *Nat.* 14. 89; for further references to Roman attitudes and Greek bemusement, see André, *L'Alimentation*, 172 n. 89.

[45] The disorder of 'opsophagy', i.e. the eating of the flavoured foods without the staple—an option only for the powerful—is discussed engagingly by James Davidson, 'Opsophagia: Revolutionary Eating at Athens', in Wilkins, Harvey, and Dobson (eds.), *Food in Antiquity*, 204–13.

[46] For general discussion see Blake Leyerle, 'Meal Customs in the Graeco-Roman World', in Paul F. Bradshaw and Lawrence A. Hoffman (eds.), *Passover and Easter: The Liturgical Structuring of a Sacred Season* (Notre Dame, Ind.: University of Notre Dame Press, forthcoming); Dennis E. Smith, 'Social Obligation in the Context of Communal Meals: A Study of the Christian Meal in 1 Corinthians in Comparison with Graeco-Roman Communal Meals', Th.D. dissertation, Harvard Divinity School, 1980, pp. 3–38; Dalby, *Siren Feasts*, 1–30.

questions were probably more important for the wealthy on a daily basis, they were not without significance for others, who would have encountered them in the context of specific festivals and in the popular social groups often referred to as *collegia*.[47]

Recent discussions of New Testament texts have emphasized Graeco-Roman meal customs, with important results.[48] The *symposium*, or drinking-party after the banquet proper, has been seen as providing a literary model for the construction of meal scenes in the Gospels.[49] Some liturgists and many New Testament scholars have also seen Jewish meal-models, and the Seder in particular, as the historical origin of the Last Supper of Jesus, and thus supposedly the interpretative key to ensuing eucharistic meals of the Christian Church,[50] yet few studies have taken the comparison of eucharistic meals with other ritual meal customs past the evidence of the New Testament period.[51] These matters deserve some brief consideration here, both to take this discussion of ancient eating past 'food' to 'meal', and also to acknowledge, albeit critically, the importance of these issues of pattern and form to the reconstruction and interpretation of early Christian meal practice.

[47] On the *collegia*, the four vols. of J. P. Waltzing, *Étude historique sur les corporations professionnelles chez les Romains depuis les origines jusqu'à la chute de l'Empire d'Occident* (4 vols.; Louvain: C. Peeters, 1895–1900), are still standard. Dining customs contained important common elements; see Smith, 'Social Obligation', 101–77. On their relation to early Christianity, see John S. Kloppenborg, 'Edwin Hatch, Churches and *Collegia*', in B. McLean (ed.), *Origins and Method: Towards a New Understanding in Judaism and Christianity*, JSNTSup 86 (Sheffield: Sheffield Academic Press, 1993), 212–38, and R. L. Wilken, 'Collegia, Philosophical Schools, and Theology', *The Catacombs and the Colosseum: The Roman Empire as the Setting of Primitive Christianity* (Valley Forge, Pa.: Judson, 1971), 268–91.

[48] e.g. Smith, 'Social Obligation', and Dennis E. Smith and Hal Taussig, *Many Tables: The Eucharist in the New Testament and Liturgy Today* (London: SCM, 1990); David Aune, 'Septem Sapientium Convivium', in H. D. Betz (ed.), *Plutarch's Ethical Writings and Early Christian Literature* (Leiden: E. J. Brill, 1978), 51–105; Kathleen Corley, *Private Women, Public Meals: Social Conflict in the Synoptic Tradition* (Peabody, Mass.; Hendrickson, 1993).

[49] Modern discussions have usually had more to say about the relationship between early Christianity and the *symposium* as literary genre, than that between the actual practice of the festive drinking-party and Christian meals. On the literary form itself, see J. Martin, *Symposion: Die Geschichte einer literarischen Form* (Paderborn: F. Schöningh, 1931); and for some fairly recent applications to NT texts, E. Springs Steele, 'Luke 11:37–54—A Modified Hellenistic Symposium?' *JBL* 103 (1984), 379–94, and Dennis E. Smith, 'Table Fellowship as a Literary Motif in the Gospel of Luke', *JBL* 106 (1987), 613–38.

[50] The classic statement of that position is that of Jeremias, *The Eucharistic Words of Jesus*.

[51] One notable exception is Charles A. Bobertz, 'The Role of the Patron in the *Cena Dominica* of Hippolytus' *Apostolic Tradition*', *JTS* NS 44 (1993), 170–84.

Graeco-Roman Banquets

While recent studies on the conventions of Greek and Roman banquets have identified various commonplaces and conventions that shed light on early Christian ritual meals, a certain hesitation is called for in the face of claims of unitary ideology and practice.[52] The meal itself and the time after provided an arena for struggles, in theory and practice, over appropriate conduct not only for eating and drinking, but also for politics, religion and sex.[53]

It is difficult or perhaps impossible to draw a clear distinction between sacral and 'ordinary' meals in Greek and Roman society. At private meals, invocations and libations were involved (Athenaeus, *Deip.* 5. 149, 15. 675 B-C). Clubs and guilds always had some form of religious element, whether or not they were specifically cultic θίασοι.[54] The difference between the religious character of one meal and another should usually be seen as a matter of degree rather than one of radical distinction, even if we sometimes allow a certain cynicism or complacency in their execution.[55] While the wealthy could turn their daily meals into elaborate and varied expressions of sociability, those of lesser means are unlikely to have participated in many formal banquets other than these occasional meetings of clubs and the public celebrations which might take place from time to time for major festivals. For the poorer members of a community, therefore, the question was not so much how in particular to banquet and with whom, but whether one could achieve access to the food and the other benefits, including things of such importance as professional advantage and assurance of decent burial, that went with these particular instances of the banquet.[56]

---

[52] e.g. in Kathleen Corley's use of Dennis Smith's work, the idea of a 'common meal tradition' meaning a tradition of communal or common meals (*Many Tables*, 21–35) seems to become a 'common meal form', apparently meaning a standard set of practices: see *Private Women, Public Meals*, 17–19.

[53] On the last of which see Corley, *Private Women, Public Meals*, 34–52.

[54] The burial society at Lanuvium (*CIL* xiv. 2112) is connected with the worship of Diana and of the divinized Antinous, Hadrian's lover.

[55] As in the case of the Arval brothers discussed by Sir Ronald Syme: *Some Arval Brethren* (Oxford: Clarendon, 1980), 111–15. The assumption that indications of revelry exclude a genuinely religious understanding of club meals is justly criticized by Smith ('Social Obligation', 175–7) and by Kane ('The Mithraic Cult Meal', 331–2).

[56] See Mireille Corbier, 'The Ambiguous Status of Meat in Ancient Rome', *Food and Foodways*, 3 (1989), 231–4. Smith, 'Social Obligation', 120, suggests that there might be some tendency for Roman clubs in particular to be associated with people of lower class and status.

The actual events can generally be seen as divided into two parts, the δεῖπνον proper, which involved various courses, followed by a συμπόσιον (*symposium*) or drinking-party. The distinction between the two parts seems to have been clearer to Greeks than to Romans, as Cicero indicates, praising: 'that relaxation of spirit most effectively brought about by friendly conversation, which is most agreeable at *convivia*. In these matters our people are wiser than the Greeks. They speak of συμπόσια or of σύνδειπνα, that is of "co-drinkings" or "co-dinings", but we say *convivia* because then life is lived together to the fullest' (*Fam.* 9. 24. 3).

Conduct at banquets could vary greatly. We have evidence of wild parties not only full of eating and drinking but replete with forms of entertainment such as dancing, intended to overcome the other senses as well.[57] Satirists and writers of comedy for the stage favoured the banquet as a place where excess could be pilloried, especially where participants had other attributes not to the writer's taste.[58] On the other hand the association between the banquet and philosophy was proverbial.

Many meal elements were capable of expressing, and even creating, patterns of relationship among diners and of these food is the most obvious. Quantity, quality, and variety of food and drink were indicators of many things: the wealth, taste, and generosity of the host, and the self-indulgence of host and guests alike. We find indications both of conscious equality of portions, and thus again of the banquet as a sort of dietary democracy, but also of clear differences in quantity and quality of food that underscore different offices or status. The former model seems to be associated with the older Greek ideal of the egalitarian city; portions of sacrificial meat might even be distributed by lot to make sure that justice was seen to be done.[59] As in the more public aspects of the practice of democracy, this emphasis on equality might serve as much to define members of an élite over and against others, as to lessen distinctions between them; the ideology of equality could be a powerful

---

[57] Xenophon's *Symposium*, not the most dissolute of ancient meal depictions by any means, ends with the titillation of the banqueters (*Symp.* 9. 7), and even the famous Platonic dialogue of the same name occurs through avoidance of a flute-girl's entertainment: *Symp.* 176 E. More generally, see Smith, 'Social Obligation', 20–3.

[58] The *cena Trimalchionis* in Petronius' *Satyricon* is a notably exuberant and tasteless event, discussed with implications for the social make-up of early Christianity by Richard Pervo, 'Wisdom and Power: Petronius' *Satyricon* and the Social World of Early Christianity', *ATR* 67 (1985), 307–25.

[59] See Plutarch, *Quaest. Conv.* 642 F. This apportioning practice seemed to some to undermine the actual commensality of the occasion, ibid. 643 A.

tool in the hands of dominant power.[60] Of course the silence or absence of those from the lower classes and women at many such 'democratic' events has all the more obvious significance.

If there was continued interest in this idea of the food of the banquet as an expression of equality, there were nevertheless exceptions which became more and more clear as time went on. Some diners were more equal than others; office-bearers in city and club were likely to be acknowledged with multiple 'equal' portions of a sacrificial animal or other meal ration.[61] Wealthy Roman patrons were more likely to use food-gifts, rather than actual commensality, to mediate their relations with lowly clients.[62] Roman usage suggests less embarrassment about giving varying portions and types of food even in private dinners. Pliny the Younger reports on a meal, apparently far from exceptional, where clear distinctions were drawn between diners on the basis of rank:

> The best dishes were set in front of himself and a select few, and cheap scraps of food before the rest of the company. He had even put the wine into tiny little flasks, divided into three categories, not with the idea of giving his guests the opportunity of choosing, but to make it impossible for them to refuse what they were given. One lot was intended for us, another for his lesser friends (all his friends are graded) and the third for his and our freed slaves. (*Ep.* 2. 6)[63]

The role of host was that of patron and ruler; if an inferior might occupy it temporarily towards a superior, this game of changing places created, again, a kind of fictive equality which served ultimately to reinforce dependence and hierarchy.[64] State banquets held under the

---

[60] See John D'Arms's discussions of the *mutitationes* or reciprocal dinners associated with religious festivals such as the *Megalensia* in Rome: 'Control, Companionship and *Clientela*: Some Social Functions of the Roman Communal Meal', *Echos du monde classique / Classical Views*, NS 3 (1984), 335–7.

[61] e.g. the lesser Panathenaea: *IG* ii². 334; and the Lanuvium group again: *CIL* xiv. 2112. See Pauline Schmitt-Pantel, *La Cité au banquet: Histoire des repas publics dans les cités grecques* (Rome: École française de Rome, 1992), 126–7.

[62] See D'Arms, 'The Roman *Convivium*', 308–9, and Bobertz, 'The Role of the Patron', 170–84. It may be more than coincidental that we have better evidence for the quantities in Domitian's food distributions (see Suetonius, *Domitian*, 5) than for his banquets.

[63] Pliny goes on to criticize this scene, and may thus seem more like Plutarch in avowing a democratic form of meal; yet the discussion suggests that his main point is that of economy. Rather than follow one set of social niceties and provide better food for the more honoured, he advocates serving all guests the sort of food and drink others would regard as appropriate only for the freed slaves. Cf. also Pliny the Elder, *Nat.* 14. 14. 91; Martial, *Epig.* 3. 60; Juvenal, *Sat.* 5.

[64] See Plutarch's description of the threats by Cato the Younger that followed failure to accept the favour of being the great one's host (*Cato the Younger*, 12), and the discussion by John D'Arms, 'Control, Companionship and *Clientela*', 332–4.

principate seem to have raised distinctions between diners to an art form, at once demonstrating an inclusiveness of participation beyond that of older convention but also a sense of internal hierarchy quite alien to it.[65]

The normal, or at least ideal, posture for the *cena* or δεῖπνον was to recline, both for men and women.[66] While the array of couches in a dining room or *triclinium* constituted a levelling force some of the time, there were still places of precedence and different opinions about their importance. Plutarch has one of his seven sages emphasize the equality of diners and the inappropriateness of contesting places of honour (*Sept. Sap. Conv.* 149 A–B), but there is a sense that the putting aside of distinctions at table may have been artificial, a subtle reinforcement of patron–client relations in some instances.[67]

In late antiquity the *symposium* is, if anything, more prominent as an institution than the meal to which it was linked.[68] Drinking earlier, i.e.

[65] See D'Arms, 'The Roman *Convivium*', 308–9. D'Arms suggests that accounts of these banquets (of Domitian) are 'artfully ambiguous' as to food and drink, emphasizing the more usefully propagandist theme of inclusiveness. Roman convention also seems to have distinguished more clearly between the expectations linked to a public *cena* and those for a private *convivium*, where something closer to the old Greek ideal might apply; see Cicero, *Fam.* 9. 24. 3, and further D'Arms, 'The Roman *Convivium*', 311–17.

[66] There seem to have been occasions when women dined without men, as well as the reverse; see Nancy Bookidis, 'Ritual Dining at Corinth', in N. Marinatos and R. Hägg (eds.), *Greek Sanctuaries: New Approaches* (London: Routledge, 1993), 50–1. On mixed occasions, the presence and involvement of women (other than servants and entertainers) seems to have been much less likely in this second part of the banquet, where clearly marked off; for the rule (for some), Plutarch, *Quaest. Conv.* 612 F, and an exception, *Sept. Sap. Conv.* 150 D–155 E. On the differences between Greek and Roman conventions regarding women's presence, see Cornelius Nepos, *Lives*, pr. 6–7, and for discussion, see Corley, *Private Women, Public Meals*, 24–34, 53–9; Dalby, *Siren Feasts*, 2–8; and Leyerle, 'Meal Customs'. The guilds may have been less likely to include women, but see Bradley H. McLean, 'The Agrippinilla Inscription: Religious Associations and Early Church Formation', in McLean (ed.), *Origins and Method*, 239–70, for a socially mixed religious group with many women members.

[67] Leyerle, 'Meal Customs'.

[68] 'It is rather the consumption of wine at the *symposion* after the *deipnon* that became the focus of elaborate ritualization, concerning the obligatory mixing of wine with water, the objects for use at the *symposion*, the serving of the drink, the order and character of singing or speaking, and the entertainments involved' (Oswyn Murray, 'Symposic History', in Murray (ed.), *Sympotica: A Symposium on the 'Symposion'* (Oxford: Clarendon, 1990), 6). Murray's suggestion that the symposium is constitutive of Greek society therefore stands as an alternative to that which sees the use of sacrifice and meat in the same way; see further 'The Greek Symposium in History', in E. Gabba (ed.), *Tria Corda: Scritti in Onore di Arnaldo Momigliano* (Como: Edizioni New Press, 1983), 263. For comparison and critique of these parallel interpretations of sacrifice and symposium, see Pauline Schmitt-Pantel, 'Sacrificial Meal and *Symposion*: Two Models of Civic Institutions in the Archaic City?', in Murray (ed.), *Sympotica*, 14–33. Sometimes the term is used to cover the whole process of the banquet, e.g. by Aune, 'Septem Sapientium Convivium',

during the meal, was not unknown, but less emphasis was placed on it.[69]
Wine had to be mixed with water, according to established principles but
also subject to the whim of the appointed individual; wine was normally
diluted with something like two or three times its volume of water.[70]
Libations had to be offered, apparently at the beginning of each *krater*,
three of which were customary, and each was expected to have been
offered to a particular god or gods.[71] Libation also seems to have been
appropriate at the end of proceedings.[72] While the prayers involved may
well have been short and simple, their omission was a serious matter.[73]
Hymns were also expected.[74]

Conversation was often associated with the *symposium* in particular,
which could also have been the time for further entertainment. Plato's
Symposium and the resulting genre of meal-dialogues may well have had
their effect on practice as well as on literature. Thus despite indications
of dissipation in the after-dinner entertainment we also find a distinct
interest in edifying conversation that takes place during and after meals,
and also a thread of discourse about meals themselves which emphasizes
moderation rather than extravagance.[75] There also seem to have been
those whose conservative catering even led their guests to 'fill up' before
coming, as Paul was later to advise the Corinthians to do.[76]

71–8; this imprecision is encouraged by the literary *symposia* but is not always helpful.
There are distinctions that could be emphasized more strongly, based on the texts
themselves; between *sympotica* (talk about the *symposium*) and *symposiaka* (appropriate
talk for a *symposium*) for instance (Plutarch, *Quaest. Conv.* 629 D). See Murray, Preface,
Sympotica, p. v.

[69] According to Pliny (*Nat.* 14. 28. 143) the taking of a cup before the main meal was a
1st-cent. innovation, but this would seem specifically to refer to a ceremonial cup. Wine
drunk unmixed during the meal (hence probably without the same ceremony) is attested
earlier, in Diodorus Siculus, 4. 3.

[70] Plutarch, *Quaest. Conviv.* 692 B–693 E; for further references and discussion, see
Leyerle, 'Meal Customs', and Dalby, *Siren Feasts*, 102–4.

[71] Athenaeus, *Deip.* 2. 36 B–C.

[72] *Homeric Hymn to Hestia*, 1. 5, Cicero, *ND* 2. 67.

[73] See Athenaeus, *Deip.* 4. 149 E (cf. 5. 179 D) and Plato, *Symp.* 176 A.

[74] Athenaeus, *Deip.* 2. 36 B–C, 14. 628 A–B.

[75] Plutarch's *Quaestiones Conviviales* and *Septem Sapientium Convivium* are good
examples; the former is a discussion of appropriate conduct and conversation, and the
latter a kind of literary model thereof, based on a legendary banquet of the 6th cent. BCE.
Aune suggests that the model of the *convivium* in Plutarch includes emphases on
'conviviality and fellowship rather than on intoxication' and 'orderliness and decorum
. . .' ('Septem Sapientium Convivium', 52). See also the description and discussion of the
rules of several *collegia* by Dennis Smith, 'Meals and Morality in Paul and his World',
SBLSP 20 (1981), 323–4; and discussion in 'Social Obligation', 39–73.

[76] The philosopher Menedemus seems to have offered such sparse hospitality:
Athenaeus, *Deip.* 10. 419. These reactions to sumptuary cuisine are not surprising,

Christian ritual meals in the Graeco-Roman world need to be understood in terms of these conventions, oppositions, and variations. This is not to say that each practice attested for eucharistic meals can be neatly explained by its reduction to another similar practice found in pagan circles. Yet Christian meals did not begin or remain as disembodied entities without relation to the culture in which they arose. On the contrary, it seems that from the outset Christian meal gatherings and their specific qualities, from types and quantities of food and drink to the range of attenders and their conversation, were comprehensible to participants and critics alike in terms at least partly drawn from other experiences and practices. The Christian eucharistic meals seem to have been somewhat like other meal gatherings held by religious associations. The fact that their qualities were not, however, entirely reducible to the practices of other rituals and gatherings may help account for their persistence and the present need to account for their development and significance.

Jewish Meal Models

Emerging from Judaism and in some instances remaining closely related to it long after the first century, Christian communities and Christian meals in particular may have owed much to specifically Jewish customs. Dietary laws need to be borne in mind, at least; despite the New Testament picture of a resolution of conflicts over food that made *kašrut* irrelevant,[77] there are indications that in practice things may not have been so simple. Questions of form and procedure are also of interest; in previous scholarship on Christian meals, these have often been asked largely in relation to the Seder or Passover meal, because of the synoptic Gospels' identification of the Last Supper as such a banquet, but other models have also been suggested: *ḥaburah*, *todah*, and *qidduš* meals have all been proposed as underlying the form of the eucharistic meals of the early Christians, and links have also been drawn to the Qumran sectarians.[78] While these issues of form are not necessarily

being found in other Eurasian cultures with highly differentiated cuisines as well; there are often two contradictory tendencies strongly at work even in the same parts of society at the same time, the sumptuary and the ascetic. See Goody, *Cooking, Cuisine and Class*, 97–153, and on these issues for ancient Rome in particular, Mireille Corbier, 'The Ambiguous Status of Meat in Ancient Rome', 239–42.

[77] See Mark 7: 19; Acts 10: 1–16; 11: 1–18; 15: 1–29; Gal. 2: 11–14.

[78] For the Seder, definitively by Joachim Jeremias, *The Eucharistic Words of Jesus*; but see now Gordon J. Bahr, 'The Seder of Passover and the Eucharistic Words', *NovT* 12

vital to the question of the use of foods in early Christian meals, the degree of dependence upon Jewish antecedents that is often posited for eucharistic meals does have wider implications; in particular for our purposes, the presence or absence of certain foods, or the significance of their use, have sometimes been assumed on the basis of supposed connections with particular meal-models.

While it has often been assumed that a reconstructed picture of Jewish meals based on the rabbinic evidence can be used as a starting-point from which formal and other characteristics of early eucharistic meals can be derived, it now seems that we cannot really systematize the evidence of the Mishna and other rabbinic texts in such a way as to project a supposedly fixed liturgy of (e.g.) the Seder back into the first century with an expectation of fitting the two pictures together. Even those who still value the mutual light the two may shed are increasingly cautious about assuming a fixed pattern of either Seder or eucharistic meal at such an early point.[79]

Despite the cultural (and particularly the dietary) distinctiveness of Judaism in the Graeco-Roman world, Jewish meal practices reflected in the Mishna cannot be considered without the wider set of conventions already discussed in relation to the banquet. The Seder itself, as well as the more general communal meal practices discussed in tractate *Berakot*, can be said to belong within the same world of dining possibilities as Graeco-Roman festive meals.[80] Viewed from this more general perspective, i.e. as a banquet in specifically Jewish circles, the Seder remains especially important for the discussion of early Christian meals. The diners are required to recline in the Greek manner, even if they are poor and presumably not used to doing so, as a sign of festivity and freedom (*m. Pesaḥ.* 10: 1–9). The meal proper had three courses, as it might have done in pagan circles.[81] The foods used were various.[82] While the

(1970), 181–202. On the other meals mentioned, see Lietzmann, *Mass and Lord's Supper*, 161–71; Dix, *The Shape of the Liturgy*, 50–102; and now Bradshaw, *The Search for the Origins of Christian Worship*, 47–55. On Qumran meals as eucharistic models, see K. G. Kuhn, 'The Lord's Supper and the Communal Meal at Qumran', in K. Stendahl (ed.), *The Scrolls and the New Testament* (New York: Harper, 1957), 65–93; more tentatively, Matthew Black, *The Scrolls and Christian Origins* (London: Nelson, 1961), 102–15, and most recently J. C. O'Neill, 'Bread and Wine', 176–84.

[79] Bahr, 'The Seder of the Passover and the Eucharistic Words', 201–2.

[80] Ibid. 181–200; Smith, 'Social Obligation', 178–9.

[81] Bahr, 'The Seder of the Passover and the Eucharistic Words', 187–8; Leyerle, 'Meal Customs'.

[82] '. . . lettuce, radishes, cucumbers, fruit, cheese, eggs etc.' for the appetizer; 'unleavened bread, lettuce, and fruit puree' as well as bitter herbs and two other dishes

emphasis placed on cups of wine at earlier points through the meal is not in accordance with the tradition of the *symposium*, it was not unknown in Rome by the first century.[83] Prayers accompany the various cups, as they might have at a *symposium* (*b. Ber.* 43a, *t. Ber.* 4, 8, 9). Thus while there are of course distinctive aspects to the Seder, we should take this meal as exemplar, rather than as exception. As depicted in the rabbinic sources, it makes use of the festive motifs common to Graeco-Roman banquets: reclining, abundance as well as variety and quality of foods, a number of ceremonial wine cups, and a set of expectations for appropriate discourse.[84]

Where doubts have been acknowledged about the connection between Last Supper and Seder, the tendency has often been to seek another specific Jewish meal-type that could serve as a model or precursor. The *haburah* (association) meal is one of the most influential of these types, especially because of its use by both Hans Lietzmann and Gregory Dix.[85] Again, however, the evidence for the procedures of the *haburot* has been used to construct too fixed a picture of Jewish ceremonial meals.[86]

What *Berakot* does provide is a discussion of procedures for blessings over food and wine. The expectation of saying blessings over foods, variations on a theme common to daily prayer and other activities also, provides a religious link between all meals, simple or elaborate.[87] This common theme is worked out in a number of different situations, i.e. for different kinds of foods (6: 1–4; cf. *t. Ber.* 4: 1–7) and for cases where proper order or the applicability of blessings to different courses may be

for the main course; 'wine and various foods such as bread and salted items' for 'dessert', Bahr, 'The Seder of Passover and the Eucharistic Words', 190, 195, 198. While the paschal lamb still holds a prominent place in the rabbinic sources, it is clear that the actual use of lamb was proscribed after the destruction of the Temple (*m. Pesah* 10: 1–9).

[83] Although seen as an innovation by Pliny (*Nat.* 14. 143), drinking unmixed wine is mentioned by Diodorus Siculus somewhat earlier (4. 3); but Pliny's reference seems to be to a mixed and hence more ceremonial cup.

[84] Of course specific meanings are given to the foods in the Seder. Reicke, *Diakonie, Festfreude und Zelos*, 108–110, attempts, without complete success, to link these with the sort of fertility imagery (*Panspermie*) found in some Greek religious contexts, by way of accounting for Christian meals emphasizing remembrance of the dead.

[85] Lietzmann, *Mass and Lord's Supper*, 161–71; Dix, *The Shape of the Liturgy*, 50–102.

[86] For that matter we know rather little about what a *haburah* was; the people called 'associates' in the Mishna are a mystery to us, and it is as hard to imagine whether their meals really had any direct influence on early Christianity as it is to assess the historical value of what the rabbis tell us about these people. See Anthony J. Saldarini, *Pharisees, Scribes and Sadducees in Palestinian Society: A Sociological Approach* (Wilmington, Del.: Michael Glazier, 1988), 216–20.

[87] Tzvee Zahavy, *The Mishnaic Law of Blessings and Prayers: Tractate Berakhot*, BJS 88 (Atlanta: Scholars Press, 1987), 1–7, 77–133.

at issue (6: 5–6). Despite the various scholarly attempts to work out a strict order of various festive meals from these texts, they seem to depict a range of possibilities, even for the important issue of saying the appropriate blessings: 'When they are sitting, each person recites the blessings for himself. When they recline, one person recites the blessings for all of them. When they bring out wine during the meal, each person recites the blessings for himself; after the meal, one person recites the blessings for all of them, (*m. Ber.* 6: 6).[88] This excerpt depicts customs much like those of Greeks and Romans. When guests recline as they would at a more formal or festive occasion, the host (we presume) takes a more formal and focused role by offering food blessings. Similarly the focus on the host offering the prayer for wine after the meal indicates that a *symposium* is envisaged, also a more festive event than if wine were merely served during proceedings.[89] In both cases this emphasis on the role of host is in keeping with the importance that this role takes as a sign of patronage and respect.[90]

Since the Mishna suggests some not-unexpected flexibility or variation in meal practices in accordance with social conventions, it may not be necessary or even wise to use later commentary or supplementary material to systematize.[91] Since the *haburot* may well be understood as local versions of the Roman *collegia*, they are important as another set of groups, rather closer to the Christian communities in space (whether or not in time), which met for meals. There is little or no value in using the

[88] Zahavy, *The Mishnaic Law of Blessings and Prayers*, 85. I understand the contrast as referring to different meals or occasions, and have therefore left out material supplied in the translation to make sense of the change in posture as indicating procedure before and during the meal.

[89] Zahavy reads the Mishna through the Tosefta, thus perhaps running the risk of anachronisms or harmonizations similar to those of which Christian liturgical historians have been guilty. The result is that the different prescriptions are taken to apply to different parts of a more formalized meal than the Mishna could be taken to portray, if read alone: *The Mishnaic Law of Blessings and Prayers*, 85–7.

[90] The Tosefta (4. 8) understands these alternative approaches to the blessings somewhat differently, apparently from a context where this contrast is no longer understood or accepted; 'sitting' is presumed to refer to the time before the meal proper, and the alternative forms of blessing for wine are made cumulative so that two forms must be offered. Without Tosefta's guidance there is doubt about the actual placement of the blessings discussed at 6. 8 and through Ch. 7, assumed by commentators to be blessings after the meal. Only at one point (7. 3) is the meal referred to as having been eaten; but at 7. 5 it seems clear that wine to be blessed has not yet been drunk and hence that the meal is in progress; Zahavy takes 7. 5 as displaced or at least as an 'appendage': *The Mishnaic Law of Blessings and Prayers*, 89–107.

[91] In Ch. 8 of the Mishna it is clear that many disputes about the proper order of proceedings were still in progress between the houses of Hillel and Shammai.

ḥaburah as source of a distinct type of meal that can be neatly separated from others, whatever it is called.[92] Other specific Jewish meal-types, the *qidduš* meal and *zebaḥ todah* or sacrifice of thanksgiving are probably of even less explanatory value for eucharistic origins.[93]

The rabbinic sources, especially the Mishna, certainly remain a valuable source for comparison, even if they do not explain questions of order and other aspects of eucharistic meals quite as neatly as has sometimes been assumed. Differences in meal elements, posture, and prayers are appropriate to the varieties of meal, simple and elaborate, which are envisaged as shared by the readers. Only the actual prayers used in the meal really depart radically from the expectations of pagan diners.

The value of the evidence concerning the forms of Jewish meals for understanding the eucharistic meals of early Christianity lies, therefore, primarily in the comparison of two groups which are both a part of Graeco-Roman society and its range of meal practice, rather than in the use of one to provide an explanation of the other. I approach two or three further, and somewhat marginal, sets of data on Jewish meals, the meal of the Therapeutae described by Philo of Alexandria and the meals of the Qumran community and/or of the Essenes, having again emphasized this point so that the value of these is not seen as dependent upon any organic or specifically genetic connections with Christian ritual meals; these, too, constitute variations within the same realm of possibility.

Philo of Alexandria describes the ritual meals of the Therapeutae, identified as a Jewish group who lived not far from Alexandria (*De Vita Contemplativa*, 37 and 64–89).[94] His description is a very conscious

---

[92] Jacob Neusner, 'Two Pictures of the Pharisees: Philosophical Circle or Eating Club', *ATR* 64 (1982), 525–38, suggests that the rabbinic traditions show no interest in ritual gatherings, which may be going too far; but his discussion does heighten the fact that the Jewish concerns about meals reflected in the Mishna are generalized, rather than specific or limited to certain occasions. On the other hand, his contrast of this type of concern with the ritualization of specific Christian meals draws heavily upon assumptions in dispute here; at least some Christians, too, may have found it hard to recognize radical distinctions between ritual meal and everyday meal.

[93] On the *qidduš* see the criticism by Jeremias, *The Eucharistic Words of Jesus*, 26–9; also Bradshaw, *The Search for the Origins of Christian Worship*, 48–51. In its more modest form (a suggestion of influence in prayer models), the *zebaḥ todah* theory need not be dismissed; but where seen as of genetic significance for the eucharist, the same objections, including that of overstandardization of the Jewish evidence, apply. See Thomas Talley, 'From *Berakah* to *Eucharistia*: A Reopening Question', *Worship*, 50 (1976), 115–37, and Paul Bradshaw, '*Zebah Todah* and the Origins of the Eucharist', *Ecclesia Orans*, 8 (1991), 255–60.

[94] For a recent debate on the nature of the meal as well as those at Qumran, see Baruch Bokser, 'Philo's Description of Jewish Practices', *Center for Hermeneutical Studies: Protocol of the Thirtieth Colloquy* (Berkeley: Center for Hermeneutical Studies, 1977), 1–11, and the

reworking of the ideal *symposium*, and he constantly pits the Therapeutic virtues, as manifest in their meal, against the vices of the famous philosophical banquets. Women are present as full participants. Before reclining in order of seniority, all pray. Frugality is demonstrated in the simplicity of furnishings, lack of servants, and purity of food and drink, which consists only of bread, salt, and water. Before the meal actually begins, a discourse and a hymn take place; the placement of these events before the meal, along with the absence of wine, appears to be a conscious reversal of the classic *symposium*, though there is also a 'vigil' which Philo likens to 'drinking the strong wine of God's love'.[95] No specific blessings are described as taking place over the foods, but it seems as though the whole scene is understood as suffused with prayer and contemplation of eternal truths.

It would seem that readers, too, might well take this meal with a grain of salt. Even if we assume that the Therapeutae did exist, the description of the meal seems to owe much to classical models, admittedly by way of contrast as much as of comparison. Philo's own philosophical bent may lessen any confidence that some real picture, even of sectarian Jewish practice, could be discerned in this description.[96] Yet the meal of the Therapeutae, whether real or ideal, does not step so far outside the bounds of expectation, given the apparent relation between other Jewish meals and the Graeco-Roman tradition.[97] Ascetic and philosophically minded Jews, whom we might expect to find in Alexandria (we know of at least one at this time!) might have celebrated meals like this.[98] Whether or not they ever did so is another question.

'Response' by Lawrence W. Schiffman in that same vol. (19–27), also revised and published as 'Communal Meals at Qumran', *RevQ* 10 (1979), 45–56.

[95] While this is a criticism of the standard symposium, we may note the similar allusion to love as host in Plato, *Symp.* 197 D.

[96] David Hay has suggested that possible differences between Philo's apparent lifestyle and that of the Therapeutae have been ignored, a conclusion which might lead us to take the picture more seriously: 'Things Philo Said and Did Not Say About the Therapeutae', *SBLSP* 31 (1992), 673–83. I am nevertheless inclined to think that the group represents ideals held, but presumably not attained, by Philo.

[97] Bokser, 'Philo's Description of Jewish Practices', 1.

[98] In reaction to E. R. Dodds's analysis of Christian and Jewish asceticism as self-hatred, the practices and motivations of the Essenes, Therapeutae, and Desert Fathers are discussed by Stevan Davies, 'Ascetic Madness', in Robert C. Smith and John Lounibos (eds.), *Pagan and Christian Anxiety: A Response to E. R. Dodds* (Lanham, NY: University Press of America, 1984), 13–26. Davies is right to dismiss the idea that the earlier Jewish models represent radical opposition to the body; but it is too much (or too little) to say that the meal and other aspects of the description are largely based on concern for health or desire for moderation (pp. 17–19).

Finally among these Jewish models we come to the meals of the Qumran community,[99] probably to be identified with the Essenes.[100] Again, the comparison of this eating and drinking with Christian ritual meals has tended to be overshadowed by the tendency to look for genetic explanations of the Christian eucharist. The argument that light is cast on the origin of the eucharist (or at least of the Matthean and Markan accounts of the Last Supper) from the meals of the Qumran community is based on the possible resemblance between the blessings for bread and wine offered together at the beginning of a meal at Qumran (1QS 6: 4–5; 1QSa 2: 11–22) and the similar conjunction of the blessings in two Gospel accounts.[101] Yet the likelihood that the order of blessings at meals was not fixed at this time means that there is no particular reason to link these accounts.[102] If the placement of the blessings before the meal means anything, it is probably that the meal was a simple or ascetic one and that there was no *symposium* envisaged afterwards.

The evidence of Josephus on the practice of the Essenes (*JW* 2 § 131) gives a similar picture of a meal presided over by a priest, before whose blessing none are to eat, and which ends with prayer rather than with a drinking-party. Philo's information on the Essenes is not as detailed as is the report on the Therapeutae. Apart from emphasizing a common table and simplicity in food as in other things, he does describe the Essene units of living as θίασοι, suggesting a link with the practice of pagan religious associations, but it is impossible to say how far that comparison could be used to construct a picture. As in the case of the Therapeutae,

---

[99] See esp. Schiffman, 'Communal Meals at Qumran', 45–56. Some comparisons between the Qumran meals and the meal practice of Jesus (rather than the eucharistic meals of early Christianity) are made by James G. D. Dunn, 'Jesus, Table-Fellowship and Qumran', in James H. Charlesworth (ed.), *Jesus and the Dead Sea Scrolls*, ABRL (New York: Doubleday, 1992), 254–72.

[100] Despite Schiffman's important criticisms of this assumption: see *Reclaiming the Dead Sea Scrolls: Their True Meaning for Judaism and Christianity*, ABRL (New York: Doubleday, 1995), 65–157, and for the more commonly held view, James C. VanderKam, *The Dead Sea Scrolls Today* (Grand Rapids: Eerdmans, 1994), 71–98.

[101] Of course the meal at 1QSa 2 is an eschatological one, but seems to draw upon the same pattern as that in the *Manual of Discipline*, and I treat them together accordingly. On the eucharist and Qumran meals see Kuhn, 'The Lord's Supper and the Communal Meal at Qumran', 65–93; Black, *The Scrolls and Christian Origins*, 102–15 (both are criticized by Richardson, 'A Further Enquiry into Eucharistic Origins', 347–66, who perhaps introduces more problematic material than he eliminates) and now O'Neill, 'Bread and Wine', 180–4, who links the eucharist not only with Qumran but with *Joseph and Aseneth* and a variety of priestly traditions. O'Neill considers food rather than form, but does not discuss the Christian evidence, merely asserting that Christian meals consisted of 'receiving token pieces of bread and token sips of wine' (p. 169).

[102] Thus Jeremias, *The Eucharistic Words of Jesus*, 31–6.

Philo suggests that there is significant concern for order; the picture of the members arranging themselves in rows according to precedence in synagogues could perhaps be applied to meals as well (*Prob.* 81, *Hypoth.* 11: 13; cf. *Contempl.* 67–9). This depiction of Essene life accords again with the evidence from Qumran (1QS 6, 1QSa, and elsewhere). The value of the Qumran or Essene evidence lies therefore, for present purposes at least, in its presentation of the way a ritual meal might be conducted within the context of a Jewish religious association, i.e. with the expected indications of formality and asceticism or restraint.

These varied pieces of Jewish evidence may thus help focus a little more on the formal questions of ancient dining as they may have applied to the early Christians. There is, however, at least as much need to disengage from various unfruitful attempts to make over-specific connections between Jewish meal models and eucharistic meals. There was a revolution of sorts when the necessity of relating Christian meals to Jewish ones was understood by modern scholars.[103] Perhaps unwittingly, this rediscovery seems nevertheless to have adopted the logic of supersessionism, and thus to have made the relationship of Christian scholarship to Judaism as one of regretfully 'despoiling Egypt'. The Jewish origins of Christian meals were therefore seen in terms of Jesus, Paul, or others taking models, above all those attested in the rabbinic literature, and adapting them for Christian use. It is not, however, adequate to extend the genetic fallacy back even beyond the Last Supper, to include a generalized and somewhat idealized picture of the Seder or meals of *ḥaburot* as somehow absorbed, along with their meanings, into the eucharist.

In fact the relations between Christians and Jews during the first few centuries were complex, and there was at least a degree of ongoing borrowing and imitation as well as differentiation and criticism.[104] It is no longer possible to assume that the Mishna or the other rabbinic materials always represent forms of Jewish belief and practice that precede Christianity. As in more contemporary forms of Jewish–Christian dialogue, the way forward for understanding seems to be in placing the two sets of meal practices side by side, rather than one above the other. Further consideration of Jewish food concerns will be

---

[103] 'Our understanding of our forms of worship underwent a radical transformation some forty years ago when it finally occurred to someone that Jesus was a Jew,' Gregory Dix, quoted by Thomas Talley, 'From *Berakah* to *Eucharistia*', 80.
[104] As e.g. in art and architecture; see R. L. P. Milburn, *Early Christian Art and Architecture* (Berkeley: University of California Press, 1988), 9–13.

necessary when some detailed discussion of Christian ritual food-use has taken place. For the moment we should acknowledge that Jewish meal practices, like other, Graeco-Roman ones, included a variety of choices and oppositions which reflect religious, social, and other differences. Among these, the uses of food and drink were not the least significant.

THE CUISINE OF SACRIFICE

The significance of eating in the ancient Mediterranean, pagan or Jewish, is not fully explained by the most careful consideration of the actions and words of those who assembled for communal meals in a *triclinium*, but also needs to be related to practice outside, in market, temple, and forum. The provision of food served not only to express and establish power in the most obvious senses already mentioned, but also to bring religion to the table, and with it a whole set of issues, not simply religious in the modern sense but political as well, related to the practice of sacrifice.

This cuisine of sacrifice was centred on meat.[105] The religious and social significance of sacrifice and meat-eating has been expounded fully in a number of fairly recent works which see these practices as socially constitutive for ancient Greece and beyond.[106] According to Marcel Detienne: 'we see in the Greeks a society in which the basic ritual acts in daily practice are of a sacrificial nature. For nearly ten centuries, guided by immutable cultic statutes, the Greeks never failed to maintain relations with the divine powers through the highly ritualized killing

---

[105] Recently Peter D. Gooch has emphasized, in connection with 1 Cor. 8 and 10, that 'idol-food' could theoretically have been other things too: *Dangerous Food: 1 Corinthians 8–10 in Its Context*, Studies in Christianity and Judaism, 5 (Waterloo, Ont.: Wilfred Laurier, 1993), 1–13, 21–6. Meat was, however, the main focus of concern about sacrificial food, and the major link between sacrifice and meals elsewhere.

[106] The importance of meat and sacrifice for the Greeks has been underscored in a series of works, in particular by French scholars associated with the Centre de recherches comparées sur les sociétés anciennes. See the representative essays in Detienne and Vernant, *The Cuisine of Sacrifice among the Greeks*, and in R. L. Gordon (ed.), *Myth, Religion and Society: Structuralist Essays by M. Detienne, L. Gernet, J.-P. Vernant and P. Vidal-Naquet* (Cambridge: Cambridge University Press, 1981). On the sometimes important differences under the Roman Empire, see Corbier, 'The Ambiguous Status of Meat in Ancient Rome', 223–64. Stanley Stowers uses these and the more cross-cultural theory of Jay, *Throughout Your Generations Forever*, in 'Greeks Who Sacrifice and Those Who Do Not: Toward an Anthropology of Greek Religion', in L. Michael White and O. Larry Yarborough (eds.), *The Social World of the First Christians: Essays in Honor of Wayne A. Meeks* (Minneapolis: Augsburg Fortress, 1995), 293–333.

of animal victims, whose flesh was consumed collectively according to precise strictures.'[107]

As the constitutive religious ritual for Greek society in particular, sacrifice was a means not only of establishing and maintaining proper relations among human beings and between humanity and the gods, but also included animals, and their meat in particular, as key elements of that ritual and those relations. Most clearly, sacrifice established cosmic order by making offerings to the gods. Although more reflective writers and observers were uneasy about the somewhat crude anthropomorphism of offering meat to divine beings, it is clear that maintenance of sacrificial ritual was important to all who valued piety.[108] Without it, there seems to have been fear not only of divine displeasure but also of a crumbling of the fabric of the material world and culture, and of the differences between human beings and animals as well as between different classes of human beings, structures understood (by those writing and defending them at least) to be cosmically as well as socially constitutive.

Sacrifice was also a political activity. Direct participation in sacrifice was often limited to free-born males; women, resident aliens, slaves, and others seem to have stood (literally and otherwise) at some distance to the central event in most cases, but were made participants in a different sense through receiving the meat of the offering, mediated through the male citizens in the quantitatively expressed hierarchy already discussed.[109] Nancy Jay's analysis suggests that as a gendered activity,

---

[107] See Detienne, 'Culinary Practices and the Spirit of Sacrifice', *The Cuisine of Sacrifice Among the Greeks*, 1–20 (quote from p. 1); and further Jean-Louis Durand, 'Greek Animals: Toward a Topology of Edible Bodies', ibid. 87–118, and 'Ritual as Instrumentality', ibid. 119–28. While Detienne *et al.* criticize universal theories of sacrifice such as those of Durkheim and Mauss (as crypto-Christian), their own insistence on a universal and uniform essence over such a long period, even for Greek sacrifice, itself risks eliminating variety under the influence of an ideal type. For present purposes, we need only accept a substantial continuity between classical and late antique times in thought and practice.

[108] Perhaps two strategies could be identified among the revisionist (rather than oppositional) pagan responses: that which sought more appropriate offerings, of which Pythagoras is presented as champion; and that represented by such as Celsus (see Origen, *Contra Celsum*, 8. 29–31), which defended animal sacrifice but linked it with lesser divine beings rather than the true God or Gods. Porphyry, *De Abstinentia*, also presents animal sacrifice as for such lesser (and less attractive) *daimones*.

[109] See Detienne, 'The Violence of Well-Born Ladies', *The Cuisine of Sacrifice Among the Greeks*, 131–2; W. S. Ferguson, 'The Attic Orgeones', *HTR* 37 (1944), 73–7. The extent to which women were excluded is a matter of present debate; discussing classical Greek evidence, Robin Osborne criticizes Detienne's radical exclusion of women even from meat-eating ('Women and Sacrifice in Classical Greece', *Classical Quarterly*, 43

sacrifice in this culture (and some others) played an important part in creating patrilineal kinship.[110] Sacrifice could therefore be a powerful expression and reinforcement of patriarchy, slavery, and the political chauvinism of the city or state. The transition from the city as locus of power to the Roman Empire seems to have involved a reordering of these same elements rather than a radical change. In sacrifice, the personal figure of the Emperor came to be the symbolic centre of the political structure constantly re-enacted in sacrifice, an earthly embodiment of the benevolent despotism of the universe (see Celsus, in Origen, *Contra Celsum*, 8. 68).[111]

Through sacrifice therefore, a most important (if not altogether common) element of cuisine was itself rendered sacral, even when bought at the meat-market rather than consumed in the temple. The association of meat with sacrifice was such that meat could be referred to as τὸ ἱερεῖον, 'that which is holy' or 'sacrificed', without further qualification (Xenophon, *Cyr.* 1. 4. 17; Oribasius, 2. 68. 6). Meat was associated with sacrifice directly and indirectly. Typically, sacrificial ritual centred on the slaughter of an animal victim and consumption of its meat by the participants. Many temples were equipped with dining areas where the feast, an integral part of the sacrifice itself rather than merely a happy but incidental event, took place. Yet the significance of the sacrifice for meals extended beyond the temple precinct. Portions were often taken home by participants. The meat of sacrificial victims seems often to have been sold, and was readily available to the point that a first-century Christian might have to assume that there was a reasonable chance that meat in a market was from a temple.[112] The sale of such meat was of considerable economic

(1993), 392–405); but, in a slightly different context, John Scheid's argument that Roman women were largely not involved in the actual ritual of sacrifice is not insubstantial; see 'The Religious Roles of Roman Women', *A History of Women in the West*, i. *From Ancient Goddesses to Christian Saints* (Cambridge, Mass.: Belknap, 1992), 377–408.

[110] Jay, *Throughout Your Generations Forever*, 30–60. Scheid, 'The Religious Roles of Roman Women', 398, points out that the usurping of the father's role relative to the city may well have been the key problem in the scandal over the Bacchanalia of 186 BCE (Livy, 34. 1). Stowers, 'Greeks Who Sacrifice and Those Who Do Not', 299–306, points out that Jay takes maternity as essential and paternity as constructed, but himself argues that they are both constructs of sacrificial ritual. These two discussions depend rather heavily on bloodshed as linking birth and sacrifice. In fact sacrificing groups are also agnatic, seemingly concerned with broader (but admittedly patriarchal) kinship, as well as with parenthood.

[111] This is illuminated by S. R. F. Price, *Rituals and Power: The Roman Imperial Cult in Asia Minor* (Cambridge: Cambridge University Press, 1984).

[112] As implied in 1 Cor. 8 and 10. Stowers, 'Greeks Who Sacrifice and Those Who Do Not', 294, Dalby, *Siren Feasts*, 9, and Smith, 'Social Obligation', 12, all assert that meat

importance to the priests, who were often also leading citizens rather than merely religious specialists.[113] There is some evidence that sacrificial meat, when identifiable as such, was preferred by those who had power to choose.[114] Even where meat was not the product of actual sacrifice, there was an association of cultic convention with roles such as that of butcher; while choice of fish for a banquet depended on host and cook, that of meat involved the μαγείρος.[115] A downturn in religious practice might well mean first and foremost a decline in meals linked to sacrifice, such as the meals of *collegia* or those of the wealthy who could afford meat. In some cases at least, clubs might own and run cook-shops through which a managed surplus might be sold ready to eat.[116]

Other foods were used in certain sacrificial rituals, but they were not as prevalent, nor used in other meals after being employed in temple ritual. In fact some foods might well be understood as conceptually opposed to sacrificial food. Despite the use of cereals in some ritual, bread was arguably the prosaic opposite of sacrificial meat: common rather than prized, bloodless not bloody, vegetable not animal, if not raw then at least often cold. This tension is expressed in the Promethean myth wherein wheat and meat are exchanged (Hesiod, *Works and Days*, 45–105, *Theogony*, 535–616).[117]

---

was normally sacrificed (Stowers: 'except under extraordinary circumstances'), but this needs to be qualified. Allowance must be made for indications that sacrificial meat was preferred, and hence there was sometimes a choice; see further below. Corbier, 'The Ambiguous Status of Meat in Ancient Rome', 223–64, also suggests historical change and increased availability, with correspondingly decreased religious or numinous significance, as time goes on during the Roman period.

[113] Pliny, *Ep.* 10. 96; see A. N. Sherwin-White, *The Letters of Pliny: A Historical and Social Commentary* (Oxford: Clarendon, 1966), 709–10.

[114] Aune, 'Septem Sapientium Convivium', 71. This conclusion can be drawn from a passage in the *Life of Aesop* where pigs' tongues are identified as coming from victims: see M. Isenberg, 'The Sale of Sacrificial Meat', *Classical Philology*, 70 (1975), 271–3, and Joan Frayn, 'The Roman Meat Trade', in Wilkins, Harvey, and Dobson (eds.), *Food in Antiquity*, 112–13.

[115] Dalby, *Siren Feasts*, 10. See further Guy Berthiaume, *Les Rôles du mágeiros: Étude sur la boucherie, la cuisine et la sacrifice dans la Grèce ancienne*, Mnemosyne Supplementum, 70 (Leiden: E. J. Brill, 1982), 17–78. These conventions may have been weaker in Rome than in Greece; see Corbier, 'The Ambiguous Status of Meat in Ancient Rome', 232–3.

[116] See *IG* ii². 1301, discussed by Ferguson, 'The Attic Orgeones', 113–14.

[117] J.-P. Vernant, 'At Man's Table: Hesiod's Foundation Myth of Sacrifice', in Detienne and Vernant, *The Cuisine of Sacrifice Among the Greeks*, esp. 35–9. There is admittedly a sense in which the opposition is taken up *within* Greek religion in the contrast of earthy or chthonic and Olympian deities and cultus, in which schema cereals are more easily associated with Demeter. It is intriguing that archaeological evidence suggests meat was not eaten in the all-female feasts of Demeter and Kore at Corinth; see Bookidis, 'Ritual Dining at Corinth', 54–5.

Where meals with a cultic aspect do not involve meat, the focus of religious concern does not necessarily move to the otherwise most important or prized food remaining. Fish, neither domestic nor likely to be brought alive to an altar, were not normally appropriate for sacrifice (see Plutarch, *Quaest. Conv.* 729 C–D);[118] they were part of an alien world far removed from that of agriculture and human sociability.[119] Rather, wine or incense, lesser but not unimportant elements of the cuisine and accoutrements considered appropriate for sacrifice, might be specified as being offered with prayer.[120]

Wine in particular features as the single most common element used to indicate the religious character of any meal, being more commonly consumed than meat. Wine formed part of the cuisine of sacrifice in a somewhat different way; its production was not itself ritualized, but its consumption was. To drink without libation, at a banquet at least, was unthinkable. More than for any other item of food or drink, the offering of wine with prayer, even in the domestic setting, was uniquely important. This practice was an echo of the more explicitly cultic use of libations as a necessary part of sacrificial ritual in temples, the creation of an analogue between the uses of food and drink in these separate but related spheres. The association of wine with sacrifice meant that libations were one of the obvious means by which a Roman magistrate might put Christians to the test (Pliny, *Ep.* 10. 96). Some religious clubs focused their attention on wine, giving portions of honour to members just as meat was commonly distributed in fixed portions after animal sacrifice.[121] Thus we might say that while wine, unlike meat, was not in itself sacralized, its use almost necessarily was; and it is therefore no accident that, as we shall see further, the qualms which various groups raised about it are in important respects similar to, and indeed joined to, those regarding meat.

Just as bread or grain was a sort of logical opposite to meat, water

[118] The exceptions are real, but serve in a sense to prove the rule; the most significant was the tuna, which bleeds like a mammal. Athenaeus reports this (7. 297, 303) and Boeotian use of eels (7. 297) as acknowledged oddities, clearly based on the usual, domestic animal, forms of sacrifice. See Durand, 'Ritual as Instrumentality', 119–28; Brian Sparkes, 'A Pretty Kettle of Fish', in Wilkins, Harvey, and Dobson (eds.), *Food in Antiquity*, 150–61.

[119] See now in particular the discussion by Nicholas Purcell, 'Eating Fish: The Paradoxes of Seafood', in Wilkins, Harvey, and Dobson (eds.), *Food in Antiquity*, 132–49.

[120] The Lanuvium funerary club uses fish for its celebrations and directs the *quinquennalis* to offer incense and wine; the fish have no part in the ritual: *CIL* xiv. 2112, col. 2. 29–30.

[121] Thus the Athenian Ἰόβακχοι, of the 2nd cent. CE, the period at issue here. Their rules are provided in *IG* ii². 1368; See Smith, 'Social Obligation', 145–6.

likewise opposes itself to wine, if for somewhat different reasons. Although natural, pure, and capable of ritual use, water was generally not to be offered in libations, whose proper element was wine (e.g. Philostratus, *Vita Apoll.* 2. 6–7). Exceptions were made with water, milk, and honey for certain divinities and occasions (*Odyssey*, 10. 519; Aeschylus, *Eumenides*, 107), but these were acknowledged as exceptional (see Plutarch, *Mor.* 132 E, 464 C) and serve to reinforce the normal association of sacrifice and wine.[122]

Theophrastus' account of the emergence of sacrifice confirms both sets of associations—of meat and wine with sacrifice, and of grain and water as their polar opposites—in a historicized fashion: as the cereal offerings of an idyllic past had made way, first for more domesticated vegetable foods (fruit and bread) and then for meat, so water libations had gradually been transformed into the pouring of honey, then oil, and finally wine (fr. 12, in Porphyry, *De Abst.* 2. 20).[123] Just as a domesticated animal, the product of human culture as well as of its own kind, was the necessary food element of sacrifice, the drink appropriate to festivity and worship was also a divine gift mediated through the processes made possible by human culture. It seems that it was not enough for an offering to be 'natural'; it had also (or rather) to be 'cultured'.[124]

The cuisine of sacrifice may therefore best be understood not merely as the varieties of food eaten in temples, but as the eating of meat and drinking of wine in temples, club meetings, festivals, and at meals generally.[125] All this means that there was a fundamental problem for those, such as Christians, who wished to participate in the social, political, and economic benefits, as well as the dietary ones, of most important meal practices of the Graeco-Roman world, but whose religious scruples prevented them from joining in meals involving sacrificial meat in particular. Gerd Theissen has suggested that the poorer members of a community might only have been able to eat meat when present at occasions of a pagan religious nature (the distribution of

---

[122] Fritz Graf, 'Milch, Honig und Wein: Zum Verständnis der Libation im griechischen Ritual', *Perennitas: Studi in onore di Angelo Brelich* (Rome: Edizioni dell'Ateneo, 1980), 209–21. On the exceptions, see further below on milk and honey.

[123] Ibid. 212–14.

[124] On this distinction and its continued importance for early Christian eaters, see Blake Leyerle, 'Clement of Alexandria on the Importance of Table Etiquette', *JECS* 3 (1995), 123–41.

[125] While Peter Gooch points out that there might have been other foods associated with idol-worship, the evidence for the unique importance of meat cannot be pushed aside simply by presenting a schema of different foods that might have had cultic significance; see *Dangerous Food*, 5–13, 53–6, 129.

meat by political hopefuls may be an exception, but even this may have been from animals ritually slaughtered (Cicero, *Off.* 2. 52)), and that the problems in regard to meat-eating in the Christian community at Corinth (1 Cor. 8, 10) between 'strong' and 'weak' groups may have had as much to do with economic and social incentives and opportunities for meat-eating as it did with religious scruples.[126]

Although wine was also clearly associated with the religious aspect of a banquet or communal meal, the different relationship between its supply and religious employment means that it did not need to be regarded as so thoroughly problematic, although there were exceptions, as we shall see. Generally however, since the wine was 'sacrificed' or made sacral in the course of the meal itself, through libations and prayers, rather than through its association or employment in temple ritual, many Jews and Christians might be expected to use it without qualms. So too, the prevalence of wine across all sections of society and its common use outside communal meals altogether could be expected to mean that it was not so immutably associated with pagan ritual. Christians and Jews also, however, would render wine sacral according to their own principles and their own traditions.

Hence the foods of the Christian meal best known and attested, the eating of bread and drinking of wine, could be understood as a compromise with or oblique response to the cuisine of sacrifice. Meat was tainted with the associations of idolatry even for Paul, the apostle of the clear culinary conscience, and so could not easily have been employed in the meals of Christian communities, even if there had been a ritual tradition encouraging such use. Wine, while free of such direct sacrificial associations, was still capable of being viewed in the light of festive and religious custom, Jewish as well as Gentile, and could therefore readily be used in a meal which, for Paul, clearly came to have overtones which were sacrificial in nature. And yet there are hints that wine also was a dangerous thing to consume, not only at Corinth, but in Rome and elsewhere. In the light of the importance of sacrifice for society as a whole, it is not surprising that consumption of meat and of wine should be a key issue for the emerging Christian communities, just as it was (as we shall see further) for other groups somewhat marginal to the mainstream of religion and society.

While these important issues of meat and sacrifice have received much

---

[126] G. Theissen, 'The Strong and the Weak in Corinth: A Sociological Analysis of a Theological Quarrel', in John H. Schütz (ed. and trans.), *The Social Setting of Pauline Christianity: Essays on Corinth* (Philadelphia: Fortress, 1982), 121–43.

attention in relation to Paul and the Corinthians, less significance has been attached to the ongoing connection (or opposition) between Christian ritual meals and sacrifice, and the highly charged choices between avoidance even of sacrificial language and thought on the one hand, and accommodation to the wider society and its expectations on the other. The importance of sacrifice as a factor in persecution and martyrdom is undisputed, but has not been fully explored in relation to eucharistic meals. Commentators have tended to emphasize the sense in which the eucharist was a sacrifice, to the exclusion of the sense in which it obviously was not. For the moment I suggest merely that these issues did not disappear, and that the ordering of diet and ritual life in the first few centuries of early Christianity may have continued to be influenced by the sorts of choices that faced Paul's correspondents in Corinth.

ASCETICISM

Introduction

To consider the significance of food as we ought, it is necessary to discuss non-consumption as well as consumption. For that matter, even the issues of structure and order already discussed could be described as matters of asceticism.[127] If there are times when modern discussions of ancient meals or other social conventions tend to generate stereotypical pictures of cultural and social practice, the issue of asceticism raises ideas and practices which are distinguished by their *resistance* to cultural norms, rather than by reducibility to the same. Of course asceticism may also, at another level, be capable of being understood as a part of the same society which it tends to resist, as a type of practice whose meaning depends very much on the opposite which it rejects;[128] whether this can still be the case when, for example, the response of the dominant culture to an ascetic individual or community is violence and repression is another question. For the moment, I suggest that when considering the early Christians as eaters we are dealing with communities often characterized by a particular asceticism with respect to the prevailing culture and its use of foods.

This may not be immediately obvious, if we tend to assume that the

---

[127] See for instance Geoffrey Galt Harpham, *The Ascetic Imperative in Culture and Criticism* (Chicago: University of Chicago Press, 1987), pp. xi-xiii.

[128] Ibid. xii-xvii.

ascetic is the extreme or the radically self-denying. Yet it is not enough to conceive of asceticism as a quantitative issue, where a one-dimensional scale going from excess through moderation to self-denial could be used to plot the situation of individuals or groups according simply to the amounts they eat.[129] Asceticism has a qualitative, as well as a quantitative, aspect. This means that issues of non-consumption must be considered in relation to the things normally consumed by different members of society, and in relation to foods with particular significance. In other words, the asceticism of those who eat as much as others but do not eat certain foods is as important as, if somewhat different from, that of those who simply eat little. Jewish food restrictions may be the best-known example of such concerns, but it is important to consider the non-consumption of other groups in ancient Greek and Roman society.

Asceticism also has a social aspect that must be included in accounts of Christian food concerns in particular. When in discussion of early Christianity, 'asceticism' sometimes becomes a synonym for 'monasticism', there is a danger that the importance of practices earlier than those of the fourth century is swept away in the rush to develop a picture consonant with the exemplary virtue of the early monks (or even with Foucault's 'construction of the self').[130] It may be important to distinguish, for instance, between forms of non-consumption intended to affect the practitioner, those directed at others (e.g. by means of prayer), and those which are customary or legal forms of community practice.[131]

The problem of meat at Corinth provides such an example. Despite the temptation to read dietary self-denial primarily in terms of concern for the individual body and its health (or mortification), indications are, as exegetes generally recognize, that the primary concerns among the 'weak' and 'strong' among Paul's addressees at Corinth may have had to

---

[129] There is a tendency to pass over these questions in considering Christian asceticism, based partly on the attraction of the monks and their practices; to quote a representative discussion, for 'the earliest Christian ascetics' (apparently meaning the monks!) 'it is the activity of eating, rather than food itself, that assumes symbolic significance for the creation and cultivation of a religious self' (Margaret Miles, 'Religion and Food: The Case of Eating Disorders', *JAAR* 63 (1995), 550). I suspect this analysis is not entirely adequate even for the famous ascetics of the 4th and following centuries (see my brief comments in Ch. 6 below).

[130] For example, the discussion by Harpham, *The Ascetic Imperative*, 27–8: 'Pagan asceticism is a public and even civic practice. Christian asceticism, by stark contrast, concentrates exclusively on the self . . .'.

[131] Bruce Malina's application of Douglas's 'group' and 'grid' concepts to the question of fasting and other forms of non-consumption gives a helpful example of the possibility of seeing the meaning of non-consumption in more contextual ways: *Christian Origins and Cultural Anthropology* (Atlanta: John Knox, 1986), 190–201.

do with their place in society (including, of course, religion). These concerns about whether or not to eat meat did not emerge with the Pauline correspondence; rather they have a history that is prominent in classical antiquity and which deserves some further consideration.

The Philosophy of Food

The main sources for Greek and Roman asceticism with regard to food are those we would term philosophical writers. In using these sources we may therefore be considering a somewhat élite sample of concerns. There are, however, indications that these matters were discussed and practised among whole communities. It may also be important to remind ourselves in this context that the philosopher was one not necessarily so much predisposed to speculation as to consideration of virtue and of the good life, i.e. with practice.

Despite the fact that the likes of Philo could pillory the classical *symposium* as devoted to lust and drunkenness (*Contempl.* 58–64), there was substantial concern for moderation and self-control in the philosophical tradition which he had inherited. Some mention of this has already been made in describing the range of possibilities for the conduct of banquets; people who were wealthy enough to feast in fine style might well choose to moderate their celebrations for reasons such as general health and well-being or the avoidance of extravagance.[132] There seems to have been significant support for the Delphic adage 'nothing to excess', a theme which finds echoes in different philosophical schools, if somewhat differently understood in practice.

If most were content to seek moderation, there were also more radical options which appeared from time to time and which had their effect on moderate or conservative discussions as well. The rejection of meat-eating is the most obvious of these radical responses to the dominant culture of bloody sacrifice, and the best-known of these critics or dissidents was Pythagoras. He and his followers were the most famous of ancient rejecters of meat-eating, but they did not appear entirely in a vacuum. There were earlier Greek understandings of primordial peace between animals and humans, and Orphic and Egyptian ideas of transmigration of souls into various bodies may have had some impact on Pythagoras and others.[133]

---

[132] Corbier, 'The Ambiguous Status of Meat in Ancient Rome', 240–2.

[133] See Daniel A. Dombrowski, *The Philosophy of Vegetarianism* (Amherst, Mass.: University of Massachusetts Press, 1984), 35–6, and for a fuller account on Orphic vegetarianism and Egyptian influences, Johannes Haussleiter, *Der Vegetarismus in der Antike* (Berlin: Alfred Töpelmann, 1935), 79–96 and 145–50 respectively.

These conceptions of ensoulment and metempsychosis have dominated general discussions of Pythagoreanism and its influence on later vegetarian diet. Typically, it is stated that because animal or other bodies were ensouled, fish as well as land animals were not eaten by Pythagoreans; and the extension of this understanding to beans, as possible receptacles for souls, is one of the popular explanations for the Pythagorean prohibition of those legumes.[134] Stories about Pythagoras also suggest that reasons of health and broader concerns about appropriate conduct were also important in his movement.[135]

In fact the Pythagorean picture is somewhat more confused than this, and while there are historical problems involved which cannot concern us here, the contradictions in the evidence may be revealing.[136] Despite the common image of Pythagoras having extended the moral concern about taking human life to include animals, there are other indications that he and his early followers were not necessarily opposed to all killing or eating of animals, but critical of certain forms of killing and eating, and specifically of certain forms of sacrifice. Some witnesses suggest he excluded not all meat or all animal sacrifice but opposed specific offerings, such as white cocks or lambs and working cattle, implying that others were acceptable (Diogenes Laertius, *Lives*, 8. 12, 20, 34; cf. Aulus Gellius, *NA* 4. 11, Iamblichus, *De Vita Pyth.* 18. 85). Wine, which obviously bore no relationship to killing animals but was characteristic of standard civic religious practice, was acceptable to some Pythagoreans but not to others (Iamblichus, *De Vita Pyth.* 97–8; cf. 107).[137] The contradictions between the 'vegetarian' picture and this more complex one may not need simply to be resolved by deciding that one or other picture is true, but may reflect different aspects of the Pythagorean tradition, as not only a religious sect but also a political reform that influenced whole cities.[138] While sacrifice is obviously an issue in either version of the Pythagorean dietary concerns, either of these regimens

---

[134] A vexed question; some have suggested that favism, a condition which prevents safe eating of beans, may have led to the exclusion of beans by Pythagoras. See J. Scarborough, 'Beans, Pythagoras, Taboos and Ancient Dietetics', *Classical World*, 75 (1982), 355–8. Detienne uses more symbolic indications of the perceived importance of the bean: 'La Cuisine de Pythagore', *Archives de Sociologie des Religions*, 29 (1970), 153–4. More generally, see Dombrowski, *The Philosophy of Vegetarianism*, 43–4, and Haussleiter, *Der Vegetarismus in der Antike*, 85–96.

[135] Dombrowski, *The Philosophy of Vegetarianism*, 37–54; Haussleiter, *Der Vegetarismus in der Antike*, 127–44.

[136] See esp. Detienne, 'La Cuisine de Pythagore'.

[137] See Graf, 'Milch, Honig und Wein', 215–16.

[138] Detienne, 'La Cuisine de Pythagore', 142–8.

may best be described as sacrificially revisionist rather than simply anti-sacrificial as such.

Ascetic critiques of sacrifice varied in their specifics, but there are some striking common elements and symbols. The idea of a golden age in which meat-eating was unknown and unnecessary was an important one, acknowledged even by those who do not seem to have paid it much practical attention (Plato, *Politicus*, 271 D–272 B).[139] Empedocles (5th cent. BCE) and the Peripatetic Theophrastus (4th cent. BCE) accepted the notion of primordial peace in advocating a diet without meat, and wine—mixed wine in particular—was also removed from this imagery of pristine eating.[140] This was no mere matter of partisan philosophy; by the third century CE the Neoplatonists Plotinus and Porphyry could claim the same understanding and practice.[141] The power of this protological basis for avoidance of meat seems to have been very real.

Not all the reasons given among the philosophers for rejecting meat-eating were related to prehistoric idylls. The affinity between humans and land animals, whether or not couched in terms of ensoulment, was also a prominent theme. Plutarch's diner Lamprias says:

As far as the land animals whose meat is here before us is concerned, we must admit at least this if nothing else, that they consume the same food and breathe the same air as we do, and drink and bathe in water no different from ours. This has in times past made people ashamed when they butchered them in spite of their pitiful cries and in spite of having made companions of most of them and shared their store of food with them. (*Quaest. Conv.* 669 D–E)

This affinity was, however, ambiguous. For the majority who accepted the value of meat-eating, as soon as the relation between humanity and other animals was rendered visible it was necessary to cover it again, or at least to restrain its possible negative implications.

Aristotle is perhaps the best representative of this position or strategy among the philosophers: while acknowledging that certain of the psychic powers were present in animals as well as humans, with the result that one should ask not whether a particular being has a soul but rather what

---

[139] Dombrowski, *The Philosophy of Vegetarianism*, 19–34. Detienne suggests that the foods attributed to Pythagoras' recommended diet (Porphyry, *Vita Pyth.* 34–6) were indicative of a time even before cultivation: 'La Cuisine de Pythagore', 148–53.

[140] Empedocles, frs. 128 and 130, in H. Diels, *Die Fragmente der Vorsokratiker*, 10th edn. (Berlin: Weidmann, 1960); Theophrastus is often cited in Porphyry, *De Abstinentia*, probably from *On Piety*. See also Graf, 'Milch, Honig und Wein'.

[141] On Porphyry, see Catherine Osborne, 'Ancient Vegetarianism', in Wilkins, *Food in Antiquity*, 218–23; and for the intervening period see Dombrowski, *The Philosophy of Vegetarianism*, 55–119.

kind of soul, he finally places most emphasis for practical purposes on the remaining distinction, that of thinking (*On the Soul*, 2. 3. 414 A–415 A).[142] This is not a surprising place to have put the stress, given his view of humanity and society, to which these attitudes to food and eating must be related here as otherwise. Aristotle is in step with the dominant social and religious tradition of Greece in seeing the line between humans and animals as thin but absolutely vital. If humans do not live in society with all that that means, including the ritualized re-enactment of the relations between gods, humans, and animals in sacrifice, then humans themselves are animals. In the famous passage he says that a human being is a 'political animal'; but also that 'the person who is naturally without a city is either something less than, or more than, human' (*Pol.* 1. 1. 9). This is the essence not only of his own cosmology but also that of the Greek city, the place that stands between animal chaos and divine transcendence; and sacrifice, the consummate civic event, is the ritualized preservation of those distinctions. Aristotle thus represents a position that makes more systematic the ambiguity of other philosophers who acknowledge some awkwardness about eating meat yet nevertheless go ahead and sacrifice.[143]

In fact the prominent dissident tradition of qualms about meat-eating is all the more remarkable given the importance of meat and sacrifice in these societies. To reject meat was possibly to reject religion, and even morality; it was to reject the distinctions recounted in mythology and re-enacted in sacrifice that rendered this affinity between animals and humans powerless, not only so that humans might eat animals, but also so that humans might not eat each other. It may also have been to reject the internal structuring of human society and the distinctions, especially that of gender, which maintained internal order.[144]

The more commonly held position of the reflective carnivore had its own version of protological eating patterns; the realm of nature was not always an idyllic prelude to history to which it would have been desirable to return, but was rather the place of primordial contest and of

---

[142] Dombrowski, *The Philosophy of Vegetarianism*, 64–72; Dombrowski, however, thinks that Aristotle should, if consistent, have been a vegetarian; it will be apparent that we differ on this.

[143] So too does the remarkable compromise of the Pythagorean community at Croton, reported on by Aristoxenus of Tarentum, who were not vegetarian; Aristoxenus also suggests that Pythagoras himself only refused to eat the domestic ox and the sheep. This is discussed in very interesting terms by Detienne, 'La Cuisine de Pythagore', esp. 142–8. See also Stowers, 'Greeks Who Sacrifice and Those Who Do Not', 325–9.

[144] Jay, *Throughout Your Generations Forever*, 30–60; Detienne, 'The Violence of Wellborn Ladies: Women in the Thesmophoria', 129–47.

cannibalism.[145] The rejection of meat in its institutional forms was thus arguably to risk promoting cannibalism, and Pythagoreans were not immune to being accused of this practice.[146] But more representative of a sort of dietary anarchy were the Cynics, to whom we should also give some attention.

The possible influence of Cynic philosophy and practice on early Christianity has recently been the subject of some serious debate.[147] As elsewhere, the purpose of raising these issues is not to adjudicate debates on the question of origins, which has sometimes tended to dominate those discussions as well, but to begin to consider the possibility of Cynic influences or comparisons in the second and third centuries. While most of the discussion about Cynics and Christians has focused on Jesus and the 'Q' community, F. Gerald Downing in particular has taken this question somewhat further in time, to the end of the fourth century. While the only issue of food and meals prominent in his discussion is that of cannibalism,[148] there is considerable evidence that will be discussed further below on the relationship between the less fantastic aspect of Cynic meals and those of early Christians.

The *Lives of Famous Philosophers* by Diogenes Laertius may serve as a primary source for Cynics, not because of its historical value for the lives of Antisthenes, Diogenes, and their early followers, but as exemplifying the reception of a tradition of philosophy and ethics in the ancient world. Cynic values seem to have emphasized disdain for authority and convention, and tradition had it that this was manifested in spectacular acts of public transgression of taboos such as defecation (Diogenes Laertius, ibid. 6. 2. 61) and sexual intercourse (6. 7. 97). With regard

---

[145] Andrew McGowan, 'Eating People: Accusations of Cannibalism against Christians in the Second Century', *JECS* 2 (1994), 428–31.

[146] Ibid. 423–5, 432.

[147] Burton L. Mack, *A Myth of Innocence*; Leif E. Vaage, *Galilean Upstarts: Jesus' First Followers According to Q* (Valley Forge, Pa.: Trinity Press International, 1994); F. Gerald Downing, *Christ and the Cynics* (Sheffield: JSOT, 1988) and *Cynics and Christian Origins* (Edinburgh: T. & T. Clark, 1992).

[148] Expanded upon in his 'Cynics and Christians, Oedipus and Thyestes', *JEH* 44 (1993), 1–10. Despite the value of some comparison with Cynicism, the connection seems to me rather less direct than Downing argues. The argument that the combination of cannibalism and incest is uniquely characteristic of Cynicism (and Christians) is weak; they are commonly, and logically, paired. There is both cannibalism and incest among the gods, and various allegations of sexual disorder in many other cases, esp. of distant and strange peoples. While he is right to say that the evidence specifically pertaining to 'secretive religious groups' is inadequate, consideration of other examples which violate boundaries such as those of nation, time, and social or cosmic order provides a fuller set of comparisons: see McGowan, 'Eating People', 418–33 and John Rives, 'Human Sacrifice Among Pagans and Christians', *Journal of Roman Studies*, 85 (1995), 65–85.

to food the equivalent disordered action was cannibalism, violation of the ultimate food taboo.

In fact the evidence suggests not only that all these actions or suggestions may have been exaggerated by critics, but that this was not the behaviour expected from or attributed to later Cynics.[149] In the case of cannibalism the most ever suggested is that Diogenes was willing to defend it (6. 2. 73–4). But while the tradition of Cynic shamelessness grew and may have had influence on would-be Cynics as well as critics, there was a more serious side to Cynic tradition and lifestyle. While it seems difficult or perhaps impossible to define an 'essence' of Cynicism, there are some common threads, especially those to do with actual practice, including use of food.[150]

These choices for Cynic behaviour seem to cohere reasonably well around concepts such as what is 'natural', 'virtuous', 'free', and 'ascetic', despite the difficulty that ought to be acknowledged in seeking to use catchwords or -phrases as the definition of Cynic views.[151] Thus while one might have expected the Cynic disdain for convention to lead to an outrageous and extraordinary diet, in fact the evidence suggests that what was more often sought was food understood to be simple and natural. An opposition of sorts between nature and culture therefore seems to have led to rejection, or at least mitigation, of the importance of certain practices, negative or positive, related to food. Anecdotes concerning Diogenes also indicate lack of concern for the serious gaffes of eating in public places (6. 2. 48, 57, 61, 69), using food that had fallen to the ground (6. 2. 35) or scavenging (6. 2. 58, 61).[152] Diogenes, a would-be savage mind it seems, is said to have spurned the opposition of the raw and the cooked by trying to eat uncooked meat (6. 2. 34), and to have died trying to eat a raw octopus (6. 2. 76).

If Diogenes had practical difficulties in chewing meat, more often it seems that principle and necessity both led Cynics to eschew it. As we have seen, meat was a most desirable and expensive component of diet. Although there seems to have been nothing Diogenes would not do on principle, he seems to have been critical of luxurious eating, and of banquets in general, for moral as well as dietary reasons (6. 2. 25–6, 28, 46, 59), and to have regarded meat-eating as wrong or at least capable of being overdone (6. 2. 49).

---

[149] Downing, *Cynics and Christian Origins*, 50–3.
[150] Ibid. 26–56.
[151] Ibid. 45–50.
[152] Cf. the picture in Ps.-Lucian, *The Cynic*, 5, where the Cynic practice is to eat whatever comes to hand.

Asked the best time for lunch, Diogenes is said to have responded 'If rich, when you like; if poor, when you can.' This seems a good summary of Cynic attitudes. Diogenes is said to have taught his pupils to be content with plain food and water (6. 2. 31), although he was not averse to drinking wine when someone else was paying (6. 2. 54). Drinking water, the pure and natural drink (Artemidorus, *Oneir.* 1. 66), went logically with avoiding meat. Necessity seems to have been able to overcome any vestiges of conscientious objection to luxurious food, in the unlikely event it was available (*Lives*, 6. 2. 55–6), but also rendered ridiculous the relative prices of a useless statue compared to much-needed flour (6. 2. 35). Antisthenes, Diogenes' teacher, preferred a bag of flour in the hand to the broader economic advantages suggested by the promise of a shipload of fish (6. 1. 9). Diogenes' rejection of tainted loaves at a sacrificial meal suggests that bread in particular took on a symbolic importance for the Cynics (6. 2. 64). The general pattern of preference for vegetable food and water is borne out in the life of Crates, who approved of thyme, garlic, figs, and loaves of bread as a good diet (6. 5. 85). Another story of Crates takes this theme further: 'When Demetrius of Phalerum sent him loaves of bread and some wine, he reproached him saying, "Oh, that the springs yielded bread as well as water!" It is clear then he was a water drinker' (6. 5. 90). Diogenes Laertius sums up the Cynic position on food: 'They also hold that we should live frugally, eating food for nourishment only . . . some at all events take vegetables and cold water only' (6. 9. 104; cf. Ps.-Lucian, *Cyn.* 5). This indicates quite clearly that there was an expected set of Cynic dietary conventions, even if we could not expect them to be held hard and fast if these adventurous souls were to emulate Diogenes in spirit.[153] Thus Lucian in *The Fugitives* can attack pseudo-Cynics who eat too much bread of too fine a quality and eat meat and drink wine with it to boot. Asceticism based on bread and water, rather than cannibalism based on raw meat, was the distinctive aspect of Cynic diet.

While the Cynic tendency not to eat meat may have been the consequence of voluntary poverty, there are some broader symbolic or religious connections that should be acknowledged. Their attitude to sacrifice seems to have been lukewarm at best, regarding it as silly rather than utterly wrong (Lucian, *Zeus Catechized*, 5) and the meals that tended to follow as extravagant (6. 2. 28), an attitude that would militate against meat-eating. Occasionally there is a hint that the eating of meat is

---

[153] Lucian, *Dem.* 5, says that Demonax was an imitator of Diogenes in dress and demeanour, but ate normally.

not natural (Ps.-Lucian, *Cyn.* 11), a view which, although arguable, is perhaps not surprising. The attitudes of Cynics seem often to align them with animals, as the 'doggishness' of their name itself suggests. Rejection or lack of enthusiasm for cooking, for implements (6. 2. 37), for normal means of obtaining food, for dedicated spaces or for conventions of separation of sexes (6. 7. 97) all seem to be related to a rejection of the animal–human distinction at the heart of sacrificial practice in particular and of meat-eating in general.

These practices were often linked to attitudes generally critical of religion, sometimes in an absolute sense but more often in the form of a disdain for institutional religion, including and especially temple-cultus and images. Criticism of idols is, if not exclusively Cynic by any means, at least to be expected in the sort of popular moralizing characteristic of Cynics in the early centuries of this era. The pseudonymous *Epistles of Heraclitus* demonstrate this view to the extent that early commentators were inclined to believe they were Jewish in origin; and interestingly enough they combine contempt for temple and images with harsh criticism of meat-eating.[154]

Thus the characteristic asceticism of the Cynics was not merely a rejection of luxury but a rejection of the symbolic centre of the society to which they wanted to relate only marginally.[155] This rejection of 'manners' in general can be understood as a radical response to the culture of eating in Graeco-Roman society;[156] yet for all its radicalism, Cynic practice seems to have drawn from existing expectations about simplicity and poverty more often than inventing conventions altogether. While the rejection of meat and wine that was characteristic of the Cynic tradition was not generally presented as a conscious affront to religion, its impact is clear enough. The rejection of sacrifice and the rejection of distinctions within society, including those of gender, seem to go together here as Nancy Jay's work would suggest.

In later antiquity it would seem that the influence of the different philosophical schools was somewhat garbled in this area as in others, as we already saw in commenting on the protological support for vegetarianism claimed by the likes of Porphyry. The most famous Neo-Pythagorean may have been Apollonius of Tyana, whose practice actually resembles the earlier Cynic picture at least as well as the

---

[154] See Harold W. Attridge, *First Century Cynicism in the Epistles of Heraclitus*, HTS 29 (Missoula, Mont.: Scholars Press, 1976), 13–23.

[155] See Detienne, 'Between Beasts and Gods', *Myth, Religion and Society*, 225–6.

[156] See Leyerle, 'Clement of Alexandria on the Importance of Table Etiquette', 123–41.

Pythagorean one.[157] According to the account of Philostratus, Apollonius refused meat or specifically 'ensouled foods', and was especially critical of animal sacrifice (*Vita Apoll.* 1. 8, 10–11). He is also said to have produced a treatise on appropriate sacrifice (3. 41). Apollonius also refused wine, but seems to have been a little less anxious about this issue, if the evidence is accurate, since the origins of wine in the grape are expressly approved (1. 8), but the effects are seen as undesirable (2. 35–7). One story suggests that the association with sacrifice and religion was a key issue for this abstinence too: one of Apollonius' companions, Damis, assumes that the sage will drink some date wine that has been given to the group because it is not from grapes. While he seems most concerned about the effects of the substance, the real test, Apollonius instructs Damis, is whether the drinker would pour a libation of the beverage (2. 6–7).

This case is one of many that confirms the continuing centrality of the cuisine of sacrifice in asceticism, even when the precise rationales and schools of thought for refusal of wine or meat shift somewhat. Porphyry represents an interesting foil for the case of Apollonius, as a conservative armchair Pythagorean perhaps, who was bitterly opposed to Christianity (the non-sacrificial religion *par excellence*) and who spends a whole book of his *On Abstinence* defending the piety of avoiding meat and arguing for alternative forms of sacrifice. Porphyry is less concerned about the justice or piety of killing animals than about the effects on the individual (*De Abst.* 4. 1–4). Interestingly he seems to have had little problem with the use of wine (*De Abst.* 2. 6, 2. 19, 4. 4). While taking a somewhat different position from that attributed to Apollonius, Porphyry thus confirms the persistence both of the cuisine of sacrifice and of the social consequences of rejecting it.

What can be said of these philosophical traditions as a whole? Like the practice of the banquet, the theory of food manifest in these discussions is very diverse. The importance of meat in various respects comes through again and again: as desired and luxurious food, but also as ambiguous and numinous. As we saw earlier, the importance of meat both economically and otherwise meant that the practices surrounding its production and distribution were somewhat sacralized; in philosophical discourse and

---

[157] Perhaps it had to, in the absence of the ordered community of early Pythagoreanism. The ascesis of autonomous individuals, however indebted they were to Pythagorean ideas, is almost bound to be compared with the paradigmatic autonomy of Diogenes. Detienne, 'Between Beasts and Gods', 227, points out that after Pythagoras 'some Pythagoreans turn into Cynics almost before our eyes'. This underscores the difficulty of pushing comparisons with Cynic tradition too far in Christian circles and elsewhere in late antiquity.

practice the ambiguity or even rejection of meat can also be understood in terms of a perceived need to control or regulate, even to the point of exclusion. In virtually all cases there is an understanding of meat as problematizing the relation between humans and animals, and of course between these two and the gods, givers of animals who demand them back in sacrifice. While some philosophers such as Aristotle were content to render this difficult and delicate relationship more systematic, so as to provide the ideology that made sense of the practice of the state and of the individual, the more radical responses were at least as important for later discussion. In some sense the philosopher was to become the paradigmatic refuser of meat.

The differences between Pythagorean and Cynic rejection of meat suggest that the usual continuum between luxury and asceticism, with moderation in between, is not an adequate scale on which to measure the various responses that dissident eaters made to the dominant cuisine of banquets and sacrifices. The Pythagoreans had a highly complex cuisine wherein specific exclusions served, whatever else, to define the community itself; 'vegetarianism' may not really have been as universal among them as usually assumed, but regulation was.[158] While Pythagorean influence was spread more widely than in groups conforming to this picture, the asceticism of Pythagoras is one of self-definition in terms of an accepted set of rules and practices. As we would expect from Douglas's models, the individual body and the social body seem to have analogous sets of boundaries.[159] On the other hand the asceticism of the Cynic is that of the autonomous individual, and the disregard for convention in foods as in other respects reflects the lack of a coherent group structure. The fact that the Cynic tends to eat simply or 'naturally' suggests that the lack of concern for boundary maintenance extends beyond human culture altogether, to include animals.

Even though it is not likely to be helpful to see the schools of the classical period as lying squarely behind particular forms of later ascetic practice, Christian, Jewish, or pagan, the distinctions between the practices of the earlier philosophical eaters are useful models for comparison in terms of the way one emergent religious group which emphasized ritual meals came to deal with questions of participation and self-definition in this complex world of ancient meals, and in particular the choice or avoidance of certain foods. For confirmation

---

[158] Detienne, 'La Cuisine de Pythagore', 142–8.
[159] Douglas, 'Deciphering a Meal', 249–75.

that Christians, the best-known of the other non-sacrificers of antiquity, could be seen in these terms, we can turn to Galen: 'For they include not only men but also women who refrain from cohabiting all through their lives; and they also number individuals who, in self-discipline and self-control in matters of food and drink, and in their keen pursuit of justice, have attained a pitch not inferior to that of genuine philosophers.'[160]

Judaism and Asceticism

Just as it seemed more fruitful not to consider the formal aspects of Jewish meals in isolation from other Graeco-Roman evidence, understanding Jewish asceticism with regard to food may benefit from being linked with the preceding discussion.[161] The question of meat was vital to dissident Greeks of various sorts; and consideration of Jewish evidence suggests that this was also, if not always, an issue among Jewish groups.

Of course the Jewish dietary laws or *kašrut* have long been the subject of analysis from all quarters. Here I will not try even to summarize the significance of these, save to say that from a social point of view at least, observance of the laws counted not only as a matter of personal piety but as a sort of community marker acknowledged by Jews and Gentiles alike. While observance of ritual purity in diet necessitated a certain separation from Gentile systems of production and exchange of foods, Jews nevertheless usually seemed to others to live in a way which was, if odd, nevertheless acceptable and not as bizarre or offensive as the Cynic responses to normal diet. Yet we do have evidence for certain groups within Judaism which may be comparable in certain terms at least; the Therapeutae and the Essenes are again foremost among these.

Philo of Alexandria describes the ritual meals of the Therapeutae as simple but solemn meals of bread, hyssop, and salt, with water to drink (*Contempl.* 37, 73–4, 81). The actual foods employed in the ascetic meal are of interest, whether that meal is real or imagined. Philo's description confirms what the general survey of foods above has already suggested, that the use of bread, with salt and water, would be seen as a frugal but perhaps not an unusual meal. It is remarkable in this case largely because

---

[160] A fragment from Galen's summary of Plato's *Republic*, preserved in Arabic; cited in R. Walzer, *Galen on Jews and Christians* (London: Oxford University Press, 1949), 15.

[161] I have not dealt with fasting as such; Grimm's discussion of Jewish fasting (*From Fasting to Feasting*, 14–33) emphasizes the unique in Jewish asceticism in this area as otherwise, but is useful.

choice is implied; like Greek philosopher-dissidents, they adopted this diet voluntarily, unlike many for whom it was all there was to choose. The Therapeutic meal also has a clear ritual or even sacral aspect,[162] but the foods used are not exceptional for the members; rather they exemplify the form of asceticism adopted by the group in all their activities. In this sense there is a parallelism between these ascetic meals and the meat meals of the cuisine of sacrifice, and the meaning of the food used at special communal meals is not so much exceptional as exemplary.

While the use of bread, water, and salt might have been easy to reconcile with Jewish food practices, these elements do not seem to be chosen because of any identifiably Jewish concern. As we have seen, they are in fact typical of Graeco-Roman asceticism, not only in their simplicity or frugality but especially in the absence of meat. Philo explains these choices to some extent; the reason that the bread is leavened and that even these modest condiments are used is to distinguish this food from that of the bread offered in the Temple, and to make it thus seem only second-best (ibid. 82). Implicit in this account is that the Temple offerings themselves are superior according to a principle of simplicity and purity, which is not that of *kašrut*.[163] In any case this comparison with the Temple cuisine makes explicit, albeit in a softened form, the opposition between the ascetic diet and cultic or sacrificial meals, present also in dissident pagan responses to religion.

Philo's descriptions of the Essenes (*Prob.* 75–87; *Hypoth.*) speak in general terms of their frugality in eating (*Prob.* 84; *Hypoth.* 11. 11), but emphasize that 'they have shown themselves especially devout in the service of God, not by offering sacrifices of animals, but by resolving to sanctify their minds' (*Prob.* 75). Josephus does not specify the drink of the Essenes, and moderation rather than abstinence could be implied by

---

[162] Thus Bokser, 'Philo's Description of the Therapeutae', 5–11, where the meal is seen to be an alternative to Temple ritual. Despite the criticism of Schiffman, 'Communal Meals at Qumran', 46, it does not seem to me that a meal need be directly related to sacrificial cult to be 'sacral' in some sense.

[163] The food of the Therapeutae has been variously interpreted as drawing upon secular motivations related to health and well-being in general (Davies, 'Ascetic Madness', 17–19), as Pythagorean in inspiration (I. Lévy, 'Parabole d'Héraclide; Héraclide et Philon', *Recherches Esséniennes et Pythagoriciennes* (Geneva: Droz, 1965) 42–4), as related to *kašrut* (Marcel Simon, 'L'Ascéticisme dans les sectes juives', in Ugo Bianchi (ed.), *La tradizione dell'Enkrateia: Motivazioni ontologiche e protologiche* (Rome: Edizioni dell'Ateneo, 1985), 408–11) or to a combination of 'asceticism' and *kašrut* concerns (R. T. Beckwith, 'The Vegetarianism of the Therapeutae, and the Motives for Vegetarianism in Early Jewish and Christian Circles', *RevQ* 13/49–52 (1988), 407–10).

his reference to their 'invariable sobriety' (*JW* 2 § 133). His description of the meal centres it on bread but implies the addition of modest amounts of meat (*JW* 2 § 130); and in one textually difficult passage (*Ant.* 18 § 19) he may even imply that they offer sacrifices.[164] The Qumran community, whether or not they are to be identified as Essenes, had no prohibition against wine or meat. Wine is envisaged as being drunk at the communal meals prescribed by the *Manual of Discipline* (1QS 6: 4–5) as well as at the banquet envisaged in the Messianic age (1QSa 2: 11–22).[165] It is true that the word used in these descriptions, *tiroš* (תירוש), could be translated as referring to some other sort of grape drink (must, sweet wine, and juice have all been suggested), but there is no indication of prohibition of intoxicating drink.[166] There is also some suggestion of further concern, in that the *Manual of Discipline* restricts new members from participation in the drink of the community for a further year beyond the time they are admitted to contact with its solid foods (1QS 6: 13–23). This may reflect a general distinction found in rabbinic Judaism also, between food and drink and in particular the understanding that liquids are seen as capable of making solids impure.[167] Meat was certainly eaten at Qumran, since plentiful but curious burials of bones have been discovered there, clearly the remains of animals (sheep, goats, cattle) that were cooked and eaten and the bones placed in jars.[168] Although difficult to explain, the care taken in the assembly of bones suggests openness to meat-eating.

Evidence of unease about meat consumption does occasionally appear in Jewish sources. There was already a tradition in the Hebrew Bible that the eating of meat was a concession made after the Flood, and that the first humans would have been vegetarian (Gen. 9: 3–4).[169] The concern for blood in sacrificial ritual and otherwise (Lev. 3: 17), and the view that

---

[164] The textual question soon becomes tied up with that of the identification of the Essenes and the Qumran community. See the notes on the text by Louis Feldman in the Loeb edn.: *Josephus*, ix. 16–17.

[165] Davies, 'Ascetic Madness', 14–15, is right to say that quantity of food and drink is not mentioned, but here again we must not assume asceticism is purely quantitative. Josephus' description and the Qumran documents suggest sobriety and moderation, at least.

[166] Despite the suggestion, e.g. by J. T. Milik, *Ten Years of Discovery in the Wilderness of Judaea*, SBT 26 (London: SCM, 1959), 105–7, that this substance might avoid Nazirite prohibitions. While it is true that vows to abstain from *tiroš* seem to have existed (*y. Ned.* 7. 1), those bound by such were allowed wine.

[167] Lev. 11: 34, 37–8, and *t. Makš.*; see Schiffman, 'Communal Meals at Qumran', 45–56; Hamel, *Poverty and Charity*, 28–9.

[168] See Roland de Vaux, *Archaeology and the Dead Sea Scrolls*, rev. edn. (London: Oxford University Press, 1973), 12–15.

[169] Alfred Marx has recently argued that the different (animal and vegetable) elements in prescriptions for Temple sacrifice can be linked with different perspectives on meat and

it was equivalent to life, seems to represent an ongoing need to qualify, to hedge around with checks and balances, the possibility of killing and eating. Rabbinic sources continue this 'before and after' contrast, but historicize it in relation to the Exodus and wandering in the desert rather than to the creation story. Even *Genesis Rabbah* (34) does not seem especially interested in changes instituted with the Noachic covenant; the commentary is mainly concerned with the types of sacrifice instituted by or at that time, linking primordial sacrifice with the later Temple cultus and martyrdoms.

On the Exodus association with criticism of meat-eating and its continued influence, the Babylonian Talmud records a comment on Exod. 16: 8: ' "When YHWH will give you tonight meat to eat . . .," a tanna teaches in the name of R. Yehoshua b. Qarḥa: the meat that they asked for indecently was given to them indecently; what they asked for decently [bread] was given in a suitable manner. Hence the Torah teaches us the manners: one must eat meat only at night' (*b. Yoma,* 74a).[170] Tractate *Ḥullin* also reflects on changes in the supposed diet of Israel after the possession of the land. Commenting on the Mishna 'all slaughter; and at any time do they slaughter' attributed to R. Ishmael, the discussion distinguishes between the time before, when killing of animals for meat at will (i.e. not within sacrificial practice) was thought to have been prohibited, and the later time when it was allowed (*b. Ḥul.* 16b). The Palestinian Targums on Deut. 1: 1 associate desire for meat with rejection of the divine gift of God's bread, manna, and with idolatry. Moses criticizes the people's grumbling, which arose (among other reasons) 'because of the manna of which you said "our soul is afflicted from this bread which is a poor food." Your corpses fell at Haseroth because of the meat which you desired. Because of the calf you made, YHWH determined by his word to exterminate you.'[171] The eventual exclusion of lamb from the Passover meal is an interesting change, given the problems that Christians, too, were to encounter in dealing with meat in the years soon after the destruction of the Temple.[172] It is possible that

---

killing, and that the Priestly code in particular emphasizes a utopian perspective without killing: *Les Offrandes végétales dans l'ancien Testament: Du tribut d'hommage au repas eschatologique,* VTSup 57 (Leiden: E. J. Brill, 1994).

[170] Hamel, *Poverty and Charity,* 26 n. 191.

[171] *Tg. Neof.* on Deut. 1: 1; *Tg. Ps.-J.* gives a similar picture. See Roger Le Déaut (ed. and trans.), *Targum du Pentateuque,* SC 271 (Paris: Éditions du Cerf, 1980), iv. 16–17, and Hamel, *Poverty and Charity,* 26 n. 191.

[172] If e.g. the economic changes that followed the military and political actions affected the production of meat that could be accepted as ritually pure, then all meat may have

some of the Christians who are attested as refusing meat do so for the reasons implicit in the Jewish refusal to eat lamb for the Passover, i.e. recognition of the end of sacrifice.

If the idea that meat-eating is a sort of historic compromise is present in Judaism, as in Greek and Roman thinking, only rarely does the radical move of excluding meat altogether arise. One instance, a story which appears in virtually identical forms in the Babylonian Talmud (*b. B. Bat.* 60b), Tosefta (*t. Soṭa*, 15: 11–12), and the Midrash on the Psalms (137: 6), is quite striking:

> When the Temple was destroyed for the second time, large numbers in Israel became *pĕrushim*, binding themselves neither to eat meat nor to drink wine. R. Joshua got into conversation with them and said to them: My sons, why do you not eat meat nor drink wine? They replied: Shall we eat flesh which used to be brought as an offering on the altar, now that this altar is in abeyance? Shall we drink wine which used to be poured as a libation on the altar, but now no longer? He said to them: If that is so, we should not eat bread either, because the meal offerings have ceased. They said: we can manage with fruit. We should not eat fruit either [he said] because there is no longer an offering of firstfruits. Then we can manage with other fruits [they said]. But, [he said,] we should not drink water, because there is no longer any ceremony of the pouring of water. To this they could find no answer . . . (*b. B. Bat.* 60b)[173]

Joshua b. Ḥananiah's logic is reasonable, as well as amusing, and the question highly relevant: why refuse these elements? While meat was offered in the Temple, so were various cereal offerings. While wine was offered, it was hardly more prominent than the use of bread or oil.[174] Of course the avoidance of wine invokes the tradition of the Nazirite vow, or of the sect(s) of the Rechabites; as takers of a vow these ascetics may be understood to be adopting something like a Nazirite vow, but its content is still mysterious. Some other reason for identifying these particular foods as appropriate to avoid seems to be at work.

Although *pĕrushim* is also the term used for the group known as

---

seemed less satisfactory. It is clear that the preferred food for a festive Sabbath meal became fish rather than meat; which, granted that fish may have had a positive association with festivity and even a religious association with envisaged eschatological meals, may also indicate a negative connotation for meat.

[173] Trans. M. Simon in I. Epstein (ed.), *The Babylonian Talmud* (London: Soncino, 1935), 245.

[174] Wine is specified for the daily offering (Exod. 29: 40), first-fruits offering (Lev. 23: 13), and burnt offerings (Num. 15: 5, 7, 10; 28: 14). In all these cases it is combined with animal and cereal offerings.

Pharisees, this is not at all likely to be the case here, since the term is used pejoratively.[175] Recent discussion of the difficulties in taking a source like this at face value must also be acknowledged; the literary setting of a debate soon after the destruction of the Temple is rather unlikely, but probably serves, as elsewhere in the Talmuds, to give weight to a judgement upon a later problem. Thus while meat and wine are prized foods, and the giving up of these delicacies for mourning purposes might make sense independently of the ritual parallels,[176] the association of the problem with the destruction of the Jerusalem Temple need not be historical.[177] Since in some texts dealing with 'Pharisees' and 'Sadducees' in the Talmud these designations could be ciphers intended to defend against Christian criticism, it is even tempting to suggest that the passage could reflect a debate between Christians and Jews, quite possibly from long after the first century.[178] It may therefore even be a testimony to meat- and wine-avoiding Jewish-Christians such as those called Ebionites. If this is too speculative, it is still more than likely that the identification of these foods as appropriate for abstinence in mourning after the end of sacrifice stems not only from their association with festivity, but from the well-established patterns of asceticism in which meat and wine were synonymous with the cuisine of pagan sacrifice.[179]

[175] There are other instances where some different sense should be sought, perhaps still related to the more basic meaning of 'separate ones'. The different uses of the term in rabbinic sources are identified and discussed by Ellis Rivkin, 'Defining the Pharisees: The Tannaitic Sources', *HUCA* 40–1 (1969–70), 205–49; on this passage see esp. 234–6. Rivkin is criticized for not considering problems within the texts themselves by Jacob Neusner, *The Rabbinic Traditions about the Pharisees before 70* (Leiden: E. J. Brill, 1971), i. 2–5, but Neusner's work only serves to underscore the need to look elsewhere for identification of the group discussed at *b. B. Bat.* 60b.

[176] Cf. *b. Sanh.* 70a; Reicke, *Diakonie, Festfreude und Zelos*, 111–18, goes so far as to suggest that wine was prescribed for mourners rather than avoided (see *b. Ketub.* 8b). These same texts, however, also witness to the opposite view.

[177] Despite Hamel, *Poverty and Charity*, 27, the choice of meat and wine need not mean that the ascetics are wealthy, since they may be giving up festive rather than common foods.

[178] This suggestion is made with regard to the lists of different kinds of Pharisees (*m. Soṭa*, 3: 4, etc.) and references to Sadducees in Pharisee/Sadducee comparisons (*m. 'Erub.* 6: 2) by Saldarini, *Pharisees, Scribes and Sadducees in Palestinian Society*, 199–237, esp. 223–4, 226, 234. He also points out the inclusion of heretics among 'separatists' in the Eighteen Benedictions (*t. Ber.* 3. 25); it seems plausible enough that Christians might be referred to here also.

[179] Grimm's suggestion (*From Fasting to Feasting*, 24–8) that this story presents 'fasting' as a substitute for sacrifice is interesting, although of course the proposed ascetic regimen is not a 'fast' in the sense the rest of her discussion (or the Mishna) presumes, i.e. abstinence from all food and drink; nor is the avoidance of wine and meat presented here as an adjunct to prayer, as the Mishnaic fasts generally are.

The story of Daniel (1: 8–16) gives an early parallel to avoidance of meat and wine, apparently connected with concerns about ritual defilement not directly related to the law but extended to include all commensality with Gentiles.[180] While the precise setting of this story is difficult to establish, it must be from the Hellenistic period despite the ostensible Babylonian setting, and the issues of the cuisine of sacrifice are quite possibly operative.[181] The implication that meat, as well as wine, was the focus of this dietary asceticism suggests some concern about sacrifice and the likelihood that such food would have been offered to idols. Later in the same book, in a passage more clearly datable to the Maccabean period (10: 3), similar avoidance of meat and wine is based on mourning, which suggests a parallel with the mysterious *pĕrushim*; here abstinence takes on the form of an instrumental asceticism, connected with Daniel's fitness to receive the vision that follows (cf. *T. Reub.* 1. 10). Josephus' retelling of the story of Daniel 1 (*Ant.* 10 § 190–4) renders explicit the avoidance of meat and develops the more personal and spiritual aspect of this dietary asceticism. These depictions of Daniel's diet seem to relate to confronting Gentile society and religion and may have borrowed Gentile expressions of dissent.

Josephus also reports that priests sent to Rome under Nero took a store of figs and nuts (*Life*, 14), presumably to avoid having to eat impure food. Jews living in Gentile cities could have resorted to vegetable foods as a diet less difficult to maintain in purity than one involving meat and wine, both perhaps not only tainted by association with sacrifice but prepared in ways not in keeping with the dietary laws.[182] Yet it is hard to imagine that these measures would really have been necessary in a city such as Rome, where a Jewish community was well established.[183] It is more plausible that Josephus himself is keen to present a model of outstanding Jewish piety in terms recognizable to his pagan associates, as

---

[180] See John J. Collins, *Daniel: A Commentary on the Book of Daniel*, Hermeneia (Minneapolis: Fortress, 1993), 141–7; and David Satran, 'Daniel: Seer, Philosopher, Holy Man', in George W. E. Nickelsburg and John J. Collins (eds.), *Ideal Figures in Ancient Judaism*, SBLSCS 12 (Chico, Calif.: Scholars Press, 1980), 33–48.

[181] On dating, see Collins, *Daniel*, 25–33.

[182] Peter Stuhlmacher, *Paul's Letter to the Romans: A Commentary* (Louisville, Ky.: Westminster/John Knox, 1994), 222–9; Ernst Käsemann, *Commentary on Romans*, ed. G. W. Bromiley (Grand Rapids: Eerdmans, 1980), 364–9.

[183] Despite the limited evidence on trade and occupations among the Jewish community in Rome, one funerary inscription (Leon 210) commemorates 'Alexander, a beef-vendor from the meat-market (*bubularus de macello*)', implying provision of meat was possible for the Jewish community. See Harry J. Leon, *The Jews of Ancient Rome* (Philadelphia: Jewish Publication Society of America, 1960), 233–8, 293–4.

well as to many Jews, than that all the Jews in ancient Rome resorted to figs and nuts for their diet.

In the same context, that of dealings with Gentiles, come the statements of 'Aboda Zara (*m. 'Abod. Zar.* 2: 3) that there is a prohibition on 'wine, vinegar of the gentiles which to begin with was wine' and that 'meat . . . which comes out [from being offered to an idol] is prohibited because it is like sacrifices of the dead'.[184] This text seems to confirm the association between these particular items of food and drink and idolatry, for Jews as well as others. Wine as well as meat featured in a number of these examples. There are other examples in Jewish tradition which suggest a more narrow asceticism excluding wine, a successor to the Rechabite pattern of avoidance perhaps, was also known to rabbinic authors. A reference to 'water-drinkers' in the *Mekilta* of Rabbi Ishmael (*'Amalek*, 4) seems to be a synonym for the Rechabites, although the identity of this group is a difficult question at any point.

To summarize, in Judaism radical moves to exclude meat and/or wine from diet altogether are certainly unusual, but not unheard of.[185] Those examples we have are rather late and may well be influenced by pagan models, but in any case seem to have to do with the avoidance of the Graeco-Roman food system in general. Where meat and wine are excluded we seem to have parallels to the Greek dissident patterns rather than anything identifiably, or at least solely, derived from the Mosaic law. The continued importance of the avoidance of wine in some specific cases, and of the form of a vow, are particularly important and distinctive links with earlier Jewish tradition. Despite these instances of radical exclusion, Jewish asceticism more typically consists of observance of the system of purity laws, which entrench an ambiguity towards meat that may have met economic needs for control of consumption, as well as the subtler need to manage a commodity both prized and feared.[186]

---

[184] NB 2: 5 'Grape pits and grape skins belonging to the gentiles are prohibited . . . And sages say, '(If) they are moist, they are forbidden. If they are dry, they are permitted.'

[185] The prohibition of shepherding (*m. B. Qam.* 7: 7) is another curiosity, but perhaps best explained in other terms; see further Hamel, *Poverty and Charity*, 118–21.

[186] See Mary Douglas, *Purity and Danger: An Analysis of Concepts of Pollution and Taboo*, rev. edn. (London: Routledge & Kegan Paul, 1976), esp. 41–57, 159–79; and Hamel, *Poverty and Charity*, 28–9.

Conclusions

Christians are often assumed to have broken free from the dietary restrictions imposed by Judaism, to have moved from a narrow and odd sort of culinary world into a 'normal' one where all foods were fit to be eaten. Whatever caricature of Judaism may be involved in such a view, its main fault may lie in the failure to acknowledge that every culture has its own sets of taboos and preferences which are not based on rational, let alone nutritional, factors alone but which are related to the whole symbolic universe in which eaters participate.[187]

The concerns and conventions already discussed have the potential to shed light on various aspects of Christian meals. Many converts shared the attitudes to food and meals acceptable to Graeco-Roman society in general as the basic framework for understanding diet in general, and ritual diet in particular. Others, Jewish by background or attracted to Judaism, saw the requirements of the Mosaic law as a more important starting-point, but were not thereby removed altogether from the same world of foods and meals. In both cases a given set of expectations, or some combination of the sets, was taken up and then used as the basis for self-expression and community maintenance.

Yet it is not enough to say that Christian attitudes and practices with regard to food and meals simply make use of existing ideas and practices, as though the similarity between one practice and another could be made equivalent to the explanation of a practice in historical terms. If certain Christian, Jewish, and pagan Graeco-Roman practices must all be understood in terms of the variety of possible conventions and prohibitions which preceded them, this is not to say that they lack original or unique elements. For the purposes of argument at least, diet and related matters can here be considered as a system (a subsystem in fact) of signs in which the significance of a particular action or object derives its significance from its place in the whole, not merely within the community in question but for that community as a part of the wider society. At times we must be open to the possibility that practices are not merely borrowings from another group or tradition that serve to illustrate how thoroughly embedded in the culture Christian communities were, but actually reactions, conscious or unconscious oppositions created in the culinary world of signs. Just as Jewish dietary law could be a means of

---

[187] There is no small irony in the appearance of Veronika Grimm's somewhat stilted picture (in *From Feasting to Fasting*) of Christianity as a sort of dietary psychopathology, emergent from the integrated eating of an all-too-monolithic Judaism.

self-definition and opposition in the face of persecution, Christian uses of food could express self-definition and separation of the group from the wider society.

This discussion of the ordering of food suggests a number of issues of importance for the early Christian communities. Many of the conventions of communal dining seem to have held good for these groups; yet the uses and meanings of food suggest various connections between the goings-on in a house-church and the wider world, just as between events in temples and those at banqueting tables. It was one thing to continue or adopt the conventions of the communal meal, but these variable conventions said little in themselves about one's allegiances or concerns, being applicable to Jews or Greeks, Christians or devotees of Mithras. Consideration of the mere form of a meal does not take us all that far into the possibilities of placing the ritual meals of early Christianity within that society.

Use or avoidance of particular foods had implications not only as to the wealth or status of the eaters, but for their positions with regard to the religious and social norms of the day. Meat and wine in particular were crucial dietary issues: consumption of these was not merely a sign of participation in the dominant culture of sacrifice, but quite literally effected that participation. There is evidence that the force of these associations extended to Jewish practice as well as to pagan. The importance of these issues may not be immediately apparent for the conduct of early eucharistic meals, but in the following chapters I will seek to indicate how for many Christians they impinged upon all meals including those of the Christian community. With these insights in mind, we now move to a consideration of the evidence for the diversity of foods used in Christian meals in the first instance, and then to the surprising indications of an enduring and widespread asceticism concerning meat and wine in certain Christian communities and their meals.

3
Food and Drink in Early Christian Ritual Meals

INTRODUCTION

In the late fourth century, at a time by when the form and elements of the eucharist are regarded by most to have been well established, Councils held in Hippo (393) and Carthage (397) seem to have been concerned not merely with the prayers or decorum of the eucharistic celebration, but also that the right foods be used:

Let nothing more be offered in the sacraments of the body and blood of the Lord than he himself delivered, i.e. bread and wine mixed with water. First-fruits of honey or milk, which are accustomed to be offered on one most solemn day for the sacrament of the newly baptized, are to be offered at the altar none the less, but have their appropriate blessings however, that they may be distinguished from the sacrament of the body and blood of the Lord. (*Brev. Hipp.* 23)[1]

There is little or no further evidence to resolve the intriguing uncertainty this canon raises with regard to the foods being offered at the ritual meal in late fourth-century Africa. The fact that it was passed, however, testifies at the very least to worrisome memories of an over-diverse Lord's Supper.

The actual use of foods in eucharistic meals has rarely been the subject

---

[1] 'Ut in sacramentis corporis et sanguinis Domini nihil amplius offeratur quam ipse Dominus tradidit, hoc est panem et vinum aquae mixtum. Primitiae vero seu lac et mel, quod uno die sollemnissimo pro infantum mysterio solet offerri, quamvis in altari offerantur, suam tamen habent propriam benedictionem, ut a sacramento dominici corporis et sanguinis distinguantur.' This is part of the text of the Canon in the *Breviarium Hipponense*, accepted as a whole by the Council of Carthage of 397 (*Registri Ecclesiae Carthaginensis Excerpta*, 34) and repeated as its own Canon 37. It concludes with a somewhat contradictory statement apparently referring to actual harvest first-fruits: 'Let nothing more be offered in the first-fruits than what comes from grapes and wheat,' which, along with a version without the reference to the baptismal first-fruits (*Conc. Carth. III*, 24) suggests interpolation at some point of the baptismal reference. Whether this was during the complex conciliar processes or the later, and also complex, literary tradition of these *Acta* is hard to say. See further F. L. Cross, 'History and Fiction in the African Canons', *JTS* NS 12 (1961), 227–47.

of serious discussion. Many seem to have thought that they cannot be treated in the sort of descriptive and comparative fashion outlined so far, since the use of bread and wine as the elements of the eucharist is determined by imitation of the Last Supper, or of Jewish meal models in which the choice of foods and the meanings thereof are related only to maintenance of a tradition. I have already argued that it is important to try and understand the use of foods without collapsing the issue into that of origins or founding intentions; participants may not always have been aware of these, and the ritual meal may have been comprehensible within the symbolic world of food and diet somewhat independently of the question of its institution.

Even in an approach to eucharistic meals which assumes the uniformity of practice generally taken for granted, there would seem to remain some potential for further reflection on the use of bread and wine in those traditions, and on the varied imagery applied to the eucharistic meals, from a perspective informed by social theory and cross-cultural studies.[2] Yet ultimately the assumption of fundamental uniformity of Christian meal practice does undermine the attempt to consider the foods themselves as culturally or socially embedded; it does so because it fails to consider their meaning in the system, in terms of choices and oppositions such as bread or meat, water or wine.

In fact there is evidence with which to challenge the normative picture precisely at the point of the use of various foods.[3] If the meals of the early Christian communities did display a diversity of use of foods, then not only would traditions have to be understood more broadly than in terms of a unitary practice, but they could more readily be conceived of in terms of choices, oppositions, and conflicts, as we would understand any other issue of diversity in early Christianity.

In this chapter I intend to try and give a broad picture of the uses of different foods in early eucharistic meals.[4] This is an attempt to pay more

---

[2] Feeley-Harnick, *The Lord's Table*, would seem to be the most notable case in point.

[3] The fullest summaries hitherto of evidence for different eucharistic foods and drinks are those of Adolf von Harnack, 'Brod und Wasser: Die eucharistischen Elemente bei Justin', *Über das gnostische Buch Pistis-Sophia; Brod und Wasser: Die eucharistischen Elemente bei Justin. Zwei Untersuchungen*, TU 7 (Leipzig: J. C. Hinrichs, 1891), 115–44, esp. 132–6, and Cyrille Vogel, 'Le Repas sacré au poisson chez les chrétiens', *RevScRel* 40 (1966), 5–7. These assume relative lack of concern regarding particular foods in the eucharist (Harnack) or a large number of fairly distinct traditions regarding food (Vogel); neither of these analyses seems adequate, as will be discussed further below.

[4] I have chosen not to deal with alleged use of semen or menstrual blood by groups such as Borborites, Coddians, and Phibionites (see Epiphanius, *Pan.* 25–6), or with cannibalism, of which Jews and Christians were accused by pagans at first and of which Christians later

attention to detail and adopt at least a 'thicker' descriptive method than has been the case in previous discussions.[5] This survey will indicate that there are serious inadequacies in beginning and ending with consideration of the Christian meal as use of bread and wine only. There are other foods which have some place in the reconstruction of early Christian ritual, either because they are clearly attested in specific cases, or because there are allusions or hints that have led some to argue that they were used. The rest of this chapter will survey these cases: cheese, milk and honey, other fruits and vegetables, oil, and salt; and, somewhat separately, the case of fish, probably more a modern suggestion than an ancient oddity.

Although some of the instances where other foods appear to have been used may seem idiosyncratic to the point of irrelevance, we should not be too quick in dismissing the 'odd' evidence for the use of different foods. If these instances are exceptional, the exceptions are not only capable of mitigating the picture of uniformity, but also help shed light on what the eventually normative tradition actually meant. Although this survey begins with the same sort of schematic method employed in the previous chapter, dealing with various categories of food and drink, the results are by no means distributed evenly across the range of available foods. The specifics of these eucharistic oddities suggest that there were particular concerns about 'ordering food' which served to shape practices, and which also offer possibilities for their interpretation.

BREAD AND WINE

There is little doubt that a tradition of using bread and wine as the central elements of a eucharistic meal emerged at a very early stage in many Christian communities.[6] This use of foods is represented pre-eminently in the stories of Jesus' Last Supper, where the identification of

---

accused Jews and each other. That 'bodily-fluids' eucharist, connected with the pounding and eating of a human foetus (26. 5. 6), seems to me a version of the supposed cannibal one, on which see my 'Eating People', 413–42. In any case, these practices do not involve foods in the sense I am employing the word here. Of course an a priori refusal to accept these possibilities is not adequate. An attempt to take the 'fluids' eucharist seriously is made by Jorunn Jacobsen Buckley, 'Libertines or Not: Fruit, Bread, Semen and Other Bodily Fluids in Gnosticism', *JECS* 2 (1994), 15–31.

[5] Geertz, 'Thick Description', 3–30.

[6] See the lists assembled by Harnack, 'Brod und Wasser', 132–6, and Vogel, 'Le Repas sacré au poisson', 6.

the meal as the Passover both accents the role of bread and implies the festive use of wine; in fact the saying (Mark 14: 25 and parallels) in which Jesus announces his abstention from further drinking of wine seems to make its use explicit. This, however, is only to present the picture assembled in the canonical texts and not to credit the possibility of a complex history of these narratives, of which the earliest literary version we have is apparently that given by Paul in 1 Cor. 11: 23–9. This account may seem to imply the same paschal chronology as the Synoptic Gospels (cf. 1 Cor. 5: 7), but some have argued that the interpretation of the meal as Passover starts with Paul, or at least in the development of the tradition after Jesus, rather than in historical reminiscence.[7] This caution is important because there may have been some eucharistic meal traditions which were aware of the Last Supper tradition in some form but seem not to have used wine, and other meal traditions which did use wine but made no reference to the Last Supper. The former case will be pursued later, but the latter may be neatly exemplified by the meal of the *Didache*, which shows no knowledge of the Last Supper but involves wine, judging by the allusion in its eucharistic prayer 'regarding the cup' to the 'holy vine of David' (9. 2).

We have seen that the use of wine, like that of bread, could be wholly unremarkable for almost any meal. This does not mean that in particular settings the use of wine did not become more important. In general Graeco-Roman custom the use of wine was appropriate to a communal festive meal, including memorial meals for the dead, as well as for particular events such as Passover.[8] Apart from the conclusions that may be drawn from the canonical form of the Gospels as to a widespread and continuing use of wine at the eucharist, there are a reasonable number of second-century witnesses confirming early use in Christian ritual meals: Papias (cited in Irenaeus, *Adv. Haer.* 5. 33. 3) who, like the *Didache*, makes use of the imagery of vines and grapes in an allusive sense; Irenaeus himself, who attacks those who refuse wine in the cup (ibid. 5. 1. 3); and Marcus, a Valentinian gnostic known to Irenaeus (ibid. 1. 13. 2). These three examples all come from the same literary work, but the diverse sources suggest a reasonably widespread use, both in terms of geography and theology. At the turn of the third century we also have the

---

[7] Lietzmann, *Mass and Lord's Supper*, 172–87.

[8] See Jeremias, *The Eucharistic Words of Jesus*, 238–43; Lietzmann, *Mass and Lord's Supper*, 180–5; Reicke, *Diakonie, Festfreude und Zelos*, 101–49; Paul Lebeau, *Le Vin nouveau du royaume: Étude exégétique et patristique sur la parole eschatologique de Jésus à la Cène* (Paris: Desclée de Brouwer, 1966), 17–65.

witness of Clement, Tertullian, and others; by that time at least, the use of wine is a self-conscious rule in many communities, and perhaps in most of what emerges as orthodox Christianity.

Despite the necessity of concluding that the use of wine was widespread in early Christian meals, the evidence that this was a general rule is certainly not as overwhelming as one might have assumed. In fact most of these earliest witnesses do not conform to all aspects of the picture of standard development, but include 'odd' characteristics such as priority or multiplicity of eucharistic cups.[9] There are also some interesting and important names that have been passed over. Ignatius of Antioch never mentions the content of the cup.[10] Justin Martyr's account is ambiguous and may originally have referred to a eucharist employing water.[11] Irenaeus, Clement, and other important early witnesses to the use of wine must all polemicize against the use of water in the cup.[12]

While the relative ease of access to wine of at least some quality, as well as the conventions related to both Jewish and pagan religious traditions, might suggest that silence regarding the contents of the cup should be interpreted in favour of the presence of wine, there are in fact numerous indications that the use of wine was controversial in early Christian communities. Not only are there plentiful examples of eucharistic meals involving water, there are others where no cup is found at all.[13] Since these questions of eucharistic meals wherein less than the expected elements are found cannot be dealt with quickly and easily, I will return to them in the next chapter after having completed the envisaged survey of different foods and the possibilities involving more, or other, than the expected meal elements. This bread-and-water tradition or pattern, however, turns out in fact to be the most important and widespread 'exception' to the use of bread and wine.

The use of bread itself ought not to be passed over altogether. It is worth reiterating that bread was the main element of most meals for most people, and that a meal of bread and wine (or water) was not in itself remarkable. In the absence of clear evidence about quantities, it is important for the

---

[9] Andrew McGowan, '"First Regarding the Cup": Papias and the Diversity of Early Eucharistic Practice', *JTS* NS 46 (1995), 551–5; on multiple cups, Irenaeus, *Adv. Haer.* 1. 13. 2; *Ap. Trad.* (Dix), 23. 1–11 (= Botte, 21).

[10] I am not sure why Harnack makes a concession in Ignatius' regard that the contents of the cup could be inferred to be wine; I can only think of the identification of the cup as 'blood' (Ign. *Rom.* 7. 3), but this could also apply to Justin, whom Harnack clearly claims as using water ('Brod und Wasser', 133–4).

[11] Harnack, 'Brod und Wasser', 115–44, and Ch. 4 below.

[12] Irenaeus, *Adv. Haer.* 5. 1. 3; Clement, *Paed.* 2. 2; and see Ch. 4, *passim*.

[13] Harnack, 'Brod und Wasser', 134–6; and see Chs. 5 and 8 below.

modern interpreter to acknowledge this pattern as rather normal, and the likelihood that there was a stage at which the meal was substantial as well as symbolic. The important questions of how and why a substantial meal became a token one will not be addressed here, but further evidence will be presented below suggesting a persistence, in some 'deviant' circles at least, of substantial eucharistic meals well into the second and third centuries. This difficult question does not, however, represent an absolute obstacle to the consideration of the eucharistic meal as 'meal', for reasons already given; the structure even of a token meal derives its meaning to some extent from the substantial meal which it recalls for the participant.

Whether in large or small quantities, bread could receive a wide variety of associations and meanings. Rabbinic and early Christian texts suggest that bread was an obvious part of images of eschatological plenty, to the extent that grain of miraculous yield (Papias, in Irenaeus, *Adv. Haer.* 5. 33. 3–4) and even 'bread trees' (*Gen. Rab.* 15. 7; cf. *b. Ber.* 38a–b) could be envisaged as part of divine providence. This sort of understanding is arguably present in the eucharistic prayer over bread in the *Didache* (9. 4; cf. 10. 5–6).[14]

In and of itself, however, the use of bread is wholly unexceptional. The New Testament texts do not use the word that would specify 'unleavened bread' (ἄζυμος), even in the depiction of Jesus' Passover meal. This might reflect the assimilation of the institution narratives to meal practices of a more everyday nature, using the bread commonly eaten, or may conversely be a remnant of a non-paschal tradition embedded in the Gospel accounts. Only in a couple of (rather later) cases are there specific indications of the use of unleavened bread in eucharistic meals, and these seem exceptional. Origen says that 'Ebionites', Jewish-Christians of whom he apparently had some firsthand knowledge, kept Passover at the same time and in the same way as (other) Jews did (*In Matt. Comm. Ser.* 79). The *Epistula Apostolorum* also depicts a community for whom the observance of Passover seems to be an ongoing practice, although we are told nothing in detail about the meal elements.[15] Of course bread might, in the normal course of events, have been unleavened, especially

---

[14] I also note the intriguing suggestion that Jesus' use of bread as a substitute for his flesh according to the institution narratives may be understood as connected with other salvific symbolism attached to bread, and especially to the substitution of *matzah* for the paschal lamb; see Lawrence A. Hoffman, 'A Symbol of Salvation in the Passover Haggadah', *Worship*, 53 (1979), 519–37.

[15] This observance raises the 'Quartodeciman' issue; celebrating Easter at Passover (on the 14th day of Nisan, hence the name applied to the controversy) would establish a clearer significance for the use of unleavened bread.

for the poor; but the lack of concern about this aspect is interesting in itself.

The actual material of the bread is rarely mentioned. The story of the 'sign of the loaves' in John 6 is often seen as having some eucharistic overtones, and specifies that the loaves are made of barley (vv. 9, 13), bread of the poor. Otherwise it seems that the substance of the bread may have been a matter of indifference, or of economic opportunity rather than religious scruple.[16]

CHEESE

The use of cheese as an element of a eucharistic meal is attested for one community at least. Epiphanius of Salamis first provides us with the key information: that there is a group known as the Artotyritai, 'bread-and-cheesers', who are associated with a group or groups known variously as Quintillians, Pepuzians, or Priscillians. These groups are derived in turn from the Cataphrygians (which seems to be Epiphanius' designation for Montanists) but differ from them in certain respects (*Pan.* 49. 1. 1). Later he seems to say that 'Artotyritai' is a designation for the group (Quintillians etc.) as a whole rather than for a subgroup (49. 2. 6). The reason for the name is that 'in their rites they set out bread and cheese and thus celebrate their rites'.

This evidence is presented in even simpler form by Filastrius of Brescia (*Div. Haer. Lib.* 74) who simply says that the Artotyritai are in Galatia and 'offer' bread and cheese. He seems to be followed by Augustine (*De Haer.* 28), 'Praedestinatus' (*Praed. Haer.* 1. 28), and Pseudo-Jerome (*Indiculus de Haeresibus*, 20) who agree with one another virtually word-for-word in adding a protological explanation, i.e. that the group say 'that the first offerings to God were celebrated by the first human beings with the fruits of the earth and of sheep', alluding perhaps to the offerings of Cain and Abel (Gen. 4: 3–4) yet avoiding any implication of an animal sacrifice.[17]

Epiphanius' witness is too odd to be a convenient invention, yet his information amounts to very little evidence for the practice.[18] While

---

[16] Ancient practice related to Passover and the ongoing tradition of the Western Church are both discussed by John McHugh, 'Num solus panis triticeus sit materia valida SS. Eucharistae?' *Verbum Domini*, 39 (1961), 229–39.

[17] The Artotyritai are also mentioned by Jerome, but as a group unknown other than by name: *Comm. in Ep. ad Gal.* 2. 3.

[18] See P. de Labriolle, *Les Sources de l'histoire du Montanisme* (Fribourg: Librairie de

agreement between Epiphanius and Filastrius was at one point seen as evidence for common use of the lost *Syntagma* of Hippolytus, this is now regarded as less likely.[19] 'Praedestinatus' anticipates the difficulties of those who would like to know more: 'there is nothing worth saying about them' (*Praed. Haer.* 1. 28). Despite the shift in locale according to Filastrius, and the addition of the protological explanation of the custom in Augustine and his borrowers, it is tempting to conclude that we merely have the one testimony (from Epiphanius), transmitted with a geographical mistake by the bishop of Brescia and an attempt at rationalization by the bishop of Hippo.[20] All that seems clear is that some group or groups, possibly connected with Montanism, were believed to have made use of cheese in eucharistic meals.[21]

Of course Augustine may have guessed correctly at his explanation, or

l'Université, 1913), pp. lxvii–lxix. A. Strobel, *Das heilige Land der Montanisten* (Berlin: Walter de Gruyter, 1980), 257–61, suggests that the name is simply a slander against Montanists, based on the sort of offerings of various foods depicted in the *Apostolic Tradition*. Yet there are other, clearer slanders against Montanist eucharistic practice, and Strobel's argument assumes greater liturgical uniformity (and especially a parallel with Novatianist asceticism based on acceptance of authentic Hippolytean authorship of the *Apostolic Tradition*) than I am willing to accept. The caution other authors apply to any Artotyrite connection with Montanism at all should also be taken into account here.

[19] See H. Koch, 'Philastrius', PW 38 (1938), col. 2130. The judgement of F. Heylen, editor of Filastrius in the Corpus Christianorum version, seems apt: 'in primis Epiphanium spoliavit' (CCL 9. 210).

[20] Augustine's dependence on Epiphanius and Filastrius, and hence the likely originality of the analysis to Augustine, is undisputed: see Augustine, *Ep.* 222. 2, and Labriolle, *Les Sources de l'histoire du Montanisme*, pp. cix–cxiv ('La phrase . . . est une explication propre à Augustin', p. cxiii). See also, with more precision on Augustine's use of Epiphanius and his *Anacephalaiosis* in particular, G. Bardy, 'Le "*De haeresibus*" et ses sources', *Miscellanea Agostiniana* (2 vols.; Rome: Tipografia Poliglotta Vaticana, 1931), ii. 397–416. Bardy also wishes to keep alive the possibility of use of Pseudo-Jerome by Augustine, rather than the reverse (pp. 408–11), but this would make little difference to the value of the additional material, since the *Indiculus* would in any case be from only a little earlier at best.

[21] Doubts about the connection with Montanism must be admitted. Filastrius discusses Artotyritai at some remove from Quintillians, but if he relies on Epiphanius for these groups to the extent that seems likely, this is hardly weighty. Still, we do not have a clear basis for deciding whether to be more suspicious of a centrifugal tendency in which heresiologists (Filastrius?) separate groups to emphasize the disorder of heretics, or a centripetal tendency that works genealogically (Epiphanius?) to link all heresy with such ultimate sources as Simon Magus. Marcionite connections also need to be considered, if with caution; see further below. Some have taken the Montanist practice to be a derivative of Phrygian paganism, given the strong associations there with the harvest-related cult of the Great Mother (cf. Firmicus Maternus, *De Err. Prof. Rel.* 3), but this seems an unnecessary hypothesis given other examples of use of odd eucharistic foods, even in orthodox sources such as the Hippolytean *Apostolic Tradition*, on which see further below. See also Strobel, *Das heilige Land der Montanisten*, 258–9.

may even have known something specific about the group; there were various speculations, Christian and otherwise, about a paradisiacal state in which meat would not have been eaten.[22] His suggestion that the choice of cheese (and bread) is a link with primeval history and a restored pre-Noachic state of abstinence from killing and eating is in keeping with other evidence about Montanism, in that use of meat in the movement was proscribed or restricted,[23] and draws upon the ascetic tradition of avoiding meat already discussed from pagan and Jewish sources. It is also possible that Augustine is applying evidence known to him regarding other groups or traditions which used this logic. Use of cheese may therefore be rather more than an oddity of local cuisine or culture, but a reasonable (if idiosyncratic) extension of the quest for food that expresses opposition to bloodshed and sacrifice, and hence to conventions of social order. It is interesting that Montanists were also among those Christian groups most at odds with the usual attitudes to gender roles, with women members who were prophets and ascetic attitudes to sexuality; thus the possible anti-sacrificial character of the Artotyrite eucharist fits well with what we know about the social organization of the group from which they may well have sprung.[24]

Later we have an odd attestation of the Artotyritai as Marcionites rather than Montanists. In the sixth century, by when we should think of the group as extinct, Timothy of Constantinople lists 'Marcionites, that is Artotyritai', along with other sectarians who need to be baptized when admitted to the great Church.[25] He goes on to say that 'The Artotyritai derive from the heresy of this Marcion, but depart from that designation in terms of differences of opinion. For they celebrate their distinctive rites mixing leaven with milk' (*De Receptione Haereticorum*).[26] Whatever

[22] e.g. Theophrastus, *On Piety*, fr. 13; Plutarch, *De Esu Carnium*, 993 B, 994 F, 996 C; and the Pseudo-Clementine version, *Hom.* 8. 15–16 etc.

[23] See Tertullian, *De Ieiunio contra Psychicos*, and further below.

[24] Cf. Nancy Jay's suggestion of sacrifice as an instrument of patriarchy and specifically of tracing patrilineal descent. Jay considers cases where sacrifice is related differently to family organization, but not where sacrifice is avoided or refused, except in the case of Hawaii (*Throughout Your Generations Forever*, 77–93), a specific instance of breakdown rather than a general pattern of avoidance.

[25] Their demise might of course have been much earlier. The implication of the repetition of the same information in heresiological catalogues is rendered explicit by Jerome (*Comm. in Ep. ad Gal.* 2. 3. 2), who says they are now unknown.

[26] Cf. *Ex Niconis Pandecte*, 2 (*PG* 86. 1. 69) where the same identification of Marcionites as Artotyritai is made. See further Adolf von Harnack, *Marcion: Das Evangelium vom fremden Gott: Eine Monographie zur Geschichte der Grundlegung der katholischen Kirche*, 2nd edn. (Leipzig: J. C. Hinrichs, 1924), 381*–2* (reference will generally be made to John E. Steely and Lyle D. Bierma (trans.), *Marcion: The Gospel of the Alien God* (Durham, NC: Labyrinth, 1990), but the asterisked numbers refer to appendices not translated).

we are to make of this claim historically, the idea that the ritual cheese-eaters may be understood to be using cultured or coagulated milk is perhaps not merely obvious but symbolically important, and finds parallels, as we shall see.

Cheese (probably a soft cheese or curd in this case) may be practically or symbolically identical with milk. Perhaps this substance would have been something to be spread on the bread, a semi-solid element evocative of milk, rather than simply a second solid food element introduced alongside bread.[27] In that case, the extent to which the Artotyrite practice is really a departure from meals involving bread and cup as sole (or at least accentuated) elements ought not to be exaggerated unnecessarily. Both Montanists and Marcionites are elsewhere attested not only as avoiding meat but prohibiting wine, including that of the eucharist.[28] Understood as a form of milk, cheese might really have been the mutated result of a quest for an appropriate form of ritual drink, rather than an additional solid food.

Although I will discuss milk and honey further below, there is another Marcionite instance involving those elements, rather than cheese as such, that bears comparison with Timothy's extension of the Artotyrite label. In the fourth century, Ephraem the Syrian attacked Marcionites for using milk and honey in the eucharist:

Instead of that bread, the presence-bread [cf. Exod 25: 30] of the new covenant,
they offered honey or milk.
Since all these things are natural, however
They could not found their error this way either.
Honey is not brought as an offering
nor is milk used for sprinkling and libation.
The presence-bread was offered symbolically,
and blood and wine purified as types.
The crucifiers and the teachers of error
Have been contradicted by the symbol of which Moses wrote.

(*Hymn. contra Haer.* 47. 6)

This attack is both interesting and obscure.[29] It seems that Ephraem was not aware that the use of milk and honey was common in the West in

---

[27] J. M. Hanssens, *La Liturgie d'Hippolyte: Ses documents, son titulaire, ses origines et son caractère*, Orientalia Christiana Analecta, 155 (Rome: Pontifical Institute of Oriental Studies, 1959), 423, suggests that this 'caillé' was to be 'uni rituellement au pain eucharistique'.

[28] See the next chapter for details of this ritual meal pattern.

[29] It is discussed briefly and descriptively in Pierre Yousif, *L'Eucharistie chez Saint Éphrem de Nisibe*, Orientalia Christiana Analecta, 224 (Rome: Pontifical Institute of Oriental Studies, 1984), 161–6.

orthodox circles also, at least in the more specific context of the baptismal rites. Although he seems to refer to a substitution of these foods for, rather than their addition to, eucharistic bread and wine, this must be rhetorical since elsewhere in the hymn bread is referred to explicitly (47. 2 for example).[30] Ephraem may either have been attacking the practice of giving milk and honey at a baptismal eucharist, which Tertullian also attests among Marcionites (*Adv. Marc.* 1. 14. 3), or may have been referring to a practice more like that attributed to the Artotyritai, i.e. of using these elements in regular eucharistic meals, presumably as a form of bloodless sacrificial cup, just as Timothy understood other Marcionites to be doing. We cannot choose between these possibilities from this evidence. This is disappointing since, unlike some of the other later heresiologists discussed, Ephraem seems to have had some firsthand experience of his opponents.[31] It does, however, add to the possibility that Timothy's evidence is more than an enthusiastic but inaccurate attribution of deviant practice to Marcionites.

In any case, the specific nature of Ephraem's attack on the Marcionites is also intriguing. Milk and honey are unacceptable, he says, because they are not sacrificial foods; honey seems to be brought into parallelism with bread (or meat) and milk with wine (ibid. 47. 6. 5–6). Of course Ephraem has in mind the sacrifices of the tabernacle and the Jerusalem Temple as types of the eucharist, but states this position on sacrificial foods as a general principle, and may also be alluding to pagan practice rather than Jewish when he argues that milk is unacceptable for libations.[32]

Later, the fifth-century bishop of Bagrawand, Eznik of Kolb, attacks Marcionite acceptance of fish and rejection of meat (from meals other than specifically eucharistic or communal ones, it seems) in the same terms; the heretics are perceived to make a fundamental mistake in removing the elements appropriate for sacrifice and adding non-sacrificial foods (*De Deo*, 407).

It is possible that the attacks of Ephraem and Eznik reflect something of the Marcionites' own anti-sacrificial rationale. Although they, like Tertullian, assume that Marcion and his followers despised all the creator's work and were hypocritical to use it, the reasons underlying

---

[30] Nor does it seem to be wineless, despite the indications that early Marcionites refused wine (see further below). Earlier in the same hymn Ephraem wrote: 'The assemblies of the "deniers" do not have the true blood of Christ . . . they have only an image which is similar, because they do not recognize the real body of Christ' (*Hymn. contra Haer.* 47. 1).

[31] See G. A. M. Rouwhorst, *Les Hymnes pascales d'Ephrem de Nisibe* Supplements to *Vigiliae Christianae*, 7 (2 vols.; Leiden: E. J. Brill, 1989), i. 13–14, 71–2.

[32] 'Libation (*nukaya*)' is also used in Syriac to refer to the eucharistic wine.

this sort of substitution seem like a rejection of the cosmos more in the sense of 'order', the shape of creation, rather than as 'matter', the fact of creation. If milk and honey were being used as additional foods, originally perhaps as substitutes for wine as we have speculated in regard to the other 'milk' or 'cheese' eucharists, their appropriateness may have been based in their difference from the wine of sacrificial practice. It also seems that Marcionites rejected the use of wine at the eucharist and elsewhere.[33] In any case, this further instance supports the likelihood of the use of such additional foods in some way, and the rebuttal is an interesting and even revealing voice from the side of the normative tradition with regard to the significance of this sort of food.

If there really were Marcionite ritual cheese-eaters, they might still have been few and late, since Marcionite conservatism or similarity to orthodoxy in liturgical matters was otherwise widely acknowledged (see (Ps-?)Cyril of Jerusalem, *Mystagogic Catecheses*, 18. 26). Yet there are other indications making it conceivable that Marcionites, too, should have understood milk or cheese as appropriate foods because of their lack of connection with bloody sacrifice, as well as because of the positive connotations that might be seen in the use of milk. There are explicit statements by Tertullian that Marcionite baptismal ritual involved use of milk and honey (*Adv. Marc.* 1. 14. 3); and Marcionites, like Montanists, avoided meat and wine, choices whose symbolic opposites might well, in terms of the cuisine of sacrifice, have been bread and milk or cheese.[34]

A more figurative example of a similar practice regarding cheese or curd is contained in the *Martyrdom of Perpetua and Felicitas* from 203, well before the first mention of Artotyritai, as well as far away in Africa. Perpetua describes a vision in which she sees a garden and in it a man dressed as a shepherd, milking sheep:

And he lifted his head and said to me 'Welcome, child.' And he called me, and from the cheese that he was milking he gave me a sort of morsel. And I took it with joined hands and I ate. And all those standing around said 'Amen.' And at the sound of the voice I was awakened, still tasting something sweet, I do not know what.   (*Mart. Perp.* 4. 9–10)[35]

---

[33] See Ch. 4 below.

[34] Explanations relying on Phrygian paganism (see Strobel, *Das heilige Land der Montanisten*, 258–9) and connections with the Great Mother (Firmicus Maternus, *De Err. Prof. Rel.* 3) are not impossible but are less necessary when we consider the appearance of cheese even in the *Apostolic Tradition*, on which see further below.

[35] My translation from the text in H. Musurillo (ed. and trans.), *The Acts of the Christian Martyrs: Introduction, Texts and Translations* (Oxford: Clarendon, 1972), 110–13;

It is hard to say how seriously we might take this as an indication of what an actual eucharistic meal might have involved in Perpetua's community. The eating clearly takes place in a vision, and the instant cheese or curd belongs with the imagery of the shepherd, a not-unexpected Christ-figure.[36] Yet the scenario must owe something to the sacral meal practice with which Perpetua and her companions were familiar, even if this debt were simply the gesture of hands and the 'Amen'.[37]

The interpretation given in the text itself seems to give the liturgical aspect of Perpetua's experience an initiatory character, that of a once-only ritual rather than a repeated ceremony, as it might be put.[38] Perpetua tells her companions of the vision; 'we understood it to be an imminent passion; and from then on we began to hold no hope in this world' (4. 10; cf. Mark 10: 38). Although the language of baptism is not used, the decisive vision seems to evoke a transformative event, rather than simply repeated eucharistic meals with which Perpetua and her community would also, we assume, have been familiar. Perpetua's own recent baptism may be seen as having played a part in the vividness of the experience. There are some more concrete instances where milk (if not cheese) and honey are known to have been given to the newly baptized; the evidence for these in Africa (i.e. from Tertullian) at the same time as Perpetua's writing adds to the likelihood that this meal is quasi-baptismal; of course this does not stop it from being quasi-eucharistic as well, but it seems to make it exceptional.

The seriousness with which the episode in the *Martyrdom of Perpetua and Felicitas* has been taken as a possible indicator of actual eucharistic meal practice has something to do with the possible links between Perpetua's account and Montanism, and hence perhaps also with the Artotyritai.[39] The emphatic pneumatology of the work and the similarities

---

the translation there resolves the awkwardness of 'milking cheese' by making the food a 'mouthful of milk', but this is misleading.

[36] Apart from canonical sources, Armitage Robinson notes points of contact that suggest the influence of the *Shepherd* of Hermas: *The Passion of S. Perpetua*, TextsS 1/2 (Cambridge: Cambridge University Press, 1891), 26–36.

[37] Thomas J. Heffernan goes somewhat further in trying to establish the plausibility of the dream in terms of Perpetua's experience, but tends to conflate various pieces of liturgical evidence; see *Sacred Biography: Saints and their Biographers in the Middle Ages* (New York: Oxford University Press, 1988), 206–11.

[38] Thus Neyrey, 'Ceremonies in Luke-Acts', 362–3.

[39] Harnack, 'Brod und Wasser', 136; Lietzmann, *Mass and Lord's Supper*, 202; *The Treatise on the Apostolic Tradition of St. Hippolytus*, ed. and trans. G. Dix; 2nd edn., rev. with preface and corrections by H. Chadwick (London: SPCK, 1968), page g; Hanssens, *La Liturgie d'Hippolyte: Ses documents, son titulaire*, 422–4.

of style with the writings of Tertullian feed each other in promoting this possibility.[40] Yet even if the Artotyritai were Montanists of some sort, the odd reports of their practice would seem to be part of the evidence for rather later, and specifically Eastern, manifestations of that movement, and must in any case be kept separate from discussion of the phenomenon as it appeared in Africa at the end of the second century.[41] The silence of the sources about actual ritual cheese-eating in earlier Montanism cannot be ignored.[42]

There is nevertheless a similarity of concern or milieu between the African martyrs and the Artotyritai. In the vision of Perpetua, the cheese offered by the shepherd expresses a vision not dissimilar to the vegetarian idylls envisioned by other opponents of meat-eating. The cheese certainly fits the sense of 'coagulated milk', being provided directly from the sheep by the shepherd; here again, therefore, the significance of cheese is really the significance of milk.

The *Martyrdom of Perpetua and Felicitas* is in fact filled with references to an opposition of sorts between blood and killing on the one hand, and milk and peace on the other. Perpetua's way up to the shepherd's paradise is a ladder; at the base are weapons and a dragon, blood-letting opposites of the heavenly realm (ibid. 4. 3–4). Perpetua's consistent depiction as a nursing mother giving milk (ibid. 2. 2, 3. 8–9, 6. 7–8) is a further element in the picture of what is life-giving, opposed to what is death-dealing, in the narrative. Even the crowd gathered to witness the spectacle of the martyrdoms is appalled to see Felicitas, just having given birth and now also with dripping breasts.[43] In the martyrdom account as a whole, these milk elements form a powerful opposition with the bloodshed of the arena, and perhaps offer a basis in experience for radical entrenchment of these oppositions in cultural contexts such as meals.[44]

[40] Robinson, *The Passion of S. Perpetua*, 47–58. Connections between Asia and African Christianity have often been suggested; see T. D. Barnes, *Tertullian: A Historical and Literary Study*, rev. edn. (Oxford: Clarendon, 1985), 276.

[41] Labriolle, *Les Sources de l'histoire du Montanisme*, p. lxvii.

[42] The Montanism known to Tertullian seems, like Marcionite Christianity, to have had a liturgical order already somewhat like that of the orthodox. He makes no attempt to defend such practices as cheese or milk in the eucharist, and the apparent use of water in the cup (see below) is no basis for imagining more flexibility in the structure or elements of eucharistic meals, but rather the opposite.

[43] Felicitas' pregnancy and birth are also highlighted (15. 1–7, 18. 3); and note the mad heifer used to torture them (20. 1).

[44] After baptism, 'mihi Spiritus dictavit non aliud petendum ab aqua nisi sufferentiam carnis' (3. 5: 'the Spirit inspired me not to seek anything from the *water* but perseverance in the *flesh*' (my emphasis)); this also seems to be an opposition related to this theme.

Sacrifice, and therefore implicitly meat-eating, is constantly presented as the key issue for the martyrs. Perpetua is asked to sacrifice, and this plea is linked solidly to the basic relationships to which she should owe allegiance, the relationships which were seen as created and sustained by sacrificial practice: "Perform the sacrifice—have pity on your baby!' . . . 'Have pity on your father's grey head; have pity on your infant son. Offer the sacrifice for the welfare of the emperors' (ibid. 6. 2–3; cf. 18. 4–5). But rather than killing animals in sacrifice, the martyrs themselves are killed by animals (ibid. 19–21) in a symbolically appropriate, if horrific, reversal.

Here again the question of gender roles is an important one. Perpetua envisions herself transformed and engaging in battle with a monstrous Egyptian warrior: 'My clothes were stripped off, and suddenly I was a man' (ibid. 10. 7). While the warrior fights in order to kill her, Perpetua's prize will not be the death of her opponent but a branch of golden apples (ibid. 10. 8–9); thus the contest represents a breaking down of the conventions of sex but clear maintenance of the oppositions of death and life, including those of food. The courage of both Perpetua and Felicitas in their actual martyrdoms similarly suggests transcendence of the expected gender roles reinforced in sacrificial ritual (ibid. 20; 21. 8–11).

Thus the *Martyrdom of Perpetua and Felicitas* may not really be a witness to the actual use of milk or cheese in ritual meals, nor is it likely to be directly connected with the case of the Artotyritai, but the oppositions presented in the account, between bloodshed, meat-eating, and sacrifice on the one hand, and idyllic peace and avoidance of meat on the other, are a valuable and enlightening source for comparison. In this case it seems that it was at least 'good to think', and to write, as though milk or cheese were an appropriate alternative to blood and meat.

A similar milk-vision is recorded in the *Martyrdom of Montanus and Lucius*, another Carthaginian source.[45] There again a woman among the imprisoned has a vision:

I saw my son that had suffered come to the prison. He sat down at the rim of the water-trough and said 'God has seen your pain and tribulation.' After him there entered a young man of remarkable stature carrying in each of his hands two drinking cups full of milk. And he said; 'Be of good heart. God has been mindful of you.' And he gave everyone to drink from the cups which he carried, and they were never empty.   (ibid. 8. 3–5)

---

[45] The parallels with Perpetua have led some to suggest that this work is a forgery, but most would seem to demur. See Musurillo, *Acts of the Christian Martyrs*, pp. xxxiv–xxxvi.

In this case the image of the giver of milk as initiator into martyrdom has probably been assimilated into a picture more like that of contemporary liturgical practice; the drinking of milk and the multiplicity of cups could both derive from baptismal liturgies.[46]

There is one other example of use of cheese in a eucharistic meal, i.e. in the prescriptions for particular food offerings in the Egyptian Church Order often identified as the *Apostolic Tradition* of Hippolytus.[47] The offering of oil, and of cheese and olives, is provided for among the prayers of thanksgiving associated with the eucharistic meal that follows the ordination of a bishop:

Likewise if anyone offers cheese and olives he shall say thus: Sanctify this solidified milk, solidifying us also unto Thy charity. Grant also that this fruit of the olive depart not from Thy sweetness, <this fruit> which is the type of Thy fatness which Thou hast caused to flow from the tree for the life of them that hope in thee.   (Dix 6 = Botte 6)[48]

The newly ordained gives thanks over bread and wine in the manner now seen as exemplifying the normative tradition. Immediately after, provision is made for 'offering' oil, and 'giving thanks', these being the same two terms used for the prayers over the bread and wine.[49] Then comes the prayer for 'cheese and olives', apparently treated as a pair; the prayer-text quoted above is to be used 'if someone offers cheese and olives', implying that this was expected, but not constant, practice.[50]

[46] Cf. Tertullian, *De Corona*, 3. 3.

[47] This view was expounded definitively by R. H. Connolly, *The So-Called Egyptian Church Order and Derived Documents*, TextsS 8 (Cambridge: Cambridge University Press, 1916).

[48] 'Sanctifica lac hoc quod quoagulatum est, et nos conquaglans tuae caritati. Fac a tua dulcitudine non recedere fructum etiam hunc olivae qui est exemplu(m) tuae pinguidinis, quam de ligno fluisti in vitam eis qui sperant in te.'

[49] 'Si quis oleum offert, secundum panis oblationem et vini, et non ad sermonem dicat sed simili virtute, gratias referat dicens . . . Similiter, si quis caseum et olivas offert . . .'

[50] The blessing for cheese is found only in the Latin version; olives are alluded to in the *Testamentum Domini* and there is a trace of the prayer in the preservation of its doxology in the *Canons of Hippolytus* (see B. Botte's notes, *La Tradition apostolique de saint Hippolyte: essai de reconstruction*, ed. and trans. B. Botte, Liturgiewissenschaftliche Quellen und Forschungen, 39 (Münster: Aschendorff, 1963), 18–19). Eric Segelberg points out that there are traces in other oil-prayers not so closely related to the *Apostolic Tradition* or dependent Church Orders; some prayers for chrism or oil of the sick bear a relationship to the prayer in *Ap. Trad.* 6 and include the imagery of 'the type of your abundance' applied in *Ap. Trad.* 5 to the olives rather than the oil: 'The Benedictio Olei in the Apostolic Tradition of Hippolytus', *OrChr* 48 (1964), 268–81, esp. 271–81. This makes it seem likely that these prayers were present in the original (if we can speak of such a thing) and removed in the subsequent versions.

This means that some distance may have to be set between consideration of the practice itself and the actual forms of prayer, which presumably came later. In any case, 'offering' seems to be the technical term for bringing a food for ritual purposes, in this part of the document at least. Although a distinction is made between these prayers and those that should be said for the bread and wine, they are clearly analogous to say the least: 'If someone offers oil, let him give thanks in the same way as for the bread and the wine, not in the same words but with the same sense . . . Similarly, if someone wishes to offer cheese and olives . . .' (ibid. 5–6).

Granted the pre-eminence of bread and wine in this meal, all these foods are eucharistic in the sense of the word 'eucharist' arguably used in the text itself, at least.[51] The 'additional' foods are here only comprehensible as part of the same meal as the elements of bread and wine, granted that we could well be dealing with prayers and prescriptions put together for programmatic reasons, rather than with a direct reflection of real practice.[52]

These actions remain something of a mystery, and the growing shadow falling over the traditional attribution and dating of the *Apostolic Tradition* does not help.[53] The now-traditional identification places the work in Rome in the early third century, but other suggestions would make the date somewhat later and the place anywhere from Egypt to Syria.[54] If the different eucharistic sections of *Apostolic Tradition* were all of the same origin, we could not easily link this use of cheese, let alone the text itself, with the Artotyritai and Montanism. Everything we can reasonably infer about the Artotyritai encourages us to think that they were avoiders of wine and anxious about appropriate food, or at least

[51] This has been recognized by C. Vogel, 'Symboles cultuels chrétiens: Les Aliments sacrés, Poisson et Refrigeria', *Simboli e Simbologia nell'alto Medioevo* (2 vols.; Spoleto: Presso la Sede del Centro, 1976), i. 215–16. A tag at the end of *Ap. Trad.* 6 seems to be from another, probably redactional, hand, referring back to these prayers (perhaps including those for the bread and wine) as 'blessings' (benedictiones) rather than the terminology which the prayer texts themselves use, which is 'giving thanks' for 'offerings'.

[52] See Bradshaw's 'Ten Principles for Interpreting Early Liturgical Evidence', *The Search for the Origins of Christian Worship*, 56–79.

[53] See Paul F. Bradshaw, 'Re-dating the Apostolic Tradition: Some Preliminary Steps', in *Rule of Prayer, Rule of Faith: Essays in Honor of Aidan Kavanagh, O.S.B.* (Collegeville, Minn.: Liturgical Press, 1996), 3–17, and *The Search for the Origins of Christian Worship*, 89–92; Marcel Metzger, 'Nouvelles perspectives pour le prétendue *Tradition Apostolique*', *Ecclesia Orans*, 5 (1988), 241–59, and 'Enquêtes autour de la prétendue *Tradition Apostolique*', *Ecclesia Orans*, 9 (1992), 7–36; Jean Magne, 'Pour en finir avec la "Tradition d'Hippolyte"', *Bulletin de littérature ecclésiastique* (1988), 5–22.

[54] Bradshaw, *The Search for the Origins of Christian Worship*, 90–1; Hanssens, *La Liturgie d'Hippolyte: Ses documents, son titulaire*, 291–7.

about appropriate ritual foods. Wine marks the *Apostolic Tradition* off as belonging to a world where avoidance of the cuisine of sacrifice was not paramount. So too, the sacrificial language of this section and of other parts of the *Apostolic Tradition* puts this work in a different milieu.

It would be easier to draw links between these cheese-and-olives prayers and the Artotyritai if, as some suspect, the Church Order is really a pastiche and not a 'treatise' at all, a collection of liturgical and legislative material; this would account for the internal incoherence and would allow different parts of the work to be read independently. The sense of cheese as coagulated milk in the prayer of the *Apostolic Tradition*, a sense found also in Timothy of Constantinople's late and confusing reference to Marcionite Artotyritai, could arguably be a link of sorts between these cheese-eaters. It could also conceivably point to the same sort of imagery as the vision of Perpetua, in the sense that the provision of milk is actually what seems symbolically important in both cases, and the cheese is actually seen as milk in a solid form. This, however, would amount only to a common understanding of what cheese is. If it is too difficult to say whether the similarity offers any clue to the origin of the practice depicted in the *Apostolic Tradition*, the language nevertheless may further support the idea that the conjunction of bread and cheese, not only in Artotyrite practice but also in that underlying the *Apostolic Tradition* itself, is a development from a meal including bread and milk, explaining the odd element as an evolved 'cup' as already suggested.

The association of milk and vegetable elements—cheese and olives— may also be seen as a link of sorts with the ritual theory of the Artotyritai. It is the combination again of elements that are 'fruits of the earth and of sheep', to borrow Augustine's understanding, that is most curious and suggestive. The olives evoke 'sweetness', 'abundance', and 'life', and the image of the cross as a tree (of Life?) plays a part, evoking original grace and its paradisiacal diet.[55] The fact that the 'fruits of the earth' are in this case olives, rather than bread, means that direct connections with the Artotyritai are not likely, but the logic of the offerings may originally have been the same, i.e. the use of cheese and olives in some communities as elements of eucharistic meals may also have some connection with the themes of primordial bliss, and of avoidance of meat-eating and its implications. A diet of cheese (or milk) and olives might have seemed appropriate to meat-avoiding Christians.[56]

---

[55] This is also suggested by Segelberg, 'The Benedictio Olei in the Apostolic Tradition of Hippolytus', 278. The *Gospel of Philip*, 91, identifies the Tree of Life as an olive.

[56] See further Chs. 4 and 5 below.

In any case, this document envisages someone offering cheese, among other things, in a manner that is clearly eucharistic, not only in the general sense that elements are offered and given thanks for or blessed in the context of a communal meal, but in clear parallelism with the pre-eminent elements of bread and wine. A perception that foods such as these were part of the eucharistic meal may have led both to the distinctions made in the *Apostolic Tradition* as it stands about the prayers for elements other than bread and wine, and to legislation such as that of the African councils which indicate concern about the use of other foods at the eucharist. Unfortunately we do not know to which foods the bishops at Carthage were referring, but it seems plausible that even distinctions like those made in the *Apostolic Tradition* might not have satisfied them.

MILK AND HONEY

The importance of cheese is likely, then, to be the importance of milk in another form. As already mentioned, we do know of some (other) instances of the use of milk, together with honey, in early Christian ritual meals, and especially in connection with baptism. Yet there is no convincing evidence for a milk-and-honey baptismal meal in the first or early second centuries.[57] The New Testament uses of milk imagery are mostly negative (1 Cor. 3: 9; Heb. 5: 12–13; but cf. 1 Pet. 2: 2), and undoubtedly figurative. Characteristically, the author of the *Epistle of Barnabas* (6) treats the milk and honey of the land of promise (Exod. 33: 3) not to prescribe contemporary practice, but to extract a spiritual meaning allegorically.

Clement of Alexandria's discussion of milk in the *Paedagogus* has been taken more seriously, but is at best a problematic witness.[58] Difficulties arise here, as often when dealing with Clement's 'sacramental' language and his ready shifts between apparently literal and allegorical or figurative statements.[59] In refuting gnostics who seem to distinguish, along lines

---

[57] The discussion by T. Schermann in 'Die Abendmahlsliturgie der Neophyten nach ägyptischen Quellen vom 2.–6. Jahrhundert', *ZKT* 36 (1912), 464–88, is certainly too accepting of allusions as real practice, apparently motivated by a desire to find very early instances of developed liturgical models.

[58] H. Usener, 'Milch und Honig', *Rheinisches Museum*, 57 (1902), 185; Hanssens, *La Liturgie d'Hippolyte: Ses documents, son titulaire*, 481–4. Hanssens acknowledges the difficulty but still reaches the opposite conclusion.

[59] See Andrew McGowan, 'Naming the Feast: The *Agape* and the Diversity of Early

suggested by Paul, between those Christians who are ready to eat 'meat' and those who can only stomach 'milk' (cf. 1 Cor. 3: 2), Clement acknowledges some difficulty in reconciling the derogatory use of the milk metaphor with the positive associations of milk and honey in the Exodus narrative (*Paed.* 1. 6. 34. 3–35. 1). Rather than providing an exegesis of the ritual use of milk, he gives a somewhat tortuous version of received physiological wisdom, arguing for the identity of milk and blood: milk is a kind of frothy or whipped (hence its whiteness) blood (ibid. 39. 1– 50. 2).[60] With blood Clement was apparently on firmer ground, closer to the sacramental imagery known to him; and from that hard-won position he could move to the imagery not only of the blood but the body of Christ (ibid. 42. 2), and of the bread of heaven (ibid. 46. 2–3). Various further examples are used, from everyday practice including food and meals, but with no clear reference to Christian rituals of initiation. The importance of milk is related rather to its supposed affinities with bread (ibid. 47. 1) and with water (ibid. 50. 3), as well as with honey (ibid. 51. 1), and even to the use of butter in lamps (ibid. 51. 3).

If Clement knew of a ritual use of milk and honey he was obtuse about it. We could only say for certain that he was referring to such a symbolic meal if that were the only explanation for his talking about mixing milk and honey at all, and this is clearly not the case; the topic is determined by his exegetical agenda. While it is true that this extended discussion of milk is also connected with baptism, this in fact renders the absence of clearer reference to a milk ritual quite incomprehensible. The apparent emphasis placed by his opponents on the 'infancy' of other Christians is more than enough to explain the fact that milk is such a vexed but important image for Clement. Like Perpetua among others, he draws on a generally accepted set of images and ideas about milk, both natural and supernatural. In neither Clement's case nor that of Perpetua does this mean that an actual ritual practice known to the Christian communities of the authors is being alluded to.[61]

Christian Ritual Meals', in Elizabeth A. Livingstone (ed.), *Studia Patristica XXX* (Leuven: Peeters, 1997), 314–18, on Clement's references to the *agape* meal, a similar case where his metaphorical language has been overread because of the desire to find uniform liturgical patterns and practices.

[60] See Brown, *The Body and Society*, 18, for the connection of various fluids in sexual contexts also.

[61] In fact we could well imagine that the Gnostic opponents would have been more likely to use such an image with its implication of gradations among the faithful. This was apparently the case with the Mithras cult. Tatian seems to have depicted John the Baptist as eating 'milk and honey' rather than 'locusts and wild honey'. See Sebastian Brock, 'The Baptist's Diet in Syriac Sources', *OrChr* 54 (1970), 115–16.

The first really clear reference to milk and honey in baptismal use is not too far away in time or space. Such was apparently known to Marcion or his followers (Tertullian, *Adv. Marc.* 1. 14. 3) and certainly to Tertullian (*De Corona*, 3. 3), according to whom the heretic's hypocrisy as to the created order was borne out in his use of these elements in baptismal ritual, wherein he fed his followers with a mixture of milk and honey after the water and anointing and before the eucharistic bread.[62] There may be some question about the accuracy of Tertullian's know-ledge of Marcionite ritual, but we have already seen there may be other evidence supporting this kind of practice in those circles, and in any case it was clearly the use of his own African community late in the second century.

We can be even clearer about these practices as they appear in the *Apostolic Tradition*. There the sort of imagery used by Clement is acted out explicitly. After the actual baptism and anointing, a eucharistic meal follows:

And then let the oblation now be offered by the deacons to the bishop and let him eucharistize the bread into the representation, which the Greek calls antitype, of the body of Christ; and the cup mixed with wine for the antitype, which the Greeks calls the similitude of blood, which was poured out for all who have believed in him; milk and honey mixed in fulfilment of the promise which was to the fathers, which he spoke of as a land flowing with milk and honey, which Christ also gave as his flesh, through which those who believe are nourished like small children, making the bitterness of the heart sweet by the sweetness of the word; water also as an oblation as a sign of the washing, so that the interior person also, which is of the flesh, may be acted upon in the same way as the body. And the bishop shall give an explanation of all these to those who receive them. And breaking the bread into pieces let him say while distributing 'The bread of heaven in Christ Jesus.' And let the one who receives respond 'Amen.' Let presbyters, and if there are not enough, deacons also, hold the cups and stand by in order and with reverence; first the one who holds the water, second the one with the milk, and third the one with the wine. And let those who receive drink three times from each, [and] let the one who gives say 'In the Lord and Father Almighty.' And let the one who receives say 'Amen.' 'And in the Lord Jesus Christ.' 'And in the Holy Spirit [and] the Holy Church.' And let him say 'Amen.' Let it take place thus for each one. (Dix 23. 1–11 = Botte 21)

---

[62] 'Sed ille quidem usque nunc nec aquam reprobavit creatoris, qua suos abluit, nec oleum, quo suos ungit, nec mellis et lactis societatem, qua suos infantat, nec panem, quo ipsum corpus suum repraesentant, etiam in sacramentis propriis egens mendicitatibus creatoris' (*Adv. Marc.* 1. 14. 3). I assume we may tentatively follow the order of use of the elements outlined as reflecting Tertullian's understanding of the practice.

It has been suggested by others that these cups of milk and honey, and of water, which feature along with bread and wine in this baptismal eucharist of the *Apostolic Tradition*, might be the remnant of a (solid) meal which was also the original setting of a separate ritual of the specifically eucharistic elements of bread and wine.[63] But while the mixture of milk and honey might seem like 'food' for infants, it would also and more immediately have been recognized as μελίκρατον, a mixture of milk or water and honey also used by pagans in certain, exceptional, wineless libations (Homer, *Odyssey*, 10. 519; Euripides, *Orestes*, 115); if unusual, this mixture was drink, really and symbolically.

Consideration of the broader meal evidence suggests in fact that three cups after the main part of a meal is quite to be expected;[64] to use more than one on the paschal feast is, apart from anything else, an appropriate marker of the occasion.[65] These cups are therefore probably a vestigial *symposium*. Hence it is the whole of this proceeding, including both the eucharistized bread and the multiple cups, which is both the eucharist proper and the remnant of a meal, rather than two sets of essentially separate acts. The prayers used for the various meal elements keep the bread and the different cups in very close relationship; thanks are given for all, and all the cups are administered with the same solemnity both of persons (presbyters or deacons; no hierarchy of cups is established, although the bishop distributes the bread) and of words. The various cups should therefore be understood as comparable, together, to the drink of a *symposium*, rather than separated into attenuated forms of the food of a *cena* on the one hand and the real eucharistic cup on the other. The whole eucharistic meal seems very much like the remnant of an older, real meal.

Similar pictures of multiple post-baptismal cups including the use of milk and honey are given in both African and Italian sources, but most of rather later date than even the opponents of Hippolytean authorship are inclined to attribute to the *Apostolic Tradition*. The *Acts of Susanna*, set during the persecutions under Diocletian but perhaps from closer to 500,[66] depict the bishop Caius blessing 'the body and blood of our Lord,

---

[63] Jungmann, *The Early Liturgy*, 35, 139.

[64] Cf. Athenaeus, *Deip.* 2. 36 B–C.

[65] Note also the multiple cups of the eucharist of Marcus the Magician (Irenaeus, *Adv. Haer.* 1. 13. 2), which could have had such sympotic overtones as well as, or instead of, the conjuring-trick atmosphere which Irenaeus suggests.

[66] See L. Duchesne, 'Les Légendes de l'*Alta Semita*', *Mélanges d'archéologie et d'histoire*, 36 (1916–17), 27–56, esp. 33–42; H. Delehaye, *Étude sur le legendier romain: Les Saints de novembre et decembre* (Brussels: Société des Bollandistes, 1936), 12, 24.

and also the milk and the honey and the spring [*fontem*] . . .'.[67] Councils at Carthage and Hippo sought to distinguish the ritual post-baptismal use of milk and honey more clearly from the (other) eucharistic elements (*Conc. Carth. III*, 24).

Jerome also mentions a similar practice, that of drinking milk along with the wine of the eucharistic meal after a baptism, but does not mention the various cups prescribed in the *Apostolic Tradition*; the implication might even be that a mixture is used. In any case, such milk ritual is apparently known in the Western churches, but not in the East by his time.[68] The textual history of the later Church Order documents dependent on the *Apostolic Tradition* also suggests some embarrassment or at least uncertainty about the multiplicity of cups, and a tendency to combine the elements in fewer where possible.[69]

The geographical extent of using milk in an initiatory cup remains somewhat obscure so long as the questions of the date and authorship of the *Apostolic Tradition* are also vexed, which may be forever. In this case at least, Roman (or at least Western) origin does not seem out of keeping with the rest of the evidence, and the alternative of an Egyptian derivation is not well supported by comparison. By Jerome's time the use of milk was unknown in Syria (if it had ever been known there) and was seen as a Western tradition; and the persistence of such practices in Coptic and Ethiopic Christianity could reflect the influence of the Church Order literature just as well as explain its content. Ephraem Syrus' reference to Marcionite use of milk and honey confirms that the practice was only Western by condemning it altogether, apparently unaware of its orthodox respectability in other places. The use of milk and honey in baptismal eucharists persists for some time in the West, and then merely fades out of existence. Blessings of milk and honey continue to appear in medieval sacramentaries even when there is apparently no ongoing practice of this kind.[70]

[67] *Acta Sanctorum*, Febr. III 63 A–B, cited in Hanssens, *La Liturgie d'Hippolyte: Ses documents, son titulaire*, 484–5.

[68] 'et non solum vinum emamus, sed et lac, quod significat innocentiam parvulorum, qui mos ac typus in occidentis ecclesiis hodie usque servatur, ut renatis in Christo vinum lacque tribuatur' (*Comm. in Is. Proph.* 15. 55. 1–2); 'lactis et mellis praegustare concordiam ad infantiae significationem' (*Adv. Luc.* 8).

[69] See J. M. Hanssens, *La Liturgie d'Hippolyte: Documents et études* (Rome: Gregorian University, 1970), 116–17, 120–1, which provides Latin text or translations in synopsis of the relevant portions of the Verona Palimpsest, the Syriac, Arabic, and Ethiopic versions of the Egyptian Church Order, and of *Testamentum Domini* and *Canons of Hippolytus* respectively.

[70] Hanssens, *La Liturgie d'Hippolyte: Ses documents, son titulaire*, 485–8; Usener, 'Milch und Honig', 187–90.

What do these various rituals signify? While it may be taken for granted that Christian use of this combination of elements drew upon the description of the promised land as flowing with milk and honey as well as on images of infancy and of sweetness (*Ap. Trad.* 23. 2; cf. *Mart. Perp.* 4. 10), earlier pagan descriptions of divine presence also make free use of these foods and associated images.[71] More particularly, similar ritual use does appear in contexts rather like those in which Christians were also to make use of the same elements, i.e. in initiatory practices.[72] Initiates of Mithras, for instance, were given honey, purportedly as a sign of purity and of immortality (Porphyry, *De Antro Nymph.* 15–16).[73] For that matter, the heroine of the Jewish romance *Joseph and Aseneth* is given as an initiatory process a divine honeycomb to eat, made by 'the bees of paradise . . . from the dew of the roses of life that are in the paradise of God', a description using imagery which, if not without biblical connections, is not evocative of the Exodus in particular.[74]

These possible connections are neither exclusive nor exhaustive. While many converts might have been able to compare their baptismal feeding with milk and honey to descriptions of Dionysiac plenty, or to the Mithraic initiations which they or others known to them might have experienced, this similarity hardly supplants use of the Exodus or other biblical stories as the basis for the particular sacramental meal. Rather, the parallel uses of milk and honey in pagan ritual serve to suggest a generalized set of meanings for the foods and practices for members of the society at large, upon which more specific traditions and motifs could be laid. Christian use of this imagery also has overtones of initiation and of participation in a tranquil golden age, easily assimilable to the land of promise or to prelapsarian innocence. More prosaic aspects ought not to be forgotten either; milk was probably not available in fresh form to many people very often; its perishability will have tended to restrict its use to the wealthy and those close to its production.[75] Milk is thus probably a sign of wealth and plenty, and more especially of an age characterized by these qualities.

---

[71] Euripides, *Bacchae*, 142; Ovid, *Fasti*, 3. 736 etc.; see Usener, 'Milch und Honig', 177–95, esp. 178–83.

[72] Usener, 'Milch und Honig', 181–3, 193–5.

[73] Ibid. 182–3; Rev. 10: 9–10 (cf. Ezek. 3: 3) also implies an initiation.

[74] See C. Burchard in *OTP* 2. 211–12, n. 8i. This interesting meal is often seen as equivalent to participation in the formulaic 'bread of life', 'cup of immortality', and 'ointment of immortality' which are mentioned often in *Joseph and Aseneth* (8. 9, 15. 5, 16. 16), but I suspect these elements have been somewhat sacramentalized by interpreters; they are opposed to the general eating practices of pagans (8. 5) and may refer to all pure food rather than to a sacral meal.   [75] Dalby, *Siren Feasts*, 65–6.

To the sense of milk and honey as signs of a young world should be added their more concrete association with young persons. The use of milk for newborns is self-evident, although the imagery perhaps most familiar to readers of the Bible is negative, based on an unfavourable comparison between infancy and maturity. Honey was also fed to newborns, at least in part because it was understood to have a purgative effect.[76] This particular sort of connection was an obvious one to make in initiatory use.

Actual use of these foods in ritual may need therefore to be read against one or more complementary sets of associations, in addition to the most general and obvious aspect of aesthetic and dietary desirability: the common feeding of newborn children with these substances; the pastoral overtones of rural life; the well-known idyllic and divine associations of pagan religion and literature; and the specific connections with the Exodus story.

But such 'essential' meanings must be treated carefully. We have already noted that libations of milk and honey were employed in certain pagan rituals in conscious contrast with the more typical use of wine, as exceptions that proved the rule.[77] Like water, the milk-and-honey mixture was a sort of opposite to wine, and its meaning dependent on that contrast, as much as on anything necessarily conveyed by milk or honey in and of themselves. Use of this μελίκρατον in pagan and Christian ritual alike could thus be seen as a device which served, by its departure from the usual form of libations, to create a sort of conceptual space to be filled by some new association which depended on the specific context and community. While acknowledging the natural symbolism to a certain extent, we must therefore seek particular meanings for the different uses of milk (and/or cheese), rather than assuming that they all mean the same thing.

The appearance of milk and honey in initiatory meals, for instance, may well need to be understood quite differently from the possible use of cheese or curd in regular eucharistic meals among some Montanists (and Marcionites?) later. Not only are the historical connections loose, the actual significance of the food in the two sorts of cases seems somewhat different.

The milk-and-honey cup is connected with the unique ritual of baptism, draws upon the idea of infancy more strongly than in the

---

[76] Soranus, *Gynaeceia*, 2. 11. 17; Oribasius, *Libri Incerti*, 20. See Leyerle, 'Meal Customs'.

[77] See further Fritz Graf, 'Milch, Honig und Wein', 209–21.

other examples,[78] and is rather closely related to pagan models. Despite the biblical connections which became the rationale for the use of milk and honey in initiatory meals, communities which adopted this practice were also constructing clear analogues to pagan ritual such as Mithras-initiations, and making use of images of abundance and luxury common in the religious imagery of the Graeco-Roman world.[79] Where the milk-and-honey cup involves a temporary contrast with the usual wine-cup of the normative eucharist, in a way not at all dissimilar to the pagan use of such libations for particular occasions, it suggests a sort of embellishment or enrichment. Other things being equal, this sort of ritual use suggests positive (although not necessarily uncritical) engagement with existing social norms, rather than radical separation.

On the other hand, when milk and honey introduce a life that contrasts radically and permanently with that of sacrifice and vinous symposium, as they do in Marcionite use, the use of that cup (alone) becomes a sign of that contrast. While milk and honey convey luxury and a restored creation, they stand in marked contrast with the problematic state of the rejected world. So too, the use of cheese in repeated eucharistic meals without the rarer and more expensive honey may best be understood as a sign of rejection of sacrifice and its present-day bloodshed, claiming instead a share in primordial bliss. These cases, the one unique and the other repeated, both express not merely a transitory contrast with the normal use of wine, but a more radical and permanent renunciation.

The differences between the ways milk or cheese is used in terms of time and occasion, i.e. whether in repeated or unique meals, is therefore potentially significant. Where cheese seems to be part of a pattern of repeated ascetic eucharistic meals, it emphasizes the allegiance of the participant to an order of foods (and of other things) somewhat removed from that of society in general; the community may see itself as an island of the New Creation, restored to ancient peace. On the other hand, the more 'orthodox' use of milk and honey at once-only baptismal eucharists suggests an ordering of time in which the symbolism of the elements is held in momentary tension with ordinary existence; in terms of ritual theory, there is a moment of removal from the previous state, but then also one of reintegration into society, or an alternative society; milk and honey belong to the transitory, dissociative state, which may be renewed

---

[78] Granted the presence of this aspect in the somewhat baptismal vision of Perpetua, who is addressed as 'child' by the divine shepherd.

[79] Usener, 'Milch und Honig', 190–2.

in the future (after death) but is somehow markedly different from daily existence.

There is ultimately a connection between these two basic forms of milk ritual in the pastoral and paradisiacal symbolism of milk, but the common symbolic aspect is mediated through somewhat different world-views. The use of this imagery in connection with Dionysus and his revellers was certainly a different sort of primordial vision from that of bloodless peace. Granted therefore that the practice seems to have been present among rigorist Marcionites as well as the orthodox, the milk-and-honey baptismal ritual suggests an analogy with pagan religion, and involves the creation of sacral initiation meals which might appeal as viable alternatives to, rather than outright rejection of, the problematic cuisine of sacrifice.

OIL

There are only a few indications that oil may have been used in Christian ritual meals, at least as a food in itself. Yet olive oil, in particular, was regarded as a food or condiment in its own right, and could be expected at tables in a variety of social and religious settings. The use of oil for anointing was also common and has been easier to trace as part of Christian ritual.[80]

Oil does appear in one of the eucharistic meals of the *Acts of Thomas* (29). There the apostle took 'bread, oil, vegetables and salt, blessed them and gave them to them', clearly echoing the actions of Jesus in Gospel accounts of the Last Supper or miraculous feedings.

This and other meals of the apocryphal *Acts* present particular problems of definition, since few or none are quite recognizable in terms of the conventional picture of eucharistic practice. They can in general be separated into two categories, although the boundaries are not absolute. Some (not including the present case) use the terminology of 'eucharist' clearly and consciously.[81] The term generally refers to the bread of a sacral meal which, however, is typically accompanied by water or no cup at all; these will be discussed further below.

---

[80] Although not without its own difficulties; there is no reference to oil for initiatory rites in the New Testament, and few indications of any continuity from the therapeutic use proposed in Jas. 5: 14–15 in the early Church. See Jeffrey John, 'Anointing in the New Testament', in Martin Dudley and Geoffrey Rowell (eds.), *The Oil of Gladness: Anointing in the Christian Tradition* (London: SPCK, 1993), 46–76, and John Halliburton, 'Anointing in the Early Church', pp. 77–91 in the same vol.

[81] *Acts of Thomas*, 27, 29, 49–51, 121, 133, 158. See further Ch. 5 below.

The case in point, however, is one of a number of meals in the apocryphal *Acts* which are less clearly sacral in nature. Thomas does 'bless' the foods, and his actions are reminiscent of Gospel meals with eucharistic overtones; but since the *Acts of Thomas* are quite capable of speaking of 'the eucharist' in the absolute, referring specifically to the broken and shared bread for which the apostle typically 'gives thanks', some distinction can be allowed. King Misdaeus, Thomas' opponent, does describe the apostle's 'sorcery' as involving 'oil and water and bread' (ibid. 152), but this mention of oil is more likely to refer to baptism (although the reference to water could apply to the eucharist, as much or more than to baptism, in this work).

While there are different types of meal in the *Acts of Thomas*, this is not to say that this meal with oil and others with additional elements do not share to some extent in the 'eucharistic' character of the more explicit bread or bread-and-water eucharists. It is clear in the *Acts of Thomas*, and in the apocryphal *Acts* generally, that there is more concern about excluding inappropriate foods (specifically meat and wine) than about including oil or anything else.[82] This meal is therefore a model of appropriate eating in which the prime element of the eucharist 'proper', i.e. bread, is also central. Oil, like salt and vegetables, is part of the typical poor or ascetic diet of antiquity. Here, as in the cases of Cynics and Pythagoreans, asceticism cannot be conceived of merely in terms of concern for health or the body generally, but has some specific relationship to the question of sacrificial cuisine.

The *Excerpta ex Theodoto* from the pen of Clement of Alexandria, which are notes and extracts from the Valentinian Theodotus, may indicate use of oil as part of a meal.[83] At a point where Clement seems to be quoting Theodotus we read: 'Both the bread and the oil are sanctified by the power of the name of God . . .' (ibid. 82. 1).[84] Nothing further is said about what is done with the oil, but the conjunction of bread and oil suggests eating. This text should be dated late in the second century and is probably from the eastern Mediterranean; Theodotus is understood to be a part of the Eastern school among the successors of Valentinus. Theodotus may well also be a

---

[82] See Ch. 5 below.

[83] Thus Aloys Scheiwiler, *Die Elemente der Eucharistie in den ersten drei Jahrhunderten* (Mainz: Franz Kirchheim, 1903), 133–5.

[84] καὶ ὁ ἄρτος καὶ ὁ ἔλαιον ἁγιάζεται δυνάμει τοῦ Ὀνόματος Θεοῦ . . . The suggestion that 'oil' be emended to read 'wine' is, as F. Sagnard (ed.), *Clément d'Alexandrie: Extraits de Théodote*, SC 23 (Paris: Éditions du Cerf, 1970), 234 n. 1, 207 n. 2, comments, quite gratuitous, but again revealing of some scholarly assumptions.

representative of the practice of using water in the eucharistic cup (on which see further below), and here as in the *Acts of Thomas* there is probably a connection between the emphasis placed on appropriate foods which seem at first glance 'additional' to the expected bread and wine, and the refusal of what seems to have been an offending element in pagan and (most) orthodox practice alike, i.e. wine.

The foods mentioned in the eucharistic prayers of the ordination meal in the *Apostolic Tradition* also include oil. After the prayers specific to the bread and wine, and before those for cheese and olives, comes that for oil. The actual text of the prayer over the oil suggests use for both unction and ingestion: 'May you grant, O God, in sanctifying this oil, that in the same way as all who use and receive it receive the sanctification with which you anointed kings, priests and prophets, so may it provide strength to all tasting it and health to all using it' (Dix 5 = Botte 5).[85]

The prayer seems to suggest a specifically therapeutic use, but this does not mean that we are dealing here with 'oil of the sick' in the more developed sense, i.e. with oil solely for anointing; the eucharistic elements are also described as 'medicinal' by Ignatius of Antioch rather earlier than this (*Eph.* 20. 2), and given the everyday uses of oil, that sort of imagery would be attractive even were the oil to be used at a eucharistic meal, or as seems more likely in this case, for medicinal use at home.[86] There are various indications in somewhat later and undoubtedly orthodox circles that blessed oil could be used therapeutically for internal purposes, as well as externally.[87]

---

[85] 'Ut oleum hoc sanctificans das, deus, san(ct)itatem utentibus et percipientibus, unde uncxisti reges, sacerdotes et profetas, sic et omnibus gustantibus confortationem et sanitatem utentibus illud praebeat.' My translation in this instance. The relation between the first and second parts of the prayer is awkward, even when one accepts the suggestion of reading 'sanctitatem' for the MS 'sanitatem' (*The Treatise on the Apostolic Tradition of St. Hippolytus*, ed. Dix, 10–11; see also Botte, *La Tradition apostolique*, 18 n. 2). Segelberg, 'The Benedictio Olei in the Apostolic Tradition of Hippolytus', 270–1, 279, suggests that while the emendation may not be necessary in the existing prayer despite both Dix's and Botte's dissatisfaction with the text, the other prayers deriving from this one support the notion that health rather than holiness may have been the theme of the archetype.

[86] This does not mean to say that this was the original context even of the prayer as it stands, let alone of this custom of blessing oil for use in eucharistic meals. The fact that at this point in the *Apostolic Tradition* there seems to be no distinction between oil for anointing and eating, while at 21 there is a very clear distinction between 'oil of thanksgiving' ('eucharistized oil', as it were) and 'oil of exorcism', reflects two quite different backgrounds for the two portions of the text.

[87] e.g., Martin of Tours's action according to Sulpicius Severus, *Dialogues*, 3. 2; see Halliburton, 'Anointing in the Early Church', 82–9.

SALT

The clearest references to the use of salt in eucharistic meals are those of
the Pseudo-Clementine *Homilies*. The literary frame or introduction of
the *Homilies* includes letters from Clement and Peter and instructions for
the *Contestatio* ($\Delta\iota\alpha\mu\alpha\rho\tau\upsilon\rho\acute{\iota}\alpha$) or 'hearing' prescribed for those who are to
be entrusted with the book that follows, i.e. the *Homilies*; but the
Contestatio may have been part of a basic writing or *Grundschrift*
underlying both the *Homilies* and the *Recognitions*, the other version of
the Clementine romance, in which case the meal elements to be discussed
here probably reflect practices earlier than the middle of the third
century.[88] This proceeding, consisting of a solemn declaration while
the candidate is standing next to baptismal water (see *Cont.* 1. 2) prior to
eating bread and salt, combines initiatory action and meal in a way
similar to that found in Justin, the apocryphal *Acts*, the *Apostolic
Tradition*, and elsewhere, although no immersion takes place; it would
seem that baptism is alluded to, rather than depicted.[89] The candidate
uses a detailed oath invoking the elements 'heaven, earth, water, in which
all things are comprehended, and in addition to all these air also, which
pervades all things . . .' The substance of the oath is that the books and
their contents are not to be divulged by any means. 'And after this, let
him partake of bread and salt with the one who handed over [the books]'
(*Cont.* 4. 3).

If the connection between the meal and baptism is merely allusive in
that first case, it is more concrete in a passage in the *Homilies* proper,
where the baptism of Clement's mother is described. There Peter,
'having broken the bread with thanksgiving ($\grave{\epsilon}\pi$' $\epsilon\grave{\upsilon}\chi\alpha\rho\iota\sigma\tau\acute{\iota}\alpha$) and
having put salt on it he gave it first to [our] mother and after her to
us, her sons. Thus we both ate with her and blessed God' (*Hom.* 14. 1. 4).
This is certainly more than an incidental meal, but is the realization of a
new relationship between the eaters; without baptism they could not
have eaten together (cf. *Hom.* 1. 22, 13. 4).

The fact of a salt eucharist here seems to imply a link with the ritual
described in the *Contestatio* and hence with the possible basic writing. If,

---

[88] The view of (e.g.) Georg Strecker, *Das Judenchristentum in den Pseudoklementinen*, TU
70; 2nd edn. (Berlin: Akademie-Verlag, 1981), 137–145, is that the *Contestatio* and *Epistula
Petri* go back to the *Kerygmata Petrou*, a source for the *Grundschrift*; but it seems to me that
apart from other factors, the salt rituals link the *Contestatio* and the *Epistula Clementis*, on
which see further below.

[89] Strecker, *Das Judenchristentum in den Pseudoklementinen*, 142–3.

as seems likely, the story in this form was a part of the source material common to both versions of the Pseudo-Clementine works, the more orthodox *Recognitions* seem to have balked at the identification of a real meal with a post-baptismal eucharist when they tell the same story, separating the initiation somewhat from a later, and less highly charged, family dinner (*Recog.* 7. 38. 2).

In the *Letter of Clement to James* (*Epistula Clementis*), another of the preliminary sections of the *Homilies* which would seem to come from that basic document underlying both versions,[90] the eating of salt stands explicitly (as elsewhere in ancient literature) for the sharing of table-fellowship. More particularly it means the creation of ἀγάπη: 'I know that these things will be done by you, if you establish love (ἀγάπη) in your mind. To this end there is one sure means, the common partaking of salt (ἡ κοινὴ τῶν ἁλῶν μετάληψις)' (*Ep. Clem.* 9. 1–2).[91]

Georg Strecker seems to understand these references to salt almost as a redactional overreading of idioms used in earlier materials—the transformation of a turn of phrase into a fictional ritual. To 'take salt' with someone certainly does represent table-fellowship and friendship generally, and in this sense it is attested in the *Homilies* and very widely elsewhere in Greek literature.[92] Yet Strecker's conclusion that the salt element is largely a literary twist seems inadequate. His own source analysis actually suggests that we have at least two layers of material, source and redaction, in which salt is prominent, a fact which makes the use of this element more than incidental.[93] All the 'salt' meals of the

[90] Strecker, 'The Pseudo-Clementines', in W. Schneemelcher (ed.), *New Testament Apocrypha*, rev. edn. (2 vols.; Louisville, Ky.: Westminster/John Knox, 1992), ii. 488. Strecker therefore places this piece one compositional step later than the other letter and the *Contestatio*.

[91] Here again the Latin is a little different; *caritas* will come about 'si frequenter inter vosmetipsos communem cibum vestrum mensamque faciatis'.

[92] In the *Homilies*, as elsewhere, the expressions τροφῆς μεταλαμβάνειν (*Hom.* 1. 22. 3 etc.) and ἁλῶν μεταλαμβάνειν (11. 34. 1 etc.) do often have similar meanings. The verb συναλίζεσθαι is also used, obviously in the general sense of 'to eat together', in the Acts of the Apostles (1: 4). In Strecker's view the compiler of the *Kerygmata Petrou* source, one of the possible precursors even to the hypothetical basic writing, replaced a baptismal eucharist with the salt meal of *Cont.* 4. 3; and the two other places where salt is an explicit and important part of proceedings (*Ep. Clem.* 9. 2 and *Hom.* 14. 1. 4) come from the redactor of the basic writing, who would have been influenced by the one instance in his source and by an alleged motif of Jewish meal practice: see *Das Judenchristentum in den Pseudoklementinen*, 209–13.

[93] There is good reason to accept that the *Epistula Petri* and *Contestatio* do predate the *Epistula Clementis*, since they construct somewhat different literary-fictional frames for the work. The *Epistula Clementis* belongs with the Clement 'romance' which provides the narrative framework for both *Homilies* and *Recognitions*.

Pseudo-Clementines have a clearly ritual or even sacral quality: one is associated with a solemn (quasi-)baptismal oath, another with baptism proper, and the other explicit reference is part of an exhortation to participation in the exclusive community meal, not to 'mere' eating. The explicit salt references are therefore best understood as indications of certain meals as especially significant, at least in literary terms; this may also, however, be a feature that we are meant to read into the other meals, all of which are clearly understood to meet standards of purity and asceticism that are not observed by those outside this Christian community.[94] Thus the importance of salt, whether for diet in general, for specifically ritual purposes, or as a symbol, apparently reflects the position of the author of the basic writing and perhaps even that of an earlier *Kerygmata Petrou*, and presumably therefore the salt meal represents the actual ritual of the community or communities from which these documents arose, rather than merely an over-literal reading of a common expression.

What does the use of salt signify? Despite the prominence of salt in these meals it would be wrong to regard the use of that element as sacral in a sense not applied to other food. Here we have an instance where more is less, so to speak. The use of salt does not necessarily imply a significant expansion of a meal consisting otherwise of bread and water only, because it was already part of the limited group of foods whose simplicity and purity was recognizable to Jew, pagan, and Christian alike. We have already seen that salt was the most basic form of the additional dish which was necessary, along with bread and drink, to form the structure of the Graeco-Roman meal. There are examples in other works where we find the conscious use of salt as a basic and ascetic food, perfectly capable of being seen and used in just the same light as a meal of bread and water, indicating voluntary poverty in a variety of social settings: this is the ideal diet of the student of the Torah (*m. 'Abot* 6: 4), of the contemplative of Philo (*Contempl.* 37), of the Cynic (Lucian, *Fug.* 14) and, in the apocryphal *Acts* as well as here, of an ascetic apostle (*Acts of Thomas*, 29). From a literary perspective also, there seems to be continuity between the different kinds of meal description in the Pseudo-Clementines, rather than a sharp distinction between the presentation of the 'salt meals' and that of others. It is probably fair to say that either these are presented as the most solemn, or are simply the most carefully described. At most, the use

---

[94] Lebeau, *Le Vin nouveau*, 161–2. Oscar Cullmann, 'La Signification de la Saint-Cène dans le christianisme primitif', *RHPR* 16 (1936), 9, goes so far as to suggest that 'sharing salt' is the technical term for the Lord's Supper in the Pseudo-Clementines.

of salt at baptism may have some special significance or emphasis, but it does not radically change the nature or meaning of the meal.

Strecker also rejects the possible conclusion that these meals should be seen as eucharistic, on the basis that a bread-and-salt eucharist is (otherwise) unattested.[95] In fact, there are arguably, as we shall see, other instances of bread-and-salt meals that can reasonably be termed 'eucharistic', granted that the answer to this question depends somewhat on terminology and assumptions. But whether there are many instances or one, Strecker's assessment is based on the familiar and unsatisfactory assumption that a eucharist must contain certain elements not present here, and for that matter on the assumption of a normative unity of eucharistic meal practice which dismisses unique evidence precisely as unique. It must be admitted that the Pseudo-Clementine works lack not only a eucharist consisting of the recitation of the institution narratives over bread and wine, but also any one meal radically distinguished from all others for its sacral quality. This does not, however, mean that these works and the communities represented indirectly in them had no connection with the Christian traditions of communal meals we might otherwise define as 'eucharistic'. It seems rather to mean that the application of any sacral emphasis to communal eating was general, rather than specific to one type of meal.

Other meals in the Pseudo-Clementines which do not contain reference to salt and which use rather prosaic language are clearly understood as exclusive (*Hom.* 1. 22. 5, cf. *Recog.* 1. 19. 3). This general exclusiveness of the table of the baptized is explained in terms of purity and pollution: 'we do not live with all indiscriminately; nor do we take our food from the same table as Gentiles, inasmuch as we cannot eat along with them, because they live impurely' (*Hom.* 13. 4, cf. *Recog.* 7. 29). Often, but not always, the language of giving thanks or of blessing (or both) is used with regard to the taking of food (*Hom.* 10. 26. 2, 12. 25. 1, *Recog.* 2. 72. 6). While there is no mention of the Last Supper or of the body and blood of Jesus, these factors along with the association with baptism (*Cont.*) all indicate that these descriptions are comprehensible as the eucharistic meal of the Christian community, or as much of a eucharistic meal as this community or communities knew or cared to know.[96]

---

[95] 'Dieser Schluß wäre nur möglich, wenn auch an anderer Stelle eine judenchristliche Eucharistie mit Brot und Salz bezeugt wäre. Aber das ist weder für die Kerygmen noch in der außerklementinischen Literatur der Fall.' *Das Judenchristentum in den Pseudoklementinen*, 210.

[96] Thus also Lietzmann, *Mass and Lord's Supper*, 195–6. See also Ch. 5 below on the exclusion of wine from the meals of the Pseudo-Clementines.

If salt is uniquely prominent in the Pseudo-Clementines, it is not completely absent elsewhere. We have already seen in the discussion of oil that salt, too, was mentioned as a food in the frugal meals of the apocryphal *Acts* (*Acts of Thomas*, 29). Granted that in the apocryphal *Acts* some real distinction may be made between descriptions of appropriate meals in general and the depiction of the breaking of the eucharistic bread in particular, it is clear none the less that there are connections, and that the more specifically eucharistic meals exemplify standards of ascetic eating that are to be maintained at all times. The *Acts* are therefore at least somewhat like the Pseudo-Clementines in their ordering of food in sacral terms. All food is a matter of anxiety, and meat and wine in particular are to be excluded. It seems that in both sets of apostolic pseudepigrapha the tremendous emphasis placed on the creation of boundaries between the community and the wider world, and between the food of the community and the food of the wider world, means that less weight is placed on certain issues of internal order; more room is left for food elements to feature in eucharistic meals as well as in other meals.

One further case where a more specific salt meal or eucharist may be at issue is in the *Acts of Philip*, probably a somewhat later collection of *Acts* modelled on the others, and especially on the *Acts of Thomas*. In their present form the *Acts of Philip* seem to date from the fourth or fifth century, although their clearly composite nature suggests that earlier materials are included.[97]

After the allocation of different spheres of missionary activity to the apostles, Philip is upset at receiving Greece: 'And Mariamne his sister (it was she that made ready the bread and salt at the breaking of the bread, but Martha was she that ministered to the multitudes and laboured much) seeing it, went to Jesus and said "Lord, do you not see how my brother is vexed?"' (ibid. 8)

The incident or practice referred to as the 'breaking of the bread' involving salt does not seem to be attested in the earlier chapters, although two communal meals involving bread and vegetables are.[98] In fact this passage introduces the figure of Mariamne and begins the second half of the collection (ibid. 8–15), generally regarded as older and more coherent than the preceding seven chapters.[99] The use of bread and

---

[97] Aurelio de Santos Otero, 'Later Acts of Apostles', in Schneemelcher (ed.), *New Testament Apocrypha*, ii. 468–73.

[98] At least in the version in the Athos MS Xenophontos 32: see the *fiche signalétique* complied by F. Bovon and B. Bouvier in Bovon *et al.*, *Les Actes apocryphes des apôtres* (Geneva: Labor et Fides, 1981), 301–4.

[99] De Santos Otero, 'Later Acts of Apostles', 469.

salt at the 'breaking of the bread' may therefore refer to another type of eucharistic meal depicted in a source for the present version of these *Acts*, and it seems problematic to link this salt meal too strongly to the other eucharists in the work. At some point in their doubtless complex redaction history, however, the *Acts of Philip* seem to allow a glimpse of a eucharistic meal where salt was used in addition to bread in a deliberate fashion. As in the Pseudo-Clementines, there is no immediate connection with the Last Supper of Jesus, and the use of salt seems likely to be related specifically to the ascetic milieu of the work.[100] While remaining little more than an intriguing hint, this salt meal confirms that those of the Pseudo-Clementines must also be taken as more than literary fictions, and that the use of salt can be understood, like that of foods such as cheese or milk, oil, and vegetables, as characteristically ascetic, rather than as a sort of carefree culinary embellishment, when found in what appear to be communal meals.

Just as there was to be a more orthodox aspect to the use of cheese or milk, i.e. their association with very specific meals of an initiatory character, salt also appears in cases from the normative stream, but which generally seem to be of later date.[101] These are again related to baptism, or rather to the preparation for it. In Africa and in other parts of the West, it was common for salt to be given to catechumens as a *sacramentum salis*. Augustine seems to allude to this once or twice;[102] it is also referred to in an African council of his time, where the bishops are apparently concerned to quash a custom of admitting catechumens to the eucharist during the paschal season (*Conc. Carth. III*, 5).[103] John the Deacon, writing in Rome in the sixth century, also attests clearly to the practice (*Ad Senarium*, 3).

While these instances are all part of a somewhat different symbolic world from that of the Pseudo-Clementines, the use of salt before baptism perhaps suggests some connection with the salt meal of the Pseudo-Clementine *Contestatio*, or hearing. It is not clear when the

---

[100] Erik Peterson suggested links with the group(s) attacked by the Synod of Gangra; see 'Die Häretiker der Philippus-Akten', *ZNW* 31 (1932), 97–111.

[101] See further Latham, *The Religious Significance of Salt*, 87–125.

[102] *Conf.* 1. 11. 17, where he speaks of being seasoned with God's salt from childhood; and *De Cat. Rud.* 26. 50 where the explicit reference to salt in the text is uncertain (some prefer to read *sacramento salis* rather than the better-attested *sacramento sane*), but even the more oblique reading could still indicate its use.

[103] There are other possibilities, since 'sacramentum' in this context could refer to some other ritual; the blessed bread or *eulogia* has also been suggested. See Latham, *The Religious Significance of Salt*, 96–101 (although Latham is too dismissive of the possibility that the eucharist was involved).

catechumenal *sacramentum salis* emerged, but it could conceivably have been a development from some other less clearly defined prebaptismal use of salt. Geographical considerations do not, however, encourage suggestion of direct links with the Pseudo-Clementines.

The fact that salt is such a common food makes it difficult to establish general symbolic significance; it is not that there is a lack of associations, but rather the opposite.[104] As with milk and honey, the significance of salt ritual must be considered in terms of the particular cases. These do, however, recall certain others which can be assumed to be relevant to early Christian communities; it is worth remembering the general significance of salt both as sign of a bond (cf. Num. 18: 19) and, as already discussed, as a symbol (whether enacted or merely as a turn of phrase) of commensality in general.

While the Pseudo-Clementine and other ascetic examples share with the orthodox Western baptismal usages some sense of salt as basic and necessary food, and perhaps of its common use as a sign of a bond, the shared meaning is put to different uses in rather different settings. The more radical use of salt conceives of asceticism positively, and as a permanent calling for all Christians; thus in the meal of the *Contestatio* the use of salt is the highlight rather than merely the preliminary phase of a ritual. This community has a sense of identity that sets it apart from the wider (pagan) society in certain respects at least.

In the later Western cases salt conveys something which again is, if not negative, at least minimal. It is interesting that the baptism-related feeding practices of salt and of milk and honey do seem to appear together, in Africa and Rome particularly, but not in the East. The fact that salt is a sign of frugality suggests that in the African and other orthodox baptismal practices where the relatively luxurious milk and honey are also used, the salt given before the initiatory rite accentuates the symbolism of the post-baptismal feeding. The use of these foods before and after baptism therefore also suggests a transition from poverty to luxury. Salt does, of course, have positive connotations in Jewish and Christian tradition as well, but the catechumen is meant to aspire to the milk and honey of new life in Christ. Christian living is constructed in terms with which the compilers and users of the Pseudo-Clementines would have been less than comfortable; as, at least symbolically, luxurious and plentiful.

As in the contrasting uses of milk or cheese, there are different

---

[104] Latham, *The Religious Significance of Salt*, 29–82.

orderings of time at work, as well as different understandings of the food. For catechumens in later orthodox circles the use of salt was apparently token, separate from a meal and intended to cease with baptism. Baptized life was symbolized by the divine gifts of milk and honey. For the community or communities behind the Pseudo-Clementines, however, salt was an appropriate expression of the baptized life, understood primarily as one of purity and ascetic disengagement from the world of sacrifice, luxury, and immorality.

FRUITS AND VEGETABLES

We have already seen that 'bread, oil, vegetables, and salt' were the constituents of a 'blessed' meal in the *Acts of Thomas*. In the *Acts of Paul and Thecla*, 25, Paul, Thecla, and companions celebrate a meal in a tomb (cf. *Acts of John* 72, 86): 'And within the tomb there was a great ἀγάπη.'[105] The meal consists of 'five loaves, and vegetables (λάχανα) and water'. The only description of their liturgical acts is that 'they were joyful over the holy works of Christ'. Again this meal seems to have a special character, but one which may be somewhat removed from that of the 'eucharist', which in these *Acts*, as in the *Acts of Thomas*, is typically celebrated with bread alone or bread and water. This is one of the earliest instances where references to *agape* and eucharist can be placed in any parallelism as distinct meals or activities, but this does not disqualify the *agape* meal of these Acts from being seen as eucharistic in the terms being used here.

Yet again the *Apostolic Tradition* provides some comparable practices. We have already seen that there was a blessing for olives, with cheese, associated with the eucharistic meal of an episcopal ordination (at least according to the arrangement of material as it stands). A prayer proper to the offering of harvest first-fruits is also included, suggesting the appropriate form of words accompanying the practice, which is impressed on the people, of giving these things to the bishop: 'We give thanks to Thee, O Lord God, and we offer to Thee the first-fruits of the fruits which Thou hast given us for food, having perfected them by

---

[105] Although all the translators I have seen render this in similar terms, suggesting only the emotional or ethical response of the participants to the events described, the use of ἀγάπη in this context suggests at least a hint of more technical meaning, and could perhaps be as well or better translated 'there was a great *agape* meal in the tomb'. The absence of this term for a ritual meal elsewhere in these *Acts* or the apocryphal *Acts* generally (except perhaps *Acts of John*, 84) must, however, urge us to caution.

Thy word, bidding the earth to send forth fruits of all kinds for the joy and nourishment of human beings and for all beasts' (Dix 28. 3 = Botte 31).

A list of fruits appropriate for blessing is then given: 'grapes, figs, pomegranates, olives, pears, apples, mulberries, peaches, cherries, almonds, plums; not pumpkins, melons, cucumbers, onions, garlic or any other vegetable (λάχανον)' (28. 6 = 32).[106] Flowers may also be blessed.

The exclusion of certain items ('vegetables', in modern Western terms at least) and the singling out of appropriate 'fruits' seem to stem at least in part from associations with Egyptian captivity on the one hand (Num. 11: 5) and the land of promise on the other (Num. 13: 24; Deut. 8: 8).[107] There are also rabbinic discussions on appropriate forms of food blessings that emphasize the importance of the 'seven kinds of foods of the land of Israel', referring to the list of Deut. 8: 8: wheat, barley, grapes, figs, pomegranates, olives, oil, and honey.[108] These connections are more satisfactory for explaining the exclusions of vegetables than for the actual content of the list of fruits. There may be some aesthetic category of 'sweetness' (or cost or general desirability for diet) at work,[109] but the list is interesting also for its omission of the most substantial of the 'seven kinds' one could derive from Deut. 8: 8, i.e. the wheat and barley. After omitting the first two, the prayer moves through four elements of the biblical list, then leaves out the three elements mentioned elsewhere in the Apostolic Tradition. It seems there is some fear of confusion of the first-fruits ceremony with the eucharistic meal; if bread or grain were to be offered, how would their blessing be understood?

The prohibition of λάχανα in general, as well as the specifically

---

[106] I read these two sections as related, but have some doubts. The importance of offering the first-fruits seems to suggest not merely fruit in the modern English sense but the more basic produce such as grains, which are quite comprehensible as ἀπαρχὴ καρπῶν (a Greek version survives in a collection of Byzantine prayers: see Botte, La Tradition apostolique, 76, 77 n. 1). While the specification of particular crops in the offering of first-fruits is also found in the rabbis, there grains are allowed (as named among the 'seven kinds of the fruit of the land of Israel'); the absence of these remains somewhat mysterious. More importantly the language of the first-fruits prayer implies that all fruits and vegetables are acceptable, while the following rubric specifies that some are not.

[107] J. B. Bauer, 'Die Fruchtesegnung in Hippolyts Kirchenordnung', ZTK 74 (1952), 71–5. Hanssens is correct in concluding that the specific fruits and vegetables mentioned offer little to the question of the setting of the document itself: La Liturgie d'Hippolyte: Ses documents, son titulaire, 491–2.

[108] m. Ber. 6: 4; m. Bik. 1: 3, 3: 9.

[109] See the discussions of the significance of vegetables on the one hand, and fruits on the other, in the Oneirocriticon of Artemidorus (1. 73 and 69 respectively).

'Egyptian' elements, makes again for interesting comparison with the sources more marginal to the mainstream. Presumably someone has, in fact, made use of vegetables in the past in order for there to be some anxiety about the appropriate foods to offer. Of course in the *Acts of Paul and Thecla* we have what might be such an example, granted that the tomb-*agape* and the harvest-blessings are somewhat different settings.[110] It may be that the blessings in the *Apostolic Tradition* are still understood to belong to a eucharistic meal setting rather than to an entirely separate cultic activity. The Church Orders dependent on the *Apostolic Tradition* are sometimes actually more open about the fruits to bless; the *Canons of Hippolytus*, for instance, specify that all vegetables and fruits are to be blessed.[111] By then, perhaps, there is no danger that the food-offerings will be confused with the defined elements of the eucharistic meal.

FISH

Gospels

The prominence of fish in Gospel feeding stories and the use of fish in early Christian art and inscriptions raise the question of the possible use of fish in ritual meals.[112] It has often been remarked that there are eucharistic elements in Gospel meal scenes such as the miraculous feedings of the 4,000 and 5,000 people (Mark 6: 30–44; 8: 1–10, and parallels) and resurrection stories (Luke 24: 41–3; John 21: 9–13). In the former group, the Synoptic Gospels are unanimous in using the language of 'breaking bread', and in the sequence of taking, blessing (or giving thanks), breaking, distributing, and eating, identified by Dix as the essential structure of all eucharistic rites.[113] We do not have to accept Dix's absolute insistence on the universality of this pattern to acknowledge

[110] Although Montanists seem to have maintained a regime of cabbage-eating (ῥαφανοφαγία; Hippolytus, *Ref.* 8. 19. 2) there is no particular indication that this was ritually emphasized; it reflects avoidance of meat more than exaltation of vegetables.

[111] Bauer, 'Die Fruchtesegnung in Hippolyts Kirchenordnung', 73–4. For synopsis see Hanssens, *La Liturgie d'Hippolyte: Documents et études*, 136–7.

[112] Vogel, 'Le Repas sacré au poisson chez les chrétiens', 1–26 (this is substantially reprinted as part (pp. 225–52) of Vogel's 'Symboles cultuels chrétiens', 197–252, with discussion, pp. 253–65; the rest of that later article is also equivalent to his 'Symbols in Christian Worship: Food and Drink', *Concilium*, 132 (1980), 67–73). Richard H. Hiers and Charles A. Kennedy discuss the same evidence without indication of awareness of Vogel's work, but with broadly similar conclusions, in 'The Bread and Fish Eucharist in the Gospels and Early Christian Art', *Perspectives in Religious Studies*, 3 (1976), 20–47.

[113] Dix, *The Shape of the Liturgy*, 48.

that the analogy is real, and that the loaves-and-fishes meals at least evoke ritual parallels. The version of the miraculous feeding in John's Gospel (6: 11–15) is not so closely related in terms of the structure of Jesus' meal actions, lacking reference to the breaking of the bread, but it is of course linked to the imagery of Jesus' body and blood through the accompanying discourse that many commentators have taken to refer to the eucharist. Other elements of the stories such as reclining, prayer, and the use of the twelve to distribute the meal elements may also seem to evoke later ecclesial practice, although they are too generally applicable to any ancient description of a formal meal to contribute much to the question of eucharistic character.[114] Similarity of vocabulary between the Last Supper stories and the feeding stories may also be a factor in considering ritual allusions or influences.[115]

The resurrection meals involving fish are not so close to the quasi-ritual form found in the miraculous feeding stories, but they are hard to dismiss as of no relevance to possible reconstruction of ongoing eucharistic meals. In the 'appendix' to John's Gospel Jesus meets a number of disciples and gives them bread and fish (21: 9–13).[116] In Luke, a meal of fish and, according to some important textual witnesses, honey-cake, is involved in one appearance (24: 41–3).[117]

These meal scenes, taken with the later archaeological evidence which will be discussed further below, have led a few scholars to conclude that there was a bread-and-fish eucharist in early Christianity, or perhaps even in the movement around Jesus during his lifetime. Cyrille Vogel suggests that the Gospel fish meals indicate a ritual meal tradition separate from the better-known bread-and-wine pattern, connected

---

[114] Hiers and Kennedy, 'The Bread and Fish Eucharist', 30, take the descriptions as indicating that the crowd 'sits', but all the words used might better be translated 'recline'.

[115] Hiers and Kennedy, ibid. 30–1. But as they acknowledge, this similarity could argue for influence in either direction; so also, it could reflect more general usage in relation to formal meals.

[116] Raymond Brown, *The Gospel According to John*, AB 29–29 A (2 vols.; Garden City, NY: Doubleday, 1966–70), ii. 1084–5, 1098–1100), like others, suggests originally separate 'catch' and 'meal' stories in John 21, which would seem to support the possibility of an independent and important tradition of a resurrection meal involving fish.

[117] Yet the fish scene does not have the fourfold ritual action which the Emmaus meal has (Luke 24: 30). John Dominic Crossan, *The Historical Jesus: The Life of a Mediterranean Jewish Peasant* (San Francisco: HarperSanFrancisco, 1991), 399–401, actually takes the stories of breaking bread at Emmaus (Luke 24: 30–1) and the meal of fish in Jerusalem as originally one, separated by Luke; Joseph Fitzmyer, *The Gospel According to Luke*, AB 28–28 A (2 vols.; New York: Doubleday, 1981–5), ii. 1577, sees the content of the meal as potentially important at a pre-Lukan stage, but not in the Gospel as it stands. On the eucharistic aspect of the fish in resurrection meals see also Cullmann, 'La Signification de la Sainte-Cène dans le christianisme primitif', 6–7.

with Jewish 'eschatological' meals centred on fish.[118] The more detailed analysis of the same texts by Richard Hiers and Charles Kennedy gives more attention to the differences between the various Gospel meal descriptions and argues that the canonical texts represent, despite themselves, a rather less ritualized tradition of fish meals which may have been suppressed even before the Gospels were written.[119] In this case the diminishing presence of fish in the different versions, from Mark 6: 40–4, where fish is mentioned five times, to other versions where there are only one or two references to it, is argued to indicate a progressive subordination of the fish element on the one hand, and accentuation of the specifically eucharistic character on the other.[120] Despite Hiers and Kennedy's contrast between fish meals and eucharistic meals in conventional terms and their discernment of a vanishing fish meal in the Gospel texts, their study joins Vogel's in also suggesting an ongoing tradition of fish meals distinguishable from the 'major' or normative eucharist.[121]

While the possibility of ritual structures in these Gospel texts (and hence perhaps some relation to an actual meal-form) cannot be ignored, the almost complete silence of literary sources outside the Gospels about the actual use of fish in eucharistic meals is damaging to either version of the hypothesis. Vogel insists that the presence of fish in these narratives is significant. This might be true, but such acknowledgement does not equal acceptance that fish was used at later meals; the connection may, as many have argued, be purely symbolic.[122] To take the most obvious example, those who understand the bread-and-fish meal of John 6 to refer to eucharistic practice must accept that the symbolism of 'body and blood' (6: 51–8) actually refers to a meal of bread and cup, rather than one of bread and fish. The tension between the depiction of the meal involving the 5,000 and the meal presumed to be known to the readers

[118] Vogel, 'Le Repas sacré au poisson chez les chrétiens', 17–24.

[119] Hiers and Kennedy, 'The Bread and Fish Eucharist', followed by Crossan, *The Historical Jesus*, 398–402.

[120] Hiers and Kennedy, 'The Bread and Fish Eucharist', 26–35.

[121] Vogel, 'Le Repas sacré au poisson', 1–5, 7, and *passim*. For Hiers and Kennedy, 'The Bread and Fish Eucharist', 23, 44–5, the fact that the fish element is all but suppressed by the time of the written Gospels makes the value of the later evidence more difficult to determine. Like Vogel they argue from the wider use of fish in Jewish meals to suggest a milieu in which the symbolism of fish was meaningful; but they also hint at survivals.

[122] The mammoth studies of Franz J. Dölger, *IXΘΥΣ: Das Fischsymbol in frühchristlicher Zeit*, i. *Religionsgeschichtliche und epigraphische Untersuchungen* (Rome: Spithöver, 1910), and *IXΘΥΣ: Das Fischsymbol in frühchristlicher Zeit*, ii–v. *Der heilige Fisch in den antiken Religionen und im Christentum* (4 vols.; Münster: Aschendorff, 1922–43), are concerned with symbolism rather than practice but remain invaluable for background and collection of sources.

and hearers of the Gospel of John is real, but perhaps no more awkward than other metaphors in that Gospel and elsewhere.

On the other hand there is, of course, no way to disprove the idea of a fish eucharist that existed (only) in the period before the writing of the Gospels, along the lines suggested by Hiers and Kennedy.[123] Since, however, the alleged subordination of the fish element is present even in Mark's Gospel, we are here speculating about the preliterary history of this tradition; there could even have been, as others have argued, an accentuation of the fish element.[124] Of course the tradition-historical argument of gradual subordination and eucharistic accentuation actually implies that fish is not seen as sacral; there is no reason to say, in this case, that the supposed original fish stories are not simply historical reminiscences of the meals of the 'Jesus movement' without any relation to later ecclesial practice. This last possibility, if accepted, gives the fish stories a certain interest regarding the practice of Jesus, but enables us to draw no links with ongoing meals.[125]

It is of course quite anachronistic to pose the question of the meaning of these accounts in terms of eucharist in the more technical sense, especially where it is only a pre-Gospel tradition that is at issue.[126] While the use of various foods in eucharistic meals in the broader sense adopted in this study, i.e. of communal meals with a ritual character, seems not only possible but quite likely in the earliest period, it is odd to suggest that fish may have had a peculiarly sacral meaning at a stage (i.e. prior to the composition of the canonical Gospel texts) when even bread and wine had not, or at least not everywhere, taken on the fully sacramental character familiar from later tradition.

[123] This seems to be the position of Hiers and Kennedy, 'The Bread and Fish Eucharist', 24–35, in the longest continuous section of their study, yet they also argue that the later artistic representations of meals involving fish may suggest a survival of the meal tradition, at least in (graphic) symbol, ibid. 43–5. These two arguments could, therefore, be considered more or less separately as I am doing. So also Crossan, *The Historical Jesus*, 398–404, limits his use of Hiers and Kennedy to suggesting the bread and fish meal in the life of the earliest communities, although he draws upon the later graphic evidence.

[124] Thus Paul Achtemeier, 'The Origin and Function of the pre-Markan Miracle Catenae', *JBL* 89 (1970), 265–91.

[125] This suggestion is probably the most interesting or promising from the examination of the NT evidence, and is taken by Crossan from Hiers and Kennedy in these terms; but the apparently technical use of the term 'eucharist' in their title and some points of the article suggests some confusion.

[126] This is where it is most difficult to be sure just what Hiers and Kennedy, 'The Bread and Fish Eucharist', 29–35, mean, since they argue for the existence of a bread and fish 'eucharist' as the title of the article suggests, but also equate the accentuation of the 'eucharistic' character of the Gospel stories with the suppression of the fish element.

Inscriptions

Even were we to allow the possibility of a communal meal involving fish in the New Testament, the second part of the fish hypothesis, that of a separate but ongoing tradition, is problematic to say the least. Even the ambiguous evidence that remains seems to leave us with absolute silence for a period of a century or more. The argument can only be sustained if we can convince ourselves that the later archaeological and epigraphic evidence involving the symbolism of fish looms close enough in time to Jesus and the Gospels, and is clear enough in nature, for us to swing a hypothetical rope from one side of this chronological gap to the other. This later evidence needs to be examined further.

Three inscriptions from the early third century, all funerary in nature, make significant use of fish symbolism.[127] The inscription of Abercius, bishop of Hierapolis in Asia Minor (*c.*200 CE), refers to the travels of the deceased and reads in part: 'I had Paul in my wagon. The faith preceded me everywhere and provided food for me, everywhere the fish from the spring, mighty and pure, whom the pure virgin caught and gave to the friends to eat always, having sweet wine, giving mixed wine with bread.'[128] While this is evidence that fish may have been pure and prized food in the mind of the writer and readers, and even a symbol of some weight, there is no reason to take 'fish' any more literally here than we need take the suggestions that Paul was Abercius' travelling companion or that a virgin caught and cooked his fish. In the second case, the inscription of Pectorius of Autun (from around the same time), we have a similar kind of text, a similar use of imagery, and must reach similar conclusions. This time we read: 'Receive the food, sweet like honey, of the savior of the holy ones. Eat with relish, holding the fish in your hands. May I fill myself with the fish, I long for it, my master and my savior.'[129] The third case is much more brief and allusive: the funerary inscription of Licinia Amias, again from the early third century, depicts two fish with an anchor between and the inscription 'Fish of the Living'.[130] In all these cases it is clear that the

---

[127] Vogel, 'Le Repas sacré au poisson', 11–14; Hiers and Kennedy, 'The Bread and Fish Eucharist', 22 n. 5, 45 n. 61.

[128] For the text and its restoration see *DACL* i. 68–83. Discussion in Dölger, *IXΘYΣ* i. 87–112, and *IXΘYΣ* ii. 454–86.

[129] Text and discussion, *DACL* i. 3195–7. See further Dölger, *IXΘYΣ* i. 177–83 and ii. 507–15.

[130] *IXΘYΣ ZΩNTΩN*. The rest consists only of the standard (but pagan) 'D(iis) M(anibus)' and the name of the honoree. See Vogel, 'Le Repas sacré au poisson', 13 and nn. 27–8; Dölger, *IXΘYΣ* ii. 573–4.

symbolism of fish is important, positive, and perhaps especially to be associated with hope for the afterlife and a heavenly banquet. It is not clear that direct reference is being made to a particular literal act of eating fish.

Paintings and Sarcophagi

The depictions of bread and fish on wall-paintings and sarcophagi raise different problems, some of which are beyond the scope of this study.[131] Research on the earliest catacomb paintings portraying use of bread and fish has recently tended to push the probable date up into the late third century, making the distance from possible New Testament evidence all the greater;[132] hence in part the need to separate consideration of this visual evidence from the question of an earlier meal tradition based on fish.

In any case it is not easy to say what the paintings should be understood to show. One type simply shows a fish, lying or swimming with a basket of bread on it.[133] More detailed banquet scenes depict diners, often seven in number, with fish, bread, and sometimes wine at the table, and baskets, also sometimes seven, beside the participants.[134] There are also sculptures with similar scenes on numerous sarcophagi (or their lids) from the late third century.[135] Some obvious connections could be made between the details of these scenes and the biblical fish stories, such as the seven baskets of Mark 8: 8, or the seven disciples fed in John 21. Yet the pictures owe at least as much to third-century dining practices and artistic conventions as to biblical models. Seven was also held to be the right number to seat at the *sigma*-style tables typically shown.[136]

[131] The most recent and most comprehensive study of these depictions known to me is that of E. Jastrzebowska, 'Les Scènes de banquet dans les peintures et sculptures chrétiennes des IIIe et IVe siècles', *Recherches Augustiniennes*, 14 (1979), 3–90. The paintings that survive are nearly all Roman; interestingly, the literary, archaeological, and epigraphical evidence for funerary meals tends to favour Africa; Jastrzebowska, 'Les Scènes de banquet', 6. See also, for a more general account of early Christian art in its social context, Graydon F. Snyder, *Ante Pacem: Archaeological Evidence of Church Life before Constantine* (Macon, Ga.: Mercer University Press, 1985), esp. 21–2, 64–5.

[132] The *Capella Graeca* of the Catacombs of Priscilla must now be dated to the late third century; the Catacombs of Callistus may be somewhat earlier, but it would now be misleading to date any such painting 'slightly before 200 AD' (Hiers and Kennedy, 'The Bread and Fish Eucharist', 21). See Milburn, *Early Christian Art and Architecture*, 23–5.

[133] Milburn, *Early Christian Art and Architecture*, 31, fig. 15.

[134] Ibid. 34–5, figs. 19 and 20; see also the collection of line drawings and detailed descriptions in Jastrzebowska, 'Les Scènes de banquet', 14–29.

[135] Jastrzebowska, 'Les Scènes de banquet', 29–35.

[136] See Martial, *Epig.* 10. 48. 6, and note of course the proverbial *Septem Sapientium Convivium*.

Aside from the allusions to New Testament stories we have to consider both the possibility that these show the envisaged life of paradise, as well as the suggestion that the paintings reflect actual eucharistic meals or more particularly the banquets for the dead which might have taken place in or near these venues.[137] Vogel takes the obvious connection with the afterlife as a basis for suggesting that the tradition of fish meals is that of a *refrigerium* or funerary meal.[138] It is clear enough that the catacomb banquets draw upon real contemporary meal practices. In some cases there is little or nothing in a picture that might not have been found in a living scene enacted nearby.[139] The foods could have been quite real; fish was seen to be appropriate for funerary meals by pagans also.[140] Artistic context raises an initial problem, however. There are few if any other themes in the catacomb paintings of this period that can be taken in a similarly literal fashion. Biblical scenes abound, many of them from the Old Testament, such as the three young men in the furnace; the good shepherd appears, so too does the phoenix of pagan myth.[141] The typical praying figure is probably at least somewhat abstract, representing 'the believer' or even a personified virtue, as in other Roman art, rather than one concrete individual. The banqueters, arrayed along with these scenes, would be uniquely prosaic figures if merely one-time participants in a meal for the dead.[142] Artistic convention suggests the contrary; there are cases where very similar scenes in pagan contexts are clearly linked with transition to the

[137] The 'celestial banquet' interpretation is still most common, it would seem; a serious case for the depiction of funerary meals is offered by A. Stuiber, *Refrigerium Interim: Die Vorstellungen vom Zwischenzustand und die frühchristliche Grabeskunst*, Theophaneia, 11 (Bonn: Peter Hanstein, 1957), esp. 120–36. For further bibliography on connections with funerary meals, see Jastrzebowska, 'Les Scènes de banquet', 7 n. 8, and for discussion of the possibilities argued in the history of scholarship, ibid. 8–13.

[138] Vogel, 'Le Repas sacré au poisson', 24–6. Snyder, *Ante Pacem*, 64–5, conflates the possible funerary meal with the *agape* and Lietzmann's Jerusalem type, which is an unlikely scenario.

[139] Not, however, in the catacomb chambers in question, it would seem. Jastrzebowska, 'Les Scènes de banquet', 80–1, points out the differences between these rooms and the *triclinia* typical of a pagan temple or necropolis, or for that matter in Christian venues in North Africa or Spain.

[140] e.g. by the burial society at Lanuvium, *CIL* xiv. 2112; the 'Vibia' painting, Milburn, *Early Christian Art and Architecture*, 45–6, 57 n. 1; Jastrzebowska, 'Les Scènes de banquet', 38–9. See further Dölger, *IXΘΥΣ* ii. 311–16, 377–410.

[141] Granted that the scenes must somehow be regarded as exceptional among the catacomb paintings, not only as less clearly related to biblical scenes if at all, but in numerous cases by their placement in the *arcosolia* of the chambers: Jastrzebowska, 'Les Scènes de banquet', 62–5.

[142] See Milburn, *Early Christian Art and Architecture*, 30–6.

afterlife. A tomb near the Catacomb of Callistus, for instance, is painted with a scene in which the occupant Vibia enters a banquet strikingly similar to the Christian ones, guided by a 'good angel'. In another scene Vibia proceeds before the thrones of Pluto and Persephone.[143] The Christian scenes are therefore also probably linked to the idea of a celestial banquet.

Christian Funerary Meals

This does not make it impossible that Christian funerary meals employing fish took place. It is clear that even if the pictures were understood to display or evoke banquets in the afterlife, they draw upon real ways of eating known to the artists and patrons.[144] It has been suggested that the alternative interpretations of heavenly and earthly banquets ought not therefore to be seen as too hard and fast.[145] Yet neither does the existence of the paintings make acceptance of a fish meal necessary. There is certainly no sign whatsoever that the typical eucharistic meal, relatively well defined at Rome by the time of the paintings, was the direct referent of the banquets depicted.[146]

---

[143] Milburn, *Early Christian Art and Architecture*, 45–6, 57 n. 1; Jastrzebowska, 'Les Scènes de banquet', 38–9. The Catacomb of Domitilla also includes a Christian 'introduction' scene where Petronilla the martyr leads a woman, Veneranda, into Paradise.

[144] Jastrzebowska's careful analysis ('Les Scènes de banquet', 62–71) suggests a development in pagan and Christian banquet scenes alike, from a type depicting daily life, with varying numbers of diners and types of food, to increasingly formal models which are more likely to represent funerary banquets; yet this recognition does not solve the problem of the realism of the scenes. We then have to ask whether it is possible that the iconography might have been taken over without the corresponding ritual; and even if not, we would then seem to be dealing with a relatively late Christian adaptation of pagan funerary meals rather than an ongoing tradition related to fish.

[145] Recognized by C. Mohrmann in 'Locus Refrigerii', *Études sur le latin des chrétiens* (Rome: Edizioni di storia e letteratura, 1961), ii. 87–8: 'D'une part les répresentations des Repas célestes sont iconographiquement très proches des anciennes représentations de repas funéraires, tout en faisant allusion à l'Eucharistie par les symboles traditionels du poisson, du vin et du panier à pain; d'autre part les paysages paradisiaques, images bucoliques, avec leurs sources et tant d'autres emblèmes rustiques à l'ombre des arbres feuillus, nous avertissent de ne plus exclure du *refrigerium* paléo-chrétien l'image du rafraîchissement terrestre.' See also the discussion of method with regard to earlier funerary banquet scenes by J.-M. Dentzer, *Le Motif du banquet couché dans le proche-orient et le monde grec du VIIe au IVe siècle avant J.-C.* (Rome: École française de Rome, 1982), 1–20.

[146] The temptation often seems to be to assimilate the uncertain funerary meals with the *agape* meal (e.g. Snyder, *Ante Pacem*, 64), but this is dubious, based largely on an assumption that a meal distinguishable from the eucharist must be called *agape*. The word *agape* does occur in some of the paintings, along with *irene*, both apparently as personified virtues who take the role of servants; but this does not make the meal an *agape* any more

Some consideration of other evidence of funerary meal practice is necessary to test the more specific suggestion that there might have been a connection between fish and Christian funerary meals. Clear indications of Christian funerary meals distinct from other eucharists are few and far between until the fourth century.[147] Two instances in the apocryphal *Acts* have been mentioned, and neither uses fish or the term *refrigerium*.[148] An inscription from Africa, the *mensa* of Aelia Secundula, is dated to 299 CE and makes clear mention of provision for commemorative meals, but once again does not help with meal elements.[149] Even these scanty references, together with the paintings and later evidence of the importance of these meals, such as the anecdote told by Augustine regarding the devotion with which his mother Monica took part in meals at martyr shrines (*Conf.* 6. 2),[150] might encourage us to consider the possibility that funerary and commemorative meals had long been celebrated by Christians more or less in imitation of pagan models, but had been a matter of private and familial action rather than the public and corporate practice of the Christian communities as such.[151]

Yet it is also possible, and I think rather more likely, that the emergence of more information about such meals in the late third and fourth centuries is a sign that the acceptance of commemorative meals was part of the tendency of Christians to assimilate and accommodate

than it makes it an *irene*. There are attempts to define the *agape* as a particular type of meal perhaps related to a primitive form of eucharist (Lietzmann, *Mass and Lord's Supper*, 161–71), or as a specifically charitable meal (A. Hamman, *Vie liturgique et vie sociale* (Paris: Desclée, 1968), 151–227). Reicke, *Diakonie, Festfreude und Zelos*, uses it as a sort of generic title, emphasizing both funerary and charitable aspects; but it might be preferable to start by considering the *agape* in terms of meals that actually use the name; see McGowan, 'Naming the Feast'.

[147] There are indications of celebrations of the anniversaries of martyrs as far back as the time of Polycarp (*Mart. Pol.* 18; Cyprian, *Ep.* 34); these might well have involved meals, but not necessarily meals so distinct from the typical eucharistic celebration of the community in question. Christians in some areas were urged to celebrate the eucharist in cemeteries (*Apostolic Constitutions*. 6. 30).

[148] See Mohrmann, 'Locus Refrigerii', esp. 82–3, and G. van der Leeuw, 'Refrigerium', *Mnemosyne*, 3rd ser. 3 (1935), 130, for the earliest inscriptions indicating a testamentary provision for holding funerary meals and the fulfilment of such obligations. Only in the fourth century does the terminology of *refrigerare*, *refrigerium*, and so forth emerge as unequivocally applicable to actual meals rather than merely as an image of refreshment or eternal peace, despite A. Stuiber, *Refrigerium Interim*, esp. 105–11.

[149] See J. Quasten, '"Vetus Superstitio et Nova Religio": The Problem of *Refrigerium* in the Ancient Church of North Africa', *HTR* 33 (1940), 253–66, esp. 257–8.

[150] He says that she took *pultes*, bread and wine.

[151] On the pagan model, see the discussion by Charles Kennedy, 'The Cult of the Dead in Corinth', *Love and Death in the Ancient Near East: Essays in Honor of Marvin H. Pope* (Guilford, Conn.: Four Quarters, 1987), 227–36.

themselves to attractive customs modelled by their pagan neighbours.[152] The appropriation of pagan artistic forms related to funerary meals suggests and exemplifies this.[153] Ambrose of Milan's reaction to Monica's piety, i.e. disapproval on the grounds that the practice was pagan, may also be an indication that this is a rather late, and localized, phenomenon. Many questions about the meaning and practice of the *refrigerium* and other funerary meals must remain unanswered for the present.

The Meaning of Fish

Why the use of the fish symbolism at all? Even though the fish eucharist seems to be a fantasy, the symbolism is a puzzle. While we should probably allow eucharistic allusions in the paintings, Vogel points out that in literary contexts it is not until the fourth century that we find clear use of fish imagery in connection with the now normative eucharistic meal.[154] The famous acrostic *ΙΧΘΥΣ* seems to be just as late.[155] Prior to the fourth century, however, there is some use of the sign as an image of Jesus himself. Tertullian says, regarding baptism, that Christ Jesus is the (big) fish and Christians are little fishes who swim in the saving water (*De Baptismo*, 1). This could perhaps make some sense of those references in inscriptions, if the Christ-fish is an allusion to baptism, rather than to a ritual meal as such. Granted, the Christ-fish is not eaten in baptism, but perhaps the connection between baptism and a eucharistic meal, involving in some cases honey (Tertullian, *De Corona*, 3. 3; *Adv. Marc.* 1. 14. 3; cf. Pectorius) and/or wine and bread (cf. Abercius) would have encouraged the language of the epitaphs. This would make the metaphors of the two inscriptions not much more muddled than they already are.

But even Tertullian's fish imagery does not emerge from nowhere. The Gospel stories may be the most important background for such usage, but there are other, broader, aspects of fish symbolism that

---

[152] Snyder's ultimate conclusion is appropriate enough: 'As a net result of these considerations, the meal can be seen as a continuation of the non-Christian meal for the dead in light of the New Testament paradigm of the Feeding of the Five Thousand', *Ante Pacem*, 65.

[153] Jastrzebowska, 'Les Scènes de banquet', 86–8.

[154] The first example of the 'eucharistic' image seems to be in Augustine, *Tract. in Io. Ev.* 123; see Vogel, 'Le Repas sacré au poisson', 7–8.

[155] The acrostic first appears in the *Sibylline Oracles*, 8. 217–50, probably from the fourth century: Vogel, 'Le Repas sacré au poisson', 10; Hiers and Kennedy, 'The Bread and Fish Eucharist', 20–1.

deserve consideration. Fish was probably a symbol of luxury, in art and otherwise.[156] Since it was very expensive in areas at all removed from the sea, its use was a sign of wealth for those who could afford it often, and of celebration for those who might eat it more rarely.[157]

There are some impressive sources that suggest fish was significant in Jewish meals such as Sabbath-eve suppers.[158] This practice may bear some relation to Christian symbolism but of course needs its own explanation. Apocalyptic literature presents legends involving the killing and eating of Leviathan in the Messianic age, drawing on the earlier tradition of the battle between God and the sea-creature, but there are few if any clear connections between this and the evidence for the Sabbath meal.[159] Most references to this practice merely reinforce the sense that fish was prized and expensive, and its use a sign of piety because it was appropriate thus to honour the Sabbath.[160]

Fish and Sacrifice

We should also consider the fish, eaten or otherwise symbolically employed by Christians and Jews, as an alternative to meat, an idea we find in the pagan sources in a variety of ways.[161] One of Plutarch's convivial company, Lamprias, adds to a discussion about the culinary

---

[156] Granted, paradoxically, the overtones of poverty associated with fishing as a living; perhaps the contrast between the effort of the fisher and the concrete result could underscore the luxury of the product; see Purcell, 'Eating Fish', 134–8. For fish as a symbol of wealth in decorative art, see Yvon Thébert, 'Private Life and Domestic Architecture in Roman Africa', in P. Veyne (ed.), *A History of Private Life* trans. A. Goldhammer (Cambridge, Mass.: Belknap, 1987), i. 364–8. See also Vogel, 'Le Repas sacré au poisson', 16.

[157] See Plutarch, *Quaest. Conv.* 668 B, Apuleius, *Apol.* 41. The parable in *Gos. Thom.* 8 seems to work in these rather general terms as well.

[158] These are usefully summarized and discussed both by Vogel, 'Le Repas sacré au poisson', 17–24, and by Hiers and Kennedy, 'The Bread and Fish Eucharist', 35–8.

[159] A commonplace in apocalyptic literature: *1 Enoch* 60: 7; *4 Ezra* 6: 49–52; *2 Apoc. Bar.* 29. See discussion by Hiers and Kennedy, 'The Bread and Fish Eucharist', 35–9, and Vogel, 'Le Repas sacré au poisson', 21–5, both drawing on E. R. Goodenough, *Jewish Symbols in the Graeco-Roman Period* (13 vols.; New York: Pantheon Books, 1953–68), v. 31–62, and Reicke, *Diakonie, Festfreude und Zelos*, 208 n. 11. In any case, there do not seem to be clear examples where the use of fish as appropriate Sabbath-eve food is linked with the Messianic or apocalyptic themes regarding the killing and eating of Leviathan. Dölger (*IXΘΥΣ* ii. 490–2) criticizes any attempt to link the two conceptions, since the Leviathan is a symbol of evil to be overcome rather than of purity; but the fact that it is eaten still has to be acknowledged.

[160] See *b. Šabb.* 118b, 119a.

[161] As e.g. in the whole of the fourth question posed in Book 4 of Plutarch's *Quaestiones Conviviales*, 667C–669 E.

and digestive benefits of fish by providing a deeper analysis of the way human beings relate to land animals and to fish as potential foods:

> But we shall say that of all delicacies the most legitimate (δικαιότατον) kind is that from the sea. As far as the land animals whose meat is here before us is concerned, we must admit at least this if nothing else, that they consume the same food and breathe the same air as we do, and drink and bathe in water no different from ours. This has in times past made people ashamed when they butchered them in spite of their pitiful cries and in spite of having made companions of most of them and shared their store of food with them. Sea animals, on the other hand, are a species entirely alien and remote from us, as if they had sprung up and were living in some different world. Neither look nor voice nor service rendered pleads with us not to eat them, for no animal can employ these pleas that has no life at all among us; nor need we feel any affection for them. (*Quaest. Conv.* 669 D–E)

Viewed from this perspective, fish belonged to an alien and mysterious world; it escaped affinity with humans, as well as other features that characterized meat, especially in terms of the ambiguity towards slaughter and what has already been described as the 'cuisine of sacrifice'.[162] While the caught and cooked product does not seem to have carried too much of an air of mystery with it, even fish as food was more like game than like the domestically produced meat associated with sacrifice, more the result of luck and nature than of order and culture.[163]

If bread was the staple food of most people most of the time, further foods would have been necessary to mark a meal as of particular importance. Reasons have already been given as to why meat was at best ambiguous to most Christians, and sufficiently tainted by association with pagan sacrifice for some to reject its use altogether. While in some cases it seems that bread took the place of meat for Christians in an apparent set of opposing categories of good and bad food, it would be plausible that fish might also have done so in certain circumstances. There are sufficient reasons to imagine that fish, a food prized yet relatively free from the associations of sacrifice (or martyrdom), might have been envisaged as appropriate for the heavenly table. The positive associations of the Gospel traditions, which might well themselves trade on the sense of fish as a symbol of luck and gratuitous abundance, would have built upon this sacrificially neutral foundation. There is no reason to think that such logic might not have applied to earthly meals as well, although it is not likely that the expense of fish could often have been

---

[162] See further Purcell, 'Eating Fish', 132–49.   [163] Ibid. 137–9.

justified, except for just the sort of occasional use that a funerary or commemorative meal might suggest.

There is one case where we do have some indication of the use of fish in precisely these terms, i.e. as an alternative to animal sacrifice. Marcion, who seems to have rejected the use of both wine and meat, allowed fish.[164] Tertullian taunts him because of this, seeing an inconsistent dualism at work : 'you also reprove the sea, but make use of its produce, which you regard as holier food' (*Adv. Marc.* 1. 14. 4).[165] So too, Eznik of Kolb understands Marcionite food practice to allow fish but not meat, and argues against this preference in a way that both makes and misses the point: that fish is an inferior food, he says, is indicated by the fact that it is not used for sacrifice (*De Deo*, 407). This was, of course, precisely the distinction that might indeed lead a Christian group to use fish.[166]

The reference to fish as 'holier' to Marcionites need not be taken to refer to a specifically eucharistic or otherwise communal Marcionite meal. Marcionites seem to have had rituals very similar to those of other Christians to the point that, later at least, in some areas there was risk of confusion.[167] Use of fish in a more well-defined eucharistic meal at this point would have come to clearer notice than it does. In context, the allocation of degrees of holiness would seem merely to be a matter of allowing fish into the general diet. This case, therefore, helps us see another aspect of fish symbolism that may help explain the references already discussed, but it is not evidence for a fish eucharist, or for funerary meals involving fish.

Fish—Conclusion

In short, the idea of a fish eucharist is not borne out by the evidence. There is at least a possibility that meals of the circle around Jesus involving fish were later understood as of some ritual significance, but no clear indication that these continued into the life of the early Christian

[164] Interestingly he is also accused of observing the Jewish Sabbath supper or *cena pura* (Tertullian, *Adv. Marc.* 5. 4).

[165] 'Reprobas et mare, sed usque ad copias eius, quas sanctiorem cibum deputas.'

[166] Arthur Vööbus, *History of Asceticism in the Syrian Orient: A Contribution to the History of Culture in the Near East* i. *The Origin of Asceticism: Early Monasticism in Persia*, CSCO 184 (Louvain: Secrétariat du Corpus SCO, 1958), 51.

[167] See further R. Joseph Hoffmann, *Marcion: On the Restitution of Christianity: An Essay on the Development of Radical Paulinist Theology in the Second Century* (Chico, Calif.: Scholars Press, 1984), 18–21.

communities. The importance of fish in Jewish Sabbath meals may have been a belief shared by some Christians, but supposed connections between these meals and Messianic expectation are less clear than the fact that fish was prized food used on festive occasions. The lack of connection with sacrificial ritual seems to have contributed to Marcionite preference for fish over meat for diet, and may also have contributed to the Sabbath use, but this choice has no clear positive connection with Christian ritual meals. Finally, the depictions of fish in the context of tombs and funerary meals may suggest the use of fish in meals to commemorate the dead, but this is not certain; what is clearer is that these meals, and any use of fish, might have drawn upon Jewish traditional symbolism, but could have been as much or more pagan in inspiration. There is simply no persuasive evidence for a fish eucharist.

SUMMARY

The evidence for foods other than the expected bread and wine in eucharistic meals is not very great, but also not insignificant. Despite having started from a broad descriptive basis, considering the range of foods employed in some degree of parallelism with those available as discussed in the previous chapter, we find that the evidence is not only sparse but markedly uneven. The form of this uneven distribution of foods is not random but suggests some correlation with the issues of order already discussed.

One general and surprising feature seems to stand out; that the instances of these supposedly additional foods tend to be linked, not by any apparent laxity of practice or lack of concern about appropriate food or ritual, but on the contrary, by their asceticism. The Artotyritai who use cheese are linked with ascetic Montanism, and their cheese or curd may well really be a version of a cup without wine, constructed in imitation of a primordial peace prior to bloodshed and sacrifice. The milieu of the African martyrs which uses the imagery, if not the actual practice, of milk opposed to flesh, is not dissimilar in its outlook. Likewise those who make use of oil, salt, and vegetables in their regular community eucharistic meals are characterized by uncompromising rejection of the wider pagan society, including its food and especially its meat, and use their meals as a sign of that rejection. The prominence of oil, vegetables, and salt in these descriptions seems to be a means of emphasizing the absence of meat. In these cases, such as the apocryphal

Acts and Pseudo-Clementine literature, there is real difficulty identifying different forms of meal along the lines of a clear opposition between sacral and ordinary or secular meals, such as the usual search for a eucharist in the absolute sense would assume. In the literary pictures at least, these communities seem not to distinguish so much between a particular sacral communal meal and all other normal eating, but between all the eating they do and the eating that all others do. Thus the relatively soft boundaries established between different non-sacrificial foods reflect the tremendous emphasis placed on the hard boundaries between the Christian communities and the rest of society. While it has been tempting to see the groups and bodies of writing in terms of their relationship to the orthodox mainstream along the lines of 'heresy', the key issue may really be their relationship with the wider society. Their oddities are comprehensible more in terms of social organization than of doctrine alone, and of sectarianism rather more than of heresy.[168]

The distinctions being expressed could be posed in various ways: Christian/pagan, poor/rich, pure/impure, ascetic/luxurious; but the underlying issue of order seems again to be that of participation in, or avoidance of, the cuisine of sacrifice. This category is to be preferred as the fundamental one because it identifies the key aspect of the actual system of provision of meat in particular.

Although there are instances where some of these elements such as salt, and milk and honey, have a place in the ritual meal practice of more accommodating and more orthodox groups, these are now very clearly fenced around as tokens belonging to very particular persons, times, and places, of salt in the catechumenal process, of oil in healing ritual, and of fruits or vegetables in seasonal or festive food offerings such as those of the *Apostolic Tradition*. These are in little or no danger of being confused with well-defined use of bread and wine in eucharistic meals carried out in remembrance of the sacrificial death of Jesus. Salt does not stand for the appropriately ascetic diet of all, but for the status of the catechumen as one who has not yet participated in the feast of salvation. Milk or cheese are not the elements of a tradition of ongoing ceremonial meals, but the marks of a unique transformative ritual. Fruit is the marker not of a present return to innocence but of past and future glories. These rather different patterns can be understood in relation to other evidence of internal ordering in the orthodox mainstream: of times (in the

[168] These questions would have to be pursued for the different pieces of evidence and groups under discussion. See further below, Chs. 4–7, on the bread-and-water tradition of eucharistic meals.

establishment of appropriate times to fast and not to fast), and of persons (in the setting apart of individuals and communities called to specific forms of asceticism), as well as of foods. The clear distinction between the eucharist and other food and meals is not unrelated to these issues of order.

By contrast, in the early ascetic cases there is a continuum of concern between ritual practice and ascetic practice concerning diet as a whole. As we shall see in the following chapters there is a very strong correlation between use of these foods in regular communal meals and the practice of using water in the eucharistic cup. It would seem therefore that in the ascetic cases, more may mean less, in a sense. The eucharistic meals of some early Christian communities were distinguished from their other meals only by emphasis, perhaps on the basis of an exclusive commensality among members of the Christian community as much as because of particular food elements. But the relative openness of these meals to at least certain foods cannot be fully explained without further consideration of the two things so obviously avoided, one clearly eucharistic and the other not in terms of the normative tradition, but more associated than distinguished in these ascetic communities: the sacrificial meal elements of meat and wine.

4
Bread and Water in Early Asian and Syrian Christianity

INTRODUCTION

Lucian of Samosata says of Peregrinus Proteus, the subject of his satire *De Morte Peregrini*, that he was rejected by the Christians who had previously hailed him as a great teacher, perhaps because he ate foods forbidden to them (ibid. 16). Lucian's easy assumption that this might explain Peregrinus' fall need not indicate confusion of Christians and Jews, or a particular case of continued association of Christians and Jews; in fact food prohibitions were of great importance to many Christians for centuries.[1]

We have seen that there are various cases where foods other than the expected bread and wine are used in ritual meals of Christian communities in the first few centuries, often in what is understood by both members and critics of the groups in question to be the eucharist, or at least the major communal or eucharistic meal of the community, rather than in any second type of meal such as an *agape*. Yet the most widespread practice other than the use of bread and wine is a case of less rather than more; many Christian groups seem to have used water rather than wine for the cup of the eucharistic meal, and for meals in general. This ritual pattern seems to be closely linked to another dietary restriction of a more general kind, i.e. the avoidance of meat. These practices may also hold some important clues to the other 'odd' uses of food in ritual meals which, it has been argued, are also generally ascetic and anti-sacrificial in character.

This and the next two chapters will have the nature of a catalogue of the cases where bread and water (or bread alone) are the elements of the eucharistic meal. Some of the material involves problems of interpretation

---

[1] See E. R. Dodds's summary of suggestions for the specific breach by Peregrinus: *Pagan and Christian in an Age of Anxiety* (Cambridge: Cambridge University Press, 1965), 60 n. 2. I think that of Labriolle, in *La Réaction paienne: Étude sur la polemique antichrétienne du Ier au VIe siècle* (Paris: Artisan du livre, 1938), 104, that Peregrinus ate sacrificial meat, is closest. But from the rest of my discussion it will seem obvious that I think all he need have done was eat *any* meat.

and location in time and space even prior to the questions of eucharistic meaning, and these will be addressed in an attempt to establish the extent and value of the evidence as clearly as possible. Granted the difficulties of evidence, the extent of the practice is surprising, and worth establishing in itself as something of historical significance regardless of the interpretation given. It seems that this ascetic pattern, which transcends the usual distinction between ritual and dietary issues, can meaningfully be linked to other aspects of the social organization of the Christian groups among whom the bread-and-water tradition is attested. Most importantly, it represents the apex of a Christian version of the anti-sacrificial asceticism already discussed.

JEWISH–CHRISTIAN EUCHARISTIC MEALS

Introduction

Instances of Jews who avoided both meat and wine have already been mentioned; the Therapeutae of Philo are perhaps the most obvious example. When such avoidance is attested in early forms of Christianity, especially where there are clear links with or influence from Judaism, we ought probably to assume some connection between the Jewish and Christian forms of this asceticism. This is not to say that Jewish tradition explains the Christian versions of the phenomenon, or even the Jewish ones for that matter. Rather, it will be argued, in both cases there seems to be some response to paganism and that characteristic religious and social eating which has been described as the cuisine of sacrifice.

Ebionites

Irenaeus is the first to attest to the existence and practices of the Ebionites, apparently a Christian group who persisted in the observance of the Torah, rejected Paul, and recognized only Matthew's Gospel as authoritative (*Adv. Haer.* 1. 26. 2).[2] Irenaeus was a native of Asia Minor and had spent time in Rome, and his reports could stem from groups there or, more indirectly, from Syria or Palestine.[3] Irenaeus says that the Ebionites used

---

[2] Justin Martyr also refers to Torah-observant Christians with an apparently adoptionist Christology (*Dial.* 47–8), but does not name them or say anything of their ritual practice.

[3] Although writing somewhat later than Justin who is discussed below (late 2nd cent.), Irenaeus' account could reflect earlier practices. See A. F. J. Klijn and G. J. Reinink, *Patristic Evidence for Jewish-Christian Sects*, NovTSup 36 (Leiden: E. J. Brill, 1973), 19–20.

only water in the cup of their eucharist. The reason for this, he says, is that they rejected the union of divine and human natures in Jesus symbolized in the mixture of wine and water in the cup (5. 1. 3; cf. 3. 21. 1, 4. 33. 4). This rationale seems unlikely, and depends upon Irenaeus' view that all groups which differed from his own rule of faith and practice were consciously deviating from a fully established doctrinal and liturgical whole which went back to Jesus and the apostles. Nor, for that matter, is it clear that all 'orthodox' Christians at this time used a mixture of wine and water (on which see further below), let alone that they all understood the mixture as symbolic of a combination of natures in Jesus.

Tertullian and Hippolytus mention the Ebionites but add little to our knowledge. Origen, however, does have some different things to say about them, including a couple of references to food. He indicates that Ebionites made distinctions between clean and unclean foods (*Comm. in Matt.* 11. 12), and that they kept Passover at the same time and in the same way as (other) Jews did (*In Matt. Comm. Ser.* 79). These practices are simply those we would expect to find in Judaism, and there is no indication on Origen's part of the problem raised by Irenaeus.

Origen also distinguishes between two Ebionite groups, one orthodox with respect to Jesus' conception and birth and the other more like those described by Irenaeus, believing Joseph to be Jesus' father (*Contra Celsum*, 5. 61; cf. *Comm. in Matt.* 16. 12). It is possible that there really were two Ebionite groups, but it is also possible, and rather more likely, that Origen is dealing with different sources, or with Jewish-Christians of his own acquaintance on the one hand and some known to him only by report on the other. He uses the term 'Ebionite' for all groups or testimonies, encouraged by the tendency to catalogue and label heretics exhibited by Irenaeus and Hippolytus and by his own etymology of 'Ebionites' as 'poor in intelligence'. Origen's own direct attacks on the Ebionites, which are at least sometimes couched in terms of first-person experience, seem usually to imply a group fairly close to his tradition doctrinally, but one which kept the Mosaic law. These do not seem to be the same group as those described by Irenaeus. Jewish observance alone would also account for his charge that they attacked or discarded Paul, given the apostle's attitude to the Torah.[4]

---

[4] Origen does not use the Gospel of the Hebrews, a text from which he cites an account of the miraculous conception of Jesus by the Holy Spirit (*Comm. in Joh.* 2. 12; cf. *Hom. in Jer.* 15. 4), as a specifically Ebionite source. Klijn and Reinink, *Patristic Evidence for Jewish-Christian Sects*, 24–5, suggest that the Gospel to the Hebrews preceded but influenced some Ebionites, who thus became the more orthodox variety known to Origen.

Although Origen's description of the Ebionites as (apparently) keeping *kašrut* and using unleavened bread for the Passover is not actually contradictory of Irenaeus' point about the use of water, neither do the two actually overlap as evidence for practice. One of the groups did keep something like the same dietary restrictions that were observed in Judaism of the time; this does not, however, explain the other's rejection of wine. And since there is reason to think of those described by Origen as relatively orthodox Christians in contrast to Irenaeus' group, both practical and doctrinal considerations mean that we are justified in treating these as two separate groups and sets of practices. Whether such Jewish–Christians were all really self-designated Ebionites must remain uncertain. It is plausible that Aramaic-speaking Christians would call themselves 'the poor', with or without a technical sense.[5]

Ebionite practice is expanded upon by Epiphanius, who adds some interesting but by no means crystal-clear information about them. According to him (*Pan.* 30. 13. 4–5; 30. 15. 3–4, 22. 3–5) the Ebionites did not eat meat. Epiphanius also reports that they had an annual eucharistic meal using unleavened bread and with water in the cup (ibid. 30. 16. 1).[6] There is some suggestion that water was regarded as significant, used for ritual washing as well as for ritual drink (ibid. 30. 2. 3–5, 15. 3, 16. 1). Unfortunately much of this information, while interesting in itself, can only with great caution be used as evidence for the Ebionites. Epiphanius' account seems to draw on earlier heresiological sources, but also on the Pseudo-Clementine literature (he refers to the *Journeyings of Peter* as a work attributed to Clement and used by the Ebionites, *Pan.* 30. 15. 1), a 'Gospel of the Hebrews', as well as some unique information, possibly involving first-hand knowledge.

It seems quite likely that all these additional sources need to be kept separate from the early information on Ebionites properly so-called. While it is possible that there was some use and development of the Pseudo-Clementine writings within Ebionite or at least Jewish–Christian circles, this cannot be assumed.[7] It is clearer that Epiphanius read some

---

[5] But note Leander Keck's criticism of the assumption that these are still the poor of the Jerusalem Church who were the subject of Paul's concern: 'The Poor among the Saints in the New Testament', *ZNW* 56 (1965), 100–29, and 'The Poor among the Saints in Jewish Christianity and Qumran', *ZNW* 57 (1966), 54–78. See also Hamel's discussion of the vocabulary of poverty, *Poverty and Charity*, 164–210.

[6] Harnack, 'Brod und Wasser', 117, and Scheiwiler, *Die Elemente der Eucharistie in den ersten drei Jahrhunderten*, 139, both take this reference to be to another, Jewish-Gnostic, group.

[7] With regard to the question of the Ebionites and the Clementine literature, see Klijn and Reinink, *Patristic Evidence for Jewish-Christian Sects*, 28–38, and G. A. Koch, 'A

materials related to this corpus, and then attributed the views and practices therein to the Ebionites. Thus while he may be a valuable source with regard to the question of the development of the Pseudo-Clementine corpus, the use of Epiphanius' material for the reconstruction of Jewish Christianity, and of Ebionitism in particular, is based on a fragile assumption about the accuracy of his application of sources to particular groups.[8] The eucharistic meals in the Pseudo-Clementines, already mentioned in the discussion of salt, will thus be examined separately in the next chapter.[9]

Similar caution should be employed with Epiphanius' witness to an Ebionite gospel which also seems to support avoidance of meat, and which he calls the Gospel of the Hebrews, a mutilated version of Matthew's Gospel (*Pan.* 30. 3. 7; 30. 14. 3). In fact Epiphanius seems confused as to whether the Ebionites themselves call it 'of the Hebrews' (ibid. 30. 3. 7; cf. 30. 13. 2) or 'of Matthew' (30. 3. 7, 13. 2, 14. 2). It certainly is not to be identified either with canonical Matthew or, for that matter, with what is elsewhere called the *Gospel of the Hebrews*.[10] Here we shall continue the modern convention of referring to this work as the *Gospel of the Ebionites* despite the fact that not even Epiphanius gives it such a name. Yet the connection with Ebionites must be regarded as unproven, and this document will also be discussed separately.

The only reference to diet left in Epiphanius' account when these two sources are sifted out is an allusion to an argument with Ebionites which Epiphanius himself seems to have conducted:

When you say to [one of] them regarding animal food, 'How then was it that Abraham set the calf and milk before the angels; or how then was it that Noah ate and heard God saying 'Sacrifice and eat,' and how is it that Isaac and Jacob sacrificed to God, or that Moses did the same in the desert?' He does not believe in these things and says 'What need do I have of reading what is in the law, when the gospel has come?' (*Pan.* 30. 18. 7)[11]

Critical Investigation of Epiphanius' Knowledge of the Ebionites: A Translation and Discussion of *Panarion* 30', Ph.D. diss., University of Pennsylvania, 1976, 268–315 and *passim*.

[8] Koch, 'Epiphanius' Knowledge of the Ebionites', 312–15; Klijn and Reinink, *Patristic Evidence for Jewish-Christian Sects*, 35.

[9] See Ch. 5.

[10] P. Vielhauer and G. Strecker, 'Jewish Christian Gospels', in Schneemelcher (ed.), *New Testament Apocrypha*, i. 134–41, 166–71.

[11] My trans.; see further *Pan.* 30. 1. 8–9. Epiphanius' odd story of Count Joseph (30. 4–12) is another original contribution, again hardly capable of being related to the Ebionites.

This seems to be a real contribution from Epiphanius, but it taxes the imagination to see how this view could come from a group who sought to be observant Jews as well as Christians. We can take this, not as evidence for Ebionitism in any specific sense, but as an indication that Epiphanius had some acquaintance with yet a further meat-avoiding group.

Epiphanius also attributes avoidance of meat and of animal sacrifice to another Jewish group he calls 'Nasareans' (*Pan.* 18). 'So they keep all the Jewish observances, but did not sacrifice or partake of animal flesh; rather it was forbidden for them to eat meat or to offer sacrifice with it' (ibid. 18. 1. 4). The existence of this group is otherwise unknown, unless we take the (plausible) view that this nomenclature indicates some confusion on his part involving Nazirites and/or Nazareans, i.e. Christians.[12] Given the uncertain state of the evidence this is just a possibility, but it serves to further emphasize the concern among some groups, Christians and perhaps Jews also, about animal sacrifice. It is also interesting that the arguments used by the Nasareans are protological in nature, and deny a dispensation to Noah to sacrifice and eat animals (ibid. 18. 3. 3–4).

The Gospel of the Ebionites

Reasons for separation of Ebionites and the *Gospel of the Ebionites* have already been given. The *Gospel of the Ebionites* did reject the eating of meat. It read ἐγκρίς (cake) for ἀκρίς (locust) in describing the diet of John the Baptist (*Pan.* 30. 13. 4),[13] and has Jesus questioning, rather than affirming, his expected desire to eat the Passover or particularly its 'meat'. Epiphanius complains at these emendations: 'They made the disciples say "Where do you want us to prepare for you to eat the Passover?" and the Lord to answer "Have I greatly desired to eat meat this Passover with you?"' (ibid. 30. 22. 4; cf. Matt. 26: 17). Jesus is even made to oppose sacrifice altogether: 'I have come to do away with sacrifices, and if you do not cease from sacrificing, the wrath of God will not cease from you' (ibid. 30. 16. 4). While commentators seem

---

[12] Cf. the use of 'Nazoreans' to designate Christians in the prologue to the *Didascalia Apostolorum*.

[13] See further on the tendency to make John a vegetarian, Sebastian Brock, 'The Baptist's Diet in Syriac Sources', 113–24. There is also some evidence for this in the *Diatessaron* and in later Syrian writers whose asceticism has become the more specialized phenomenon of monasticism; but these emulators of the Baptist are probably to be understood as the successors of early avoiders of meat and wine.

generally to take this as a reference to the Temple cult in Jerusalem, this only makes sense if the work is read as a 'Jewish-Christian Gospel' in the context of the first or early second century.[14] Since we know it only through citations in a fourth-century work whose accuracy in linking texts and communities is rather questionable, the setting could be understood rather more broadly. Ongoing concern with sacrifice might well have been understood to refer to pagan practice rather more than to the sacrifices of the Jerusalem Temple, even (and especially) if some reference to the destruction of 70 CE is granted. Whether these references arose originally in conjunction with the Temple cult remains uncertain at best.

In these cases, as in those involving supposedly odd eucharistic foods discussed in the previous chapter, it is clear that a merely liturgical or ritual analysis of these texts and practices does not allow us fully to grasp the meaning even of the application of this sort of asceticism in a liturgical context. Both ritual and general diet are affected by the same principles of avoidance of meat and wine. With this in mind, we should not leave this set of witnesses to a bread-and-water eucharistic tradition without some attention to another important case, that of James the Just, the brother of Jesus.

James the Just

According to the early Christian historian Hegesippus (2nd cent.), who is excerpted in Eusebius' *Ecclesiastical History*,

James, the brother of the Lord, succeeded to the government of the Church in conjunction with the apostles. He has been called the Just by all from the time of our Saviour to the present day; for there were many called James. He was holy from his mother's womb; and he drank no wine nor strong drink, nor did he eat flesh (ἔμψυχον). No razor came upon his head; he did not anoint himself with oil, and he did not use the bath. He alone was permitted to enter into the holy place; for he wore not woolen but linen garments . . . (2. 23. 4–6)

It seems obvious that this portrait has been assembled with some reference to the Nazirite tradition and particularly to the biblical portraits of Samson (Judg. 13), Samuel (1 Sam. 1), and John the Baptist (Luke 1). Yet James's abstinence from meat is not part of the ancient Nazirite tradition, at least. While it may be understood as a development of the prohibition of unclean foods, the specific extension of this concept

---

[14] Vielhauer and Strecker, 'Jewish Christian Gospels', 168.

to include anything 'animal' or 'ensouled' must, especially given the terminology, owe much to a sense of ascetic resistance to animal and sacrificial food developed originally in pagan thought.[15]

It is also revealing that, as Ernst Zuchschwerdt points out, James's Nazirate is depicted in terms other than the sacerdotally ordered ones of the temporary Nazirate (Num. 6), and further that the authority which derives from this asceticism is specifically contrasted with priestly ordination: he wore linen (cf. Lev. 16: 4) but neither bathed nor was anointed (cf. Lev. 16: 4, 32) as priests were. Yet despite this he is depicted as entering the holy place, and even as the sole person qualified to do so.

Even leaving meat-eating and sacrifice aside, James is therefore presented as a somewhat anti-cultic and anti-sacrificial figure. The addition of the avoidance of meat makes this anti-sacrificial picture all the stronger; it is not simply one of James's piety in the sense of self-denial or frugality, but depicts his separation from a system which is deemed corrupt or redundant.[16] It is hardly an emphasis on his Jewishness as such, since meat-eating in the time of the Temple's existence was not only allowable, but necessary for observance of Passover and other sacrifices. Rather it is a picture of a very specific type of Jewish asceticism, and one with strong pagan analogues.[17]

In this case we have no reason to assume that Hegesippus himself reflects a tradition which bans meat and wine for all Christians altogether, since James is certainly presented as an extraordinary figure rather than as a straightforward model for conduct.[18] The logic of avoidance of meat and wine, however, is clearly depicted in this episode as a matter of the cuisine of sacrifice.

---

[15] The term ἔμψυχον is not biblical; see E. Zuchschwerdt, 'Das Naziräat des Herrenbruders Jakobus nach Hegesipp (Euseb, h.e. II 23, 5–6)', *ZNW* 68 (1977), 278.

[16] See Zuchschwerdt, ibid. 276–87. James's avoidance of oil is also worth comparing with evidence for similar Essene/Qumran practice (*JW* 2 § 123; cf. CD 12. 15–17).

[17] I am not concerned here to rule on the historical value of the picture of James from Hegesippus (see e.g. Johannes Munck, *Paul and the Salvation of Mankind* (Richmond, Va.: John Knox, 1959), 109–19, for a negative view and Roy B. Ward, 'James of Jerusalem in the First Two Centuries', *ANRW* 26/1 (1987), 800–3, for a more circumspect one), but I do not find the difficulty of assimilating this asceticism to rabbinic Judaism to be an obstacle in itself.

[18] Compare the figure of Peter in the Pseudo-Clementines and the apostles of the apocryphal *Acts*, on whom see further below in the next chapter. Clement of Alexandria also attributes this sort of vegetarian asceticism to the apostle Matthew (*Paed.* 2. 1. 16. 1).

Summary

There are other (including some earlier) references to food concerns like these among Jewish groups not linked closely to Christianity, some of which were already discussed in the second chapter. It seems reasonable to link Jewish-Christian forms of asceticism involving meat and wine with traditions such as those of the Nazirate and the Rechabites to some extent, yet it is also tempting to suggest that in Jewish-Christian as in (other) Jewish circles, the bread-and-water tradition owes more to pagan ascetic models, or at least to the need to respond to the pagan cuisine of sacrifice. The Qumran and/or Essene communities whose food restrictions are a matter of inner-Jewish self-definition were unconcerned about meat and wine as such. The Therapeutae and the odd *pērushim* of the rabbinic sources were likely to have been influenced by issues associated with Greek and Roman religion. Again, it seems necessary to regard both Christianity and Judaism as very much religions of the Graeco-Roman world, not least when marked by an asceticism that was earlier characteristic of pagan social and religious dissidents.

JUSTIN MARTYR

Justin Martyr's possible testimony to a eucharistic meal involving water rather than wine is not altogether clear. In fact Justin's descriptions of eucharistic meal practice, written in the middle of the second century, are often used as firm elements of the more conventional picture of liturgical development, since he provides not only the eucharistic actions emphasized by Dix but also shows knowledge of the imagery of Jesus' body and blood in terms that suggest the institution narratives (*1 Apol.* 65–7; *Dial.* 70). Yet Justin's apparent references to wine are problematic, and deserve examination.

In a rather neglected piece published in 1891, Adolf von Harnack cast the harsh light of his textual criticism of Justin's work on to the passages relevant to eucharistic meals.[19] In two instances (*1 Apol.* 54, *Dial.* 69), both passages dealing with the Dionysiac mysteries and their resemblance to Christian ritual, there is evidence that ὄνος (donkey)

---

[19] Harnack, 'Brod und Wasser', 115–44. See also Harnack's rejoinder to criticism in his review, *TLZ* 17 (1892), 373–8, of F. X. Funk, 'Die Abendmahlselemente bei Justin', *Kirchengeschichtliche Abhandlungen und Untersuchungen* (2 vols.; Paderborn: Schöningh, 1897), i. 278–92.

was changed to οἶνος (wine).[20] The copyist who wished to have Justin speak of wine in these texts was perhaps unaware of the place of the donkey in Dionysiac imagery and, more culpably, oblivious to Justin's argument about the resemblance of the pagan rites to Jesus' ride into Jerusalem upon a donkey. Yet ignorance may not be the sole or best possible explanation for the apparent textual changes. These textual oddities might also be accounted for by the hypothesis that elsewhere Justin had referred to the use of water alone in the cup of the eucharistic meal, and that the enthusiasm of the process of 'correction' went too far.

If this were the case it would be less remarkable that Justin, deriding pagan ritual as imitating Christian practice, mentions Dionysus as supposed giver of the grapevine, yet makes nothing of any resemblance between this element of the mysteries and Christian eucharists.[21] Although the absence of that comparison may be explained in other ways, Justin does compare the rites of Mithras with the Christian meal he knows, and wants to make the use of a cup of water (not wine) by the Mithras cult into a point of similarity (*1 Apol.* 66).

Justin's use of biblical traditions contributes to the puzzle. The same suspicious, if not conclusive, silence where comparison is invited reigns in discussions (*1 Apol.* 32, 54; *Dial.* 52–4, 63, 69, 76) of Gen. 49: 8–12, the blessing of Judah, according to which the patriarch is said to 'wash his robes in wine'. Again, a positive 'water' comparison is made, without comment, when Justin uses the words of Isa. 33: 16 to describe the eucharistic elements: 'Bread will be given him, and his water [will be] trustworthy' (*Dial.* 70).

Finally we must deal with the cases where the text seems to refer explicitly to the use of wine in the eucharistic cup. These are all in the one passage, *1 Apol.* 65–7, which is the most detailed account of the eucharist Justin gives. Twice in this extended description (both in 66) he refers simply to the cup (τὸ ποτήριον), which is also the term he uses elsewhere (cf. *Dial.* 41, 70). According to most texts, at *1 Apol.* 65 the president offers bread and a cup, ὕδατος καὶ κράματος, which ought to mean 'of water and of wine mixed with water', an odd phrase at least. In fact καὶ κράματος is actually missing in Codex Ottobianus, which simply leaves the elements as bread and water. Interpolation, perhaps heedless of context again, may seem to be a likely path to this less than satisfactory text.[22]

---

[20] Harnack, 'Brod und Wasser', 127–8.
[21] Ibid. 127–9.   [22] Ibid. 130–1.

The two remaining cases, in *1 Apol.* 65 (again) and 67, refer explicitly to the offering of (previously unmixed) wine along with water. There is no text-critical basis for removal of these references to wine, but Harnack argued that on the basis of the other evidence of interpolation, these instances could also be the result of later emendation.[23] The positive comparison with Mithraic water-ritual mentioned above also takes place in the middle of this passage.

In summary, Justin compares the eucharistic meal known to him to both biblical and pagan models involving water, and to none involving wine, despite the opportunity; and the transmission of his works shows evidence of interpolation which could conceivably account for all the references to wine in the meal. It must be admitted that few have been convinced by this evidence so far as to accept Harnack's thesis fully.[24] Within a few years of its publication there was a flurry of attempts to rebut.[25] The exegetical silence on Judah's blessing was mistaken; there were others who had interpreted it without reference to the eucharist.[26] Some suggested that the reading of Codex Ottobianus was *facilior* and should be rejected,[27] and/or that κράμα could simply mean 'wine', that 'a cup' should be assumed to contain wine,[28] and that Justin's phrasing was meant to emphasize sobriety.[29] Others argued, comparing this evidence with later indications of a separate cup of water at baptismal eucharists, that the reference was to two different cups, one of water and another of mixed wine.[30] All in all, these arguments served not to make Justin's position clearly orthodox so much as to leave the question open. There is

[23] Ibid. 131.

[24] The debate is summarized, with references to the most important participants and their work, by C. Ruch, 'La Messe d'après les pères, jusqu'à St Cyprien', *DTC*, x. 898–907, a work close enough in time to the debate to have been interested in it.

[25] Most notably by Th. Zahn, *Brot und Wein im Abendmahl der alten Kirche* (Leipzig: A. Deichert, 1892), by F. X. Funk in 'Die Abendmahlselemente bei Justin', and by A. Jülicher, 'Zur Geschichte der Abendmahlsfeier in der ältesten Kirche', *Theologische Abhandlungen: Carl von Weizsäcker zu seinem siebzigsten Geburtstage* (Freiburg: J. C. B. Mohr (Paul Siebeck), 1892), 217–50.

[26] Irenaeus, Clement, Hippolytus, and Origen had all done so; see Zahn, *Brot und Wein*, 74.

[27] Zahn, *Brot und Wein*, 14, and Jülicher, 'Zur Geschichte der Abendmahlsfeier', 221–2, both suggest an instance of *homoteleuton*, the scribe of Ottobianus being deceived by the similarity of endings between ὕδατος and κράματος.

[28] Funk, 'Die Abendmahlselemente bei Justin', 278–92.

[29] Thus Zahn, *Brot und Wein*, 14; Jülicher, 'Zur Geschichte der Abendmahlsfeier', 221.

[30] A. Greiff, 'Brot, Wasser und Mischwein die Elemente der Taufmesse', *TQ* 113 (1932), 11–34. The same conclusion was reached rather later, and apparently independently, by L. W. Barnard, *Justin Martyr: His Life and Thought* (Cambridge: Cambridge University Press, 1967), 177–9.

at least sufficient reason to be circumspect about using Justin's account as positive evidence of the use of wine.[31]

Elsewhere Justin exhibits the same sort of strong opposition to sacrifice already noted in other cases of ascetic meal practice:

But the angels . . . were captivated by love of women, and begat children who are those that are called demons; and besides, they afterwards subdued the human race to themselves, partly by magical writings, and partly by fears and punishments they occasioned, and partly by teaching them to offer sacrifices, and incense, and libations, of which things they stood in need after they were enslaved by lustful passions . . . (*2 Apol.* 5. 3–4)

Justin's use of a protological and demonological explanation is neither original nor unique; what is of interest is the presence here of a connection we will often find made between the origins and purpose of sacrifice and that of meat-eating, not only in Christian but also in other circles.[32] In this particular case there is possibly a link with the generation by the 'sons of God' of the 'giants' of Gen. 6: 1–4; this story is itself set in a time before meat-eating is sanctioned in the primordial narrative, and a 'fall into meat-eating' is perhaps envisaged. The apparent criticism of sacrificial meat and of wine is what we might already expect in connection with a eucharistic practice that avoided wine in the cup.

Although Justin's (other) liturgical evidence has usually been applied to the reconstruction of eucharistic meals in Rome generally, it has been pointed out that this may be somewhat misleading.[33] Rome was the *cosmopolis*; it contained communities of many different ethnic groups, not least Syrians such as Justin himself, who maintained important aspects of their culture.[34] Justin's *Acta*, the account of his trial and martyrdom, suggests that while his eucharistic community might not have been exclusively Syrian, it was at least Eastern in membership (4. 7–8),[35] and

---

[31] See esp. Harnack, 'Brod und Wasser', 142–3. The tendency for Protestant scholars to seek a primitive Christianity characterized by freedom and charismatic leadership, later choked by a legalism supposedly characteristic of Judaism and Roman Catholicism, was perhaps an incentive to consider evidence such as this more seriously, but also involved what now seem to be serious distortions. See Burtchaell, *From Synagogue to Church*, on the history of this tendency and its application to the area of early Christian leadership and offices.

[32] See esp. on the Pseudo-Clementines in the next chapter; cf. Porphyry, *De Abst.* 2. 36 and Iamblichus, *De Mysteriis*, 14. 5.

[33] Hamman, 'Pour une lecture concrète des textes', 285–92.

[34] Juvenal, *Sat.* 6. 32: 'iam pridem Syrus in Tiberim defluxit Orontes . . .'

[35] Euelpistos' parents were Cappadocian, and Hierax was from Iconium in Phrygia. References are to the Short Recension, 'A' in *Acts of the Christian Martyrs*, 42–7.

that he was acquainted only with the practice of this one assembly (3. 3). Since he seems to have been baptized in Ephesus, his witness may refer to a community related to Ephesus, to Asia generally, or at least to the East. This question of provenance becomes more significant as we proceed to see just how widespread similar water practices are in Syria and Asia.

In the end it is difficult or impossible to reach a firm conclusion as to Justin's possible witness to the bread-and-water tradition from this material alone. The evidence of his successor Tatian may help tip the scales of probability in the more radical direction.

TATIAN AND FRIENDS

With Justin's associate Tatian we are on firmer textual ground, at least. Tatian left only the *Oratio ad Graecos* and some fragments, notably of the Gospel harmony or *Diatessaron* which had great popularity even where its author's reputation was not so well received. By itself the *Oratio* might not lead us to think that Tatian was more than an advocate of self-control in diet as well as otherwise, but there is one passage which suggests opposition to meat-eating: 'You sacrifice animals in order to eat meat and you buy men to provide human slaughter for the soul, feeding it with bloodshed of the most impious kind' (*Orat.* 23).[36] As we might have expected, sacrifice and meat-eating are closely linked and equally to be abhorred.

It is in others' reports of Tatian that his ascetic regime becomes clearer. Irenaeus links Tatian with the Encratites, saying that these ascetic Christians could in turn be traced back to Marcion and Saturninus, and that some of them did not eat meat (*Adv. Haer.* 1. 28. 1).[37] Tertullian is an early witness to Tatian's prohibition of meat and wine (*De Ieiun.* 15. 1).[38] Hippolytus reproduced the concerns of Irenaeus without adding anything (*Ref.* 8. 9). Clement of Alexandria had more specific knowledge of Tatian's writings, but makes no mention of dietary issues.[39] His own asceticism may have made Clement wary of

---

[36] Θύετε ζῷα διὰ τὴν κρεωφαγίαν καὶ ἀνθρώπους ὠνεῖσθε τῇ ψυχῇ τὴν ἀνθρωποσφαγίαν (sic) παρεχόμενοι . . .

[37] See further below on Saturninus.

[38] He includes Tatian in a list (with Marcion and some Neo-Pythagoreans) of those whose radical exclusions indicate the reasonableness of Montanist fasts and xerophagies, and the context suggests that meat and wine are at issue (cf. *De Ieiun.* 15. 3).

[39] He attacks (*Strom.* 3. 12. 81) Tatian's treatment of marriage in a lost work, *Perfection*

criticizing those who were more self-disciplining than members of his own audience. Jerome mentions that Tatian excludes some God-given foods (*Adv. Jov.* 1. 3).

Epiphanius, Jerome, and Theodoret all report that Tatian's severe asceticism included the exclusion of wine. Jerome actually describes Tatian as 'head [or first] of the Encratites', but only to identify him (*Comm. in Amos*, 1. 2. 11–12). Jerome not only refers to a practice of refusing wine, but specifically says that Tatian based his case on Amos 2: 13, apparently responding to a polemical exegesis of that verse directed against Christians who did use wine.[40] Since Tatian was the author of many exegetical works, it is at least possible that Jerome is not merely abstracting Tatian's position from vague knowledge of Encratite practice, but was acquainted with the argument at first hand from Tatian's writings. This passage may suggest adaptation of the Nazirite tradition.[41] It may also indicate that Tatian regarded those Christians who used wine as the innovators, rather than that he himself took a stance that parted from the norm known to him previously. Epiphanius (*Pan.* 46. 1–4) and Theodoret (*Haer. Fab.* 1. 20) add little to the specifics of Tatian's exclusions, apparently repeating the digests of Irenaeus and Hippolytus, but both include the practice of using water in the eucharist in their accounts of his heresy.

The *Diatessaron*, Tatian's harmony of the Gospels, is also a witness to his views on these matters, although the text is often hard to establish, given a complex tradition-history.[42] Ancient commentators are clear that Tatian, like the *Gospel of the Ebionites*, understood John the Baptist to be a vegetarian. It seems that according to the *Diatessaron* John ate 'milk and honey' rather than locusts and honey.[43] Tatian's opposition to marriage was well known, and the version of the saying regarding marriage in the kingdom of God (Luke 20: 27–40) was extended to exclude wedding-feasts; the implication may be understood to extend to the embarrass-

---

According to the Saviour. It has been suggested that Clement's reference to an 'Assyrian' teacher may indicate he sat at Tatian's feet. Clement's own clear preference for an ascetic approach to eating may have blunted any potential attack; see Grimm, *From Feasting to Fasting*, 90–113.

[40] 'De hoc loco haeresim suam Tatianus, Encratitarum princeps, struere nititur, vinum asserens non bibendum . . .'

[41] The Nazirite tradition is of course evident in the depiction of John the Baptist in the Gospels, and in that of James the Just discussed earlier.

[42] In general see William L. Peterson, 'Tatian's *Diatessaron*', in H. Koester, *Ancient Christian Gospels: Their History and Development* (London: SCM, 1990), 403–30.

[43] Brock, 'The Baptist's Diet in Syriac Sources', 115–16.

ingly well-provisioned wedding-feast at Cana.[44] There are also instances where references to wine were removed. Jesus' self-identification as the 'true vine' became 'I am the tree of the fruit of truth'.[45]

The treatment of the Last Supper is particularly revealing. In the canonical texts of the Gospels, the vow of abstinence from the fruit of the vine which Jesus makes after the cup (Mark 14: 25, Matt. 26: 29, Luke 22: 18 (after the first of two cups in this case)) includes (in the cases of Mark and Matthew) the implication that there would be a renewal of such drinking in the Kingdom, but Tatian's curtailed reading excludes the expectation of this backsliding.[46] Further, he transfers the exhortation to 'do this in remembrance of me' to a later position, after the vow of renunciation, thus apparently making the ascetic lifestyle, rather than the liturgical ritual alone, the authentic *anamnesis* of the saviour.[47]

It is worth considering this information about Tatian's attitudes to food and drink in conjunction with what little we know about him and his theology generally. The heresiologists from Irenaeus onwards were keen to pursue a 'before and after' approach to Tatian. It was known that he had been a companion of Justin, and they argued that he fell away from orthodoxy after the death of this more sound figure. The *Oratio ad Graecos*, Tatian's only fully extant work, does suggest a Christianity which can easily be reconciled with the sort of uncompromising asceticism associated with the Encratites. It also seems likely that his theology had tendencies which are comparable with Valentinianism.[48] But the idea that these supposedly heretical tendencies necessarily arose from external influences, or were formed only subsequent to Justin's death, can be questioned.[49]

Other studies have questioned the plausibility of Tatian's 'fall' in terms of the more clearly theological issues such as his quasi-Valentinian syzygies or salvific pairings.[50] Regarding ascetic practice and food in

---

[44] Vööbus, *History of Asceticism in the Syrian Orient*, 43.

[45] This is from the Persian version; see *Diatessaron Persiano*, ed. G. Messina, Biblica et Orientalia, 14 (Rome: Pontifical Biblical Institute, 1951), 322.

[46] Vööbus, *History of Asceticism in the Syrian Orient*, 41–2, and esp. n. 50.

[47] The testimony of the Arabic version; *Diatessaron de Tatian*, ed. A.-S. Marmadji (Beirut: Imprimerie catholique, 1935), 430–1.

[48] Robert M. Grant, 'The Heresy of Tatian', *JTS* NS 7 (1956), 246–8; L. W. Barnard, 'The Heresy of Tatian—Once Again', *JEH* 19 (1968), 1–10. These indications could also help explain the appearance of the bread-and-water tradition in Theodotus.

[49] See Vööbus, *History of Asceticism in the Syrian Orient*, 30–9.

[50] Robert M. Grant, 'The Date of Tatian's Oration', *HTR* 46 (1953), 99–101, and 'The Heresy of Tatian', 246–8; G. W. Clarke, 'The Date of the Oration of Tatian', *HTR* 57 (1964), 161–88; Barnard, 'The Heresy of Tatian—Once Again', 1–10.

particular, the question is similar: whether or not Tatian's probable participation in this bread-and-water tradition of eucharistic meals is really a sign of an innovation or digression in comparison to the tradition represented by Justin. It should already be apparent that the answer is not a clear 'yes'. If Justin's eucharistic meal used water in the cup, then both Justin and Tatian may represent a Syrian tendency to prefer water to wine in this context and in others.

Another case which deserves mention is that of the Syrian Saturninus (or Saturnilus), who may have preceded Justin and Tatian. We know nothing of his specifically eucharistic meal practice, but he was known to have preached and even to have popularized abstinence from meat (Irenaeus, *Adv. Haer.* I. 24). If it seems bold to infer that he rejected wine as well, it is reasonable to take Saturninus as one more instance confirming a general Syrian asceticism which was likely to have had an impact on eucharistic as well as other meal elements.[51]

Somewhat later, probably at the end of the second century or early in the third, one Severus also taught the same kind of asceticism, specifically including abstinence from wine (Epiphanius, *Pan.* 45. I. 6–8; cf. Eusebius, *HE* 4. 29, Theodoret, *Haer. Fab.* I. 21). Eusebius and Epiphanius make vague or even misleading statements about the supposed family tree of his heresy, connecting him with Tatian and with Marcion's disciple Apelles respectively, yet Eusebius' witness to his apparent rejection of Paul's writings seems to give Severus some affinity with Jewish Christianity rather than with those figures. In this case Epiphanius provides a report of a protological myth sustaining avoidance of wine:

Thus spinning his fables to support their nonsense, [he wishes] to make the serpentine roundness of the vine significant, saying that on account of its twistedness the plant resembles a snake . . . And the grapes of the vine are like drops of poison because of their roundness . . . The wine on this theory darkens the human mind and sometimes leads to lustful desires, sometimes stirs to frenzy, or again arouses anger because the body is made foolish from the power of wine and the poison of the dragon just mentioned. Thus these people abstain from wine completely. (*Pan.* 45. I. 6–8)

This, if accurate, appropriates the same sort of traditional moral objections to wine found in Tatian, but couches these in a mythological

---

[51] The indications that he had a speculative cosmology and soteriology might also suggest more specific links with Tatian.

frame with demonic overtones. Epiphanius also believes that the Severians accepted apocryphal books, which is plausible.[52]

Whatever the judgement on Justin's case in itself then, Jewish–Christian and other ascetic meal models in the same region suggest that there were some traditions with affinity to water-drinking in Syria in the second century. Tatian's clearer opposition to wine also makes it more likely that Harnack's proposal regarding Justin's water-drinking was right. Given the recent studies that have questioned the radical nature of any specifically theological break with Justin on Tatian's part, we could reasonably work on the basis that the use of water in the cup was normal for Justin and for Tatian, as well as for Severus (and Saturninus?), rather than presuming that Tatian only acquired a taste for water when he returned to the East and broke from orthodoxy. Granted a certain circularity in this argument, the broader context of Syrian asceticism can also be used to support these conclusions. In fact it would be somewhat remarkable if a Syrian Christian of the early centuries did not practice and advocate an asceticism more radical than that generally found in the Western Church. Peter Brown suggests that 'while Tatian's break with the Church of Rome, in 172, was long remembered in the Graeco-Roman Mediterranean, he merged back without remark into a Syrian Christianity that may always have been as radical as himself'.[53]

Thus even if Tatian's asceticism were more uncompromising than Justin's, there is no need to posit a radical change in Tatian's position after Justin's death, at least in regard to the eucharistic meal. But the presence of the same pattern in Ebionite circles as well as in the practice of Tatian and perhaps Justin too, should make us wary of quick resort to the traditional 'ascetic modification' explanation for the use of water in the cup.

While these practices certainly deserve to be called ascetic in the sense used here, we must resist the temptation to characterize all Christian asceticism as individualistic or moralizing. This evidence suggests rather a community-based asceticism, where non-consumption serves as self-definition, not for the individual only but for the individual as part of the Christian community. Justin's and Tatian's concerns are less a matter of 'Is this food good for me?' than 'Whose side am I on?'

A second ascetic problem or fallacy to be resisted is that which takes

---

[52] See Ch. 5 below.
[53] *The Body and Society*, 87; see also Vööbus, *History of Asceticism in the Syrian Orient*, 37.

ascetic (or specifically Encratite) tendencies as a later imposition on earlier forms of Christian life. If recent study of early Syrian Christianity makes this view less tenable, the implications of that work have nevertheless not been fully digested. The presence of a similar pattern of ritual and general diet in two somewhat different Christian groups or trajectories already discussed (the Jewish–Christian and the Syrian tradition of Justin and Tatian) need not mean that they adopted similar emendations to a normative meal tradition of using bread and wine; rather it may suggest that both inherited a primitive tradition along these lines. Further examples will have to be discussed before a definitive answer to this question of origins can be given.

ENCRATITES, *HYDROPARASTATAI*, AND APOSTOLICS

Irenaeus describes the group known as 'Encratites' not as water-drinkers, but as avoiders of meat; in the process of making this point, however, he undercuts his own attempts to lump such ascetic Christians together. Only 'some' of the Encratites do not eat meat (*Adv. Haer.* 1. 28. 1). We are apparently dealing with more than one group, and must ask whether all the people he criticizes for this sort of diet were really self-designated Encratites, even though it is plausible that a group or groups should describe themselves as 'ascetics' or 'self-controlled'.

Clement of Alexandria only mentions Encratites who refused wine, pausing in his generally pro-abstinence discussion (*Paed.* 2. 2) to note that contrary to the Encratite opinion, Jesus did indeed partake of the fruit of the vine, if in strict moderation (2. 2. 32; cf. *Strom.* 1. 19. 96). It is Hippolytus who brings these elements together: for him the Encratites reject both meat and wine, as well as marriage; and he draws a scornful but very interesting conclusion, i.e. that they are not really Christians, but rather Cynics (*Ref.* 8. 20). This not only confirms the picture of Cynic dietary ascesis suggested above, but has some value for interpreting the practice of the Encratites. Granted that it is an exercise in labelling rather than a careful or accurate designation, Hippolytus provides a category which serves to indicate the position of the Encratites relative to the mainstream of society. By refusing to conform to normal standards of behaviour regarding diet and sex, these Christians made themselves appear lawless and subversive.[54]

---

[54] Cf. his claim that the Elkesaites are 'Pythagoreans' (*Ref.* 9. 14. 1).

Later, Epiphanius and Theodoret both draw close links between Tatian and the Encratites, but both also suggest reasons to recognize further divisions between the water-drinkers rather than to lump them all together. Theodoret says clearly that there are two groups who can be considered together as offspring of Tatian's example, the Encratites who use no wine, and the *Hydroparastatai* of whom he says simply that they 'offer' water, i.e. he understands them to use it for the cup of the eucharistic meal (*Haer. Fab.* 1. 20). This suggests that, later at least, there were some for whom the prohibition was only for ritual purposes. Basil of Caesarea also treats the *Hydroparastatai* as a schismatic rather than heretical group (*Ep.* 188, can. 1), apparently limiting the extent of their perceived deviance.[55] They seem to be a relatively late manifestation of the bread-and-water usage, and there are other earlier examples which we need to consider first.[56]

Epiphanius also says that the groups quibble and are somewhat different from the master, Tatian (47. 1. 1). Epiphanius associates these 'quibbling' Encratites with the apocryphal *Acts* (47. 1. 5). As in the case of the Ebionites, it seems that Epiphanius used the similarities between a body of literature and the earlier heresiological descriptions to match these (admittedly similar) opponents of marriage. While it is not impossible that he was right, it still seems preferable to set the extended literary source aside for the present, and to deal with it as a separate manifestation of the bread-and-water tradition. Epiphanius reports that the Encratites abound in his time in Pisidia and other parts of Asia Minor: 'burnt Phrygia', Isauria, Pamphylia, Cilicia, and Galatia (47. 1. 2–3). They are also present in Rome and in Syrian Antioch. This continues the evidence for the bread-and-water tradition as something of an Eastern, and specifically Syrian and Asian, phenomenon.

There are also the obscure Apostolics or 'Renouncers', to whom Epiphanius applies the same set of attributes (*Pan.* 61); they are linked to Tatian, the Encratites, the 'Tatianites', and the Cathars.[57] These are rigorists on marriage, use the *Acts of Andrew* and the *Acts of Thomas*, and 'their rites too are different'. Since the immediate context is discussion of groups such as the Encratites, we should probably interpret this as 'their

---

[55] Basil does, admittedly, treat the Encratites and the Cathari in the same fashion; but his comments are not the most important source of our information on the earlier Encratites.

[56] See Ch. 6 below.

[57] The 'Tatianites' as a group are not discussed in the text proper, but in the summaries (*Pan.* Prol. 4. 4, Anac. 46) they stand where the discussion of Tatian himself (cf. *Pan.* 46) ought to be, and are mentioned in the discussion of the 'Apostolics' (*Pan.* 61. 1. 2).

rites differ [from ours] also [along the same lines]' and assume that they were water-drinkers.[58] We know nothing else of them.

While there may be dangers in taking Epiphanius as the main evidence for a broad picture of the bread-and-water tradition, his catalogue of water-drinking Christians certainly adds to the sense that the merely geographical connections are the strongest among these groups apart from their actual asceticism. By his time there are both thoroughgoing ascetics and also those concerned only with ritual use; there is a variety of names, but a tendency for the regions of Syria and Asia to be the home or origin of these groups. So far at least this fits with the other evidence as well. Yet these cases do not yet span the theological diversity of the bread-and-water tradition.

VALENTINIAN BREAD AND WATER: THEODOTUS

The obscure *Excerpta ex Theodoto* by Clement of Alexandria on the theology and practice of the Valentinian Gnostic Theodotus may also indicate a sacramental practice in keeping with the emphasis on bread and avoidance of wine. We have already noted the relevant passage in discussing the use of oil: 'Both the bread and the oil are sanctified by the power of the name of God . . .' (ibid. 82. 1). It goes on to say: 'Thus also water, which becomes both that which is exorcized and also baptism . . .' (82. 2).[59]

This arrangement is somewhat curious, but in any case the absence of reference to wine in what is clearly a description or analysis of the eucharistic meal, probably held in conjunction with baptism, is in no doubt. The mention of oil along with bread at this point gives pause for thought, and as has been argued already, may possibly be taken to mean that the oil is associated with the bread as a food, rather than being used for anointing. Similarly there is some doubt with regard to the water: is it all and always for baptism, or could it be for ritual drinking? The distinction between 'that which is exorcized' and 'baptism' seems to suggest that two different uses are described. While it is true that a similar duality of negative and positive, exorcized and renewed, is apparent elsewhere in the *Excerpta*,[60] in this case there is no suggestion of a temporal distinction, such

---

[58] Thus also Klijn and Reinink, *Patristic Evidence for Jewish-Christian Sects*, 36.
[59] Οὕτως καὶ τὸ ὕδωρ, καὶ ἐξορκιζόμενον καὶ βάπτισμα γινόμενον . . .
[60] See Clement, *Excerpta*, 76–7; Sagnard, *Extraits de Théodote*, 229–39.

as 'first exorcism, then baptismal regeneration'; rather, the extract implies that there are two different uses of water, in both of which the action of the Spirit is comparable. In each case, the water 'not only loses what is inferior, but also acquires holiness' (ibid. 82. 2).[61] So it is possible or likely that Theodotus used water rather than wine in a eucharistic cup, and even clearer that wine did not come into the picture in any event. The question is not whether wine was used but whether a cup featured at all; there are other cases where the cup seems to have a secondary importance or simply does not appear at a eucharistic meal.[62]

This would all be more significant if we had a clearer context in which to place the evidence. We know only that Theodotus was active during or before Clement's time, and it seems reasonable to accept both that he was a successor of Valentinus and that, as the extended title of the *Excerpta* indicates, he was one of the 'Eastern' school of the Valentinians. Although this division between Eastern and Italian Valentinian Gnostics has mainly been seen as a matter of their Christology, it is by no means surprising, given the geographical tendency already identified in the bread-and-water tradition, that this ritual meal pattern is associated with someone who was Eastern. In fact this affinity with Syrian and Asian eucharistic meals may be a hitherto unnoticed indication of Theodotus' background, if the pattern can continue to be seen as geographically focused. Of course the association of the ritual use of bread and water in a eucharistic meal with Valentinian Gnosticism, or with some part thereof, expands the theological borders of the tradition significantly.

There are other possible connections between Valentinian Gnosticism and the bread-and-water tradition, notably in the *Acts of John* (and perhaps the *Acts of Thomas*), which makes some use of Gnostic imagery as well as depicting eucharists involving water rather than wine or no cup at all; these will be discussed further.[63] Yet there is no reason to think that we are dealing with a peculiar Valentinian practice here. It seems more likely that Theodotus presents what aims to be a deeper under-standing of practices known to an outer, as well as an inner, circle, in the manner of the *Letter of Ptolemy to Flora*.[64] The practice Theodotus

---

[61] ... οὐ μόνον χωρ⟨ίζ⟩ει τὸ χεῖρον, ἀλλὰ καὶ ἁγιασμὸν προσλαμβάνει.

[62] See discussion in the next chapter on the Pseudo-Clementines.

[63] Oil is also prominent in the *Acts of Thomas* particularly; this could add to the case for a baptismal use of oil being alluded to here, and for the possible connection between Theodotus and the Christianity of these *Acts*.

[64] This difference of interpretation rather than practice is the tone, at least, of Ptolemy's *Letter*, and is more or less explicitly stated by Irenaeus (*Adv. Haer.* 1 Prol. 2). On other connections between Gnosticism and the asceticism characteristic of the East, see Vööbus, *History of Asceticism in the Syrian Orient*, 54–61.

describes may well be typical of the wider Christian communities known to him, and might arguably tell us as much about the general prevalence of such a ritual pattern in Syria or Asia as about any specifically Valentinian or Gnostic ritual traditions.

MARCION, TERTULLIAN, AND MONTANISM

Tertullian and Marcion

Explicit suggestions that Marcion refused the use of wine in the cup of a eucharistic meal are late: Epiphanius (*Pan.* 42. 3. 3) is again the crucial witness. Rejection of wine may also, however, be adduced from Tertullian's attack on Marcion, in which he criticizes the hypocrisy of the use of created elements by one who spurns the creator God (*Adv. Marc.* 1. 14. 3).[65] Tertullian gives a series of ritual practices which seem to follow the procedure of a baptism: Marcion does not disdain to use water for the washing, oil for anointing, or milk and honey as a food for the newly baptized, nor does he refuse to use bread for the ritual meal; yet there is no mention of wine.[66]

Under the circumstances, it might seem odd for Tertullian to miss the opportunity to add wine to the list of Marcion's sacramental hypocrisies. In fact the ascetic and acerbic African, already influenced by Montanist rigorism at this point, might have been expected to equate the use of wine with its abuse, and to take this as a sign of debauchery. The silence is significant; it probably means that Tertullian did not believe that Marcion's eucharistic meal associated with a baptism would have made use of wine.

Even then, Tertullian's silence demands further reflection on his own practice, as well as that of Marcion. The *Apology* (39) makes it clear that moderation, rather than abstinence, was the norm at Christian meal assemblies. If Tertullian was still used to wine at the meal, why not

---

[65] On the date of *Adversus Marcionem* see T. D. Barnes, *Tertullian*, 37, 255–6, 326–7; Barnes eventually accepts G. Quispel's dating of Book I–III, as now extant, to 208.

[66] 'Sed ille quidem usque nunc nec aquam reprobavit creatoris, qua suos abluit, nec oleum, quo suos ungit, nec mellis et lactis societatem, qua suos infantat, nec panem, quo ipsum corpus suum repraesentat, etiam in sacramentis propriis egens mendicitatibus creatoris.' Tertullian also talks of the wine of the cup of the Last Supper (*Adv. Marc.* 4. 40) without indicating much of his own or Marcion's views on the eucharist. In that case he debates the reality of Jesus' flesh and blood and argues the importance of wine (of that past event) as a type of Jesus' (actual) blood, rather than in terms of ongoing eucharistic symbolism. This passage might imply that Marcion avoided the imagery of body and blood in the eucharist.

attack Marcion for innovation, i.e. the omission of wine, at this point as at others? In his later *De Ieiunio contra Psychicos* the now fully Montanist Tertullian clearly prefers abstinence to moderation. The 'psychics', i.e. the 'average' Christians, charge that the followers of the New Prophecy impose fasts and xerophagies (periods without drink) which amount to Judaizing or 'Galaticizing' behaviour (ibid. 1. 4; 14. 1). And while Tertullian defends these disciplines as reasonable by comparison to those of other groups (led by Tatian, Marcion, and a contemporary Pythagorean, ibid. 15. 1) he nowhere confronts the charge that the Montanists will not even eat anything with a wine-like character (cf. 1. 4).[67] Rather he goes on the offensive, citing the prohibitions of the Hebrew Bible involving prophets, priests, and the Nazirite vow, and using the same passage from Amos which Jerome linked to Tatian, again with a strikingly contemporary application to the foibles of the psychics: 'Thus too in recent times he upbraids Israel: "And you used to give my holy ones wine to drink"' (ibid. 9. 8).[68] The unspecified prohibitions for which Marcion is criticized (15. 1) may also add to the likelihood of a refusal of wine.

However much his views may have hardened as time went on, it is not a difficult thing to read the basic sentiments of this teetotal Tertullian back into the already-Montanizing *Against Marcion*. Thus by the time he was writing against Marcion, Tertullian was taking a dimmer view even of moderate drinking than he had done in the *Apology*. He would not have missed the opportunity to accuse Marcion of drunkenness, and his silence can only really be explained thus: he thought that on this point Marcion was on the higher ground. Tertullian allows us (bearing in mind the supporting evidence from elsewhere) to suggest both that Marcion did not use wine in the meals of his community, and that the New Prophecy of Montanus was likewise opposed to drinking wine. He also implies that there may have been Christians of the more accommodating eucharistic tradition for whom the use of wine was embarrassing.[69]

A certain suspicion must be employed before taking Tertullian's picture of Marcion's baptismal liturgy as literally accurate. Nevertheless it is hardly likely that Tertullian would walk into so large a trap as to attack Marcionite baptism without any idea of what took place. Either Tertullian

---

[67] 'nec quid vinositatis vel edamus vel potemus' (1. 4).

[68] 'Sic et Israeli proximo exprobat et potum: "Dabatis sanctificatis meis vinum."'

[69] Despite this Tertullian seems to regard wine as an appropriate symbol of the blood of Jesus in a *literary* form; at *Adv. Marc.* 4. 40 he links Jesus' words at the Last Supper to OT texts referring to bread and wine, but makes no comment on liturgical practice as such, merely defending the reality of the incarnation against Marcion.

has some account of Marcionite practice, or he generally regards it as preserving at least the outward appearance of his own Montanizing understanding of orthodoxy. Later witnesses also attest to the similarity between Marcionite and other Christian worship, including Marcionite baptism, which was often regarded as legitimate by the orthodox.[70] Tertullian also links Marcion with the solid side of the bread-and-water tradition, seeking to draw a favourable contrast between the Montanist fasts, scheduled only for particular days in the year, and the complete prohibitions observed by Marcion and others with regard to *cibum*; Marcionites held that meat was to be avoided altogether (*De Ieiun.* 15). It is also interesting that Tertullian believes that Marcion regarded fish more highly (*Adv. Marc.* 1. 14. 4; cf. Eznik, *De Deo*, 407), another indication of opposition to the cuisine of sacrifice.[71]

Epiphanius' direct but late statement that Marcion used water in the sacramental cup has value as corroborating evidence. It does not seem to be dependent on Tertullian's non-argument. The only reason we might cite confusion or conflation here is the fact that Irenaeus, who is silent on Marcion's attitude to wine, had earlier traced a link between Marcion and other water-drinkers, the Encratites (*Adv. Haer.* 1. 28); yet this is one genetic link that Epiphanius himself does not make. Marcion can reasonably be seen as having maintained a bread-and-water tradition for the eucharistic meal, as well as a radical ascetic stance on the use of meat and wine generally.[72]

It is worth noting that the tendency to see Marcion's asceticism as derived from his dualistic world-view is hardly supported by the evidence. On the contrary, this use of the created elements was obvious and unapologetic, even if puzzling to his ancient opponent. In hindsight it seems probable that such sacramental practice did go back to Marcion, and was traditional to this Asian Christian rather than innovative. Further, his refusal of wine and meat may have had less to do with their origins from the Creator God than with their use in worship of the pagan gods.[73] As I suggested earlier, there may be room for reflection on

[70] See Cyprian, *Ep.* 73. 4; Augustine, *De Bapt. contra Don.* 3. 15; Harnack, *Marcion: The Gospel of the Alien God*, 93–4; Hoffmann, *Marcion: On the Restitution of Christianity*, 18–21.
[71] See Vööbus, *History of Asceticism in the Syrian Orient*, 51.
[72] The 5th-cent. Eznik knew some Marcionites who used wine, but was surprised by this (*De Deo*, 409).
[73] Although discussions often emphasize the link between Marcion's hatred of creation and his asceticism (Harnack, *Marcion: The Gospel of the Alien God*, 93–7; Vööbus, *History of Asceticism in the Syrian Orient*, 93–7), it seems clear that in terms of the ritual meal (and perhaps in other terms as well) he was maintaining tradition rather than innovating.

how this meal pattern reflects Marcion's attitude to cosmic order as much or more than his problems with material substance.

Montanism

Back, then, to Montanism. Origen is a further early witness to Montanist refusal of wine; he cites a composite prophecy with biblical echoes, specifically of the Nazirite vow again as the basis for abstinence (*In Epistolam ad Titum* (fr.)).[74] Origen also refers to the general tendency of prescribing abstention from foods, probably with reference to Montanism, in *De Principiis* (2. 7. 3). Hippolytus knows not only of Montanist xerophagy of the kind that Tertullian defends, but also of ῥαφανοφαγία—'cabbage-eating'—as a formidable culinary discipline in the movement (*Ref.* 8. 19). Epiphanius also discusses the Montanists, but in now-familiar fashion seems content to combine what he knows about the designations and practices of groups known as Cataphrygians, Quintillians, Pepuzians, Priscillians, and Artotyrites, some of whom may be equivalent to one another, in order to construct a *stemma* of heresy (*Pan.* 48–9). The Artotyritai or 'bread-and-cheesers' already discussed are probably also part of this broad picture of Montanist variety.

An accusation of ritual murder of infants and cannibalism appears in writings by orthodox opponents of Montanism.[75] Some of these later authors also raise less bizarre qualms about Montanist ritual. Filastrius mentions both the infanticide and a 'cynic mystery' (*Div. Haer. Lib.* 49),[76] very probably a reference to a bread-and-water meal.[77] Theodoret (*Haer. Fab.* 3. 2) is more circumspect, saying merely that 'certain people complain somewhat about their mysteries; they do not agree, but rather call the charge a misrepresentation'.[78] This might refer to the allegation

[74] 'Non accedas ad me quoniam mundus sum: non enim accepi uxorem, nec est sepulchrum patens guttur meum, sed sum Nazareus Dei, non bibens vinum, sicut illi.' This fragment is preserved in the *Apologia Pro Origene* of Pamphilus (*PG* 14. 1306).

[75] The accusation against Montanism also appears in authors dependent on Epiphanius, Filastrius of Brescia (*Div. Haer. Lib.* 49), Augustine (*De Haer.* 26), Jerome (*Ep.* 41. 4), and 'Praedestinatus' (*Praed. Haer.* 1. 26). If there is a real connection with meals here at all, it might be in abstinence from meat, the sign of integration and sociability. Earlier objects of such accusations, both Christian and Pythagorean, also rejected meat, which suggests an ironic but significant link between abstinence from all meat and being labelled as cannibals. See McGowan, 'Eating People', 423–5, 437–8.   [76] 'Mysterium cynicon'.

[77] Cf. Hippolytus' judgement on the Encratites, *Ref.* 8. 20: after describing their lifestyle of water-drinking and refusing animal food he concludes that 'such people are judged Cynics, rather than Christians'.

[78] ... περὶ δὲ τῶν μυστηρίων τινὲς μὲν θρυλλοῦσί τινα, ἐκεῖνοι δὲ οὐ συνομολογοῦσιν, ἀλλὰ συκοφαντίαν τὴν κατηγορίαν καλοῦσι.

of ritual murder, but could conceivably reflect other objections raised with regard to ritual meals, such as the 'Cynic' accusation of using bread and water. The Montanists seem to have had a basis for responding to criticism, but we do not know what Theodoret had in mind. The historical *plat principal* of Montanist deviance in meals seems therefore, despite the accusations of bizarre and murderous ritual, to have been little more than bread and water, with some cabbage on the side.

It is not clear that these restrictions were more than seasonal for Montanist Christians. Although our fullest source, Tertullian, plainly regards the exclusion of meat and wine as altogether beneficial and appropriate, he is also keen to point out that the Montanist fasts and exclusions are temporary. This is supported by other evidence of controversies over the length and number of fasts (Hippolytus, *Ref.* 8. 19; 10. 25–6).[79] Montanist meals are therefore a different sort of witness to the bread-and-water tradition. Abstinence from particular food and drink is used as a marker of important times, as well as being seen as generally beneficial for spiritual (and perhaps physical) health.

This need not mean that the origins of Montanist meal practice are vastly different from the other examples of bread-and-water eucharists. Although Tertullian seems to be a Christian from the normative bread-and-wine tradition being persuaded to adopt another practice for ascetic reasons, this is not to say that Montanus, Priscilla, and Maximilla had removed wine from the pattern known to them. Given the other examples of bread-and-water use under discussion, and especially the possible geographical connections that are already apparent (Syria-Palestine and parts of Asia predominate), this may be one aspect in which Montanism reflects ancient Phrygian Christian practice. Yet the apparent shift in the use of the bread-and-water tradition, from absolute prohibition and marker of community to marker of times, is a further warning for us not to be completely consumed by the question of links with other instances of the practice. Having come about under one set of circumstances, a meal practice could take on a somewhat different meaning in another.

[79] Claude Aziza, *Tertullien et le judaisme* (Paris: Belles Lettres, 1977), 183–6, and Grimm, *From Feasting to Fasting*, 119–39, both suggest specific Jewish influences on Tertullian, the former in terms of idol-offerings (from *m. 'Abod. Zar.*) and the latter regarding fasting and otherwise. While Barnes (*Tertullian*, 331) reasonably criticizes Aziza for not distinguishing between similarities and direct influences, Grimm may be right to point to the similarity in fasting motivation and practice between *Apol.* 40. 14 and *m. Ta'an.* 1: 4–7 etc. The possibility of ongoing influence does not, however, amount to an explanation of the significance of these practices for Christians in Tertullian's Africa, let alone in Montanism generally.

So then, by the time we include Marcionites and Montanists, the sense of a theological incoherence and an equal-but-opposite geographical focus in the bread-and-water tradition becomes all the more strong. With Marcionites on the one hand and Ebionites on the other we have hyper-Pauline and anti-Pauline Christianity linked by ritual practice and the association of most of the evidence with Syria and Asia.

VIENNE AND LYONS

The letter of the churches of Vienne and Lyons to those of Asia and Phrygia preserved in the *Ecclesiastical History* of Eusebius describes the diet of one Alcibiades, an imprisoned Christian, as bread and water alone; in this case the attitude of the author is disapproving yet not absolutely condemnatory:

> For a certain Alcibiades, who was one of them, led a very austere life, partaking of nothing whatever but bread and water. When he endeavored to continue this same sort of life in prison, it was revealed to Attalus after his first conflict in the amphitheater that Alcibiades was not doing well in refusing the creatures of God and placing a stumbling-block before others. And Alcibiades obeyed, and partook of all things without restraint, giving thanks to God. For they were not deprived of the grace of God, but the Holy Ghost was their counselor. (*HE* 5. 3. 2–3)

The rejection by Attalus of the bread-and-water tradition fits with the position of Irenaeus, bishop of Lyons not long after the martyrdoms and the letter (177). We can assume that most local Christians were used to wine in the cup of a eucharistic meal, and were perhaps even not otherwise notably ascetic, since Attalus and their companions apparently had some variety and perhaps even abundance of food.[80] On the other hand, the prominence of issues of sacrifice, and hence of meat, in persecution is obvious.

The facts of Alcibiades' presence in Gaul and his dissent from this accommodating approach to food are interesting; so too is the fact that his practice is highlighted in a letter to churches where it was probably more common. Eusebius lifts this passage out of its context; it was apparently somewhat separate from the martyrdom account he also reproduces, but still part of the same letter. Perhaps the Gallic Christians were offering encouragement and advice to their Asian counterparts on a

---

[80] Cf. Lucian, *De Morte Pereg.* 12–13, and Tertullian, *De Ieiun.* 12.

series of issues, as indeed Eusebius goes on to say that they did on the question of Montanism (*HE* 5. 3. 4). The possibility that Montanism is the issue behind this portion of the letter would arise even without Eusebius' arrangement of material. The addressees are in the Montanist heartland; the emphasis on the action of the Spirit through Attalus, bestowing personal revelations, is very strong; and as we have seen, Alcibiades' asceticism is probably consistent with, if not necessarily derived from, Montanist practice. Were this supposition correct, the critique of Montanism offered by the confessors seems to be based on a somewhat different form of spiritual authority (that of martyrdom) rather than a denial of the possibility of miraculous charismatic activity.

Whether Alcibiades is to be seen as a Montanist or someone influenced by Montanism, or simply as a representative of a fairly common Eastern practice that need not be linked with a particular person or movement, the account of his conversion to a more accommodating diet by Attalus serves to confirm both the relative oddity of such practices in the West before Montanism, and the anxiety about such matters in 'Asia and Phrygia'.

The case of Attalus does not contain any specifically ritual issues, at least not explicitly. Yet it may be assumed that someone who refused to drink wine under any circumstances would have included the eucharistic cup in his asceticism. Further, it should be clear by now that in the cases under discussion, the issues of wine in ritual diet and meat in general diet are very closely linked, and that while these communities or tendencies show great concern about the difference between their diet and that of others, they might well look for continuity rather than contrast between the content of the eucharistic meal and that of other meals.

Elkesaites and Manichees

There are a few points of contact between the testimonies already discussed and the evidence for Elkesaite practice, although there are no especially clear statements about the meal practice of this tradition. Elkesaites are generally understood as a Jewish or Jewish–Christian group who emphasized baptisms and observed the Sabbath and circumcision.[81]

Epiphanius does state that the Elkesaite 'Osseans' rejected sacrifice

---

[81] See further Klijn and Reinink, *Patristic Evidence for Jewish Christian Sects*, 54–67. Origen is cited by Eusebius (*HE* 6. 38) as saying that they rejected Paul.

(*Pan.* 19. 3. 6) but revered water (19. 3. 7), although whether this was only in reference to baptism, a prominent aspect of the group's practice, is unclear. Epiphanius gives a similar picture of another Elkesaite group whom he calls Sampseans; these also reject meat and revere water (*Pan.* 53. 1. 4, 7). These indicators of similarity with the bread-and-water tradition make it worth considering the other, admittedly rather oblique, meal evidence a little further.

Hippolytus discusses the teachings of one Alcibiades from Apamea in Syria who brought to Rome teachings derived from a book transmitted through Elkesai (*Ref.* 9. 13. 1). He gives no clear information about dietary restrictions or ritual meals, but Hippolytus and Epiphanius both give lists of 'witnesses' invoked at Elkesaite baptisms, which lists could conceivably include meal elements within a ritual schema, although the reports simply indicate that these authorities are to be invoked by the one to be baptized. Hippolytus' list (*Ref.* 9. 15. 2) gives the order: heaven, water, holy spirits, angels of prayer, oil, salt, and earth. We could imagine a ritual where some of these powers are invoked more or less verbally or by gesture alone; the use of water and oil could be something like that in orthodox baptism. 'Earth' is obviously problematic.[82] These invocations may be compared with that in the *Contestatio* of the Clementine *Homilies*, already discussed in connection with salt.

Manichaeism is not within the general terms of this discussion, but the links with Elkesaite belief and practice, particularly important since the discovery of the *Cologne Mani Codex* and the likely identification of Mani's background as Elkesaite, make some brief comment desirable.[83] According to the tenth-century *Fihrist* of al-Nadim, Mani's father was converted to the group described in that work as 'Mughtasilah' or 'baptists' (cf. *CMC* 5) who were still known in al-Nadim's time and who practised ablutions and washed their food.[84] His conversion resulted from the experience of hearing a voice that called to him:

---

[82] Epiphanius has different versions of a list (*Pan.* 19. 1. 6 (two); 19. 6. 4; 30. 17. 4). One version has the order salt, water, bread, air, wind, earth, and heaven (19. 6. 4); another salt, water, earth, bread, heaven, air, and wind (19. 1. 6 (a)); still another heaven, earth, salt, water, winds, angels of righteousness, bread, and olive oil (30. 17. 4); and another the same elements and order as Hippolytus (19. 1. 6 (b)).

[83] On Elkesai and the evidence of the Codex, see A. F. J. Klijn, 'Alchasaios et CMC', *Codex Manicaicus Coloniensis: Atti del Simposio Internazionale* (Consenza: Marra Editore, 1986), 141–52. On Mani and Elkesaite influence, Samuel N. C. Lieu, *Manichaeism in the Late Roman Empire and Medieval China*, 2nd edn., WUNT 63 (Tübingen: J. C. B. Mohr (Paul Siebeck), 1992), 33–50.

[84] Ibn al-Nadim, *The Fihrist of al-Nadim: A Tenth-Century Survey of Muslim Culture*, trans. B. Dodge (New York: Columbia University Press, 1970), ii. 811.

'Oh, Futtuq, do not eat meat! Do not drink wine! Do not marry a human being!'[85] Samuel Lieu comments that the lack of an asceticism of this nature in Zoroastrian or pagan Semitic cults suggests a link with Christianity and figures such as Tatian.[86]

The *Cologne Mani Codex* indicates that the 'baptist' sect, which Mani himself also joined, did not eat meat; there may have been other food and drink prohibitions as well (*CMC* 91–4). Mani's further objection to harvesting, in which cutting plants is likened to blood-letting and murder, seems to have cast his co-religionists in the sort of light in which we may imagine they saw other, more conventional, eaters (*CMC* 6).[87]

There is no sign of one specifically sacral meal among these apparent Elkesaites; all eating and various other activities are accompanied by ritual washings (*CMC* 80–1). This evidence is thus rather hard to link with the wider tradition(s) of Christian meals, and indeed the lack of clear evidence of Christian teaching and tradition altogether means that is not wholly surprising, but the generalized concern about all food and meals fits well with the other evidence discussed.

Later Manichaean food practices go in the direction already mentioned, the rejection even of harvesting, resulting in the practices and distinctions familiar to readers of Augustine.[88] Yet the continued interaction between Christianity and Manichaeism seems to have led to some further contact with the bread-and-water tradition. In the fifth century Pope Leo could warn the faithful against the presence of Manichaeans in their midst by describing their practice when coming to the eucharist: although they would grudgingly take the host, they would absolutely refuse to drink from the cup.[89] It seems unlikely that this avoidance stems from specifically Manichaean objections to food and drink, since bread should have been as problematic as wine. A specific objection to wine therefore suggests something more like the tradition under discussion, whether somehow maintained in Manichaean tradition or (re)gained through observance of what more ascetic Christians practised.[90]

---

[85] al-Nadim, *Fihrist*, ii. 773–4.   [86] Lieu, *Manichaeism*, 35–6.

[87] Ibid. 38 n. 33, 45–6.   [88] See e.g. *Conf.* 3. 10.

[89] 'ore indigno Christi corpus accipiant, sanguinem autem redemptionis nostrae haurire declinent' (*Sermon*, 42. 5). See Harry O. Maier, '"Manichee!": Leo the Great and the Orthodox Panopticon', *JECS* 4 (1996), 441–60.

[90] I stop short of discussing connections with the interesting water-drinking practices of Mandaism, on which see E. S. Drower, *Water into Wine: A Study of Ritual Idiom in the Middle East* (London: John Murray, 1956). While I am sceptical of positing universal ritual design as Drower seems to, it may well be that the emergence of Elkesaite practices involving water, as well as some Jewish–Christian ones, can best be comprehended in the

CONCLUSIONS

A number of preliminary conclusions can already be drawn from the materials discussed. The first and most obvious is that the bread-and-water pattern is not simply a rare and extreme case of 'encratite' adaptation of the Christian eucharist, but an important and widespread tradition in early Eastern Christianity, and especially in Syria and Asia, at least. While there are also witnesses there to the normative tradition, or what eventually becomes that, these do not seem much greater in number and scope at this point than are the indications of the bread-and-water tradition.[91]

The geographical clustering of these witnesses (which will be seen further in the next chapter), along with the theological diversity of the groups discussed, also suggests that the pattern may not actually be an ascetic emendation of a normative ritual pattern at all, but rather was the primitive tradition in these areas or communities.[92] While I have suggested that the significance of the tradition can generally be understood in terms of resistance to the cuisine of sacrifice, and hence that similar ordering of food might well be expected among groups which took the same attitude to sacrifice and society, the geographical convergence of the evidence suggests that we have not so much a case of convergent evolution but one of a common origin. It is implausible that all the groups here independently and coincidentally adopted the same ascetic and ritual practices. While they are all, or virtually all, characterized by their asceticism, this consists largely of these practices themselves, rather than in an abstract concern for the self or the body which is then merely reflected in their food practices.

To call this pattern 'ascetic' is merely to state the obvious; the point is to relate this asceticism to other aspects of social life and of thought. It is clear that the bread-and-water tradition cannot be reduced to a matter either of ritual practice or of general diet; it is both. The constant association of these two practices, as we would see them, of avoidance of

---

light of widespread baptist movements in the Near East. See Gabriele Winkler, 'The Origins and Idiosyncrasies of the Earliest Form of Asceticism', in W. Skudlarek (ed.), *The Continuing Quest for God: Monastic Spirituality in Tradition and Transition* (Collegeville, Minn.: Liturgical Press, 1982), 13–15.

[91] See Harnack's lists, 'Brod und Wasser', 132–6.

[92] Lebeau's discussion of the water-eucharist (*Le Vin nouveau*, 142–88) recognizes its extent and early date, but errs, I think, in attributing one theological agenda to the different cases.

meat in diet and of wine at the eucharistic meal, seems in fact really to be the constant reiteration of one. Both meat and wine are rejected as inappropriate, above all because of their association with sacrifice. From the point of view of the champions of a single normative tradition, whether ancient or modern, this consistent dissident cuisine is separated into two elements which are discussed separately. In modern terms, the use of water in the eucharist has been the preserve of the liturgists, and the rejection of meat from all diet has been discussed by the theorists and historians of asceticism. This disciplinary separation, which reflects the ordering of the orthodox communities and individuals rather than that of their opponents, has prevented the full implications of either aspect of the practice from being developed.

For many or even most of the bread-and-water Christians there was no absolute distinction between the communal meal or eucharist and the common, as in day-to-day, meal. The cases discussed in the previous chapter of more, rather than less, in the eucharistic meal can fruitfully be brought to bear on the consideration of this pattern. In some cases at least the groups are the same; this will become clearer in discussion of the Pseudo-Clementine literature and apocryphal *Acts* in the next chapter. Since in these cases exclusion of certain foods is part of a somewhat generalized sacralization of eating, what matters is the distinction between the meals of these communities and other meals, rather more than between the meals of the average day and the meals of Sundays or other times of assembly. Hence, once particular foods and particular persons are excluded, the possibility of including other foods becomes less problematic. These suggestions are preliminary, and may seem to apply more to some cases than to others. Completion of the survey of the bread-and-water tradition is necessary to test and develop them.

5
Bread and Water in Radical Pseudepigrapha

INTRODUCTION

The examples of the bread-and-water tradition discussed so far have been somewhat disparate, and consist largely of passing indications or polemical descriptions from authors to whom the ascetic meal tradition was a curiosity or a danger. The next two cases are rather different, being whole bodies of literature whose ritual meal descriptions are plentiful, if still problematic, and which seem clearly to belong in the same tradition.

The Pseudo-Clementine *Homilies* and *Recognitions* are two versions of an earlier work, a romance concerning the early life of Clement, the bishop of Rome. These also include significant material on the preaching of the apostle Peter, which may come from yet another, earlier source.[1] The various apocryphal *Acts*, despite similarities of genre and apparent literary interdependence, are increasingly seen as the products of various milieux and of a variety of theologies.[2] Yet all the works in both these 'collections' are witnesses to eucharistic meals involving no wine, and to avoidance of meat. Some attention has already been paid to their evidence for foods other than the expected bread and wine; further discussion of the individual documents, particularly in terms of the absence of wine in their eucharistic meals, is necessary to establish the extent and meaning of these meal practices.

If these works can be considered as emerging from the milieu of the bread-and-water tradition already discussed, they may have an extraordinary value for its reconstruction and interpretation. While the bulk of the evidence considered in the previous chapter was from heresiological and similarly indirect sources, these works can be regarded

---

[1] See Johannes Irmscher and Georg Strecker, 'The Pseudo-Clementines', in Schneemelcher (ed.), *New Testament Apocrypha*, ii. 483–6, 488–93.

[2] See discussion by Wilhelm Schneemelcher, 'Second and Third Century Acts of Apostles', *New Testament Apocrypha*, ii. 75–86.

as something more like the *ipsissima verba* of at least some of the water-drinkers. It is from these, therefore, that we should expect to find confirmation of the hypothesis of a basically anti-sacrificial rationale for the tradition.

THE PSEUDO-CLEMENTINE LITERATURE

Meals in the Clementine Homilies and Recognitions

The romances attributed to Clement of Rome but of manifestly later origin have often been considered as evidence for Ebionite Christianity.[3] The enormously complex questions concerning the origins and development of the Clementine *Homilies* and *Recognitions* cannot be fully entered into here, but I have already indicated reasons for separating consideration of these works from discussion of groups designated as Ebionites.

The *Homilies* and *Recognitions* are, in effect, two different versions of the same document or corpus, each being a series of discourses (hence 'Homilies') involving Peter the Apostle and Clement, strung together with a narrative involving the separation and providential reunion (hence 'Recognitions') of Clement's family. Although they may, in their present forms, date from a time outside the general scope of this study, there seems little doubt that the Pseudo-Clementine works contain elements from as early as the second century, or at least the first part of the third.[4]

The use of salt in what may broadly be called eucharistic meals in the *Homilies* has already been discussed. The meals of the Pseudo-Clementines not only add salt in some cases, but remove wine from what might otherwise be the expected pattern. I will here consider further some of the material already examined in the discussion of salt, and it is also necessary to look at other aspects of the texts that can give us a fuller picture of the concerns about food and meals reflected in the Pseudo-

---

[3] See Koch, 'Epiphanius' Knowledge of the Ebionites', 47–57, 268–84; and Ch. 4 above.

[4] The bewildering array of positions and hypotheses are marshalled in F. Stanley Jones, 'The Pseudo-Clementines: A History of Research', *SecCent* 2 (1982), 1–33, 63–96, and, more recently and with attention to a more specific section of text, also by Jones in *An Ancient Jewish Christian Source on the History of Christianity: Pseudo-Clementine Recognitions 1. 27–71*, SBLTT 37 (Atlanta: Scholars Press, 1995), 1–38. Georg Strecker's *Das Judenchristentum in den Pseudoklementinen* is the most recent and impressive attempt, also presented in summary in his introduction to Pseudo-Clementine extracts in 'The Pseudo-Clementines', ii. 485–93.

Clementine corpus. The *Homilies*, which are generally considered to be somewhat closer to the (or at least their own) original form, will again usually provide the texts for discussion.[5]

The *Contestatio*, or initiation ceremony for a candidate who is to be entrusted with the Clementine books themselves, is part of an introduction or frame for the *Homilies*. 'Let him be brought to a river or fountain where there is living water and the regeneration of the righteous takes place' (*Cont.* 1. 2). The candidate then uses, as we saw, a detailed oath invoking the elements 'heaven, earth, water, in which everything is comprehended, and also in addition the all-pervading air . . .' (2. 1). 'And thereupon let him partake of bread and salt with him who hands over the books to him' (4. 3). No cup is mentioned. The invoked elements of heaven, earth, water, air, and the eaten bread and salt all occur in one or more of the Elkesaite lists of witnesses provided by Hippolytus and Epiphanius.[6] In another case Peter breaks bread 'with thanksgiving (ἐπ' εὐχαριστίᾳ) and having put salt on it he gave it first to [our] mother and after her to us, her sons. Thus we both ate with her and blessed God' (*Hom.* 14. 1. 4).[7]

These cases seem to represent the basic sacral meal pattern known to the Christian communities involved. I have already argued that in this and other cases in the *Homilies*, including those where salt is highlighted, identification as a 'eucharistic' meal is justified.[8] The fact that there is no mention of the Last Supper or of the body and blood of Jesus should not be an absolute obstacle to the use of such language on the part of the interpreter. As elsewhere, the lack of such imagery may well need to be understood in terms of the avoidance of all sacrificial symbolism and practice by these communities, or more simply perhaps as maintenance

---

[5] The *Recognitions* have survived in full only in a Latin version, translated by Rufinus, which seems to have been rendered more palatable to orthodox tastes. There is also a Syriac version, without bks. 4–10. Jones, *An Ancient Jewish Christian Source*, 39–49, defends the value of the two (as witnesses to the common source) as more or less equal and fairly high.

[6] They are particularly close to one of Epiphanius' versions (19. 1. 6; 19. 6. 4). Yet there is no evidence that the Elkesaites ate the elements in their oaths; the Pseudo-Clementine oath and meal 'invokes' baptism by having the participant stand next to water, whereas the Elkesaites seem to have practised regular ritual baths. H. Waitz, *Die Pseudoklementinen, Homilien und Rekognitionen: Eine quellenkritische Untersuchung*, TU 25 (Leipzig: J. C. Hinrichs, 1904), 127, suggests that the *Kerygmata Petrou* source was Elkesaite. Strecker and others demur: see *Das Judenchristentum in den Pseudoklementinen*, 143. The precise nature of the link cannot really be established with the present evidence.

[7] Often the language of giving thanks or of blessing (or both) is used with eating (*Hom.* 10. 26. 2, 12. 25. 1, *Recog.* 2. 72. 6 etc.).

[8] See on salt in Ch. 3 above.

of a tradition of 'eucharistia', of giving thanks after the example of Jesus, rather than of reciting words of institution.

This may therefore be a case where the lack of any more explicit marking-off of particular meals reflects thinking on food and drink rather different from that of the more accommodating tradition of the eucharist. While the meals of the community of the *Homilies* must be clearly distinguished from the meals of the Gentiles, all the eating done by the community has a somewhat sacralized aspect. As was argued in Chapter 3, the separation of liturgical or ritual food concerns from the general ones of diet and asceticism is not recognized in the text.

This different sense of order in food and meals is hardly one of indifference. Meals are certainly regarded as of great importance to the community, as we find not only in narrative sections such as that just quoted, but also in more clearly prescriptive parts of the texts as well. In his charge to the unwilling Clement, about to be ordained bishop by him, the apostle Peter exhorts: 'I know that these things will be done by you, if you establish love (ἀγάπη) in your mind. To this end there is one sure means, the common partaking of salt (ἡ κοινή τῶν ἁλῶν μετάληψις)' (*Ep. Clem.* 9. 1–2). Again, this reference from the literary 'frame' of the *Homilies* seems to suggest a continuation of concerns reflected in the older narrative section into the necessarily somewhat later introductory material.

Meals, both those involving salt and others, seem to bear a significance that is not only positive for the participants but negative for outsiders. The community meal is seen as exclusive (*Hom.* 1. 22. 5, cf. *Recog.* 1. 19. 3). This general exclusiveness of the table of the baptized is explained in terms of purity and pollution: 'we do not live with all indiscriminately; nor do we take our food from the same table as Gentiles, inasmuch as we cannot eat along with them, because they live impurely' (*Hom.* 13. 4, cf. *Recog.* 7. 29). This language is of course taken directly from traditions of Jewish self-definition, but its application in the Pseudo-Clementines cannot be directly correlated with the practice of the Jewish dietary laws. As in the more radical cases of Jewish and Christian asceticism discussed earlier, meat and wine are the specific instances where a radicalized concern to avoid pollution and dealings with the wider society becomes concrete.

The *Homilies* also provide pictures of individual diet and ascesis otherwise in keeping with the bread-and-water tradition, for example in statements by Peter about his diet: 'Those who have determined to accept the blessings of the future reign have no right to regard as their own the things that are here, since they belong to a foreign king, with the exception only of water and bread, and those things procured with sweat to maintain life . . . and also one garment' (*Hom.* 15. 7. 6).[9] Peter's discussion of refusing earthly goods in political terms, as the possessions of a foreign power, is particularly stark. Bread and water are separated even from the other things allowable that could be procured by labour; despite the obvious work involved in producing bread, both these elements seem again to be symbols of a natural order, free from what is imposed by human society or malign supernatural power. Again, at *Recog.* 9. 6. 6, Peter praises the lack of expense incurred by those who use only bread and water.[10] A slightly different testimony also survives in both the *Homilies* and *Recognitions*, where Peter describes his diet as 'only bread with olives and only rarely vegetables', and his dress again as simple (*Hom.* 12. 6; *Recog.* 7. 6. 4).[11] Although there is no mention of salt here, Peter's diet and dress according to these statements seem in keeping with Cynic models in particular, and we know from other sources that bread, water, and salt could be seen as appropriate Cynic staples, or at least as signs of radical disengagement from the fabric of society.

These are of course statements of a rather different kind from those concerning ritual meals, apparently being prescriptions for the individual's lifestyle rather than for community ritual practice. Yet even if these accounts of Peter's diet are somewhat separate in form from the meal descriptions, they are certainly not incompatible with those meals. In fact if these texts do give us any real insight into the meal practices of a community and not just those of individuals, they reinforce the impression that the difference between appropriate eating in general and the appropriate content of specific ritual meals is only one of emphasis, and certainly not of radically different diet or foods as such.

It is also worth considering some more negative statements in the Clementine works which render in starker relief the critical position about the use of meat and wine implicit in these positive pictures of the use of bread, salt, and vegetables. Meat is always put in a bad light, associated with debauchery (*Hom.* 7. 3. 1; 11. 15. 6) and prohibited along with participation in pagan sacrifice (*Hom.* 7. 4. 2, 8. 19. 1; *Recog.* 1. 29–30; 8. 48. 5). Wine is similarly associated with pagan sacrifice and immorality (*Hom.* 7. 3. 1; 11. 15. 6; *Recog.* 10. 27. 4). The case of the

---

[9] . . . οὐκ ἔξεστιν ἢ ὕδατος μόνου καὶ ἄρτου . . .

[10] 'Quantus enim sumptus est, aqua et pane utentibus et hunc a deo sperantibus?'

[11] 'Panis mihi solus cum olivis et raro etiam cum oleribus in usu est'.

arch-villain Simon Magus centres on meat and wine as sacrificial foods, as Peter recounts: 'I have been told . . . after he had sacrificed an ox he feasted you in the middle of the forum, and that you, being carried away with much wine, made friends with not only the evil demons but their prince also . . . For the demons would never have had power over you, had you not first supped with their prince' (*Hom.* 7. 3. 1).

This notion of sacrificial feeding of demons bears comparison with the position of Justin (*2 Apol.* 5. 3–4) and also with similar understandings held by pagan theorists of sacrifice such as Porphyry (*De Abst.* 2. 36) and Iamblichus (*De Myst.* 14. 5). There is also a particular link in the *Homilies* with blood and a ban on shedding or eating blood, with apparent reference to the prohibition in Genesis (9: 4) and elsewhere in the Hebrew Bible: 'And the things which are well-pleasing to God are these: to pray to him . . . to abstain from the table of devils, not to taste dead flesh, not to touch blood . . .' (*Hom.* 7. 4. 2). Although some commentators have suggested that there are different degrees of concern about meat and blood in the sources, and that some layers might reflect concerns simply about particular forms of unclean meat and blood, as one might have expected in a Jewish–Christian environment, these distinctions are in fact very difficult or even impossible to make.[12] It seems more likely that the *Grundschrift* or basic document for the two Pseudo-Clementine works made use of traditional arguments concerned with establishing purity (prohibition of strangled meat and blood), but did so to argue against meat-eating altogether. Anti-sacrificial thought is also very prominent in the different source identified in *Recognitions* 1. 27–71.[13]

The protological aspect of avoiding meat in accordance with a paradisiacal state, already seen in the discussion of pagan and Jewish anti-sacrificial asceticism and probably alluded to by Justin as well, is developed in the *Homilies* into a detailed version of the doings of the giants (cf. Gen. 6: 1–4) who are held responsible for the 'fall' into meat-eating and into the (virtually identical, it seems!) crime of cannibalism (*Hom.* 8. 15–16).[14] Both Pseudo-Clementine works also give versions of the story of Noah and develop the dispensation of meat-eating (Gen.

[12] Strecker, *Das Judenchristentum in den Pseudoklementinen*, 182–3.

[13] This is described, and placed prior to the basic writing, by Jones, *An Ancient Jewish Christian Source*, 157–68.

[14] This picture combines a number of elements common to ancient descriptions of cannibals, such as its ascription to the ancients (as throughout Greek mythology), association with sexual disorders, and construction of a myth of primordial vegetarianism. See McGowan, 'Eating People', 423–5, 427–31.

9: 1–5) into an aetiology of idolatry and sacrifice (*Hom.* 9. 3–23, *Recog.* 4. 13–36).[15] These different versions of a primordial vegetarian myth are strong evidence for prohibition of meat at the earliest point in the tradition-history of the works.

Summary

The different sources and versions of the Pseudo-Clementines do not prevent us from saying that the documents as we have them give a reasonably coherent picture of meal practice. However we deal with the complex tradition-history of the documents, there is no sign of disagreement on the key issues of appropriate ritual eating and of diet in general. The authors or redactors seem to agree in their rejection of meat and wine, and the ritual meal associated with Christian community is consistently celebrated with bread, and sometimes with salt. The interest in salt need not have been present in all sources or shared by various redactors, but is not inconsistent with the bread-and-water tradition as found elsewhere, although it is somewhat distinctive and should at least be regarded as a particular development thereof.

It must also be acknowledged that there is little or no concern for a eucharistic cup here. While the polemic against wine may allow us to assume that water was drunk at ritual and other meals, the absence of a cup in what seem to be ritual meal descriptions is not insignificant. Lietzmann had suggested that there were some eucharistic meals in early Christian circles wherein the cup was very much the secondary element, and where its contents were a matter of indifference.[16] The Pseudo-Clementines allow us to entertain the former notion, but certainly not the latter. While the greater stress laid on the bread in these writings (and in the apocryphal *Acts*) is evident, there is in fact as much anxiety about proper drink as about proper food. We ought not to envisage a community where there was flexibility sufficient to allow water in the cup when some balked at wine, but rather one where wine was strictly excluded.[17] While it is theoretically possible that a cup has been removed

---

[15] The version of this section in the *Recognitions* (4. 14–20) makes moderation in food and drink the issue, rather than eating meat and drinking wine, but it seems very likely that this is part of the 'orthodoxizing' tendency, whether by Rufinus or before him (bk. 4 is not extant in Syriac for comparison).

[16] Lietzmann, *Mass and Lord's Supper*, 195–203.

[17] Lietzmann, ibid. 200–3, also conflates the absolute exclusions of the Pseudo-Clementines and apocryphal *Acts* with the concern for convention about times to drink wine mentioned in Cyprian's *Letter* 63, on which see further below. These are not without connections, but function quite differently for those involved.

from this meal pattern, there is no sign of that; it seems more likely that it was never there, at least not in the emphatic sense suggested even in the other bread-and-water eucharists.

The foods proper to eucharistic meals are the same as those which should define the diet of the Christian at all times. Commensality among the faithful is urged, but eating with unbelievers is to be avoided. Blessing and/or thanksgiving are ritually appropriate for all meals. There is no basis for radical separation of a specifically sacral meal from eating in general, all of which has a somewhat sacral character. Particular occasions such as baptism (and perhaps other mystagogic events; see *Cont.* 1. 2) are especially important; and it is possible that the use of salt is a distinguishing feature of the meals associated with these solemn occasions.

Perhaps the most important insight that examination of the Pseudo-Clementines brings to the picture of the bread-and-water tradition and its meaning is the explicit sense that bread is an ascetic and pure food which can be contrasted specifically with the meat of sacrificial cuisine. Here we have the beginnings of a clearer exposition of an idea that may already have been present in some of the other instances where the exclusion of wine is linked to that of meat. While eucharistic meals without wine have usually been explained in terms of 'ascetic' concern about wine and its effects, the concern for what is *eaten* is as strong or stronger in these documents.

As we have seen, both meat and wine are characteristic foods of pagan sacrifice, and of Jewish sacrifice for that matter. The exclusion of both these elements is thus not really a characteristically Jewish aspect of meal practice, granted that in some instances (not in the Pseudo-Clementines or other sources usually seen as connected with Jewish Christianity, but rather in Tatian and Tertullian) we have seen the possible influence of the Nazirite vow. Nor does the use of the prohibition of blood as an argument for abstinence from meat explain why one should argue for this abstinence in the first place. Rather these exclusions are linked to the refusal to eat with 'pagans' at all, which seems also to be a refusal even to eat as those pagans eat. Bread here is opposed to meat, and although not ritually prominent, water is opposed to wine. The ritual cuisine of the Pseudo-Clementines is thus a thoroughly oppositional one, in which the community not merely separates itself from dealings with pagan food but seeks to construct an independent picture of pure foods.

The *Pseudo-Clementine* Epistulae ad Virgines

The two letters *ad Virgines* which claim Clement of Rome as author are generally admitted as being pseudonymous, may well be of Syrian origin, and can perhaps be dated as late as the third century.[18] There is no organic connection between these and the Pseudo-Clementine romances, but they may reflect a somewhat similar milieu, and may be conveniently, if briefly, discussed here. The two letters offer instruction for the conduct of women and men committed to virginity, and there are a number of references to meals.

At various points concern is expressed about those with whom one should eat. There is anxiety about eating with members of the opposite sex (2. 3–5; cf. 1. 10) and with the heathen (1. 10; 2. 6). The content of diet is mentioned once, and it is bread and water (2. 2), although there is also the possibility of further elements as they are available. The eucharist is also mentioned as a good food that should be taken often. Thus the concern for food in these letters is perhaps largely comprehensible in terms of the importance of sexual abstinence for the author and addressees, and of the link between food and sexuality characteristic of a more individualized asceticism. As elsewhere, bread and water reflect the best and safest diet for those who maintain continence; but there is no clear sense of exclusion here of all other foods.

THE APOCRYPHAL *ACTS*

Introduction

Although this is manifestly a diverse body of literature, various common elements justify considering the apocryphal *Acts* (or at least those of Andrew, John, Paul, Peter, and Thomas) together, as is typically done even by those scholars who object to possible over-generalization with regard to origin or social setting.[19] While the traditions about the various apostles may have arisen across a fairly wide time and space, the complex history of transmission has presented us with a corpus whose literary nature and theological content form a real, if not unqualified, whole.

---

[18] Brown, *The Body and Society*, 196–7; Vööbus, *History of Asceticism in the Syrian Orient*, 64–5.

[19] Thus Schneemelcher, 'Second and Third Century Acts of Apostles', ii. 81–3.

The apocryphal *Acts* share a set of attitudes to food and to the ritual meal of the Christian community. As in the Pseudo-Clementines, eucharistic meals of bread alone or of bread and water are the natural ritual expression of general prohibitions on meat and wine. In this case, however, the bread of the eucharist is often (if not always) more clearly distinguished, even from other 'good' food, and the cup is often present. Although this picture is complicated by an apparent variation in intensity of concern about these issues among the different *Acts*, the patterns of non-consumption make best sense if there was some such ascetic meal practice among the communities or authors of the earlier *Acts* at least. While there have been suggestions that the milieu of the *Acts* in general may have been ascetic communities such as the 'order of widows', the general character of the works could also reflect, as is stated more often, a form of Christianity where sexual and dietary asceticism was more generally expected.[20] A survey of the major *Acts* helps demonstrate this unity in diversity.

While it is possible to draw links between the different sets of *Acts* based on theories of literary dependence, here I will present them in three loose groupings according to the picture given of ritual meal practice and concern about proper eating. All the *Acts* give some picture of appropriate ritual food; the *Acts of Paul (and Thecla)* and the *Acts of John* are only moderately concerned about the negative side, i.e. eating wrong foods and eating with pagans. The *Acts of Peter* place more emphasis on charity and the necessity of provision of food than on purity concerns, even encouraging utilitarian dealings with unbelievers. The *Acts of Andrew* and the *Acts of (Judas) Thomas* represent a rigorous position involving radical critique of meat-eating as demonic or bestial behaviour, and outright condemnation of commensality with pagans. Thus we may be dealing with the use of similar stories or models within somewhat different social and theological contexts. The last of these groupings seems to be of most interest to the bread-and-water tradition, but all have some connection with it.

[20] Stevan Davies, *The Revolt of the Widows: The Social World of the Apocryphal Acts* (Carbondale, Ill.: Southern Illinois University Press, 1980); Virginia Burrus, 'Chastity as Autonomy: Women in the Stories of the Apocryphal Acts', *Semeia*, 38 (1986), 101–17, and *Chastity as Autonomy: Women in the Stories of Apocryphal Acts*, Studies in Women and Religion, 23 (Lewiston, NY: Edwin Mellen, 1987).

The Acts of Paul

The *Acts of Paul* are preserved in a number of fragmentary witnesses, and some portions such as the *Acts of Paul and Thecla* circulated independently.[21] In the *Acts of Paul and Thecla* (5), Paul's arrival at the house of Onesiphorus in Iconium is greeted with 'great joy, and bowing of knees and breaking of bread and the word of God about abstinence and the resurrection [and] Paul said: "Blessed are the pure in heart"'. This somewhat vague description obviously draws upon the 'breaking of the bread' attested in the canonical Acts of the Apostles (Acts 2: 42, 46; 20: 7, 11; 27: 35; cf. Luke 24: 35), but either or both the apocryphal and canonical references may seem to suggest a pattern where bread was more important, and possibly unaccompanied by a cup.[22]

Later in these adventures (25), Paul, Thecla, and companions celebrate a meal in a tomb (cf. *Acts of John*, 72, 86): 'And there was great love (ἀγάπη) in the tomb', or perhaps 'a great *agape*-feast', in which 'they rejoiced in the holy works of Christ'. The meal consists of 'five loaves and vegetables (λάχανα) and water'. Beasts, not humans, are the expected eaters of flesh (*Acts of Paul and Thecla*, 27–8).[23]

Elsewhere in the *Acts of Paul* the bread-and-water eucharist appears once or perhaps twice. The more doubtful case is in the story of a dropsied man, Hermocrates (4), to whom Paul gives (without mention of actions or prayers) bread which heals him, after which he is baptized. Clearer is the case of the conversion of Artemilla, during the episode at Ephesus (7). Paul 'broke bread and brought water, gave her to drink of the word, and sent her to her husband Hieronymus'. This seems quite clearly to be a reference to water as the drink of the eucharistic meal. This eucharist is depicted as part of a familiar type-scene in the *Acts* wherein a wealthy woman seeks to disengage herself from a prominent and powerful man.[24] In this case Hieronymus intends Paul to be a victim of wild beasts, and his purpose is thwarted by Paul's reunion with a baptized lion (apparently on the run from Aesop's fables). Ironically it is Hieronymus who is at least symbolically dismembered, losing an ear while Paul is unharmed. While somewhat sensational to say the least, there is a discernible opposition in this account between bread and water,

[21] Schneemelcher, 'Second and Third Century Acts of Apostles', ii. 220–2.

[22] Lietzmann, *Mass and Lord's Supper*, 161–71, 195–203. See Ch. 7 below.

[23] One MS of the *Acts of Paul and Thecla* contains an episode concerning the remainder of Thecla's life, of which it is said that she 'dwelt in a cave seventy-two years, living on vegetables (λάχανα) and water'.

[24] On these see esp. Burrus, *Chastity as Autonomy*.

the food of the holy, and the bloodshed of the circus, not altogether dissimilar to the contrast visible in the *Martyrdom of Perpetua and Felicitas*.[25]

The *Acts of Paul* also express concern about food in other respects: fasting is emphasized (*Paul and Thecla*, 8, 23; *Acts of Paul*, 7), and rich food and wine are criticized. Thamyris, Thecla's betrothed, wines and dines the pseudo-disciples Demas and Hermogenes to get information (*Paul and Thecla*, 13); this participation in the table of pagans leads to betrayal. At Sidon (*Acts of Paul*, 5) the locals bring food for a feast while Paul chooses the better part and fasts.

The *Acts of Paul* thus present a stark opposition between meat and wine on the one hand and bread and water on the other, a distinction which seems to stand alongside the glimpses in the narrative of extraordinary animal life; both perhaps invoke the distinctions between humans, beasts, and gods established in sacrificial ritual. Over and against the world of pagan violence in which animals hurt and harm stands the pure world of Christian eating, a sphere of restored harmony between humans and beasts.

The Acts of John

The *Acts of John* are, in the form generally reconstructed, the most gnostic of the apocryphal *Acts*, with remarkable material such as the Hymn or Dance (92–4), which has a far more mystical character than the narrative sections. The picture of ritual meals is, however, similar to that of the other *Acts*.

Chapter 46 makes brief reference to a 'eucharist': 'After John's homily to the brethren, prayer and eucharist, and the laying of hands on each person assembled . . .', but no details emerge. Later, in the story of the attempted sexual violation of the dead Drusiana, the circumstance of the apostle's presence at the grave is a plan to 'break bread' there, apparently linked with the third day after death: 'On the following day John and Andronicus and the brethren went at the break of day to the tomb in which Drusiana had been for three days, so that we might break bread there' (72). After effecting his miracles at the scene, John gives a speech which names the benefits of Christian life, including both 'eucharist' (or thanksgiving) and 'agape' (or love) along with other things both abstract and concrete. John then proceeds with the plan to celebrate the meal: 'After these words John prayed, fetched a loaf of bread to the tomb to break it and said, "We praise your name, who have converted us from error and unmerciful lusts . . ." Having thus prayed and praised [God] he made all the brethren partake of the Eucharist of the Lord and then left the tomb' (85–6).[26]

A similar eucharistic meal follows in ch. 109, where preparations for John's death are under way:

> And having asked for bread, he gave thanks saying, 'What praise or sort of offering or what thanksgiving shall we invoke as we break the bread, but you only, Lord Jesus? . . .' And having broken the bread, he gave it to us, praying for each of the brethren, that he might be worthy of the grace of the Lord and his most holy Eucharist. He also partook it and said 'To me also let there be a portion with you, and peace be with you, my beloved'.

Again the sole element is bread, and the dominant elements of the prayer are thanksgiving and glorification.[27] Overall, these *Acts* seem to present a broadly similar ritual picture to that of the *Acts of Paul*, although there is a pattern of bread alone here rather than bread and water. Whether coincidentally or not, both mention meals at tombs and speak of the 'breaking of the bread'. The issues of sexual renunciation (*Acts of John*, 48–54, 63–86) and polemic against pagan sacrifice (38–45) also occur, but are not clearly linked to meals.

The Acts of Peter

A surviving Coptic *Act* concerning Peter's daughter is generally regarded as a witness to part of the original *Acts of Peter*. In this story Peter has healed and taught a crowd (explaining that it is better for his daughter to be crippled, so as to avoid being an occasion of sin, than for her to be healed), and then 'praising the name of the Lord Jesus Christ, he gave of the bread to them all; [and] when he had distributed it he rose up and went to his house' (Codex Berolinensis 8502).

In the Latin version which also probably reflects a Greek original with reasonable accuracy, Paul (*sic*) presides at a bread-and-water eucharist (*Act. Vercell.* 2): 'And they brought bread and water to Paul for the sacrifice that he might offer prayer and distribute it among them.' The elements themselves are described as 'the eucharist' and the worshippers come 'to

---

[26] K. Schäferdiek, 'The Acts of John', in Schneemelcher (ed.), *New Testament Apocrypha*, ii. 200–1.

[27] The eucharistic prayer, *Acts of John*, 109, contains elements which have led some editors and commentators to regard it as secondary: Schäferdiek, 'The Acts of John', ii. 164.

the altar of God'. The sacrificial overtones of these phrases are quite exceptional in the apocryphal *Acts*, and indeed among the instances of the bread-and-water traditions discussed. The sexual anxiety of the *Acts* is illustrated on this occasion in the case of the would-be communicant Rufina, who is struck down because of her illicit domestic arrangements.

Despite the concern about qualifications to participate in the eucharistic meal conveyed in that story, the *Acts of Peter* also contain less clearly rigorous elements. As Peter voyages to Rome to combat Simon Magus he is invited to dine by Theon, the ship's captain. Peter seems not to balk at eating with Theon prior to the latter's baptism, and no mention of particular foods is made (5). In fact the baptism of Theon and the eucharist following seem to be connected with Theon's invitation to dine: 'and Peter took bread and gave thanks to the Lord [and prayed . . .] ". . . I give to him in your name your eucharist, that he may for ever be your servant, perfect and without blemish."' Yet we are told that all others aboard were in a drunken stupor.

There are no other such eucharistic meal scenes in the extant *Acts of Peter*. Bread and water do appear in one or two other places. Peter is miraculously fed with a loaf of bread in a vision (ibid. 17). A list of titles or attributes of Jesus calls him 'the bread, the water' among other things, many of which can be traced to the Gospel of John. Another of the titles is 'the refreshment', *refrigerium*, which later referred to cult meals at the graves of martyrs. This could conceivably be a link of sorts with stories of grave-meals in the *Acts of Paul* and the *Acts of John*.

There are other references to food, some of which may add to the sense that the *Acts of Peter* are less uncompromising in their asceticism. Fasting is clearly approved; Peter embarks for Rome without provisions, and the few in the city who do not succumb to Simon fast and mourn (ibid. 5; cf. 6, 18, 22). Still, the provision of food for the poor is put in a positive light (8), as is the need for a son to provide food for his widowed mother (25) and for former slaves to have provisions (28). In two cases enormous gifts are made for the benefit of widows and the poor, and the moral qualifications of the giver are of little import (29, 30). These suggest greater concern for familial and civic duty than we encounter elsewhere in the bread-and-water tradition; it may not be accidental that the notion of 'sacrifice' has been used, if in a reconstructed sort of fashion.[28]

---

[28] Robert F. Stoops, 'Patronage in the *Acts of Peter*', *Semeia*, 38 (1986), 99, suggests that the *Acts of Peter* reflects a concern to deal with the question of patronage, implying closer links with the wider world than are reflected in other apocryphal *Acts*: 'The differences suggest [the *Acts of Peter* and the *Acts of Paul*] derive from significantly different social worlds'.

When Peter dies, the noble convert Marcellus has him embalmed with spices and myrrh as well as milk and wine; yet this action is criticized by Peter who visits him in a dream, whether because of the foods used we cannot tell. As in some of the other apocryphal *Acts*, there is use of imagery involving eating and animals to criticize inappropriate behaviour or belief. Peter's enemies are circling dogs (ibid. 7; cf. Ps. 21: 17 LXX), the spurned Albinus is like a wild beast, and Simon is a devouring wolf (8; cf. John 10: 12). Yet some of these images are more clearly biblical than in other cases, and the animal/human interactions of some of the other *Acts* do not appear so clearly here. A dog becomes a messenger (9, 12). Preserved fish are revived and eat bread; this odd story cannot be made to imply either criticism or endorsement of the use of fish as food.

The *Acts of Peter* may therefore be understood as a rather weaker witness to the social rigorism of the bread-and-water tradition. There is still no clear approval of use of meat or wine, and the eucharist is celebrated with bread and water, but in the form we know them these *Acts* involve a somewhat more positive and engaged view of society expressed in uses of food, as well as in other terms including the logic of sacrifice.

The Acts of Andrew

The *Acts of Andrew* are preserved only in fragments, but a reconstruction is possible making use of Gregory of Tours's adaptation.[29] Two important meal scenes are preserved only in Gregory's *Liber de Miraculis Beati Andreae Apostoli*. These exemplify the 'bread eucharists' also found in the other apocryphal *Acts*. After healing a woman 'The apostle broke bread and gave it to her. She thanked God and believed in the Lord with all her house' (5).[30]

Later, Andrew learns of his coming passion and death, and holds his own last supper: 'He took bread, broke it with thanksgiving, and gave it

---

[29] See Jean-Marc Prieur and Wilhelm Schneemelcher, 'The Acts of Andrew', in Schneemelcher (ed.), *New Testament Apocrypha*, ii. 101–17. The cannibal episodes of the *Acts of Andrew and Matthias*, while intriguing for questions of food and meals, are somewhat different in character from the other *Acts* material. See further the attempt by Dennis R. MacDonald to argue for the integrity of the cannibal episode (and the rebuttal by Prieur): 'The *Acts of Andrew and Matthias* and the *Acts of Andrew*', *Semeia*, 38 (1986), 9–33; and MacDonald's text and translation of the materials: *The Acts of Andrew and the Acts of Andrew and Matthias in the City of the Cannibals*, SBLTT 33 (Atlanta: Scholars Press, 1990).

[30] 'Beatus autem apostolus fregit panem et dedit ei. Quae gratias agens, accepit et credidit in Domino cum omni domo sua.'

to all saying: 'Receive the grace (*gratiam*) which Christ the Lord our God gives you by me, his servant' (20).[31] This case looks especially 'eucharistic'.[32] It is interesting that, as in the *Acts of John*, despite the clear evocation of the Last Supper there is no use of the quasi-sacrificial language of body and blood. While of course it is Andrew's supper and it would be absurd to imagine him presenting his own body and blood, this silence helps throw into high relief the absence of allusion to the institution narratives in the apocryphal *Acts* as a whole.

Gregory's version of the *Acts of Andrew* must, admittedly, be taken as something other than a direct witness.[33] Nevertheless the very oddness of these eucharists in the later milieu, and their similarity to what is found in the other *Acts*, argues in favour of the text being close to the original in these meal depictions. While it can hardly mean that these practices would have been generally acted upon in sixth-century Gaul, it is possible that the ascetic character of the *Acts* was seen as appropriate in the circles of developed and well-defined monasticism.

Those sections of the *Acts of Andrew* more directly attested give interesting information about attitudes to food on the part of the author or community. The villain Aeagates who wishes to enjoy sexual relations with his wife Maximilla is a ravenous, in fact a 'bestial (ὡς θήρ)', eater (ibid. 46) who suffers from stomach problems because of his appetites (13). The only other apparent flesh-eaters among the characters are dogs, who eat the unfortunate and unchaste servant Eucleia, and who are also intended by Aeagates to devour Andrew after he dies on the cross (54). Christian characters eat only bread and vegetables (25, 27).

Most interesting is an explanation by the apostle of the power gained by demons from meat-eating or from the sacrificial killing of animals necessary to it:

I will tell you and the brethren walking with me something else about people alien to us. As long as the demonic nature lacks its bloody food and cannot suck up its nutrition because animals are not slain, it weakens and recedes to nothingness, becoming entirely dead. But if it has what it longs for, it strengthens, expands, and rises up, growing by means of those foods it enjoys. (ibid. 53)

This is the most explicit statement so far, bearing in mind the similar examples presented earlier, of what seems to be the implicit logic of the

[31] 'Et accipiens panem, gratias agens fregit et dedit omnibus, dicens: "Accipite gratiam quem vobis tradit per me famulum suum Christus dominus Deus noster."'

[32] Perhaps *gratia* might translate εὐχαριστία in this case.

[33] See Prieur and Schneemelcher, 'The Acts of Andrew', in Schneemelcher (ed.), *New Testament Apocrypha*, ii. 106–8, 118–23. Note Gregory's apparent reversal of attitudes to marriage typical of the apocryphal *Acts* (*Liber*, 11).

bread-and-water tradition all along: that pagan sacrifice is indeed, as the likes of Aristotle would have had it, a structuring of the polis and the cosmos, but one which is evil in character and which Christians must resist. Here we have the radical ascetics' answer to the pagan topos which sees (mostly) beneficent *daimones* as feeding on the sacrifices of the pious (Iamblichus, *Myst.* 14. 5; cf. Porphyry, *De Abst.* 2. 42; Origen, *Contra Celsum*, 8. 30–1). The depictions of Christians who eat no meat and drink no wine can hardly be mere idealized sketches in this case at least; the question of what to eat and drink is an urgent one, and one with dire consequences. Bread and water stand in this narrative as they would have in practice, as pure and pious foods to be opposed to the meat and wine of pagan sacrifice and debauchery.[34]

The Acts of (Judas) Thomas

The *Acts of (Judas) Thomas* are somewhat different from the others in their theology and literary development in the narrative; their dependence on at least some of the earlier *Acts* is very likely. The traditions concerning the main character, Judas Thomas, are striking, and imagery such as that of the bridal chamber and of sacramental anointing is quite distinctive and fully developed. Prayer texts such as *epicleses* are more common and fuller in form; only the *Acts of John* come close to the same kind of liturgical or prayer elements. Traditions about eating and meals, however, are in keeping with the picture provided by the other *Acts*, and in fact are at the more radical end of the scale.[35]

Thomas's ascetic conduct is very similar to that of Peter in the Pseudo-Clementines: 'He continually fasts and prays, and eats only bread with salt, and his drink is water, and he wears one coat . . .' (*Acts of Judas Thomas*, 20). The celebration of eucharistic meals is depicted a number of times in close association with baptism (of which the most prominent element is use of oil) and as in previous cases suggests a close relationship between issues of diet and those of appropriate ritual food. Bread alone is mentioned in four cases (ibid. 27, 29, 49–51, 133), water in one (121), and the contents of a cup are unspecified in another (158). King Misdaeus also describes Thomas's 'sorcery' as involving 'oil and water and bread' (152). The blessed bread

---

[34] Note the persistence of the tradition in the interesting juxtaposition near the beginning of the *Acts of Andrew and Matthias* (1): 'The people of that city ate no bread and drank no water, but ate human flesh and drank their blood.'

[35] See Vööbus, *History of Asceticism in the Syrian Orient*, 83–5.

itself seems to be called 'eucharist' (51), and the term *agape* is applied in one instance to the event or gathering (50).

Two references to Jesus' body and blood are the only ones in the whole of the apocryphal *Acts* to employ this terminology in something like the (later) normative fashion. One and possibly both of these are secondary, although this does not necessarily exclude them from interest. In chs. 49–50 Thomas presides at a eucharistic meal whose element(s) he refers to as 'body and blood of Christ', but the meal turns out to involve only bread. This is of course awkward, but certainly suggests an amendment in the direction of orthodoxy, of which there were many in these *Acts*.[36] From this example, we might conclude that the other case (ch. 158) could also have occurred in the same fashion. In any event, it arises in a context that suggests the imagery was not radically separated from other symbolic references to Jesus' death and resurrection:

When they came out of the water, he took bread and a cup, blessed, and said, 'We eat your holy body, crucified for us; and we drink your blood, shed for our redemption. May your body be redemption for us, and your blood be the forgiveness of our sins! For the gall which you drank for our sakes, may the gall of the devil around us be taken away; and for the vinegar which you drank for us, may our weakness be strengthened; for the spittle which you received for our sake may we receive the dew of your goodness . . .' And he broke the bread of the eucharist and gave it to Vazan, Tertia and Mnesara, and to the wife and daughter of Siphor, and said, 'May this eucharist be to your salvation and joy and to the healing of your souls!' And they said 'Amen'.   (ibid. 158)

Thus while the 'body and blood' language is most important, it seems that the elements might also have been understood as representing other substances, such as gall, vinegar, and spittle, which feature in the passion narratives. Even were we to take the reading as authentic or early, there is certainly no need to assume that wine, rather than water, was used. Either way, it is intriguing that an interest in the eucharistic elements as Jesus' body and blood does not affect the actual practice depicted.

Another meal which seems to be separate from the 'eucharist' proper involves bread, oil, herbs, and salt (29). The apostle blesses these foods and gives them to a crowd on the evening before a eucharist; he himself fasts. This instance has been discussed in the earlier sections on oil and salt.

As in the *Acts of Andrew*, inappropriate food and drink are signs of vice and of the demonic. The apostle preaches that all, regardless of

---

[36] Lietzmann, *Mass and Lord's Supper*, 198–200.

age or station, should 'abstain from fornication and avarice and the service of the belly; for in these three heads all lawlessness is comprised' (28; cf. 126). A demon with whom Judas Thomas contends describes the role of pagan sacrifice in very similar terms to those provided in the *Acts of Andrew* and the Pseudo-Clementine *Homilies*: 'And as you enjoy your prayer and good works and spiritual hymns, so I enjoy murders and adulteries and sacrifices offered with wine upon the altars . . . the multitude worships [idols] and does their will, bringing sacrifices to them and offering wine and water libations as food and presenting gifts' (76–7).

It is tempting to see 'libations of wine and water' as a reference to other Christians' practice and to the mixed chalice, as much as to pagan ritual. Certainly the emphasis placed on wine here as a form of sacrificial food is very interesting, and confirms what is implicit elsewhere, i.e. that disdain for wine was not only a matter of moral concern at its effects on the individual and the body, but religious concern at its association with paganism.

The negative estimate of wine and feasting is confirmed by the fate of a cupbearer who hits Thomas and is devoured by a lion and dogs (6–9).[37] Here again, as in the *Acts of Andrew*, it is only the beasts that may reasonably eat flesh. In the episode concerning Mygdonia and Charisius, food and sex go closely together; for Mygdonia to refuse to eat with her husband is also to refuse to sleep with him (90, 95–8).

Along with the *Acts of Andrew* in particular, the *Acts of Thomas* provide us not only with striking pictures of uncompromising asceticism related to the bread-and-water tradition, but provide a fuller theological (or rather demonological) rationale for the anti-sacrificial nature of the tradition. Wine is as firmly associated with sacrifice as is meat, and use of both feeds demons. This anti-sacrificial concern extends from the temple to the *triclinium*, just as the positive models of ascetic eating include both the distinct eucharist and other food and meals. The continuum of ritual and general dietary concerns thus provides a structural parallel to the feared and hated pagan meat-system, which as we have seen extended the numinous character of sacrificed meat from the sanctuary into the realm of polite dinner-parties.

---

[37] This makes for an intriguing connection with the cryptic logion 7 of the *Gospel of Thomas*: 'Blessed is the lion that the human being will eat, and the lion will become human; and cursed is the human being whom the lion will eat, and the lion will become human.' See further Howard M. Jackson, *The Lion Becomes Man: The Gnostic Leontomorphic Creator and the Platonic Tradition* (Atlanta: Scholars Press, 1985).

Summary

This survey of the various apocryphal *Acts* of apostles has sought to acknowledge the differences between the various works at the same time as pointing to one of numerous common points in the genre, the form of celebration of eucharistic meals. In this aspect of the *Acts* as a group, as in others such as attitudes to sexuality and use of particular narrative elements, we are dealing with variations on a theme within the body of works, rather than substantially different pictures or positions.

The eucharist of the *Acts*, which is in most cases clearly identifiable, is typically celebrated with bread and water, or bread alone, with the apostle presiding and with prayers, where indicated, emphasizing praise and thanksgiving. The influence of the Last Supper story is present in a number of cases, but is no more prominent overall than are allusions to miraculous feeding stories from the Gospels. Where Andrew and John hold their own 'last suppers' in apparent imitation of their master's action, the *Acts* come no closer to evoking 'body and blood' language, but tend to think of actual element(s) of the sacred meal, rather than the act itself, as 'eucharist' (*Acts of John*, 109; Gregory of Tours, *Liber*, 20). This may well be understandable as part of the resistance of the tradition as a whole, and of these communities particularly, to the imagery of body and blood and its similarity to sacrificial and meat-eating symbolism.

The exceptions to this are perhaps the *Acts of Peter*, which have a more accommodating view of society in other respects also, and the rather late *Acts of Judas Thomas*, which are otherwise uncompromising in their anti-sacrificial position yet contain one substantial reference to the eucharist meal as the body and blood of Jesus (ibid. 158). In the latter case it is tempting to see the coexistence of what would otherwise be conflicting tendencies as a late and redactional element, but in any case it testifies to the possibility of the bread-and-water eucharist being celebrated in settings where the better-known interpretation of the meal based on the Last Supper was known and accepted.

In the *Acts of Peter*, on the other hand, there is an appropriation of the notion of sacrifice accompanying a general *rapprochement* with society. The more radical *Acts of Andrew* and *Acts of Judas Thomas*, as well as the *Acts of Paul*, demonstrate a particular concern about eating with pagans at their meals. This may suggest a setting where there are incentives for Christians to take part in banquets or other pagan meals, but perhaps little likelihood that pagans would seek or find the Christian eucharistic meal celebration.

Conclusions

The Pseudo-Clementines and the apocryphal *Acts* present eucharistic meals using bread and water (or bread alone) as a matter of course. The two bodies of literature also have in common the understanding that this use of food represents an alternative to pagan sacrificial meals, which in some cases are characterized as demonic.

A shared difficulty in using these writings is the question of the nature and historical value of their meal descriptions. These are effectively works of fiction, compared often with ancient novels, containing stock elements that can hardly be taken uncritically to refer to the real lives and experiences of the authors or audiences.[38] The meal scenes of both collections might seem to owe more than a little of their detail to Gospel parallels. Often the meals are linked with miracle stories, and often the apostles of the *Acts*, in particular, seem to be continuing the practice of Jesus as depicted in stories such as the feeding of the 5,000 or resurrection appearances.

While it is necessary to acknowledge a fair amount of idealizing and of borrowing from Gospel and other literary traditions, the eucharistic meals both of the apocryphal *Acts* and of the Pseudo-Clementines do contain peculiarities which suggest that some form or forms of the bread-and-water tradition were known to the authors or compilers. Both depict eucharistic meals involving bread, and none with wine. They show hostility to all use of meat and of wine, and include the most explicit statements of anti-cultic theory to be found in this connection. Further, these documents are, as was already indicated, a major source of instances where a variety of foods may be seen as part of eucharistic meal practice, broadly considered. These features cannot be explained on the basis either of Gospel parallels or of other literary influences, but must be understood as somehow a reflection, even if an idealized one, of practices known at least to the earliest of the various compilers or authors. The ritual meal patterns depicted in the works are best understood as idealized versions of the bread-and-water tradition as actually known to the communities in question.[39]

---

[38] The works were compared to novels especially by Rosa Söder, *Die apokryphen Apostelgeschichten und die romanhafte Literatur der Antike*, Würzburger Studien zur Altertumswissenschaft, 3 (Stuttgart: Kohlhammer, 1932). Schneemelcher is critical of the tendency to emphasize novelistic aspects of the works: 'Second and Third Century Acts of Apostles', ii. 78–83.

[39] On the general question of the use of the *Acts* to reconstruct their authors' and audiences' concerns, see Burrus, *Chastity as Autonomy*, 81–109.

References in the discussion to authors, compilers, and communities beg questions which cannot be fully answered here. In both cases we must posit complex literary traditions, with various sources, hypothetical basic documents, and tortuous lines of interdependence. It is not always possible to say whether we can take the meal practice implied in a particular case to be that of a source document, or that of a redactor, or of both. In fact the persistence of the meal patterns suggesting the bread-and-water tradition across the different versions of the Pseudo-Clementine romance and across the different *Acts* might well be an argument for the persistence of these practices; it is at least a clear indication of the tradition in the source documents or early versions. On the other hand, the fact that even the meal descriptions of late and very orthodox versions such as Gregory of Tours's shortened *Acts of Andrew* still have the same characteristics is a warning that we cannot assume that the communities or authors which produced the versions known to us understood the works in the same way as the originators.

The figure of the ascetic apostle, a common element between the two sets of writings, may also encourage circumspection as to the relationship between the asceticism of the writings and that of the readers. This characterization of the holy man or woman as an extraordinary figure raises the possibility that there is some degree of specialization within the communities behind the documents. One suggestive if not wholly persuasive analysis has suggested that the apocryphal *Acts* might stem from communities of celibate women such as the 'order of widows'.[40] Our still-growing sense of the asceticism characteristic of Syrian Christianity suggests that a radical disengagement from society, including avowal of celibacy, may have been a prerequisite in some cases, but that these ascetics gradually came to have a more well-defined place within less radical Christian communities.[41] This is not the place to seek to develop an answer to the complex questions of the social worlds of these works, but food practices need to be taken into account in any fuller picture.

There are sufficient differences between them to prevent us from attributing the apocryphal *Acts* and Pseudo-Clementines to the same community or seeing them as reflecting quite the same concerns. The radical sexual renunciation of the *Acts* is not a concern of the Pseudo-

---

[40] Davies, *Revolt of the Widows*.

[41] See Brown, *The Body and Society*, 97–102; Vööbus, *History of Asceticism in the Syrian Orient*, 14–30; Winkler, 'The Origins and Idiosyncrasies of the Earliest Form of Asceticism', 21–7.

Clementines, for instance. In the *Acts* this concern about food is more closely connected with other issues of asceticism, in that links are drawn between eating and sexual practice. The *Acts* also provide the sort of transcendence of gender roles that might be expected in a community that rejects the ordering logic of sacrifice, while the Pseudo-Clementines seem fairly conventional in this respect, emphasizing separation rather than radical reordering.[42] The *Acts*, when considered as a corpus, allow the apostle Paul a place of honour (in the *Acts of Peter* as well as the *Acts of Paul (and Thecla)*, but the Pseudo-Clementines are often taken to refer to Paul in hostile fashion through the person of Simon Magus (see *Ep. Pet.* 2).

But more importantly for our purposes, the not-dissimilar food concerns do themselves diverge at certain points. Although there is some element of continuity between eating in general and eucharistic or communal eating in the apocryphal *Acts*, the eucharistic meals of the *Acts* are clearly defined, as for instance in the fairly common use of 'eucharist' as a term for the bread of the meal, rather than simply for the act of thanksgiving. The meals of the Pseudo-Clementines, while solemn and exclusive at times, are less clearly distinguished from other meals either in the practice depicted or in the use of specific terminology. 'Eucharist' for the community in this case is still the literal act of thanksgiving, little more than 'saying grace'. Yet all eating in the Pseudo-Clementine picture presents what is arguably a sacral quality, to which others cannot readily be admitted. This unity in diversity therefore confirms both the central meaning of the bread-and-water tradition as an anti-sacrificial ritual practice, and also the inadequacy of an analysis which reduces the practice to any one single group or theological tendency.

Although there are many uncertainties about these works at various points, it is thus reasonably clear that the Pseudo-Clementine *Homilies* and *Recognitions* and the apocryphal *Acts* reflect the same bread-and-water tradition of eucharistic meals represented by the evidence presented in the previous chapter. Not only do they consistently present communal meals involving bread and water alone or bread without mention of a cup, they also have other characteristics which enable us to connect them with the tradition discussed. Liturgical and general uses of food blend into one another, so that there seems at times to be more concern about non-consumption in all meals, and non-participation in pagan meals, than for the distinction of a particularly sacral eucharistic meal among others. The cuisine of sacrifice is named and rejected in the

[42] See Jay, *Throughout Your Generations Forever*, 30–60.

texts, as are various aspects of the social ordering that it is assumed to bring about: gender roles, at least in the *Acts*, and the animal–human structures which are reversed in the awkward fates of villains in the same works, and in the Pseudo-Clementines a thorough disengagement from society and creation of a new, pure social order.

Finally and most prosaically, we must note the fact that most informed suggestions as to the provenance of both bodies of literature allow us to include them in the sort of 'ascetic crescent' that began to take shape in the survey already started, i.e. in Asia and Syria. This last point may also be a further encouragement to acceptance that the meal descriptions of these works bear some resemblance to meals actually held. While there has been a tendency to place their witness to eucharistic meals to one side as 'encratite', and hence somehow to be marginalized as of limited value for the reconstruction of the whole picture of early liturgy and meal practice, the findings of the two previous chapters suggest that the horizon against which these documents may need to be read is somewhat broader than glib talk of encratism tends to allow.

There are, however, cases in these works where not all the elements we might expect appear. The *Acts of Peter* in particular may represent a case where the literary usefulness of the bread-and-water pattern seems to have outlived the social conditions in which it found meaning. The figures of the apostles raise the question of asceticism as a more specialized role with the Christian community. Both the literary persistence of the tradition and the possible signs of its passing or narrowing in some quarters lead us into the third category of witnesses to the use of bread and water in the eucharist, to which we now turn: appearances of the same ascetic pattern in unquestionably orthodox sources, at a point somewhat later than the heresiological and apologetic evidence in the last chapter and perhaps not far removed in time from some of these radical pseudepigrapha.

6

Orthodox Use of Bread and Water

INTRODUCTION

The texts discussed so far all, with the controversial exception of Justin, seem to have some direct connection with groups considered heretical or marginal to the emerging mainstream of normative or orthodox Christianity. If Justin can be included in the bread-and-water tradition, his practice can be accounted for in terms of his connection with some aspect of Syrian asceticism, reflected more clearly in the life and reputation of his associate Tatian. There are, however, other cases where the use of bread and water in eucharistic meals appears in what are otherwise orthodox sources. While the uncertainty as to the dates of such works as the apocryphal *Acts* and Pseudo-Clementines makes a relative time-line somewhat difficult, it seems likely that the prominence of orthodox use of water actually increases for a while, but the sparse nature of the sources makes this difficult to confirm.

PIONIUS OF SMYRNA

The third-century *Martyrdom of Pionius* is a clear witness, from what seems an impeccably orthodox source, to a bread-and-water eucharist.[1] Pionius was a presbyter of the Church of Smyrna, associated with the

[1] On the date (250) see T. D. Barnes, 'Pre-Decian *Acta Martyrum*', *JTS* NS 19 (1968), 509–31, esp. 529–31. This seems to be the date of the martyr account, even to those who dispute the authenticity of the dating of the martyrdom itself. According to Eusebius (*HE* 4. 15. 47), Pionius was a near-contemporary of Polycarp, and both were martyred under Marcus Aurelius. See, in favour of this early dating, H. Grégoire, P. Orgels, and J. Moreau, 'Les Martyres de Pionios et de Polycarpe', *Academie royale de Belgique: Bulletin de la classe des lettres et des sciences morales et politiques*, 5th ser. 47 (1961), 72–83. The choice is therefore between seeing the events as reflecting the time of Marcus Aurelius, in which case we could have considered this material along with the evidence assembled in Ch. 4, or reading them in the apparent literary context, whether this is close to the time of Pionius or not. The latter seems more reasonable. The narrative and its significance is discussed at length by Robin Lane Fox, *Pagans and Christians* (New York: Alfred A. Knopf, 1987), 460–90. Text and translation in Musurillo, *Acts of the Christian Martyrs*, 136–67, but note my qualification of the translation of the key text, below.

tradition of Polycarp.[2] The events take place during the persecutions under Decius, in the year 250. The evidence is fairly simple: 'After they had prayed and taken holy bread and water ($\mathring{\alpha}\rho\tau o\nu$ $\mathring{\alpha}\gamma\iota o\nu$ $\kappa\alpha\mathring{\iota}$ $\mathring{\upsilon}\delta\omega\rho$) on the Sabbath, Polemon the temple officer and those with him arrived to seek the Christians and force them to sacrifice and eat abominated meat' (ibid. 3. 1).

The very baldness of this account of the sacral foods of Pionius and his companions has been troublesome to scholars, leading to solutions at once anachronistic and speculative, similar at least in their refusal to accept this as a eucharist in the strict sense.[3] There is no doubt that Pionius was orthodox, or indeed that the category of orthodoxy is an appropriate one to use here, since both Marcionite and Montanist Christians also appear in the narrative as victims of the same persecution: a Montanist, Eutychianus, is among the imprisoned (ibid. 11. 2), and a Marcionite, Metrodorus, apparently faces death at the same time and with the same courage as Pionius (21. 5). By this point in time and in a community as well-attested as this one it is unlikely that we can plead the same sort of continuity between all meals and the specifically eucharistic meal characteristic of the communities such as those of the Pseudo-Clementines or at least some of the second-century manifestations of the practice.

While the description of the actions of Pionius and his companions could allow interpretation as some sort of domestic or low-key celebration of a eucharistic meal, it is inappropriate to suggest this should be seen as a sort of 'reserved sacrament' communion, especially if that means that the element of water is excluded from what is understood to be sacred food. The mention of water in the text is clear and deliberate, even if there may arguably be greater emphasis on the bread. That very feature, of course, also suggests some affinity with the other bread-and-water eucharists. It is inappropriate to invoke the idea of an *agape* here as a sort of second-class meal into which this case could fit because it has no wine; we have no clear idea as to whether wine would have been used in

---

[2] See *Mart. Pion.* 9. 1–2. Pionius has often been regarded as responsible for the preservation or even the composition of the *Martyrium Polycarpi*.

[3] e.g. Sr. Cyrilla CSMV, 'Pionius of Smyrna', *Studia Patristica*, 10, TU 107 (1970), 281–4: 'What seems to me a far more likely explanation is that they made their communion from the Sacrament reserved, of course, under the kind of bread only, and drank water as a kind of ablution' (p. 282). Musurillo's translation also emphasizes the bread above the water even more than the text seems to me to allow: 'after they had . . . taken the sacred bread with water' (*Acts of the Christian Martyrs*, 137). H. Leclerq thinks that since Pionius was no 'Aquarian heretic', the meal must be an *agape* related to the commemoration of Polycarp ('Agape', *DACL* i. 817).

an *agape* either, or indeed whether 'eucharist' and *agape* existed as separate traditions in this Church.[4]

The context of the martyrdom account as a whole, and of the other evidence concerning the bread-and-water tradition, may help to explain the apparent oddity. Pionius, Sabina, and Asclepiades were arrested by the temple officer and expected to eat (μιαροφαγεῖν) the abominated roasted meat of the imperial cult (ibid. 3. 1).[5] The opposition of pure and impure foods is very clear in the arrest passage quoted, and in fact throughout the martyrdom account the act of inappropriate eating is the very heart of what the faithful Christians will not do.

Here as elsewhere, the bread and water characteristic of the Christian meal are contrasted with the meat and wine of sacrifice to idols. In the situation of persecution and martyrdom which is more obvious in this text than in most of the others already discussed (though it can scarcely have been far away from some of the others either), the absence of wine may also have been an important sign of willingness to suffer rather than to be drugged and incoherent as at least some less stalwart Christians seem to have been as a result of rather lavish provision for martyrs-in-waiting (Tertullian, *De Ieiun.* 12. 3; cf. Lucian, *De Morte Pereg.* 12–13).

In the narrative the Jews of Smyrna, with whom Pionius had a conflict, are tarred with what may now seem an expected brush—the accusations of sacrificing to the Baal of Peor, eating the offerings of the dead (*Mart. Pion.* 4. 11; cf. Ps. 105: 28 LXX) and sacrificing their children to idols, i.e. as participating in sacrificial ritual. Pionius reports on a visit he had made to Palestine and the region across the Jordan. His description of the landscape draws on the same opposition between the deadly imagery of sacrifice and the peaceful nature of the bread-and-water eucharist in the form of a metaphor: 'I saw smoke rising even until now, and a land scorched by fire, deprived of all produce and water' (ibid. 4. 19; cf. 4. 21–4).

Food is also an issue at a more basic level throughout the *Martyrdom of Pionius*. There had been a famine at Smyrna, there was significant popular unrest as a result, and a renewal of the trial of the martyrs is ruled out at one point because there is some fear of the question of the

---

[4] McGowan, 'Naming the Feast', 314–18.

[5] In fact it is not clear which cult, and since the ensuing scene takes place in the temple of Nemesis this deity could be inferred; but other knowledge of Smyrna and of the persecutions leads J. Den Boeft and J. Bremmer to favour the imperial cult: 'Notiunculae Martyrologicae III: Some Observations on the Martyria of Polycarp and Pionius', *VC* 39 (1985), 110–30, esp. 118–19.

bread ration being raised in a public assembly (7. 1).[6] Pionius interprets these problems as divine judgement, but a bystander calls out to Pionius: 'You too went hungry with us' (10. 7); but at this time the issue is Pionius' refusal to eat, not inability to do so. When they are in prison, Pionius and his companions take their abstinence further, refusing the customary gifts of food even from believers (11. 3). Most strikingly, Pionius declares judgement on the city in ascetic terms: 'Now again is Hamman made drunk (cf. Esth. 3: 15), and Esther and the whole city is in terror. Once again there is no hunger or thirst for *bread and water* [my emphasis] but rather for listening to the word of the Lord' (12. 6–7). The unwanted abundance of meat and the desired fragments of bread thus stand in stark opposition in this narrative.

Yet it is not altogether clear from the text that Pionius would always have refused meat. The focus of anxiety is very clearly on the specific temple offerings, although these are presented as a system of slaughter, cooking and taking home to eat, not simply of token sacrifices; the turncoat Euctemon even takes a cooked lamb home (18. 13), clearly illustrating the link between public religion and domestic diet. Whether in Pionius' water-drinking we have an instance of something like the rest of the bread-and-water tradition, i.e. a combination of general and liturgical asceticism, or a more narrowly focused concern about the proper elements of the Christian sacral meal (or appropriate times to eat or drink) in the face of persecution, is unknown. Nevertheless Pionius' actions fit very well within the shape of the ascesis typical of the bread-and-water tradition. His odd sacramental practice is firmly associated with rejection of sacrifice, and his Asian origin is by now no surprise.

There is some difficulty in harmonizing a Smyrnean ascetic tradition of this sort with the fact that Irenaeus of Lyons, a critic of the bread-and-water tradition, was also associated with Polycarp and gives no hint of a controversy of this kind in Asia.[7] It is possible that in some communities

[6] Following the text, rather than the emendation of Gebhardt (accepted by Musurillo) from 'an investigation about the bread (ἄρτου)' to one 'about the person (ἀνθρώπου)'. The change is unnecessary when the importance of the issue is appreciated; cf. *Mart. Pion.* 12. 7, where Pionius draws on the idea of famine ('not from bread and water but from hearing the word of the Lord') to lament the treatment of the Christians.

[7] Polycarp's *Letter to the Philippians* gives no clear indication of eucharistic practice, but is concerned with fasting (7. 2) and abstinence (11). Its affinity with the Pastoral Epistles seems to place Polycarp in a more accommodating position than that of the bread-and-water tradition. The *Martyrium Polycarpi* does not come from his hand of course (see above on Pionius), but the narrative uses positive sacrificial imagery in juxtaposition with the sacrificial practice demanded by the authorities. The powerful image of him 'not as burning flesh but rather as bread being baked' (15. 2) certainly fits with the general opposition maintained here.

the practices of using water and avoiding meat were not original but were introduced by more rigorist tendencies. The sort of interaction attested between the moderate Attalus and the radical Alcibiades in Gaul (Eusebius, *HE* 5. 3. 2–3) qualifies Irenaeus' silence, however, and might not always have been resolved in the same direction. These examples also provide some evidence for a porousness of practice even across boundaries that might otherwise be assumed to be well fixed. We have seen that there were Montanists and Marcionites in Smyrna who joined Pionius in martyrdom. Tertullian's incomplete treatment of Marcionite practice in his earlier writings has already been provided as a possible example of intimidation of the orthodox by the radical rejecters of the cuisine of sacrifice (*Adv. Marc.* I. 14. 3).[8] But we need not restrict ourselves to these well-known and readily defined ascetic groups to seek such influence in Smyrna.

Ignatius of Antioch's *Letter to the Smyrneans* indicates the presence of a different group, usually labelled 'docetists' by commentators because of their apparent Christology, who had qualms about the form of eucharist promoted by Ignatius and his allies. 'They remain aloof from eucharist and prayers because they do not confess that the eucharist is the flesh of our saviour Jesus Christ which suffered for our sins' (Ign. *Smyrn.* 7. 1, Schoedel, 238). Despite this disengagement it seems that the opponents do have their own eucharistic meal gatherings (cf. ibid. 8. 1). The criticism that they have no regard for charitable works may also be an indicator of a more sectarian social practice.[9] Of course Ignatius himself never specifies what the content of the eucharistic cup ought to be, but this controversy would fit neatly, in space and time as well as conceptually, with the bread-and-water tradition. In any case, the earlier arguments at Smyrna are a reminder that different liturgical as well as theological tendencies could have been present at an early stage and thus had the potential to go on influencing each other; it is not necessary to think of an outside or later group as bringing about the sort of ascesis demonstrated by Pionius.[10] Pionius might have been following the

---

[8] See Ch. 4 above.

[9] William R. Schoedel, *Ignatius of Antioch*, Hermeneia (Philadelphia: Fortress, 1985), 238–42, points out that Ignatius may be exaggerating the attitude of the dissenting group, and that to withdraw from the other community might necessarily have meant disengagement from acts of charity associated with the eucharistic assembly. See above on the way this issue features as an exception in the *Acts of Peter*.

[10] Since I give this by way of example rather than as a specific instance of the bread-and-water tradition, I suspend judgement on the question of how accurately the Ignatian correspondence depicts the situation in Smyrna. In any case, we can safely say that the issues discussed in the letter were real in parts of Asia and/or Syria in the 2nd cent.

established tradition of his church, or acting out a set of oppositions present in his society as a whole and well known in his region, under the influence of other local practices.

CYPRIAN

Water in the Desert

The letter of Cyprian of Carthage to Caecilius regarding the proper celebration of the eucharist (*Ep.* 63) also dates from around the persecution of Decius, and hence is remarkably close in time, if not space, to the story of Pionius.[11] Like the last text discussed, it gives clear evidence of the use of bread and water as elements of the eucharistic meal among Christians who were regarded as doctrinally orthodox and in no (other) way isolated from catholic Christianity.[12] While the letter is of interest for a number of reasons, not least that it is the first extended discussion of the meaning of the eucharist, it is the position and practice of those whom Cyprian opposes which concern us immediately.[13]

Cyprian acknowledges that while 'for the most part bishops who by the grace of God have been set in charge over the Lord's churches throughout the world' (ibid. 63. 1. 1) follow what he regards as the dominically instituted practice of using a mixture of wine and water in the 'cup of the Lord', 'there are some who, whether through ignorance or naïveté' offer water (ibid. 1). The 'some' must therefore also be among those divinely acknowledged bishops, and given the clarity of Cyprian's picture of the Church as visible institution the impact of this point ought not to be lost. This is certainly no tirade against heretics or schismatics, but a correction of an error which, however grave he takes it to be, is a matter of mainstream practice.

Cyprian's concern to argue his own position in a charitable though uncompromising way reinforces the impression that the problem is fairly close to home for him, literally and otherwise. The fact that the addressee is Caecilius, presumably the bishop of Biltha, a senior episcopal colleague who seems to be above reproach in this respect as

---

[11] See the notes on the letter as a whole in the translation of G. W. Clarke, *The Letters of St Cyprian of Carthage*, ACW 46 (New York: Newman, 1986), iii. 286–301; on dating, 287–8.

[12] Despite the judgement of G. G. Willis, 'St Cyprian and the Mixed Chalice', *Downside Review*, 100 (1982), 110, who is more candid, if no more accurate, than some others in calling the opponents 'members of some cranky sect'.

[13] Clarke, *The Letters of St Cyprian*, 288.

in others, and that there is reference in the letter to a general instruction to bishops (63.17), suggest that it has the character of an encyclical, and hence that the practice or problem may also have been quite widespread rather than a single or rare aberration.[14]

The letter is fairly complex, and it is not clear at every point whether Cyprian is directly refuting an argument or simply creating one of his own in order to knock it down. The first five exegetical sections (63. 3–7) present Noah (Gen. 9: 20–1), Melchizedek (and Abraham; Gen. 14: 18), the personified Wisdom of Proverbs (9: 1–5), the blessing of Judah (Gen. 49: 11), and the wine-press image of Isa. 63 as types of the use of wine in the cup.[15] Of these, only the troublesome Noah story invites the thought that Cyprian might be refuting an exegesis that rejects the use of wine as improper or immoral. Noah, he acknowledges, had become drunk and was shamed, but his experience was a type of the passion of the Lord (63. 3).

Two later sections, however (63. 8. 1–2), may address exegetical traditions that see references to water in scripture as figures of a eucharistic cup containing only water.[16] The first deals with the promise of water in the desert accompanying Isaiah's miraculous way (Isa. 43: 18–21; 48: 21). Cyprian counters that all references to water in scripture (typological interpretation of the Old Testament is largely in mind) indicate baptism, not the eucharist (63. 8. 1). This implies that his opponents do take some passages, these Deutero-Isaiah texts among them, as types of a eucharistic cup with water. Cyprian himself is inconsistent on this point; for instance, he takes the waters of Rev. 17: 15, already interpreted in that text itself as indicating various peoples, to refer to the water of the mixed cup of the eucharist (63. 12–13). This is perhaps a further indication of an occasional rhetorical strategy put to use in addressing the exegesis of opponents, rather than of a solid and positive typological tradition of his own.

Cyprian uses the institution narratives from the Gospel of Matthew (26: 28–9) and from Paul (1 Cor. 11: 23–6) to shore up his argument (*Ep.* 63. 9–10). From the former he takes up the clear statement, made after the words of institution, that Jesus would not drink again from the fruit of the vine, which implies that the preceding cup was indeed of wine. In the Corinthian correspondence Cyprian finds the more general point which recurs throughout his own letter, i.e. that it is the following of this pattern of Jesus' command that makes the offering legitimate (*Ep.* 63. 10. 2).

---

[14] See ibid. 291.
[15] See the discussion above, Ch. 4, of Justin's approach to the blessing of Judah.
[16] Clarke, *The Letters of St Cyprian*, 294 n. 18.

As many have pointed out, the actual words of institution do not refer to the contents of the cup in any of the New Testament versions, and it could be that a liturgical use of the narrative lacking the vow of renunciation might not have seemed to conflict with use of water. Yet at a number of points we are given reason to wonder whether those being criticized were not simply selective in their communal reading of the Last Supper stories, but may have had a quite different basis for the understanding of the eucharistic meal, less beholden to Jesus' sacrificial death and the imagery of his body and blood. Cyprian's constant reiteration of the need to follow that 'institution' is the most general reason to think so; in some sense at least, he seems to regard them as following another tradition, even though it is hard to tell just what that was.

The Cup of the Blood of Christ

The mistaken do seem to be squeamish about the idea that the cup was the blood of Christ:

> It may be that some feel apprehensive at our morning sacrifices that if they taste wine they may exhale the smell of the blood of Christ. That is the sort of thinking which causes our brethren to become reluctant to share even in Christ's sufferings in times of persecution, by thus learning in making their oblations to be ashamed of the blood that Christ has shed himself . . . How, I ask then, can we shed our blood for Christ's sake, if we blush for shame to drink Christ's own blood? (*Ep.* 63. 15. 2)

Perhaps Pionius could have answered the question. Although the passage could be taken to mean that the participants feared to have the smell of wine on them at that time of the day and thus to be detected as Christians,[17] we should also consider the possibility that there is here at least a remnant of a conscientious objection of sorts: a refusal to participate in what seems to be a sacrificial ritual, or to share in a cup that is identified as the blood of Christ and thus also in guilt for Christ's death. The fact that the text of the letter was later glossed in the direction of the simpler explanation about the smell of wine encourages us to consider this other possibility all the more.[18] It is worth

[17] Thus (e.g.) ibid. 297 n. 36.

[18] For 'ne per saporem vini redoleat sanguinem Christi' some versions read something along these lines: 'ne per saporem vini odore fraglantia odor vini horis matutinis fuerit agnitus et cognoscatur esse christianus dum nos sanguine christi in vini oblatione confundimur'. See the apparatus of Hartel in CSEL iii. 713.

remembering that among the other cases of the bread-and-water tradition we have seen little use of body and blood imagery. There have also been few indications of a link with the idea of the eucharistic meal as a Lord's Supper; the prominent terminology is that of eucharist and breaking of bread, which could perhaps look back to the miracle stories or resurrection appearances as much or more than to the Last Supper. It seems reasonable to conclude that the refusers of wine are not so much, or at least not only, objecting to the smell of wine but to the stigma of blood. Whether this objection still has all the same implications that it did in the other examples of the bread-and-water tradition is another matter.

In any case, Cyprian's link between an acceptance of the blood of Christ and willingness to accept martyrdom may be one of the innovations of the letter. In the story of Perpetua as much as that of Pionius (as well as in the apocryphal *Acts*), the oppositions of bloody sacrifice and the arena on the one hand, and the peaceful realm on the other, are very prominent. So too, the rejection of the logic of sacrifice and various aspects of the social and cosmic order that depend upon it was very strong in those accounts.[19] Cyprian's opponents might well have been inspired by the example of these—Perpetua was certainly known to them—and have taken bread and water to be the appropriate food of the martyr Church, as did their Smyrnean contemporary.

The prominence in Cyprian's letter of the body and blood imagery of the institution narratives as well as of the language of sacrifice itself may not be incidental. The term 'sacrifice' is mentioned literally dozens of times. He insists on following the example of Jesus with fidelity, but construes this as faith in the efficacy of the eucharist as sacrificial act: Jesus is 'the author and teacher of this sacrifice' (ibid. 63. 1. 1). Although there may have been sacrificial aspects of Paul's teaching to the Corinthians and even of the Gospel accounts of Jesus' Last Supper, Cyprian takes this sense of the meal as sacrifice further than ever before. As we have seen in discussion of other cases where water was employed in the eucharist, the connection between sacrifice and use of wine is to be expected, and is rather more to Cyprian and his readers than a case of blind obedience to specifically Christian tradition; it is also a necessary

---

[19] Discussions of the idea of sacrifice and martyrdom in early Christianity seem often to look quickly for 'implicit' sacrificial logic in places where it might be better to acknowledge there is none; thus Robert J. Daly, *Christian Sacrifice: The Judaeo-Christian Background Before Origen* (Washington: Catholic University of America Press, 1978), 373–88, tends to equate sacrifice with self-offering or with combat. Of course there are also cases where sacrificial logic does seem to be present: *Mart. Pol.* 14; Ign. *Rom.* 2. 2.

connection to be inferred from the world of food, ritual, and symbol known to them.

The positive meaning for Cyprian of constructing the eucharist as a sacrifice is not of primary importance here, but some initial suggestions can be made. Despite the fact of persecution and martyrdom, Cyprian sees the Church not as counter-cultural but as a means of social order; he is concerned as much for its unity as for its place in the rest of the world. As a great figure in the emergence of ecclesial order, Cyprian promulgates a teaching on the eucharist with implications that have as much to do with real power as with real presence.

A Time for Drinking

There is another indication of objections to the mixed cup which might fit less easily into the pattern of the other witnesses to the bread-and-water tradition:

> But some may possibly deceive themselves with this comforting reflection, that even while it is clear that water only is offered up in the morning, yet (they claim) 'when we come to supper we offer a cup that is mixed' . . . Then again, it may be further objected, it was not in the morning but only after supper that the Lord offered the mixed cup. Are we, therefore, to celebrate the Lord's sacrifice after supper so that we may then offer a mixed cup with the brethren gathered all together at that time for the Lord's sacrifice? Now it was only proper that Christ should make his offering toward the evening of the day . . . Whereas for us, we celebrate the resurrection of the Lord in the morning. (ibid. 63. 16)

Cyprian's diffidence in introducing this argument before refuting it may be rhetorical, but it is the only indication we have on this aspect of the views being refuted. The position opposed here seems to distinguish between appropriate times for drinking water and drinking wine. This would have been a very respectable moral position, and one for the understanding of which no great exertion of cultural sensitivity is required; drinking in the morning was inappropriate.[20] It is possible that this sort of concern came originally from the same kind of source as the more radical position, but that it has changed in form and is no longer opposed to the general cultural norms; on the contrary, it is the manifestation of the accepted standards of society as a whole. Any

---

[20] Cf. Apuleius, *Apol.* 57, where midday carousing is attacked; Cicero, *Phil.* 2. 34. 87; Acts 2: 15; 1 Thess. 5: 7–8.

connection with broader dietary exclusions seems likely to have been lost.[21]

Although it is tempting to read it in, Cyprian gives no indication of a recent move from evening assemblies to morning ones, which might otherwise explain a new objection to this use of wine; it is simply that the whole Church cannot possibly attend a normal *cena*. It would be wrong for us to take the absence of wine from the cup of a morning gathering as having resulted from such a move in time, or at least to reach such a conclusion from this evidence alone. Rather, for its proponents, the cup of water and the hour of the day it is taken are simply natural correlates, and their complaint is more likely to be related to the desire to maintain a tradition. No teetotallers these, Cyprian's ritual water-drinkers use the different beverages as markers of the difference between day and night, just as their respectable neighbours do. However they came to adopt or preserve these traditions, if they are represented with any accuracy by their opponent, these are actually more accommodating Christians than the orthodox, rather than radical separatists. The fact that there is no mention in the letter, or in other evidence from Cyprian, about eating meat may also be an important indication that this is now, at least, a rather mitigated form of asceticism that owes more to general notions of moderation and respectability than it does to social separatism. We must, however, at least leave open the possibility that these contemporaries of Pionius would also have shared his determination not to sacrifice or to celebrate their eucharist in a way that reeked of the shedding of blood; like him perhaps, they may have refused meat only in the context of sacrifice, and wine only at the eucharist.

Conclusions

How are Cyprian's opponents historically related to the other, earlier, water-drinkers already discussed? There is no certain answer to this question. It is tempting to see them, or at least their practice, as historically somehow an offshoot of Montanism, since that movement is the clearest evidence prior to this of the bread-and-water tradition in Africa.[22] If this were so, we would have to assume that Montanists were reabsorbed into catholic Christianity, or that the moral superiority

[21] So also P. Battifol, 'Aquariens', *DACL*, i. 2652.

[22] Lebeau, *Le Vin nouveau*, 180–1, suggests a Jewish-Christian group, linking these practices with Augustine's testimony to 'Symmachians' (*Contra Cresconium Donatistam*, i. 31). This seems to give too much credence to centripetal tendencies in heresiological writings.

claimed by Tertullian and his associates influenced some other Christians sufficiently for them to adopt the use of water alone in the cup. The second passage quoted at length above (ibid. 63. 16) might give some oblique support to this more indirect possibility. At least some of the water-drinkers are concerned that they be seen to be highly moral and respectable people. It is not hard to imagine the same sort of rhetoric that we find in the earlier Tertullian being used by those concerned to maintain the standards of the African communities with regard to proper times to drink. We saw that even Tertullian at his most rigorous defended the fact that Montanist fasts and xerophagies were temporary, in contrast to those of Tatian, Marcion, and others (*De Ieiun.* 15. 1). In this whole discussion of the bread-and-water eucharists, concern with the right times at which to exercise various ascetic disciplines has in fact only come up otherwise in connection with Montanism, although this would be a tenuous link at best. Otherwise, we have already seen that in socially accommodating circles it was normal to mark particular times, places, and persons by the use of the same ascetic practices that were typical of the whole lives of radicals.[23]

The other passage cited, on the question of drinking the blood of Christ (*Ep.* 63. 15), is more difficult to interpret in terms of a connection with Montanism. Cyprian's argument does seem to imply that the opponents were hostile to the identification of the eucharistic cup with the blood of Christ. Why, or indeed whether, this was a more heinous matter than the eating of the body of Christ is not stated, but it may be that the elements are not understood by the opponents as the body and blood of Christ at all. More clearly, the argument is focused on the cup simply because this is where the practical difficulty arose; they objected to wine. Bread was not a matter of contention and could be interpreted in various ways. The fact that this objection focuses on the cup and not the bread, and hence not purely on the imagery but the concrete elements of the meal, also may well be a link with the earlier water-drinkers.

All this implies a tradition which, originally at least, used bread and water and which did not construct the eucharistic meal primarily as an *anamnesis* of Jesus' Last Supper and sacrificial death. Cyprian's sometimes ponderous insistence on the importance of the form of institution, and on the sacrificial understanding of the meal, encourages us to think of a group or tradition similar in this respect at least (i.e. the absence of concern for the Last Supper) to those represented in the Pseudo-

---

[23] See esp. Ch. 3 above.

Clementines and the apocryphal *Acts*. But these features could also have been present in Montanism, and we simply do not have enough evidence to reconstruct a specifically Montanist theory of eucharistic meals. Whether or not these links with Montanism are sufficient to explain the genesis of the practices Cyprian refutes, the actual form of belief and practice known to and opposed by him is obviously quite different from those of radical ascetics fifty years or so earlier.

AQUARIANS

This seems the appropriate point at which to return to the Aquarians and *Hydroparastatai*.[24] Like (some of?) Cyprian's ignorant or simple addressees, these were apparently Christians for whom the tradition of using water in the cup was a more narrowly ritual concern; we know little about either group, and indeed they could be the same one, but there is no implication that they held any of the other opinions about meat and wine generally found in the earlier forms of the water tradition. The tendency for discussion to label virtually all the water-drinkers already discussed as Aquarians is obviously anachronistic at best; there is no indication that this term was used by the people in question, or even by their opponents, until this rather late stage, i.e. in the fourth century.

Theodoret's *Hydroparastatai* are actually distinguished by him from Encratites by the specifically sacral-meal focus of their concern about wine (*Haer. Fab.* 1. 20). The *Aquarii* are introduced by Filastrius (*Div. Haer. Lib.* 77) in the same sort of terms, but without the comparison with more radical types; they are those 'who offer water in the heavenly sacraments, rather than what the catholic and apostolic Church counsels'.[25] This same description is taken up by Augustine (*De Haer.* 64). John Chrysostom also mentions a heresy which consists of using water alone in the eucharist, but gives no details (*Hom. in Matt.* 82. 2). None of this evidence need be based on firsthand knowledge, but Cyprian's letter and Pionius' example make it quite plausible that these otherwise orthodox and accommodating groups did exist and had existed for some time.

---

[24] See Ch. 4 above.

[25] 'Aquarii sic dicti sunt, qui in sacramentis caelestibus offerunt tantum aquam, non illud quod ecclesia catholica et apostolica facere consuevit.' Jülicher, 'Zur Geschichte der Abendmahlsfeier', 223, dismissed this witness as derivative of Cyprian ('er hatte eben Cyprians 63. Brief gelesen oder davon gehört.'), but I think this is too quick an association to draw. The relatively neutral designation *Aquarii* does not come from Cyprian, nor need it be a derisive heresiological invention.

Basil of Caesarea's discussion of the possible need for rebaptism for such people (*Ep.* 188, can. 1) is a more concrete indication that there were some for whom this was a real pastoral problem. Basil distinguishes between those he regards as heretics such as Marcionites and Montanists, whose doctrine and baptismal practice differed so markedly from the orthodox, and sectarian groups, specifically *Cathari*, Encratites, and *Hydroparastatai*, who were seen as merely schismatic and not in need of rebaptism. The real existence of these people and their apparent orthodoxy in other respects is, therefore, clear enough. Whether there really were well-defined groups with all these names is another question. In particular, *Aquarii* and *Hydroparastatai* may well have been nicknames rather than self-designations. As with the earlier and more radical water-drinkers, there is certainly no good reason to collapse all the evidence into one group and one set of practices and beliefs.

It is not insignificant that at this later stage there is as much or more evidence for Christians who differ from (other) orthodox only in this specific ritual sense, than for the radical water-drinkers. This may serve to confirm, if negatively, the sense that the continuance of the broader dietary restrictions attested earlier was related to a general dissent from the normative pattern of sacrifice. These later Christians, in the time of Basil or Theodoret, are rather more a part of what becomes the theological and social mainstream, and have no need to maintain that opposition. Their preference for water in the cup of the eucharist is maintenance of a tradition whose earlier rationale is increasingly alien to their actual existence. It persists in the form of an asceticism which represents nothing more radical than the stricter end of the generally accepted spectrum of behaviour, and of the use of wine in particular; this shift is arguably present already among Cyprian's opponents. The remnants of an objection to drinking 'blood' and to sacrifice in the case of the African water-drinkers suggests genetic links between these people and the earlier ones, but now the very same thing which had distinguished their forebears from other Romans seems more like the respectable objection raised against the Christian eucharistic meals by second-century critics. Not surprisingly, this position is increasingly rare and seems to become more a matter of heresiological lists than of active practice and belief.

AFTERWORD: LATER ASCETIC MOVEMENTS AND THE BREAD-AND-WATER TRADITION

The dissipation of the radicalism of the bread-and-water tradition into the sort of awkward and merely ritual asceticism, emerging among the opponents of Cyprian and fully developed for the *Aquarii*, represents a convenient place at which to end the survey. This end-point is not, however, by any means the end of food concerns in Christianity or even of the bread-and-water tradition itself. It is rather a point at which, or at least soon after which, the ordering of food in orthodox Christianity moves into a different phase. The bread-and-wine tradition of eucharistic meals has now (more) clearly become the normative pattern of ritual practice. In this pattern, attested from the New Testament onwards, meat is eaten with the proviso that it has not been sacrificed to idols; wine is drunk on condition that it is in moderate quantities. The eucharistic meal is clearly distinguished from other meals and has a token rather than a substantial character and quantity; it derives its criteria of appropriateness not from the general rules for eating, but from the tradition represented most clearly by Cyprian, who goes back to Paul and interprets the Pauline catechesis on the Lord's Supper to construct a meal which is *sui generis*, ordered according to the unique command of Jesus and the logic of sacrifice rather than the general demands of asceticism.

The emergence of the more sacrificially understood eucharist as normative and the emergence of the great Church and of Christianity as a state religion-in-waiting are not linked by coincidence alone. Cyprian's detailed formulation of the meaning of the eucharist, the first of which we know, goes further than the statements of Justin, Clement, or Tertullian about the Christian meal as a sound and sober gathering. Now the meal is a sacrifice in a new sense; if this is not the first application of the logic of sacrifice to the meal, it is nevertheless a telling and historic one.[26] Cyprian's work does not effect the social changes in Christianity, but provides the eucharistic meal with a logic that ultimately proved effective.

Prior to the triumph of the sacrificial (and hence wine-using) eucharistic tradition within Christianity and of Christianity within the

---

[26] See Frances Young, *The Use of Sacrificial Ideas in Greek Christian Writers from the New Testament to John Chrysostom*, Patristic Monograph Series, 5 (Philadelphia: Philadelphia Patristic Foundation, 1979), 278–82.

Empire, the various patterns of eucharistic meals can be understood to have vied for supremacy, at least in certain parts of the East. The bread-and-water tradition had been the single most important alternative pattern, not only of ritual practice but of ascesis, of construction or ordering of the world of food, and for that matter of the other aspects of social and cosmic order also. After that point, however, it would be wrong to say that the tradition is simply quashed; rather it is reordered in various ways.

First, there are continuing appearances of radical ascetic interpretations of Christianity in which this same dietary and ritual tradition is accepted. In the fourth century the Priscillianist and Messalian movements are forms of Christianity with at least some affinity to the bread-and-water tradition. Priscillian and his followers seem to have been rather theologically orthodox despite the claims of their detractors, but were certainly ascetic, and seem to have been inspired at least in part by the apocryphal *Acts*.[27] Priscillian was accused of magic and Manichaeism, perhaps because he pronounced incantations over fruit (Priscillian, *Tract*. 1. 27–8), and might not have been surprised or dismayed to follow Perpetua and Pionius to martyrdom after a civil trial, the first Christian to suffer thus at the hands of Christian authority.[28] There is some evidence that the Priscillianists were ascetic in the specific context of the eucharist. The Council of Saragossa (380) insists on the reception and consumption of the elements, apparently because some are not doing this.[29] The possibility of some organic connection with the earlier bread-and-water tradition would be supported by indications of Eastern origins or influence.[30]

More definitively linked with the East were the Eustathian ascetics and their successors the Messalians, groups who had an uneasy relationship with the churches in Asia Minor in the mid- to late fourth century. The Synod of Gangra, probably held in 340, condemned a number of practices or beliefs which correspond closely with the forms of asceticism discussed above. These included refusal to eat meat (Can. 2), to recognize marriage or the validity of the office of married clergy (Cann. 1, 4, 5), to

[27] Henry Chadwick, *Priscillian of Avila: The Occult and the Charismatic in the Early Church* (Oxford: Clarendon, 1976), 61–9; B. Vollman, 'Priscillianus', PWSup xiv. 494–5.
[28] Raymond Van Dam, *Leadership and Community in Late Antique Gaul* (Berkeley: University of California Press, 1985), 101–6.
[29] See Chadwick, *Priscillian*, 23, and now Virginia Burrus, *The Making of a Heretic: Gender, Authority and the Priscillianist Controversy* (Berkeley: University of California Press, 1995), 36–7, 43–4.
[30] Van Dam, *Leadership and Community*, 90 n. 9.

accept conventional distinctions of dress between the sexes (Cann. 13, 17), to participate in the *agape* meals held by the rich for the poor (Can. 11), and to allow or accept participation in popular ceremonies of martyr-cultus. As a set, these refusals bear a strong resemblance to the bread-and-water tradition.[31] Basil of Caesarea continued to give counsel about Encratites and others (*Ep.* 199). Even late in the fourth century, ascetic Christians near Laodicea could cast aspersions on the orthodox simply by defining them as 'wine-drinkers' (οἰνοπόται).[32]

Even the designation of these groups as heresies and condemnation of their practices did not mean the end of the influence of the anti-sacrificial ascesis, even within the mainstream. In the case of the Asian ascetics in particular, the problem seems to have been the fact that they would have prescribed their own pattern of life for all Christians. Basil the Great, pillar of orthodoxy, seems in fact to have been very deeply influenced by Eustathius and to have upheld forms of asceticism very much like those condemned at Gangra, with the all-important difference that they were, in his model, channelled into the emergent phenomenon of monasticism.[33]

The monks were successors of the early ascetics, restored apostles in the tradition of the heroes of the pseudepigrapha. We read of the diet of the great Anthony: 'His food was bread and salt, his drink, water only. Of flesh and wine it is superfluous even to speak' (*Vit. Ant.* 7). Indeed![34]

---

[31] The resemblance between the practices condemned at Gangra and the *Acts of Philip* in particular was noted by Erik Peterson, 'Die Häretiker der Philippus-Akten', 97–111. Later groups such as Bogomils and Cathars may also have some organic links with the tradition. A popular account of these and later groups with similar characteristics is provided by Colin Spencer, *The Heretic's Feast: A History of Vegetarianism* (London: Fourth Estate, 1993), 149–79; see now also Dianne M. Bazell, 'Strife Among the Table-Fellows: Conflicting Attitudes of Early and Medieval Christians toward the Eating of Meat', *JAAR* 65 (1997), 85–94. Bazell's discussion does not deal with much of the material at issue here, but illustrates the way superficially similar ascetic food practices (and the avoidance of meat in particular) could have quite different meanings.

[32] An inscription cited by Lebeau, *Le Vin nouveau*, 147 n. 6, but not traceable further.

[33] K. S. Frank, 'Monastische Reform im Altertum: Eustathius von Sebaste und Basilius von Caesarea', in R. Bäumer (ed.), *Reformatio Ecclesiae: Beiträge zu kirchlichen Reformbe-mühungen von der alten Kirche bis zur Neuzeit* (Paderborn: Schöningh, 1980), 35–49; J. Gribomont, 'Saint Basile et le monachisme enthousiaste', *Irénikon*, 53 (1980), 123–44; G. Kretschmar, 'Die Theologie der Kappadokier und die asketischen Bewegungen in Kleinasien im 4 Jahrhundert', in P. Hauptmann (ed.), *Unser ganzes Leben Christus unserm Gott überantworten: Studien zur ostkirchlichen Spiritualität* (Göttingen: Vandenhoeck & Ruprecht, 1982), 102–33.

[34] The persistence of controversies in Egypt concerning the real presence of the body and blood of Jesus may also suggest a survival of the liturgical aspect, if only conceptually rather than in foods: see Elizabeth Clark, *The Origenist Controversy: The Cultural Construction of an Early Christian Debate* (Princeton: Princeton University Press, 1992), 63–6, 156–7.

Theodoret's *History of the Monks in Syria* shows an even more uncompromising asceticism, in food as in other areas. When the Syrian monks eat and drink at all, their preferences are for bread, vegetables, and water, and to avoid cooking; their asceticism again a sort of preference for nature over culture.[35] Since these athletes of virtue have been given such expansive treatment there is little need to pursue their practice here, but there may be some value in noting its genealogy to a greater extent than has previously been the case. In monastic circles the bread-and-water tradition took on a somewhat different meaning, it must be acknowledged; yet one might ask whether this metamorphosis of the liturgical and dietary tradition could have taken place without the emergence of the Christian society, and the corresponding possibility or need for an uncompromising group to take up a stand of disengagement or opposition to the dominant culture and its cuisine. Of course in this case the dissidents and the society functioned rather better together than the earlier proponents of the tradition had done, but as previously the dietary ascesis marked this group as different, and as refusers of much of what the society and its rulers offered.[36]

The era of Christian ascendancy also arguably sees a shift of focus towards the individual body as a locus of concern. This was not, of course, altogether absent in such as Clement or Tertullian, but the more expansive writers of the fourth and following centuries, who have provided much of the source material for the recent flurry of scholarly activity on Christian asceticism, theorize in a way which perhaps parallels the rise of the monastic movement, and allows rejection of meat and wine to have a real but circumscribed place. While concerns for food as a basis of medicinal and (individual) moral integrity may perhaps have been implicit in the bread-and-water tradition as discussed above, they were hardly prominent; but with a Jerome or an Augustine, as with the Desert Fathers, food is very much part of the problem of desire and of sexuality, and meat and wine are symbols of luxury and causes of lust.[37]

[35] Theodoret, *HE* 1. 2; Sozomen, *HE* 6. 33. See further Aline Rouselle, *Porneia: On Desire and the Body in Antiquity*, trans. F. Pheasant (Oxford: Basil Blackwell, 1988), 160–78.

[36] On the Syrian holy men and their diet Peter Brown, 'The Rise and Function of the Holy Man in Late Antiquity', *Society and the Holy in Late Antiquity* (Berkeley: University of California Press, 1982), 131, remarks that their 'attitude to food itself rejected all the ties of solidarity to kin and village that, in the peasant societies of the Near East, had always been expressed by the gesture of eating'.

[37] Jerome, *Ep.* 22. 8. See Brown, *The Body and Society*, 220–4, 366–86; Bazell, 'Strife Among the Table-Fellows', 76–81.

One final aspect of the heritage of the bread-and-water tradition and the limited acceptance of the rejection of meat and wine may be noted in the tendency for all Christians to be called at particular times to a temporary asceticism rather like the earlier radical and permanent one. The use of food as a marker of times and seasons was already noted with regard to the use of foods other than bread and wine in eucharistic meals, especially as testified to in the *Apostolic Tradition*. Thus the fourth-century *Apostolic Constitutions*, for instance, prescribe for the average believer a diet of bread, salt, water, and vegetables during Holy Week, specifically forbidding meat and wine (5. 18). Just as monasticism provided a place for the dissident diet by dividing the population, fasting practices did so by dividing times. In both cases these orderings of food were more sustainable, allowing the expression of the concerns inherent in the tradition without absolutizing them. The end of the bread-and-water tradition was therefore not oblivion but reordering, just as Christianity itself was being reordered in the vastly changed circumstances of the fourth and following centuries.

7
Bread and Water and the New Testament

INTRODUCTION

At the end of the previous chapter we reached what seemed to be an end of sorts, a change in the meaning and manifestations of the bread-and-water tradition perhaps having much to do with changes in the relationship between Christianity and society as a whole, as well as with the emergence of stronger and more centralized forms of ecclesial authority. The examples of orthodox use of bread and water and the acknowledgement of a continuing ascetic meal tradition in monastic and other specialized ascetic circles has seemed an appropriate place to end the survey; but questions of various kinds remain about its beginning.

In the earlier discussions of asceticism it became clear that there were also forms of the bread-and-water meal tradition, or something like it, in earlier contexts such as those of Hellenistic Judaism and of philosophically minded forms of dissident Greek practice, well before the first clear examples indicating the use of water in the eucharistic cup of Christian groups such as Ebionites. While the primary purpose of this study has been to contribute to the study of food in Christian meals between the New Testament and the fourth century, there are questions which must now be raised, if perhaps not fully answered, about the possibility of tracing the bread-and-water tradition through the New Testament also.

This chapter will consider the New Testament as a source for the tradition in two senses: first, as a possible repository of earlier evidence for similar ascetic and ritual meal practices in Christian circles; second, as providing models or other bases for meal practice in the bread-and-water tradition as attested in the following two centuries or so. The first major section of the chapter will accordingly examine the possible evidence for the ascetic meal tradition in the New Testament. In the second, I will consider the other side of the coin; the influence and use of New Testament meal models in the bread-and-water tradition. In both sections some attention is given to the broader questions of the origins and development of eucharistic meals and especially to hypotheses of dual origins, for which the evidence of the eucharistic meals using bread and water, or bread alone, have been particularly important.[1] The purpose here is not, however, to develop a generalized theory of the emergence of eucharistic meals from the New Testament evidence, but rather to continue the project of interpreting the use of foods and of considering a particular set of meals in their own terms.

BREAD AND WATER IN THE NEW TESTAMENT

Origins

In the process of describing above the use of bread and water as the elements of a eucharistic meal in a variety of (originally) Asian and Syrian traditions of the second and third centuries in particular, the likelihood of an explanation along the lines of ascetic modification, in the sense of removal of an offending element (wine) from a normative pattern of bread and wine, has been assessed as rather low. While it may be true that ascetic tendencies are common to all the instances discussed, it is asking too much to imagine that the great variety of groups attested, some clearly opposed to one another, all independently took on practices that seem remarkably similar. It is more likely that the use of water in the eucharistic meal was a very early tradition on which the different groups all drew. The geographical focus already established for the bread-and-water tradition also increases the likelihood of a common origin, rather than convergent evolution. This means that the usage in question was probably established in Christian circles at or before the time of some of the New Testament writings; being attested in a diversity of groups in the mid- to late second century, the tradition might reasonably be assumed to have emerged no later than the end of the first. In fact it seems likely that it may really go back even further, since divisions similar to those among the various exponents of the tradition on issues such as their attitudes to Judaism and to the apostle Paul are already evident in the New Testament writings.[2]

A number of passages in the New Testament suggest concerns remarkably similar to those of the bread-and-water tradition. Most

---

[1] Lietzmann, *Mass and Lord's Supper*, 195–203.

[2] See Galatians, *passim*. There are indications of polemics within the bread-and-water tradition: Justin opposes Marcion (*1 Apol.* 26), as do the Pseudo-Clementines (*Hom.* 2. 43 etc.) and Bardaisan, who can be linked with the Elkesaites (Eusebius, *HE* 4. 30).

obvious and important are references in the genuine Pauline epistles to members of the Christian communities who have difficulties with eating meat offered to idols (1 Cor. 8, 10), and to some who reject not only eating of all meat but also drinking wine (Rom. 14), the precise combination of concerns characteristic of the dissident ascetic pattern. In deutero-Pauline letters there are two further references to situations or practices which may also be linked, in 1 Timothy and Colossians. The phrase 'breaking of the bread', used as a designation for eucharistic meal gatherings in Luke–Acts, has been considered an indicator of wineless eucharists.³ Other possible indications of emphasis or concern regarding the cup in the redaction history of the institution narratives, in the Letter to the Hebrews, and in the Gospel of John may suggest disputes related to the same ascetic tradition.⁴

We have already seen that the bread-and-water tradition had pre-cursors in paganism and Hellenistic Judaism. The most likely origin of the pattern in Christian circles may be that it was a continuation of such asceticism from Jewish practice, already existing in different commu-nities around the Mediterranean before the arrival of Christian preach-ing. The theoretical possibility that a bread-and-water meal has some specific link with the practice of Jesus may be noted, but will not be pursued here. There is no indication of such a form of asceticism in the 'Jesus movement' or in Gospel traditions, whatever conclusions one reaches about the reliability of various stories and sayings.⁵ Despite the romantic appeal of a simple Galilean peasants' meal persisting in a dissident stream of Christianity, it seems more likely that the bread-and-water tradition is substantially different from any communal meal pattern attributable to Jesus. While it may be as early as the sacrificial meal of the Pauline Lord's Supper, the bread-and-water meal does show marked contrasts with the 'gracious table' likely to be discernible in the practice of the historical Jesus. The ongoing debates about the relation-ship between the meals of Jesus and the meals of the early Church must

---

³ Lietzmann, *Mass and Lord's Supper*, 195–203.

⁴ See Edward J. Kilmartin, 'A First Century Chalice Dispute', *ScEccl* 12 (1960), 403–8; Heinz Schürmann, 'Das apostolische Interesse am eucharistischen Kelch', *MTZ* 4 (1953), 223–31; Johannes Betz, *Die Eucharistie in der Zeit der griechischen Väter* (2 vols.; Freiburg: Herder, 1955), i. 26–34.

⁵ The basic argument may seem again to be *ex silentio*, but Jesus seems to have been characterized as a not sufficiently careful eater and drinker, and he may well have invested wine with special significance as a sign of the reign of God: See John P. Meier, *A Marginal Jew: Rethinking the Historical Jesus* (2 vols.; New York: Doubleday, 1991–4), ii. 146–52, 302–9. The related question of fasting seems clear enough; Jesus and his followers were criticized for refusing to fast: ibid. ii. 446–50.

be left to one side here.[6] This discussion of the New Testament is therefore not by any means exhaustive, but is an attempt to pursue different assumptions about the form, origins, and meaning of the types of dietary asceticism attested in those writings in cases where we have reason to posit some real connection, or at least parallelism, with the bread-and-water tradition.

Corinth

While the First Letter to the Corinthians is certainly an important source for early eucharistic meal practice because of the discussion of appropriate behaviour at the Lord's Supper (1 Cor. 11), our interest is primarily in the indications that some Corinthians ate food, presumably meat,[7] known to have been offered to idols, and that others refused to do so.

Since some have become so accustomed to idols until now, they still think of the food they eat as food offered to an idol; and their conscience, being weak, is defiled. 'Food will not bring us close to God'. We are no worse off if we do not eat, and no better off if we do. But take care that this liberty of yours does not somehow become a stumbling-block to the weak. For if others see you, who possess knowledge, eating in the temple of an idol, might they not, since their conscience is weak, be encouraged to the point of eating food offered to idols?

(1 Cor. 8: 7–10)

The question of idol meat at Corinth is a particularly well-trodden path for commentators, and most recent discussions owe something to the analysis of Gerd Theissen, who has argued that the 'strong' (1: 27, 4: 10) and the 'weak' (8: 7–12) are to be identified with the members of upper and lower classes present in the community,[8] and that the implications of meat-eating might have been somewhat different for the two groups. The Corinthian correspondence and its context are perhaps unique in the opportunity they give to correlate rhetoric with other indications of social standing, even with prosopographical data from such hard evidence as inscriptions.[9] This evidence seems to favour

---

[6] A summary of these issues with relevant bibliography is found in J. W. Riggs, 'The Sacred Food of *Didache 9–10* and Second Century Ecclesiologies', in Clayton N. Jefford (ed.), *The Didache in Context: Essays on Its Text, History and Transmission*, NovTSup 77 (Leiden: E. J. Brill, 1995), 257–62.

[7] I note the possibility of other foods being included (as suggested by Gooch, *Dangerous Food*, 5–13, etc.), but meat is still clearly the main issue at hand.

[8] Theissen, 'The Strong and the Weak in Corinth', 137–9.

[9] See Theissen, 'Social Stratification in the Corinthian Community: A Contribution to the Sociology of Early Hellenistic Christianity', *The Social Setting of Pauline Christianity*,

a socially mixed community, in which 'not many' may have been wise or powerful or of noble birth (cf. 1: 26), but at least some apparently were. In Theissen's reconstruction, the strong who wished to eat freely are more likely to have been wealthier members for whom the implications of refusing to participate in banquets would have been devastating in more than gastronomic terms.[10] The weak are the poor, those for whom rare opportunities to eat meat came almost entirely from explicitly religious public festivals or distributions, and for whom there was less incentive to overcome what might have been more formidable associations between meat-eating and pagan religion.[11]

This analysis has recently been criticized for overlooking the cook-shops (*popinae* or *ganeae* in Latin) which potentially gave poorer people some regular access to meat.[12] Nor were the economic and social differences between meat-eaters and others as simple as a matter of rich and poor. There was an expectation, attested even by the opponent of meat-eating, Porphyry, that certain occupations (athletes, soldiers, and manual labourers) needed meat (*De Abst.* 2. 4. 3). The association of meat-eating with soldiery was notorious, and probably not a positive connotation.[13] There were, therefore, some well-known patterns of meat-consumption among the less well-off members of a city such as Corinth.

Yet the importance of social status and economic power may survive as a central issue for interpretation of the passages related to idol meat, if only with significant qualification.[14] A more nuanced account of the consumption and meaning of meat among rich and poor is necessary, and a more careful correlation of that account with the apparent positions of strong and weak. The poor and the rich would both have been affected by the problem of idol meat, albeit in different ways. Neither the private

69–119. The appendix to Andrew Clarke, *Secular and Christian Leadership in Corinth: A Socio-Historical and Exegetical Study of 1 Corinthians 1–6* (Leiden: E. J. Brill, 1993), 135–57, is a good source of data.

[10] Theissen, 'The Strong and the Weak in Corinth', 130–2.

[11] Ibid. 128–9.

[12] Justin J. Meggitt, 'Meat Consumption and Social Conflict in Corinth', *JTS* NS 45 (1994), 137–41. On these see also Corbier, 'The Ambiguous Status of Meat in Ancient Rome', 226–34.

[13] See Corbier, 'The Ambiguous Status of Meat in Ancient Rome', 229–30, 242–4, and Meggitt, 'Meat Consumption and Social Conflict in Corinth', 137–41.

[14] Theissen's thesis may also survive as a viable interpretation for meat-eating in Corinth at the time of the correspondence on the more narrowly historical grounds of prohibitions on the sale of cooked meat in such shops by Claudius (Cassius Dio, 60. 6. 7, cf. 62. 14. 2, and Suetonius, *Nero* 16).

banquets of the rich nor the cook-shops escaped the implications of the cuisine of sacrifice.[15]

The rich would not merely have had an intellectual freedom to eat, based on education in philosophy or some form of esoteric knowledge (cf. 1 Cor. 8: 1–7); they might have been able to exercise conscience in the markets even more actively than Paul suggested. It seems that the rich would have had more choices, even the possibility of choosing meat that was not sacrificed.[16] Of course Paul does argue with some for whom it is apparently a matter of indifference to eat meat known to have been sacrificed, and even to eat it in a temple precinct (8: 10). But we might well ask whether this was, however obviously problematic from a religious point of view, anything more than the logical consequence of willingness to eat meat generally available, whether in markets or at banquets, since the association of all meat with sacrifice was so strong. The distinction that Paul seeks to make between the eating of meat in a temple and doing so in a dining-room (8: 9–13; 10: 14–33) is arguably one of his own making, at least in so far as he can encourage one and fulminate against the other. Commentators have perhaps been too quick to overlay a sacred–secular distinction that does not really do justice to the extent of the cuisine of sacrifice and its ideology.[17]

On the other hand, if the poor would have been the main clientele of the cook-shops, and if they could buy at least some forms of meat there, this is by no means to say that they had access to a secular or otherwise safe source of meat any more than wealthy diners escaped the religious connection when they entered a private dining-room. The meat of the cook-shops had to come from somewhere. While sacrificial meat may have been more highly prized and hence less likely to end up in a *popina*, the tendency of these establishments to serve offal and other lesser cuts, too coarse for the palate of the wealthy but present in every animal regardless of form of slaughter, suggests that temples might have supplied them, too. There even seem to have been cases

---

[15] See also the discussion by Wendell Lee Willis, *Idol Meat in Corinth: The Pauline Argument in 1 Corinthians 8 and 10*, SBLDS 68 (Chico, Calif.: Scholars Press, 1985), 7–64. While Willis concentrates on other specifically cultic meals in his description of the significance of 'eating with the god', his discussion helps illustrate the difficulty in drawing clear boundaries of the sacred versus the secular.

[16] There are indications of the possibility of exercising the choice in reverse, i.e. of choosing sacrificial meat; see Plutarch, *Quaest. Conv.* 729 c and further Isenberg, 'The Sale of Sacrificial Meat', on the reference in the *Life of Aesop*.

[17] See Dale Martin, *The Corinthian Body* (New Haven: Yale University Press, 1995), 182–3.

where cook-shops were directly connected with sacrificial practice, e.g. through guilds which offered sacrifice and ran cook-shops too.[18]

On a somewhat different but important note, those shops were notorious places of ill-repute (Juvenal, 8. 167–78; Martial, 7. 61; Plautus, *Poenulus*, 4. 2. 1–13). A poorer member of the community might have been more conscious of risking morality and reputation than of peril to religious affiliation when entering such an establishment. Meat-eating may thus have seemed to poorer Christians, who had fewer choices, to be a dangerous culinary course, steering between a religious Scylla and a moral Charybdis.[19]

How do these structures for production and consumption of meat seem to fit with the picture of the strong and the weak and their concerns? Most of the attention in the scholarly debate has been given to the position of the Corinthian strong, since they are apparently Paul's addressees more of the time, and because their behaviour is judged by him to be the more problematic. It has also been suggested on such rhetorical grounds, independent of the class or status questions, that the strong are probably the leaders of the congregation.[20] There is no basis on which to question Theissen's central claim about the relative social importance of eating meat to the wealthier members and the corresponding likelihood of some degree of rationalization about doing so. Yet the attitude of the strong to meat-eating is not so much a matter of placement in society, but of posture towards society, as it were. The strong are content, or even eager, to take up the opportunities of social engagement, whether or not they can already be identified as leading members of the wider Corinthian community.

But what of the weak? These are akin to the water-drinkers of the later Christian evidence in their concern about meat-eating. Paul's use elsewhere (1 Cor. 1: 26–9) of similar 'weak and strong' rhetoric in explicit reference to the power and social standing of the members of the community does seem to make it likely that the weak of chs. 8 and 10 were largely Corinthians of lower status. Yet the evidence from the later bread-and-water tradition and from other examples of dissent from the cuisine of sacrifice suggests caution in taking that assumption too far.

---

[18] *IG* ii². 1301, and Ferguson, 'The Attic Orgeones', 113–14.

[19] There were sumptuary laws aimed at preventing the poor from obtaining access to meat, a characteristic product of Roman attitudes: see Corbier, 'The Ambiguous Status of Meat in Ancient Rome', 224, 226–7, 240, 242, 244–5.

[20] Theissen, 'The Strong and the Weak in Corinth', following M. Rauer, *Die 'Schwachen' in Korinth und Rom nach den Paulusbriefen*, BibS(F) 21; (Freiburg: Herder, 1923), 2–3, 36.

Pythagoreans, Cynics, and Jews had avoided eating sacrificial meat for reasons which were arguably of social importance, and even of class significance, but which defy a deterministic correlation of class, knowledge, and interests. The later, post-New Testament examples of the bread-and-water tradition in Christianity also seem to suggest that there could be choices involved in such asceticism, and that voluntary poverty might have been at issue, rather than just making a ritual virtue of necessity.

The position of the weak might then be best understood not as a form of excessive scrupulousness, easily dismissed as fearful or lacking in initiative because of Paul's dismissal (and that of the strong), but rather as a form of protest or disengagement from the dominant culture.[21] Here in first-century Corinth, as in other periods and other societies, patterns of resistance to the dominant ideology were likely to emerge not solely from the oppressed, but from members of the dominant group who resisted the norm and created dissident forms of practice, 'cultural space' where alternatives were possible. This is true in culinary terms as much as for politics; both sumptuary and ascetic tendencies seem likely to emerge in the same societies and from similar social strata.[22] Rejection of meat was of course not merely a religious issue but a social one, since the poor had less access to meat, however far we qualify Theissen's argument. Those who reject meat are at least taking up a set of practices perceived to be more akin to those of the poor. Yet were the weak only to be seen as entrenching a dietary position that was more or less theirs by default, we might wonder what the fuss was about.

While Paul's argument is directed to the strong and may imply their leadership and high status, we need not therefore jump to conclusions about the place of the weak, or at least of all of them. While the position of the strong on the question of meat makes sense for high-status readers, the position of the weak might well be understood as sophisticated rather than as fearful, and does not make any less sense for people of higher social backgrounds. It is, however, a clearly dissident stand rather than one which would reflect the existing material interests of either rich or poor. The differences between strong and weak thus have as much or more to do with the social implications of their actions as with their social

---

[21] Hans Conzelmann's judgement, *1 Corinthians: A Commentary on the First Epistle to the Corinthians*, Hermeneia (Philadelphia: Fortress, 1975), 147, seems unwarranted: 'The "weak" are neither Jewish Christians nor any closed group at all. They do not represent a position. They are simply weak'.

[22] This is discussed in a particularly helpful way by Jack Goody, *Cooking, Cuisine and Class*, 97–127, drawing upon both Graeco-Roman, Indian, and Chinese examples.

origins. It may be that the interests of the members of the Corinthian church helped suggest their placement along the weak–strong axis, but it would be reductionist at best to see this possible correlation as exhausting the social significance of the controversy.

The difference between the implications of meat-eating or refusal for the higher- and lower-class Christians, while important, is not as absolute as Theissen might seem to suggest. Neither the lousy cook-shops nor the decorous *triclinia* escaped association with the cuisine of sacrifice. The choice between religious and social explanations for the problems at Corinth is a false one, and one which assumes ultimately that to be religious was not a social matter. Acceptance or rejection of the cuisine of sacrifice was not merely a symbolic enactment of social conflict but constituted conflict itself; to be Christian or to be a good citizen was a profoundly social question as well as a profoundly religious one. To eat or not to eat was not merely a question of signalling allegiance, but of acting that allegiance out in the most important and obvious way. Paul's catechesis on the Lord's Supper shares this understanding with his criticism of the eating of such food; in either case, to eat is literally to internalize the reality of the gods whom one served (1 Cor. 10: 16–21). Paul's failed attempt to separate these questions even in his own mind is an indication of the depth of the connection.

There is no question, therefore, that what is at issue at Corinth is the cuisine of sacrifice (even though there is no mention of the weak excluding wine). The fact that Corinth is a rather long way from the 'ascetic crescent' already described may lead us to hesitation in suggest-ing a direct historic link with the later Christian bread-and-water tradition. Nevertheless the same opposition, of pure bread and defiling meat, seems to be present in this controversy.

Rome

At Romans 14 we may have the earliest clear example of something like the bread-and-water tradition, in the sense of combined avoidance of both meat and wine, in specifically Christian circles:

Welcome those who are weak in faith, but not for the purpose of quarrelling over opinions. Some believe in eating anything, while the weak eat only vegetables. Those who eat must not despise those who abstain, and those who abstain must not pass judgement on those who eat; for God has welcomed them. . . . Everything is indeed clean, but it is wrong for you to make others fall by what you eat; it is good not to eat meat or drink wine or do anything that makes your brother or sister stumble. (Rom. 14: 1–3, 20–1)

In this case both elements of the typical dissident response to the cuisine of sacrifice are present.[23] Notably, there is no direct reference to sacrifice or idolatry, in contrast to 1 Corinthians, yet this need not be taken as indicating a different set of concerns so much as confirming the obviousness of the issue.[24] And while there is no clear connection in this case with the celebration of a communal meal, the general concern about diet referred to in the Romans passage may well need to be linked with issues of liturgical practice, as in the later examples already discussed. There is no basis for thinking that a person who was unwilling to drink wine at all would somehow make an exception for the cup of a eucharistic meal.

The weak Christians of Romans 14 have often been identified with Jewish members of the community, more so than now tends to be the case for the analysis of the Corinthians, where Theissen's social approach has won many converts. This has more to do with the history of scholarship than with inherent differences between the issues in the two cases. The Letter to the Romans has tended to elicit responses drawing on the 'history of religions' approach, wherein connections with religious movements and traditions are seen as of prime importance for interpretation.[25] Yet the link that has been established already between the avoidance of meat and that of wine suggests that some social implications could also be drawn for the Roman situation too, if not so

---

[23] Rauer's, *Die 'Schwachen'*, 97–100, exclusion of wine (from the situation rather than from diet) is tendentious and unnecessary to the case which his work sought to promote, i.e. that the 'weak' were Gentiles influenced by pagan religion. One of the reasons why he excludes the possibility is that if there were no wine, there could be no eucharist!

[24] C. E. B. Cranfield, 'Some Observations on the Interpretation of Romans 14, 1–15, 13', *Communio Viatorum*, 17 (1974), 195, finds this inconceivable, but the specific terminology in 1 Corinthians seems to come from the list of issues addressed in the letter (see 1 Cor. 1: 1), perhaps from the Corinthians rather than from Paul.

[25] Both Jewish and Gentile customs involving meat-avoidance such as those discussed in Ch. 2 have been mentioned by commentators, but Jewish-Christians tend to be seen as the weak and Gentiles as the strong, on the assumption that restricted diet signals kosher concerns: this is the position taken by Joseph Fitzmyer, *Romans: A New Translation with Introduction and Commentary*, AB 33 (New York: Doubleday, 1992). Others are more circumspect: Ernst Käsemann may be right to suggest that this is too simple (although his diagnosis of an essential and recurrent conflict within all Christianity also needs to be questioned); see *Commentary on Romans*, 364–9; C. K. Barrett, *A Commentary on the Epistle to the Romans*, 2nd edn. (London: A. & C. Black, 1962), 256–7, acknowledges the lack of a good fit with Jewish asceticism.

much in terms of the social placement of the addressees, then at least in terms of the poles of accommodation and dissidence.[26]

As has already been pointed out, the rejection of wine and meat does have a specifically Jewish manifestation, but is hardly an exclusively Jewish issue in either origins or practice. The demands of *kašrut* are not in themselves likely to have led to such prohibitions in a place such as Rome.[27] The issue of Jewish–Gentile commensality, acknowledged as a distinct issue by some scholars, may take us a little further.[28] In this view the objections would have had to do with idolatry (and therefore with the cuisine of sacrifice) rather than with the Levitical food laws, and the attitudes to idolatry and food characteristic of the strong and the weak, while perhaps based on Gentile and Jewish positions or tendencies, need not have been strictly ethnic divisions.[29]

Yet if there is no clear basis, apart from evidence of some anxiety about food, to conclude that the issue is one of division between 'weak' Jewish and 'strong' Gentile factions, there is less indication again that the groups are divided over commensality itself. The problem at Rom. 14: 20 is not whose meat to eat and whose wine to drink, but whether to eat meat and drink wine at all. To see the issue in terms of commensality seems to imply that meat would have been eaten, and wine drunk, if it could have been found in an appropriate form. This is certainly not clear from the text itself, and comparison with the other examples of bread-and-water asceticism would encourage us to consider the contrary. The strong in this case are not people who eat in temples, since they are not criticized by Paul, but simply people who eat in terms Paul finds

[26] Peter Lampe's analysis of the Roman community makes use of the disputed Rom. 16 as well as later evidence to develop a prosopography which favours a community dominated by the lower strata. See his *Die stadtrömischen Christen in den ersten beiden Jahrhunderten: Untersuchungen zur Sozialgeschichte*, WUNT 2/18 (Tübingen: J. C. B. Mohr, 1987), and the summary of this discussion in 'The Roman Christians of Romans 16', in K. Donfried (ed.), *The Romans Debate*, 2nd edn. (Peabody, Mass.: Hendrickson, 1991), 216–30.

[27] Cf. the case of Alexander the *bubularus*; see H. J. Leon, *The Jews of Ancient Rome* (Philadelphia: Jewish Publication Society of America, 1960), 233–8, 293–4. Others (e.g. Barrett, *Romans*, 256) have recognized the unlikelihood of such difficulties. Francis Watson, 'The Two Roman Congregations: Romans 14: 1–15: 13', in Dronfield (ed.), *The Romans Debate*, 204, suggests that the upheavals of 1st-cent. life might have made ceremonially pure meat and wine more difficult to obtain, but even if true this begs the question of the association of meat and wine.

[28] Alan Segal, *Paul the Convert: The Apostolate and Apostasy of Saul the Pharisee* (New Haven: Yale University Press, 1990), 231, 234.

[29] Thus Watson's 'two congregation' analysis of the problem acknowledges that one group might contain proselytes and the other 'non-observant' Jews like Paul. See 'The Two Roman Congregations', 203–4.

uncontroversial, in homes and perhaps even with ceremonially pure food. By implication the weak have some more specific discipline than this. Some members of the Christian community at Rome, whether Jewish or Gentile, understood the idolatrous associations of meat and wine to be so deep-seated that their consciences were affronted by all meat and all wine.

The fact that the earliest Christian communities are not merely linked to Judaism but, despite the presence of Gentile members, 'embedded' in it, does makes it more likely that the genetic links with other avoiders of meat and wine come through Jewish ascetic practice rather than directly from Greek dissident asceticism.[30] There are also other possible indicators of characteristic Jewish concerns such as observance of particular days for feasts or fasts (Rom. 14: 5–6) and perhaps some specific terminology.[31] It is, however, erroneous to exclude the influence of pagan ideas and practices. Immediate Jewish origins neither prescribe the meaning of the bread-and-water tradition in this case, nor do they mean that a Jewish–Gentile split is at issue. It is perfectly possible that the two tendencies represent more and less accommodating Jewish responses to Roman society, and particularly to commensality and integration, tendencies that even predate Christianity. Of course we cannot rule out the possibility of a mediation of these concerns through more specifically Gentile channels such as Cynic philosophy.[32] All in all, however, the ongoing attempts to deal with the identity of these individuals or communities in terms of religious traditions are not especially helpful, and depend upon rather simplistic pictures of the relationship between dietary ascesis and the different religious influences.[33]

The connection between, or rather identity of, the characteristic

[30] See Dieter Georgi, 'The Early Church: Internal Jewish Migration or New Religion', *HTR* 88 (1995), 35–68.

[31] On the use of κοινός and καθαρός and their possible connections with Greek philosophical terminology and the Hebrew Bible, Cranfield, 'Some Observations on the Interpretation of Romans 14, 1–15, 13', 196–7, says: 'In our opinion it is not possible to decide with absolute certainty between the last two suggestions; but we incline to the view that (the latter) is the more probable of them'.

[32] It is not necessary to link this issue to the question of whether Gnostic groups existed at this time, as some earlier attempts at identifying the weak as Gentiles seem to have done; see Rauer, *Die 'Schwachen'*, and the comment of Fitzmyer, *Romans*, 687.

[33] 'It is impossible to pick out from the many examples of religious scrupulosity to be found in antiquity any single group of persons corresponding exactly to those described here by Paul' (Barrett, *Romans*, 257). This is a good summary statement, but the futility of the quest illustrates the need to go past questions of *Religionsgeschichte*. Thus also Robert J. Karris, 'Romans 14:1–15:13 and the Occasion of Romans', in Donfried (ed.), *The Romans Debate*, 65–70; the alternative method here is of course rather different.

asceticism of the bread-and-water tradition and social withdrawal or dissidence has some further potential to shed light on the passage. The situation depicted in Romans fits well with the possibility of a group or individuals with firm convictions about disengagement from the wider society and its cuisine. The 'weak' at Rome seem to be regarded by Paul as presenting more of a challenge to him and to other members of the community than do the similar group at Corinth. The weak Christian is capable of putting up an argument (14: 1), of passing judgement on others (14: 3, 10, 13), even of speaking of the eating habits of the others as 'evil' (14: 16). After apparently toying with the suggestion that each should do as they please (14: 2–6), Paul eventually gives the weak the upper hand in practice (14: 23–15: 2).

All this suggests not only that their position was actually a firmly held one, rather than a sort of half-heartedness about food, but that the individuals or group referred to had the capacity to divide the community and may have done so literally.[34] It is more likely in this case that the rhetoric of 'weakness' may be Paul's attempt to disarm a group whose rigorism is actually quite a powerful force for him to contend with. In this conjunction of strength of conviction (if not of 'faith' as Paul understands it here) and exclusion of both meat and wine, it is even easier than in Corinth to see some forerunner of the bread-and-water tradition. Although we have no idea what meal traditions were practised in these groups, the insistence on avoidance of wine must imply that communal meals did not use wine in a cup. Again, however, the lack of clear historic links between Rome and the later examples (except perhaps the difficult case of Justin) suggests an analogue, rather than an ancestor, for the later wineless eucharists and meatless meals.

The weak at Rome are therefore easy to imagine as an entrenched and articulate group, whose weakness is largely a matter of Paul's rhetoric, rather than of strength of conviction or even of social origins. Of course there are other problems concerning the Letter which must make us circumspect about its value for reconstructing the situation at Rome.[35] Yet the discussion of wine and meat in Romans 14 is at least plausible as a response to a situation about which Paul had some concrete knowledge from informants. In this case again, consideration of the social meaning

---

[34] The insistence on purity (and withdrawal from impure eating) characteristic of the bread-and-water tradition could well support Watson's suggestion of two congregations: 'The Two Roman Congregations', 205–6. These specific characteristics of the weak may also add to the argument that the letter is occasional rather than a generalized paraenesis based on (the somewhat different argument of) 1 Cor. 8 and 10.

[35] See Karris, 'Romans 14:1–15:13 and the Occasion of Romans', 65–84.

of the bread-and-water tradition as an oppositional practice, deriving its meaning from the cuisine of sacrifice which it refuses, leads to a fuller analysis of the text. The significance of the ascesis of the weak Roman Christians was less a matter of the influence of the religious tradition through which it was mediated, than of adoption of a stance towards the dominant culture and its primary rituals.

1 Timothy

A reference to drinking not only water but wine in the First Letter to Timothy (1 Tim. 5: 23) may be another example of resistance to rigorous asceticism from the Pauline tradition. When the writer urges the addressee to 'Keep yourself pure. Do not drink water only, but take some wine because of your stomach and your frequent ill-health', we seem initially to be in the realm of medicinal advice. This sort of understanding of the power of wine is well known in antiquity (Hippocrates, *De Medic. Antiq.* 13; Plutarch, *De San. Praec.* 19). Yet the real and implied readers and authors need some separation in this later attempt to harness Paul's authority to the establishment of order in the household of God.

The position of the addressee (or of those addressed through the literary fiction of a personal address) is implicitly religious or ascetic in a technical sense. 'He' is urged not 'to drink water (ὑδροποτεῖν)', which term is used elsewhere in the exclusive and conscious sense conveyed by the addition of 'alone' or 'only' to 'drink water' in most English translations. That is to say, it means 'Do not be a water-drinker.'[36] The implication could well be association with some tradition or practice, or at least a sort of ascetic self-definition, rather than an incidental personal habit. Again it would seem that any eucharistic meal practice would be affected by this stance, and water must have been the content of the cup (if any) in the practice of the addressees or of those whom the author fears may influence them.

The immediate context gives no motive or other explanation for this practice. In fact the lack of obvious connection between the advice and the surrounding text, an exhortation on appropriate choice and practice of community leaders, is somewhat embarrassing for commentators.[37]

---

[36] See M. Dibelius and H. Conzelmann, *The Pastoral Epistles*, Hermeneia (Philadelphia: Fortress, 1972), 80–1.

[37] See A. T. Hanson, *The Pastoral Epistles*, New Century Bible Commentary (Grand Rapids, Mich.: Eerdmans, 1982), 104.

Here the possibility of choosing between, say, Jewish or Gnostic influences offers little to an understanding of the reference.[38] The water-drinking referred to could conceivably be the more self-conscious and individualized form of asceticism wherein avoidance of inappropriate foods and drinks (especially wine and meat) is seen as an aid to education or spiritual growth (Plato, *Leges*, 6. 782 C). Elsewhere in the letter, excessive wine-drinking seems a potential problem (3: 3, 9), but there are also false teachers to contend with whose message includes forbidding marriage and advocacy of abstinence from certain foods (4: 3). Asceticism is also attacked, or at least played down, in more general terms (4: 8). The conjunction of issues therefore suggests not merely a shared concern between writer and addressees for personal growth, but a veiled conflict involving radical asceticism.

If we are dealing with something like the bread-and-water tradition here, then the dietary and sexual ascesis seems unlikely to be based on philosophical dualism, but on an ethic of purity based on rejection of dominant culture and cuisine. While we can know little more for certain about the position of the false teachers, the accommodating position taken by the author of the letter towards rulers (2: 1–4) and conventional relations between the sexes (2: 8–15) is in very clear contrast with that of the opponents mentioned in ch. 4, and for that matter with the uncompromising shape of the bread-and-water tradition. Whether there is any specific evidence of the later bread-and-water tradition here, the advice to 'Timothy' not to be a water-drinker fits very well with the author's attempt to present his Christianity in terms most acceptable to respectable pagans. The author demonstrates not merely approval for the medicinal use of wine, but an openness to the culture from which this understanding comes. In wider contexts than that of medicine the two different drinks seem to fit well with the two world-views, one accommodating and the other ascetically aloof.

This letter professes to have been written by Paul, who has travelled to Macedonia, to Timothy, who has remained in Ephesus. While this is not likely, the association with Ephesus is probably not meaningless, and most scholars acknowledge some connection either with that city or with the Asian churches of the Pauline mission.[39] In turn, this makes a historical link with the later bread-and-water tradition far

---

[38] The discussion by Dibelius and Conzelmann, *The Pastoral Epistles*, 80–1, cf. 65–6, distances itself only mildly from a sort of pan-Gnostic approach characteristic of scholarship earlier in the century.

[39] See Hanson, *The Pastoral Epistles*, 11–14, 21–2.

from unlikely. The similarity of these charges to the picture of the apocryphal *Acts* and to specific heresies or factions attested elsewhere has often been noted.[40] Some have gone so far as to suggest that Marcion is the source of the problems addressed in this and the other Pastoral Epistles, and that Polycarp of Smyrna may have been their author.[41] Such a judgement must be made taking into account factors other than those at issue here; it should be said that the widespread Asian-Syrian ascetic tradition already outlined does not help, since there are many other candidates. Marcion may have been the hidden opponent of the Pastoral Epistles, but it is also possible (and I think more likely) that their absence from his canon simply reflects his ignorance or rejection of them.[42] Tatian also seems to have rejected 1 Timothy as uncanonical (Jerome, *Comm. in Ep. ad Tit.* Praef.). The attitudes of the respective parties to wine, marriage, and pagan society generally make these choices easy to understand.

The 'Breaking of the Bread'

A number of times in the Gospel of Luke and the Acts of the Apostles (Luke 24: 35; Acts 2: 42, 46; 20: 7, 11; 27: 35), a meal of apparent significance for the Christian community is referred to by the simple phrase 'the breaking of the bread'. The verbal focus on this action as the key element of a shared meal led Lietzmann and others to see in this a type of eucharistic meal in which wine was not used.[43] In the cases where the meal is not merely named but described to any extent, as in the encounter between two disciples and the risen Jesus at Emmaus (Luke 24: 25) and in Paul's meal with the community at Troas (Acts 20: 7–11), no mention of wine is made. In fact the Acts of the Apostles mention wine at all only once, in allegations of drunkenness against the Christians at Pentecost (2: 13). Nor does wine seem to feature particularly strongly

[40] Dibelius and Conzelmann, *The Pastoral Epistles*, 64–7; P. Dornier, *Les Épitres pastorales*, Sources Bibliques (Paris: Lecoffre, 1969), 75–6.

[41] Most notably Bauer, *Orthodoxy and Heresy*, 213–28, and Hans von Campenhausen, 'Polykarp von Smyrna und die Pastoralbriefe', *Aus der Frühzeit des Christentums: Studien zur Kirchengeschichte des ersten und zweiten Jahrhunderts* (Tübingen: J. C. B. Mohr (Paul Siebeck), 1963), 197–252. See the criticism by Dibelius and Conzelmann, *The Pastoral Epistles*, 2. This thesis has been revived with a different chronology by Hoffman, *Marcion: On the Restitution of Christianity*, 281–305.

[42] Tertullian, *Adv. Marc.* 5. 21. See von Campenhausen, 'Polykarp von Smyrna und die Pastoralbriefe', 204 n. 22.

[43] Lietzmann, *Mass and Lord's Supper*, 195–6.

in Luke's Gospel.[44] The Paschal chronology of the Last Supper which Luke shares with the synoptic tradition implies the use of wine at that meal, but this fact is at least balanced, for ethical purposes, by Jesus' vow of renunciation (22: 18). Yet the Lukan version of the Last Supper with its longer text referring to two cups (22: 17–20) may also be a witness to eucharistic meals with priority of the cup or with an additional cup, rather than with none.[45] It is particularly hard to imagine Paul as a practitioner of a wineless eucharist (see Acts 20: 7–11).[46]

If the position these works take on wine is ambiguous, that on meat is not; they seem to have a position somewhat like (if not identical to) the Pauline one, in distinguishing between meat in general and that strangled or with blood or offered to idols (Acts 15: 20, 29). It would therefore be difficult to argue for a clear or substantial connection between Luke–Acts and the bread-and-water tradition. It is possible in theory that the 'breaking of the bread' is a different tradition again, one marked not by refusal of wine (or meat) but simply by indifference to the presence of wine, perhaps in continuity with meals celebrated by Jesus.[47] Such a hypothesis is necessary to Lietzmann's case, in that the only instances of a wineless eucharist he is able to link with the Luke–Acts model, other than the clearly wine-avoiding ones of the bread-and-water tradition, are those where wine is actually present (!), such as the *cena dominica* of 'Hippolytus' (*Ap. Trad.* 26. 1–12).[48] There are no cases, despite Lietzmann's argument, of eucharistic meals with the use of bread alone reflecting indifference to the matter of a cup. As we have them, Luke–Acts can at best be seen as a rather indirect witness, perhaps by way of use of earlier materials and historical reminiscence, to a practice which these books no longer systematically present by any means. This evidence is not, however, without value, as a possible trace of eucharists

---

[44] John the Baptist renounces wine from the womb (Luke 1: 15); Jesus speaks of the new wine and wineskins (5: 37–9). Jesus does seem to drink wine, according to the slander of 'glutton and drunkard' (7: 34); wine (vinegar) features negatively at the cross (23: 36).

[45] McGowan, '"First Regarding the Cup"', 551–7.

[46] A. J. B. Higgins, *The Lord's Supper in the New Testament* (London: SCM, 1952), 56–7.

[47] Xavier Léon-Dufour, *Le Partage du pain eucharistique selon le Nouveau Testament* (Paris: Seuil, 1982), 30–41, argues for a broader interpretation of the Acts picture, in which eucharistic action and other characteristics of the early Christian community are presented as a whole.

[48] Eduard Schweizer, *The Lord's Supper According to the New Testament* (Philadelphia: Fortress, 1967), 95, argues that the eschatological aspect of early eucharistic celebrations was generally associated with the wine, where present. This begs the question of what 'eschatological' means, but a motif of joyous anticipation may make better sense accompanying wine than without it; see further below.

of this kind at a very early point. There may be some link between a meal form of this kind and the eucharistic meals of the Pseudo-Clementines (and some of those in the apocryphal *Acts*) where there is no cup at all; yet this connection is impossible to be sure of, let alone describe.

Others

There are numerous other passages which invite some comparison with the bread-and-water tradition, but the lack of references as direct as those just discussed leads me simply to note them with brief comments. The first three examples given above were all possible indications of the existence of the ascetic meal tradition, or at least of similar responses to the cuisine of sacrifice, by way of what seems to be a polemic directed against it. There are a few more of these, and at least one canonical book that might appear to fit rather well within the tradition rather than to be opposing it.

The opponents of the author of the Letter to the Colossians are apparently advocates of an asceticism regarding 'food and drink' (Col. 2: 16) which leads to slogans repeated or parodied by the author such as 'do not handle, do not taste, do not touch' (2: 21), and which, as commentators have noted, are likely to refer to prohibitions of meat and wine.[49] In this case there is rather more information about the theology of the ascetics, and they seem to be involved with 'worship of angels', a difficult thing to interpret.[50] Recent studies have suggested a link with Jewish visionary mysticism, in which case the abstinence from meat and wine would perhaps have an instrumental or at least symbolic connection with attempts to achieve mystical experiences (cf. Dan. 10: 3).[51] It is difficult to say whether these ascetic-mystics also have the more rigorous social characteristics of the bread-and-water tradition, and there seems to be no obvious corroborating information. The concern about 'a festival or a new moon or a sabbath' suggests some connection with the issues in Romans (cf. Rom. 14: 5–6).

---

[49] Eduard Lohse, *Colossians and Philemon*, Hermeneia (Philadelphia: Fortress, 1971), 114–15; Eduard Schweizer, *Der Brief an die Kolosser*, EKKNT (Zurich: Benziger, 1976), 119–20.

[50] See now Harold W. Attridge, 'On Becoming an Angel: Rival Baptismal Theologies at Colossae', *Religious Propaganda and Missionary Competition in the New Testament World: Essays Honoring Dieter Georgi* (Leiden: E. J. Brill, 1994), 481–98.

[51] See Fred O. Francis, 'Humility and Angelic Worship in Col 2:18', *ST* 16 (1963), 109–34, and more recently Thomas J. Sappington, *Revelation and Redemption at Colossae*, JSNTSup 53 (Sheffield: Sheffield Academic Press, 1991).

The Letter to the Hebrews presents a highly sacrificial thought-world with a perplexing lack of any indication as to real practice. A community in which a writing such as this could emerge might well regard sacrifice as done with, and ongoing cultic practice as non- (if not exactly anti-) sacrificial; sacrifice is, at least, 'good to think'.[52] Hebrews does, however, contain reference to 'strange teachings' connected with foods (Heb. 13: 9), and is critical of teachings overly concerned with elementary forms of faith and outward and passing things such as food (5: 12–6: 2; 9: 10).[53] More than one commentator has suggested some reaction to avoiders of the eucharistic cup in criticism of those who 'profane the blood of the covenant', although this language is difficult to interpret.[54] Hebrews does seem more likely to represent criticism of ascetic tendencies (as well, of course, as ongoing sacrificial ones) than to be the seedbed for the bread-and-water pattern.

The Johannine tradition is particularly interesting in its use of water imagery and the idea of 'living water' as drink (John 4). Those inclined to read other discourses such as the 'bread of life' section (John 6) sacramentally might well find some possibility of concrete ritual practice behind the talk of 'living water'.[55] Of course the same Gospel includes the imagery of abundant water changed into wine (John 2: 1–11), which certainly does not seem to be a model of avoidance, and could even be a polemic against water-drinkers. The insistence on the drinking of Jesus' blood (6: 53–6; cf. 1 John 5: 5–8) may come from a dispute over

[52] See John Dunnill, *Covenant and Sacrifice in the Letter to the Hebrews*, SNTSMS 75 (Cambridge: Cambridge University Press, 1992).

[53] On the strange foods, see Harold W. Attridge, *The Epistle to the Hebrews*, Hermeneia (Philadelphia: Fortress, 1989), 394–6.

[54] Betz, *Die Eucharistie*, 29–33; summarized by Kilmartin, 'A First Century Chalice Dispute', 404–5.

[55] Brown, *The Gospel of John*, acknowledges a sacramental possibility for John 6 (pp. 231–304, esp. 246–9, 272–5), and for John 4, but mentions only baptism (pp. 178–80); Francis McCool, 'Living Water in John', *The Bible in Current Catholic Thought* (New York: Herder & Herder, 1962), 226–33, is interesting: 'It will be wise here to note how John opposes the bread and water given by Jesus with their counterparts in nature. He who drinks the water that I will give him will never be thirsty—and the reason for this is quickly given—for the water that I will give him will become a spring of water within him, bubbling up for eternal life. The reality referred to is clearly permanent and inexhaustible—it is a constant spring which gives eternal life. Equally so is the reality figured under the bread. It is a food which lasts for eternal life (6,27) . . . I am the bread that gives life. No one who comes to me will ever be hungry, and no one who believes in me will ever be thirsty (6,35). Now, granted the strong unity of symbolic thinking which runs through the fourth gospel, it is not unreasonable to suppose that these extremely similar symbols point to the same reality' (p. 229).

eucharistic practice.⁵⁶ But some further consideration of this language, and of the link between 'blood and water', both in John's Gospel (19: 34) and in the First Letter of John (5: 6–8), may become necessary in the light of evidence for ritual water-drinking at an early stage.⁵⁷

The best possibility for a canonical book friendly to the bread-and-water tradition is the Revelation to John, whose author seems to speak of wine often, but only negatively, as an image of wrath or immorality (Rev. 14: 8–20; 17: 2; 18: 3; 19: 3). Meat is not dealt with very clearly, except within the imagery of carrion and cannibalism (17: 16; 19: 18–21). The imagery of water, however, is used positively in the same work, and explicitly in terms of the use of water as a drink (7: 17; 8: 10; 21: 6; 22: 17) rather than merely as a means of washing or baptism. More generally, the Revelation to John also presents the sort of world-view of social and political dualism, and especially rejection of imperial power, which might be expected to go hand-in-hand with the bread-and-water tradition.

This book could also be seen as a witness to an ordering of the sacral somewhat similar to that found in the bread-and-water tradition. Aside from its resolute, uncompromising emphasis on moral and religious purity, the vision given of the New Jerusalem is telling; there will be no Temple (Rev. 21: 22), which implies not only a rejection of sacrificial practice, but a generalization of the sacral rather than its focusing in specific places, persons, and times. The apparent asceticism of the book could also be linked with the visionary-mystical avoidance of these foods that seems to be attested in the Letter to the Colossians. Last but not least, its interest in Asian affairs, clear from the letters to the Churches of Asia (Rev. 1: 4–3: 22), further suggests the possibility of a direct historical link with the later bread-and-water users in that region.

This may also be the best point at which to mention the Gospel of Thomas, which speaks of being drunk from living water (*Gos. Thom.* 13), of the need to shake off wine and drunkenness in order to find true thirst (28), of the weakness of the grapevine (40), and which is apparently negative toward meat-eating (60; cf. 7). Recent suggestions of conflict

⁵⁶ Kilmartin, 'A First Century Chalice Dispute', 406–8. It should be obvious that, while I am cautious about Kilmartin's conclusions (and those of Betz regarding Hebrews) these would strengthen the case for a primitive bread-and-water tradition; and that (against Kilmartin) I see no reason to assume these would be of substantially different origin to the later examples.

⁵⁷ Greiff, 'Brot, Wasser und Mischwein', 28–34, sees an allusion to a separate baptismal water cup, along the lines of the multiple cups of the Hippolytean baptismal eucharist, in Johannine water. See also Richardson, 'A Further Inquiry Into Eucharistic Origins', 240–6.

between the communities represented by the John and Thomas traditions could help make sense of the different positions of the works on
these issues.[58] The common attributions of the work to Syria and
connections with the *Acts of Thomas*, as well as the positive pictures
not only of the apostle Thomas but of James the Just (*Gos. Thom.* 12), fit
well with the later bread-and-water tradition.[59]

Summary

These New Testament texts have varied connections and degrees of
relevance to the bread-and-water tradition. The cases mentioned in the
last subsection are too oblique in their possible links with the tradition to
be of much use for further reconstruction, but do not take anything away
from the general picture of the tradition as possibly having existed in
Asia and Syria at an early point. Among these, the Revelation to John is
at least a promising candidate for further enquiry.

The instances of avoidance of the cuisine of sacrifice at Corinth and
Rome have important similarities with the bread-and-water tradition,
but geography makes them difficult to connect directly with the later
forms of anti-sacrificial ascetic meal practice in Christianity. These are
reminders that the later examples of the use of water and avoidance of
meat in Christian circles stand in some continuity with earlier pagan and
Jewish ascetic practices. If there is some real connection to be posited, it
may be at this pre-Christian level, i.e. that there were ascetic tendencies
in Jewish communities which persisted in the earliest Christian groups
but fared rather differently in various places. In any case, consideration
of the problems in Corinth and Rome in the light of the key question of
opposition to the cuisine of sacrifice casts some light on these situations
which goes beyond either a deterministic correlation of class and status
interests or *religionsgeschichtlich* analysis to further consideration of
meaning in social context. This dietary (and perhaps eucharistic) ascesis
suggests individuals or groups who were holding themselves at a distance
from the wider society and its central ritual and cuisine, in a way
somewhat different from, and opposed by, the Pauline compromise

---

[58] See Gregory J. Riley, *Resurrection Reconsidered: Thomas and John in Controversy*
(Minneapolis: Augsburg Fortress, 1995).

[59] Stephen Patterson's discussion, *The Gospel of Thomas and Jesus* (Sonoma, Calif.:
Polebridge, 1993), 158–70, of Thomas in relation to the Synoptic tradition argues that the
Thomas community represents a continuation of the sort of *Wanderradikalismus* suggested
by Theissen and others for early Christianity.

embodied in the construction of the eucharistic meal as a meatless sacrifice.

Only in the case of 1 Timothy can we be reasonably confident of a connection with the bread-and-water tradition as attested later. Given earlier suggestions of opposition to Marcion or Encratism in the Pastoral Epistles, this is no great historical surprise. Whatever stance we were to take on those specific identifications, the evidence of the letter fits well with the picture of the tradition as a widespread and early pattern in Asia and Syria.

THE NEW TESTAMENT IN THE BREAD-AND-WATER TRADITION

Introduction

With the exception of the 'breaking of the bread' references, the texts just discussed are rarely cited by New Testament scholars or liturgical historians for evidence of early eucharistic meals, being seen largely as evidence for ascetic practices rather than for ritual ones. I have tried to suggest that this division of texts and concerns is not as immediately applicable to the ritual meals of early Christianity as we might have assumed. Yet even an introductory survey or invitation to consider the New Testament documents in the light of the bread-and-water tradition would not be complete without some consideration not only of texts that seem to deal with avoidance of meat and wine in general, but also of those which have often been understood specifically to underpin eucharistic meal practice. This is not the place for a complete survey of such a large question, but one issue in particular arises as being of special importance and interest.

I have already noted the tendency for the texts discussed in the last three chapters not to make much obvious use of the Synoptic and Pauline Last Supper stories in connection with their eucharistic meal traditions. The centrality of the symbolism of body and blood in those narratives seems to make it quite understandable that exponents of an anti-sacrificial practice and world-view should resist the construction of their communal meals in terms that seem analogous to those of pagan sacrifice.[60] The

---

[60] Young, *The Use of Sacrificial Ideas in Greek Christian Writers*, 243–9, distinguishes between the body and blood imagery and (other) sacrificial traditions in the NT, arguing that the former is not sacrificial in origin or function, but 'the communicants' personal

question remains as to how the exponents of the bread-and-water tradition did understand that story, and on what other bases they might have constructed their eucharistic practice. The following section is not, therefore, an examination of those New Testament texts in themselves or in some attempted reconstruction of the historical Last Supper, but a study of reception and exegesis. These issues do, however, have significance for New Testament interpretation as well as for the history of second- and third-century groups, as early and important readings of the texts in something close to their original context.

The Last Supper

The apparent absence of interest in the Last Supper as a direct basis for eucharistic meals in the bread-and-water tradition could feasibly be explained in four ways: first, the communities and authors did not know these Gospel traditions; or second, they knew them but did not accept them as normative or authentic; third, they knew and accepted them in forms different from the canonical ones and thus drew different implications from them; or finally, they did know them in the canonical forms, but did not interpret them as formally prescriptive for communal meals in quite the sense argued by Cyprian or assumed in most modern scholarship.

There are only a few cases among those discussed where the first or second options could be considered seriously. When Paul writes to the Corinthians he cites the institution narrative against their current practice which ignores it (although he says they already knew the tradition: 1 Cor. 11: 23). Of course in this case their eucharistic disorder seems to have been excess rather than abstinence (11: 21), and the meat-eating 'strong' seem to be the addressees. The Corinthians may nevertheless have had a more literally 'eucharistic' understanding of the meal, based on the fact of 'blessing' or 'giving thanks' for the cup and bread (perhaps in that order: see 10: 16) rather than identifying them as the body and blood of Jesus; if not strictly ignorant of the Last Supper tradition, they ignored it and the more sacrificial interpretation for which Paul argues. The 'breaking of the bread' in the canonical Acts of the

participation in the spiritual food of Christ's body and blood'. This distinction, however, seems to be based on sacramental theories used to interpret other mystery cult meals in terms of theophagy. Apart from the fact that this theory of mystery cult meals may be faulty (see Ch. 1), this imagery is still of meat and blood, hence arguably sacrificial in this society.

Apostles and its parallel in the Pseudo-Clementine novels also indicate no knowledge of the Last Supper or death of Jesus as a basis for the celebration of communal meals.

There are more candidates for the third category, where amended (or simply different) versions of the Gospel story might have been connected with different practices such as those of the bread-and-water tradition. Irenaeus says that the Ebionites knew a form of Matthew's Gospel; if this is an accurate report, it probably implies awareness of the story and of the institution narrative, but more we cannot say. Epiphanius' testimony to the *Gospel of the Ebionites* includes a passage from the Last Supper story (*Pan.* 30. 22. 4; cf. Matt. 26: 17), where Jesus seeks to avoid the paschal sacrifice rather than to participate in it. This suggests an edited version of the text rather than outright rejection thereof, and hence probably knowledge of the institution narrative in some form. We could speculate that the authors of the *Gospel of the Ebionites*, who had also taken the locusts from John the Baptist's diet and condemned all sacrifice, might also have changed the story at least to remove references to 'body' and 'blood', which would have been problematic in view of their vegetarian and anti-sacrificial stance; but there is no indication of this from Epiphanius, who was looking for deviations from his norm. It is also possible that this imagery could have been tolerated if not seen as the heart of continuing meal practice.

Marcion was regarded as a very fast-and-loose user of the New Testament, to say the least. The passages amended in his version of Luke's Gospel seem to have included parts of the Last Supper story.[61] In his polemic against Marcion, Tertullian attributes to his enemy an expansion of the words of institution: 'This is my body, that is, the figure of my body' (*Adv. Marc.* 4. 40).[62] This suggests an attempt to play down any realistic sense of identifying Jesus' body or blood with the eucharistic elements, and would therefore seem to lessen the sacrificial overtones of the passage. Harnack also judged that Marcion's text lacked the statements by Jesus about renunciation of the Passover (Luke 22: 16; see Epiphanius, *Pan.* 42. 11. 6) and of the fruit of the vine (Luke 22: 18).[63] If this last suggestion is correct, the omission might have been based on refusal to accept that Jesus had ever drunk wine at all.[64]

---

[61] This issue becomes somewhat confused with the problem of the shorter and longer versions of the Lukan text in any case.

[62] On the attribution of these words to Marcion rather than to Tertullian, see Harnack, *Marcion*, 163 n. 4.

[63] Ibid. 39–40. See further the appendices (only in the German edn.), 214*-15*.

[64] Cf. Ephraem the Syrian's response to the contempt for the Wedding at Cana story by

Epiphanius' list of changes, which also indicates (unspecified) alterations to Luke 22: 8 and 22: 15, could indicate that all references to Passover were removed. There is also no indication of the exhortation to 'do this in memory of me' in Marcion's text.[65]

Tatian was aware of the tradition of the Last Supper and conveys it in the *Diatessaron*, albeit with some significant modifications. Not only does he remove any implication that Jesus' vow of abstinence from wine might be temporary, but the crucial command to 'do this in memory of me' follows the vow of abstinence, with serious implications for Tatian's possible understanding of the prescriptive nature of the text. As we know it from the Arabic version at least (45. 16), the *Diatessaron* implies either that the whole passage, including renunciation from the fruit of the vine, dictates the appropriate form of liturgical re-enactment ('do this in memory of me'), or even simply that the implicit asceticism, rather than the explicit ritual, is the prescriptive point of the story.[66] Tatian's interpretative strategy is therefore somewhat different from Marcion's; it is less radical (despite possible dislocation), and suggests that the vow of renunciation was taken as a historic turning-point rather than as a scandal.

Among the possible exponents of the bread-and-water tradition, Justin provides a model of the final set of possibilities suggested, in which the institution narratives feature in the canonical form or something close to it, but do not seem to provide the sole basis or model for eucharistic meals.[67] Justin seems to make use of the Last Supper story in his *Apology*, quoting a version of the words of institution and describing the food of the eucharist as the body and blood of Christ (*1 Apol.* 66). Yet Justin does not actually set these references at any point in the story of Jesus, and his interpretation emphasizes not the death of Jesus but his incarnation.[68]

---

later Marcionites: *Hymn. contra Haer.* 47. Origen also indicates that there were Marcionites who used Johannine traditions; see Harnack, *Marcion*, 54–5.

[65] See also Richardson, 'A Further Inquiry Into Eucharistic Origins', 246–54; but this account seems to be based entirely on Tertullian, *Adv. Marc.* 4. 40.

[66] Richardson's objection to their awkwardness at this position does not take into account the ascetic factor: 'A Further Inquiry Into Eucharistic Origins', 235–7.

[67] Justin's own form of the narrative is not one of the canonical ones. On Justin's Gospel traditions, see Helmut Koester, *Ancient Christian Gospels*, 360–402, and on the institution narrative, Richardson, 'A Further Inquiry Into Eucharistic Origins', 237–46. The argument in this section is expanded beyond the bread-and-water tradition, with further reference to 1 Corinthians and to the *Apostolic Tradition*, in my forthcoming article for *JBL*: '"Is There a Liturgical Text in This Gospel?": The Institution Narratives and their Early Interpretive Communities'.

[68] 'Not until red wine had come to be thought of as the vivid representation of life-blood could the cup acquire a sacramental significance of its own and the eucharist become

Any allusion to the institution narrative as an actual liturgical prayer or recitation in Justin's case is a controversial one, depending on the interpretation of the phrase 'through prayer of a word [or discourse] which is from him',[69] which is Justin's explanation of the mechanism by which the meal elements are understood to become the body and blood of Jesus.[70] While it is possible that this refers obliquely to such a recitation, Justin immediately goes on to quote the institution narrative as a sort of practical catechesis rather than as a prayer, i.e. as instructions for what to do rather than what to say (66. 3).[71] It is this practice, given by Jesus to the apostles, which the rites of Mithras imitate (66. 4). This implies that what derives from Jesus, according to Justin's phrase, is the instruction to take bread and cup and to give thanks as he himself had. Apart from giving the narrative a different use for Justin, this catechetical quotation also removes the possibility of any esotericism that might be alleged as a reason for leaving out the text of the prayer.

Justin not only seems to have a use of the narrative which is catechetical rather than liturgical in the narrower sense, he also describes the prayer offered over the eucharistic meal in terms rather different from those of the institution narrative, as extended thanks and praise, after which all respond 'Amen' (65. 3–4). It is difficult to find room for transition to a recitation within that prayer-pattern. While there is no denying the presence of the sacrificial imagery of body and blood in Justin's account, it is therefore possible to discern other patterns also. The actual thanksgiving prayer of the presiding leader has no clear sacrificial or 'body and blood' aspect; the food of the meal is understood to be the body and blood of Christ (66. 1) but is actually called 'eucharist'. We may wonder just how far that interpretation in terms of flesh and blood really went among the members of the community.

Justin's account may then testify to a mixture of understandings or liturgical traditions: an interpretative one somewhat like (but perhaps less developed than) the Pauline memorial of the death of Jesus; and a

---

primarily a memorial of the Passion' (Richardson, 'A Further Inquiry Into Eucharistic Origins', 244).

[69] δι' εὐχῆς λόγου τοῦ παρ' αὐτοῦ (*I Apol.* 66. 2).

[70] See the discussion by G. Cuming, '*Δι' εὐχῆς λόγου* (Justin, Apol. 1. 66. 2)', *JTS* NS 31 (1980), 80–2, and the convincing response by A. Gelston, '*Δι' εὐχῆς λόγου*: Justin, Apology 1. 66. 2', *JTS* NS 33 (1982), 172–5.

[71] The various possibilities even for a literal acceptance of the institution narratives are expanded on by the Quartodeciman practice and indications of groups who held a yearly Passover, presumably understanding themselves as having been told to 'do this in memory of me'.

formal or practical one which is not dependent on the actions of Jesus at the Last Supper, except in so far as these exemplify a very general pattern of taking bread (and cup) with thanksgiving or blessing. While Justin's meal is therefore no perfect example of a meal understood wholly in non-sacrificial terms, it may witness to such indirectly. It is clear that for Justin the theology of the meal included the body and blood imagery of the Last Supper story, yet the actual form and especially the words of his eucharist need have had no basis in the institution narratives.

Rather later, Cyprian's opponents may give evidence of a somewhat similar pattern, in their objection to the symbolism of blood (*Ep.* 63. 15). The acceptance by the addressees of the canonical texts referring to the Last Supper is assumed throughout the argument by Cyprian. What seems to be at issue is not the authority or authenticity of the narratives but the way in which they are understood to function in eucharistic meal practice. Cyprian's ponderous insistence on the character of the meal as a repetition of the Last Supper and as a sacrifice suggests some other emphasis on the part of the water-drinkers. At that point in time it would not be at all unthinkable that they might still have been using eucharistic prayers based on blessing or thanksgiving, not including the recitation of the institution narrative.[72]

It is not always easy to tell into which of these hermeneutical categories to put other examples of the bread-and-water tradition, but generally speaking it seems reasonable to think of them in the third and fourth of those previously outlined, i.e. to think of the communities as knowing some version of the institution narratives but interpreting them in ways which did not exert the sort of controlling or recitative significance in the practice of eucharistic meals manifest in the argument of Cyprian. For this conclusion we are somewhat dependent on an argument from the very scale of the silence involved in, for example, the eucharists of the apocryphal *Acts* which seem to owe little or nothing to the actions of Jesus' Last Supper or to the quasi-sacrificial imagery of his body and blood. The major exception in that group of witnesses is a eucharistic prayer of the *Acts of Thomas* (158), also a prayer of thanksgiving or blessing in which reference to this imagery is made

---

[72] The somewhat later eucharistic prayer of Addai and Mari seems not to have used the institution narrative either; see A. Gelston, *The Eucharistic Prayer of Addai and Mari* (Oxford: Clarendon, 1992). A recent, more conservative rejoinder to the notion of late eucharistic prayers without recital of the institution narratives (E. Yarnold SJ, 'Anaphoras without Institution Narratives?' in E. Livingstone (ed.), *Studia Patristica XXX* (Leuven: Peeters, 1997), 395–410) is content to argue that such prayers cannot be attested in the *late fourth century*.

along with other aspects of Jesus' passion and death; it is still not at all a recitation of the institution narrative, even though it clearly suggests awareness of the texts.[73] So too the 'Last Suppers' celebrated by the apostles themselves (*Acts of Andrew*, 20; *Acts of John*, 109) are clearly modelled on that of Jesus to some extent, yet they make use of the story for form, rather than for content.

It seems that it was possible for at least some of the Christians of the bread-and-water tradition to avoid what the orthodox understood to be implicit (or even explicit) in the institution narratives without rejecting them altogether. Whether they were actually 'liturgical texts' for these groups, in the specific sense of formulae for recitation at the time the bread and cup were taken, seems doubtful.

Even if they did not remove them from their scriptures, it is not surprising that the bread-and-water Christians avoided the institution narratives as liturgical guides. Their sacrificial language seems palpable from the first instance we know of, Paul's catechesis in 1 Corinthians. The idea of eating Jesus' body and blood, however symbolically, does not fit well with an ethic that rejects all meat-eating. If, however, the actions described in the narratives were understood as unique and unrepeatable rather than as a prescription for ongoing liturgical practice, then the reference made to Jesus' own death may have been understood primarily as a historical event in the past, just as Protestant interpretation has tended to assert against Catholic use. Those more recent debates indicate how different assumptions brought to the texts can lead to vastly different interpretations of the sense.

Eucharist and 'Eucharistia'

It would seem that the Christians of the bread-and-water tradition had a somewhat uneasy relationship with the implications of the institution narratives as a basis on which to construct eucharistic meal practice. Was there then another authority from within Christian tradition which led bread-and-water Christians to celebrate their eucharistic meals as they did? Lietzmann, Cullmann, and others argued, we have seen, that there were different primitive eucharistic meal traditions, discernible even in the New Testament itself, represented especially by the duality of the Pauline and Synoptic pictures of the Last Supper on the one hand, and

---

[73] Cf. *Acts of Thomas*, 49, a clearly secondary reference to the 'body and blood' of Christ applied to a eucharist without a cup; in this case a descriptive statement separate from the eucharistic prayer is involved. See Ch. 5 above.

material such as the miraculous feedings, the resurrection meals, and the Luke–Acts breaking of the bread on the other.[74]

While the reconstruction of the bread-and-water tradition that has been attempted so far may seem to be a form of the dual origins argument, the correlation between this ascetic meal pattern and the traditions and understandings supposed to have underpinned Lietzmann's 'Jerusalem' form of eucharist, to which he allocated much or all of the evidence for the bread-and-water tradition, is not very great. According to Lietzmann's hypothesis the forms of eucharist which emphasized bread and lacked clear reference to Jesus's death as sacrifice derived from a different source or sources from those which emulated the Last Supper of Jesus depicted in the Synoptic Gospels. What we have seen so far is that the difference may not be so much a matter of the sort of traditions employed, as of the way they were employed. While the bread-and-water tradition does not use the Last Supper narrative in the sense of a recitation or of celebrating the eucharist as a sacrificial meal, its exponents do tend to be aware of the story and its importance.

This does not mean that other Gospel elements may not have had an influence. The links with resurrection meals and miraculous feedings have, however, generally been understood to consist of the shared emphasis on thanksgiving or blessing and the absence of influence from the Last Supper narratives. It is true that the prayers of the bread-and-water tradition seem to follow this pattern. The Pseudo-Clementines, for instance, which are the clearest case of the total absence of influence from the Last Supper traditions, emphasize thanksgiving and blessing of food at meals (*Hom.* 14. 1. 4), and the fact of commensality itself, in conjunction with exclusion of the 'Gentiles' (ibid. 13. 4). Yet these elements tell us very little about alternative positive influences from Gospel traditions; they are formal aspects of much Jewish prayer inherited by early Christian practice. This particular case may therefore be less a meal based on specific Gospel elements other than the Last Supper, than a somewhat enigmatic meal practice without specific links to the Gospels at all.

[74] Lietzmann, *Mass and Lord's Supper*, 193–208; Cullmann, 'La Signification de la Sainte-Cène dans le christianisme primitif', 1–22. This has been expanded upon recently by Bruce Chilton, *A Feast of Meanings*, 146–9 and *passim*, who suggests five successive eucharistic models in the New Testament itself; these allow for some diversity of order (cup first: pp. 111–13) and of regularity or timing (yearly in some instances: pp. 93–108), but not of meal elements. Chilton's concern is with the NT, which means he does not deal with many of the texts of interest here; but the results are not always convincing, and there is little allowance for ongoing diversity in his picture of one tradition taking over from another.

The apocryphal *Acts*, we have seen, also seem to emphasize the acts of blessing or thanksgiving. These depictions often bear some resemblance to the actions of Jesus in the feeding stories or resurrection appearances, but the specific similarities must be acknowledged as literary, as a part of the depiction of the apostle as an *alter Christus*, rather than as straightforwardly ritual or liturgical.

The formal aspect of the bread-and-water tradition and its prayers therefore merely places them in the broad tradition of banquets with Jewish elements. The patterns of blessing or giving thanks are simply too general, being present in the Last Supper stories themselves (Mark 14: 22 and parallels), in the resurrection appearances (Luke 24: 30), feeding stories (Mark 6: 41 and parallels), exhortations (Rom. 14: 6; 1 Tim. 4: 3), and other references to eucharistic meals (1 Cor. 10: 16), and for that matter in common practice. They are not a distinctive aspect of particular traditions but a commonplace of all formal or communal eating and drinking.

Eschatological Meal?

The connections with the 'breaking of the bread' tradition have sometimes been couched in terms of the eschatological, meaning especially that the meals in question are supposed to be characterized by expectation of the Lord's return or by recognition of the risen Christ in or at the communal meal, both joyful aspects contrasted with the solemnity of a memorial or sacrificial meal.[75] It is not my purpose here to pronounce judgement upon all possibility of eschatological elements in the practice of early eucharistic meals, but once again the importance of the bread-and-water evidence for this alleged strand of eucharistic understandings and practices demands some comment.

The assumption that the meals of the bread-and-water tradition, as well as those involving milk or cheese, are joyful feasts is as misplaced as the often-accompanying idea that the contents of the cup are a matter of indifference to the participants. If there is any indication that the elements of bread and water mean anything as far as the mood or emotional content of a communal meal is concerned, it is that they are signs of mourning, in Jewish circles at least. The ascetic *pĕrushim* of the Talmud (*b. B. Bat.* 60b) who avoid meat and wine do so as a sign of

---

[75] Lietzmann, *Mass and Lord's Supper*, 203–4; Cullmann, 'La Signification de la Sainte-Cène dans le christianisme primitif', 2–3 and *passim*.

mourning; so too Daniel's abstinence (Dan. 10: 3) is attributed to the
same motivation.

These parallels or antecedents to the bread-and-water tradition need
not determine its meaning, but they would suggest that the onus of proof
is on those who take these meals as joyful Messianic banquets to indicate
just how this is the case. Without undertaking another survey of the
evidence with the question of eschatology in mind, I suggest merely that
there is a strong sense of the 'not yet', rather than of the 'already', in the
wineless eucharists. There are cases, that of Tatian for instance, where it
seems Jesus' vow of abstinence from wine is understood still to be in
force. The tendency to play down the cup, or simply not to have one,
also suggests a recognition of contrast between present restraint and
future blessing, rather than an anticipation made ritually concrete. These
meals may therefore be said to have an eschatological character, but not
in the sense generally assumed; the eschatology at work is premillennial,
so to speak, and the eucharistic meal expresses the tension between the
present and the promised future rather than being an anticipation
thereof.[76]

In this case the scholarly concern for a fundamental duality (rather
than unity) has led, strangely enough, to a reading forward, rather than
back, of evidence. The character perceived to be conveyed in the meals
associated with the ministry (and especially the resurrection) of Jesus has
been transferred to these other cases where a certain similarity of form
has been discerned. While there may be a need to consider further the
implications of the meals linked with resurrection appearances and other
indications of more joyfully eschatological orientations such as that of the
eucharistic meal of the *Didache*, these questions must be separated from
the ascetic meal tradition discussed here.

Summary

What connection, then, can be drawn between the meal patterns of the
water-drinkers and particular biblical traditions? The answer is probably
'not much'. While it seems reasonable to suggest that different meal
traditions attested in the New Testament could have had greater or lesser
influences in different times and places, there is little basis for making an

---

[76] The discussion of Lebeau, *Le Vin nouveau*, on the vow of renunciation is of no small
interest to this question, but his specific conclusions bear largely on the bread-and-wine
tradition, suggesting the arrival of the reign of God, and thus the fulfilment of the vow, at
Easter, Pentecost, and in ongoing eucharistic meals.

absolute distinction between them or between the communities dependent on them for ritual inspiration. The probable knowledge of the Last Supper traditions in most of the communities of the bread-and-water pattern cautions against too radical a dichotomy of scriptural traditions and resultant models. Knowledge of, and influence from, the tradition of the Last Supper need not have prevented some Christians from celebrating their ritual meals with water rather than wine. The difference may well have been in the kind of use made of the text, rather than in a fundamentally different set of authorities. Nevertheless, it is reasonably clear that the meals of the bread-and-water tradition show less direct interest in and influence from the Last Supper than one would expect if all eucharistic meals were understood primarily as repetitions of that meal. If the influence of other New Testament meal traditions or motifs such as the 'breaking of bread' or the miraculous feedings may be real here, it does not seem to explain the more rigorous or exclusive element in the bread-and-water tradition.

CONCLUSION: MANY TABLES

Thus while the bread-and-water tradition presents itself in terms that invite some analysis in terms of a duality of meal traditions, with the ascetic refusal of the cuisine of sacrifice representing a stance that can be contrasted not only with the meat and wine of pagan sacrifice but also with the more clearly sacrificial meal of the eventually normative tradition and its generous use of the imagery of Jesus' body and blood, this is not the same duality suggested by theorists of eucharistic origins earlier this century. In fact the evidence of this tradition presents some specific problems for theories of dual eucharistic origins.

First, the uneasy but real connection between the ascetic meal tradition and the institution narratives is a difficulty for the theory that eucharists without wine would have stemmed specifically from a different tradition based on blessing or thanksgiving. While this ritual element is real enough, it is also no less prominent in meals where wine seems to be emphasized, both those of the eventually normative tradition and the small group of meals where the cup was taken first.

Second, the clear avoidance of wine in eucharistic meals of this sort bears little or no resemblance to the supposed joyful or eschatological character generally attributed to the wineless type suggested by Lietzmann. In specifically Jewish settings, this kind of meal seems to have had clear overtones of mourning. While it is possible that there was some historical continuity between the open meal practice of Jesus, or the meal traditions associated with resurrection stories, and the bread-and-water eucharists, the differences between the meanings of these meals as we find them is sufficient to render these possible links virtually meaningless in any case.

The implications of the bread-and-water tradition for the larger task of reconstructing the forms of early eucharistic meals are therefore not favourable to interpretations of particular meals in terms of either single or of dual origins. They suggest rather that it is necessary on the one hand to acknowledge a real, if somewhat broad, unity of meal practices and traditions in Graeco-Roman culture, and then on the other hand to pay equal or greater attention to the specifics of a particular meal or practice in its own terms.[77] Within that broad unity it would be better to speak of many eucharists rather than of two. This study of the different meal elements employed in eucharistic meals cannot simply be aligned with differences in form of prayers or order of proceedings in order to come to a neat picture of different tendencies. What continues to be necessary is further specific attention to particular aspects, including form and meal elements but also issues such as participation, presidency, times, and places. The picture that seems likely to emerge is an increasingly diverse one, rather than a simple or dual strand of common development. The link that has been drawn here between different meals using bread and water or bread alone serves only to establish a fairly loose grouping of meals which may have been historically linked but whose unity is as much or more negative (the rejection of the culture and cuisine of sacrifice) than it is positive or essential.

[77] So also Smith and Taussig, *Many Tables*, 20–69.

8
To Gather the Fragments

INTRODUCTION

A more adequate historical picture of early Christian meals would seek to be more comprehensive in terms of actions, participants, and other aspects of eucharistic meals than has usually been the case, and would take diversity seriously as a part of the probable picture. These suggestions have been taken up for the specific, and hence limited, question of the use of food and drink in the eucharist. In pursuing these issues I have attempted to give serious attention to different practices, not simply on the basis of assumed prevalence or importance for later eucharistic liturgy, but in terms of the possibilities available to ancient eaters. While it is obvious that I have sought to present evidence for diversity, it is certainly not the case that the picture of food and meals that has emerged is simply disparate or unfocused.

While the tendency for scholarship to disregard some of the evidence in the quest for a normative pattern is problematic, I have not taken issue with the possibility of tracing the early stages of a bread-and-wine pattern of eucharistic meals or even with the working assumption that this tradition or type might have been the more prevalent, regardless of the greater theological importance that may be attributed to it. More familiar, mainstream, Christian attitudes to meat and other foods outside the eucharistic meal, themselves hardly free from ascetic aspects, also developed through this period, and may well have been more typical. At the same time I have suggested that there were important alternative practices to these. In any case, quantity of evidence is not the only point at issue. The survey of different food practices associated with early eucharistic meals suggests that there is a distribution of sorts in terms of levels of accommodation or dissidence with regard to the normative pagan meal tradition and the cuisine of sacrifice, which sheds light on both normative and alternative practices.

This distribution of possibilities for the use of food in eucharistic meals bears a sort of inverted resemblance to the main theory of diversity suggested previously, that of Hans Lietzmann. Whereas Lietzmann, like

Adolf von Harnack before him, understood the use of food and drink more or less than bread and wine to indicate lack of concern about the elements of the eucharist, I have suggested the reverse: that these cases, both more and less, indicate anxiety about the content of the meal, and that the more accommodating bread-and-wine tradition was in fact the more normal meal, constructed by analogy with the sacrificial banquets of Graeco-Roman society, as well as in terms of continuity with the Last Supper of Jesus.

In this last chapter I will summarize the results of this quest for use of eucharistic foods more fully, and consider further some of the questions of both origin and meaning that have already been raised along the way. Here again, understanding the ascetic meal traditions more fully offers new possibilities for comprehension of the accommodating one also, as one set of choices within the range offered by a society dominated by sacrifice and its cuisine.

DESCRIBING THE BREAD-AND-WATER TRADITION

Bread Alone; Bread and Water; Bread, Water, and More . . .

While there is a discernible connection between the different instances of ascetic eucharistic meals, both in terms of the shared understanding of opposition to sacrificial cuisine and in terms of the probable common origins suggested by the geographically focused evidence, we cannot afford to ignore the differences between the various texts assembled here even in terms of the actual use of eucharistic foods. I have used the terminology of a 'bread-and-water tradition' as the most adequate available, because that seems to be the most typical pattern. Some earlier commentators such as Lietzmann emphasized the cases where bread alone was used, arguing the need to account for a form of eucharistic meal in which the bread was the more important element. Yet even Lietzmann's analysis acknowledged links between witnesses to the supposedly paradigmatic bread eucharist and those in which water or other elements appear as well.[1]

The distribution of the uses or patterns seems to go like this: bread and water are, as far as we can tell, both present and perhaps more or less equally emphasized in the usage of the Ebionites, the (problematic) case of Justin, Tatian, the Encratites, Theodotus, Marcion, Montanism, in

[1] *Mass and Lord's Supper*, 193–208.

some of the instances in the apocryphal *Acts*, and in the later orthodox groups such as the *Aquarii*. There are some cases where it is less clear, but we might add the martyr Alcibiades in Gaul who refuses wine, but whose ritual practice and background must remain uncertain.

Bread alone is attested in some of the apocryphal *Acts*. Unless we take the terminology of 'breaking of bread' in the New Testament as a further witness, this is not really a particularly strong indicator of a bread-only eucharist, even if some of the other cases might arguably emphasize the bread somewhat. Bread with other elements is used in the Pseudo-Clementines (with salt), the Artotyritai (with cheese or curd), in the less clearly eucharistic meals in the apocryphal *Acts* (with vegetables, oil, and salt) and in the curious collection of festive eucharistic meal prescriptions in the *Apostolic Tradition*.[2] Of these, only the obscure Artotyritai seem likely to have celebrated a eucharistic meal involving the sacralization of the additional element, which might well take the place of a cup; that case of course is one in which we must allow for some degree of error or misrepresentation, not to say obscurity. The other cases such that of as the Pseudo-Clementines suggest not so much a specific sacralization of the additional elements, or for that matter of the bread itself, but rather a lack of clear distinction between eucharistic and other eating, and a more generalized understanding of the sacral aspect of food that extends to all community meals, or even to all meals celebrated by baptized Christians. In this they are perhaps, paradoxical as it may be, a clearer parallel to the pagan patterns of eating meat to which they are so bitterly opposed. In both, the implications of eating were not restricted to one meal above all others, but rather centred on a meal of special communal significance and extended from the focal point to other eating at which the same elements featured.

This summary seems to confirm the suggestion that 'bread and water' is at least as useful a notion, and as typical a pattern, as is that of 'bread alone'. The criticism already made of the suggestion that the use of water actually indicates indifference to the content of the cup makes the case for a eucharistic rite greatly emphasizing bread over wine (or water) seem rather less strong. The varying emphases on bread and cup in different traditions may also have to do with the somewhat different under-standings and uses of food and drink in *cena* and *symposium*; they do not stand strictly in parallel in typical formal meal practice in the Graeco-Roman world either. Bread may indeed be the more important element

---

[2] See the lists suggested by Harnack, 'Brod und Wasser', 132–6, and Vogel, 'Le Repas sacré au poisson', 5–7.

in a number of cases in the ascetic ritual meal tradition, as it has often been in the normative tradition since, but the distinction is not all that evident; not clearly limited to the ascetic forms of eucharistic meal, and not clear enough to support the quests that have taken place for a second type of primitive eucharistic meal characterized by the use of bread alone, or by a unique emphasis on the bread.

The Geography of Asceticism

There was, then, a widespread and well-attested tradition of the use of bread and water in eucharistic (and other) meals of some early Christian communities. The evidence suggests a set of practices which are as clearly established in some cases as was the eventually normative tradition of using bread and wine. This tradition is both theologically diverse and geographically focused; it encompasses Ebionites, Encratites, Marcionites, Montanists, and Gnostics, as well as otherwise orthodox groups, but seems to be linked in most cases, and probably all the earliest, with Syria and Asia.

This geographic aspect has a number of implications. One has to do with the broader questions of diversity in early Christianity and especially with the tendency now to acknowledge that in parts of the East especially, Christian communities were often more ascetic than others either knew or would have been comfortable with.[3] Some might still argue that the bread-and-water tradition is a matter of heretical practice; it is certainly true that there are significant differences between most of the communities and authors of the bread-and-water tradition and those of emerging orthodoxy, not only on the question of the contents of the cup but on other matters as well. Yet this position is difficult to maintain in the light of the orthodox examples discussed in Ch. 6. One could perhaps maintain that Pionius' meal is ambiguous or atypical, and that Cyprian's troublesome water-drinkers were late innovators, but the fact that the heretical tradition in Syria looks as though it was the antecedent to the saintly ascetics of the fourth century should give pause for thought. In fact the problem with this defence of an orthodox uniformity of eucharistic practice is that it is virtually beside

---

[3] The argument of an influence from Manichaeism on full-blown Eastern asceticism is found esp. in Arthur Vööbus, *History of Asceticism in the Syrian Orient*; the more recent discoveries relating to Manichaeism seem to rule this out, but might provide Manichaeism and some forms of Eastern Christianity with a common pedigree. See Gabriele Winkler, 'The Origins and Idiosyncrasies of the Earliest Form of Asceticism', 9–43.

the point, from all the evidence. Use of water in the cup was, despite the heresiologists' assumptions, rarely an attempt to distance practice from that of the 'great Church', because as far as we can tell the communities in question were themselves often that Church, to the extent that it existed in these places at times as early as the mid-second century.

Whether the bread-and-water tradition can be neatly linked to the emerging scholarly construct of Syrian Christianity is another matter. The scope of the meal tradition seems to be a little too broad to subsume under this title; rather the ritual and dietary concern may need to be traced not only to Syrian but to forms of Asian (such as Phrygian) Christianity, and to tendencies or trajectories in early Christianity that cannot be fully encompassed in geographical terms. Nevertheless there seems to be some scope for further consideration of this evidence in developing the picture of early Eastern Christianity in particular, and for exploration of the suggestion that in these communities ritual and other dietary issues might not have been so clearly divided as many have tended to assume.

On the other hand, while the bread-and-water tradition may lend support to the need to consider distinctive local forms of Christianity, it does not provide evidence even of local uniformity. There was also use of wine in eucharistic meals from both Asia and Syria in very early sources, and indications of local conflicts which suggest that a narrowly ethnic or geographical approach would not do justice either to the questions of asceticism, which are asked at least of the Syrian evidence now almost as a matter of course, or to the questions of the development of eucharistic ritual. The New Testament documents and other early witnesses such as the *Didache* and correspondence of Ignatius of Antioch all indicate local divisions over matters including the conduct of communal meals.[4]

An analysis of different patterns of Christian meal along geographic lines is not new in itself. Lietzmann in particular saw such an element in his identification of two primitive eucharists, one 'Roman' and the other 'Egyptian'.[5] But as I have already argued, his attention to ideal types arguably prevented acknowledgement of just how diverse early Christian meal practice really was, and just what particular forms that diversity took. 'Formal' considerations, such as the order of proceedings and of ritual actions, which dominated the discussions earlier this century have, of course, largely been left to one side here; a fuller reconstruction of early eucharistic meals would need to give these matters attention as well.

[4] See 1 Cor. 11: 17–34; Jude 12; *Did.* 11: 9; Ign. *Smyrn.* 7–8, etc.
[5] Lietzmann, *Mass and Lord's Supper*, 204–15 and *passim*.

A Primitive Tradition

Apart from what has already been said about the mere fact and extent of the bread-and-water tradition, perhaps the most important implication for the history of eucharistic meals is that this pattern of the ritual use of food was probably primitive, rather than a late ascetic response to an early normative tradition. The geographic aspect is an important part of what leads to this conclusion, in that the combination of theological diversity and geographical focus already outlined would seem to make a very early origin the most likely basis on which the number and variety of examples attested could have come about. I have, admittedly, argued that the cuisine of sacrifice involved a set of oppositions which might have led to the establishment anywhere of an ascetic ritual meal tradition like this one, simply on the basis of a reaction to the general place of meat and wine in pagan culture. In theory, that is to say, a number of different groups could all have independently adopted such an ascetic pattern in response to the same issues in reaction to, and adaptation of, the normative tradition of the use of bread and wine.

In fact this seems far-fetched. What is most likely is that an existing pattern of asceticism, present already in Jewish communities around the Mediterranean and far from alien to Gentile Christians also, manifested itself within Christianity in response to the challenge of constructing Christian identity in a pagan world. It would be unhelpful to make judgements about a supposedly essential meaning of the bread-and-water eucharist on the basis of its inheritance from other sources; it may at least be said to be essential to the self-identity of the groups in question.

INTERPRETING THE BREAD-AND-WATER TRADITION

Introduction

The position developed through the earlier chapters on the significance of the bread-and-water tradition has been that it is generally comprehensible as an anti-sacrificial tradition of eucharistic meals analogous with, and probably ultimately derived from, other similar forms of Graeco-Roman asceticism. There remain a number of questions relating to the origins and meanings of the meal, and in the process of addressing these I will take the opportunity to address some alternative accounts of the tradition.

A Kosher Meal?

The question of the relationship between these meals of bread and water and the traditions and practices of Judaism is a particularly important one which crosses boundaries between questions of origin and ongoing meaning. We need to consider further the common suggestion that the bread-and-water tradition had specifically Jewish origins and inspiration, as well as questions of the relationships between Jewish and Christian communities in the early centuries and the ways in which diet may have come up as an issue of self-definition.

At least some of the instances of the ascetic eucharistic meal do belong to communities which might be described as 'Jewish-Christian'. Yet as has already been indicated, the exclusion of meat and of wine from diet does not represent the Mosaic law as presented in the Pentateuch and/or as interpreted by the rabbis. Neither do what seem to be our best or most important examples of Jewish asceticism from the first centuries of the common era, the Qumran community and/or Essenes, provide indications of the immediate origins of such practices. The Therapeutae described by Philo of Alexandria do represent something very similar to the bread-and-water tradition, but remain a mysterious or even dubious group, perhaps more in keeping with Philo's Hellenism than with actually existing Judaism in any case. Whether real or fictional, their ascetic meals seem likely to be modelled on those of philosophical groups such as Pythagoreans, rather than those of earlier Jewish models such as Rechabites or Nazirites. Nevertheless, the example of the Therapeutae indicates that, as in the questions of banquets and their appropriate procedures, one may have to exercise caution in separating Jewish and pagan models too radically.

Some similar concerns to those of the ascetic Christians emerge in Judaism when we have to do with issues of Jewish-Gentile commensality.[6] It is arguable that under certain circumstances, Jews might have adopted forms of diet more ascetic than otherwise required, specifically in terms of removal of meat and wine, in order to keep kosher under circumstances where the provision of appropriate food was problematic. Such an explanation has been invoked to explain both the refusal of the hero of the book of Daniel and his companions to eat the King's food or drink his wine (Dan. 1: 5–16) and the vegetarian diet of priests undertaking a mission to Rome (Josephus, *Life*, 14).

---

[6] Segal, *Paul the Convert*, 228–36.

Jews living in Gentile cities could perhaps have resorted to bread, water, and other vegetable foods as a diet less difficult to maintain in purity than one involving meat and wine, both not only tainted by association with sacrifice but prepared in ways not in keeping with the dietary laws.[7] Yet it is hard to imagine that these measures would really have been necessary in a city like Rome where a Jewish community was well-established. It is more plausible that the scrupulous priests of Josephus' story might have been understood to have taken special provisions out of uncertainty as to what they would find, than that all the Jews in ancient Rome resorted to figs and nuts for their diet. In these cases a diet of vegetables alone might possibly have helped the eaters avoid problems specific to slaughter under *kašrut*, but the association between meat and idolatry, i.e. the same concern found in the bread-and-water tradition of eucharistic meals, seems likely to have been more important. In the same context, that of dealings with Gentiles, comes the statement of tractate '*Aboda Zara* (2: 3) of the Mishna that there is a prohibition on 'wine, vinegar of the gentiles which to begin with was wine' and that 'meat . . . which comes out [from being offered to an idol] is prohibited because it is like sacrifices of the dead'.[8] This text seems to confirm the association between this food and drink and idolatry for Jews as well as others. The stories of Daniel's diet (Dan. 1: 8–16) and the meat- and wine-avoiding *pĕrushim* indicate that there was at the very least a Jewish aspect or version of the anti-sacrificial pattern. The fact that these examples are rather late and are conceivably linked with concern about cultus and sacrifice seem to suggest that this ascesis was either derived from pagan models or at least a response to pagan pressure. This means that in these cases we are dealing not merely with a question of commensality, but with one of idolatry and the cuisine of sacrifice.

There are some further possible points of contact between Judaism and the bread-and-water tradition in Christian circles. It is true that the avoidance of wine can be linked to the Nazirite tradition and to John the Baptist. We saw that there was some evidence for use of that tradition by such as Tatian. There are other indications that forms of Nazirite vow were current in the first century, given Paul's use of something similar (Acts 18: 18), although the specific provisions may have been too varied

---

[7] Stuhlmacher, *Paul's Letter to the Romans*, 222–9; Käsemann, *Commentary on Romans*, 364–9. See also the discussion on Romans above, Ch. 7.

[8] Cf. *m. 'Abod. Zar.* 2: 5 'Grape pits and grape skins belonging to the gentiles are prohibited . . . And sages say, "[If] they are moist, they are forbidden. If they are dry, they are permitted." '

for us to be clear on a specific diet connected with such vows.[9] The clearest instance of this sort of asceticism in Judaism, apart from the awkward Therapeutae, is that of the just as historically troublesome meat- and wine-avoiding *pěrushim* (*b. B. Bat.* 60b), who do in fact take a vow of abstinence, and the more straightforward but historically dislocated picture of Daniel, also apparently binding himself with a vow (Dan. 1: 8). If avoidance of meat had become a typical part of Nazirite vows by the Hellenistic period, that would only serve to underline further the amalgamation of specifically Jewish concerns with the pagan ones suggested by the cuisine of sacrifice and opposition to it.

Avoidance of meat could have been linked in certain cases to the destruction of the Temple and the consequent end of sacrifice, which is the narrative occasion for the vow of those *pěrushim*. The removal of the paschal lamb from the Seder has already been noted, but this action does not seem to have led to, or reflected, wholesale rejection of meat. If we were to accept, for the sake of argument, that there might have been Jews who advocated such a diet as an appropriate response to the disaster of the conquest of Judea, it is again hard to avoid the likelihood that their actions would have been somewhat informed or influenced by the earlier pagan models in which avoidance of these foods is determined by their importance in sacrifice and cultic meals.

Two aspects of this Jewish form of the bread-and-water pattern are more distinctive perhaps: one is the connection with mourning attested both in Daniel (10: 3) and in the Talmud; the other is the link between avoidance of meat and wine and the avoidance of all commensality. Of these, the former leaves no very clear trace in the bread-and-water tradition. If renunciation of bread and wine was a sign of refusal to celebrate, whether because of the destruction of the Temple or for any other reason, it has lost this significance for the Christian communities discussed above, although I have already suggested this parallel should warn us not to characterize the meals as joyful. It seems more likely that both versions reflect a choice involving voluntary poverty as a sign of disengagement and protest. The other aspect, that of commensality, seems to be a significant link between Jewish and Christian manifestations of the ascetic meal; the picture of eating provided in the radical pseudepigrapha includes some strong, if not altogether consistent, indications that avoidance of eating with pagans was important.

[9] See Segal, *Paul the Convert*, 238–9, 346 n. 23.

There were, therefore, Jewish versions of this form of ascesis, and the likelihood these provided the beginnings of such practices in Christianity has been acknowledged. This connection must, however, be qualified. If we should see the bread-and-water tradition in Christianity as an offshoot of specifically Jewish opposition to pagan foods, it would seem to be on the basis of literary models or the practice of extraordinary figures, rather than of common custom. Second, the suggestion that these forms of avoidance are characteristically Jewish rather than pagan, and serve to identify either Jews or Jewish Christianity when we find them in early Christian literature, is fallacious.

One further suggestion that has been made regarding a connection with Judaism ought to be acknowledged, less a matter of asceticism than of historical accident. Felix Cirlot's analysis of the bread-and-water tradition made use of the discussion of the Sabbath meal by Ismar Elbogen, who had analysed the Talmudic sources to suggest that wine was scarce in Babylonia and therefore that 'wineless kiddushes' might have been introduced in Jewish meal gatherings in that region.[10] The link between the *qidduš* blessing and early eucharistic practice is of interest to some liturgical scholars, as we have already seen. These 'wineless kiddushes', however, seem to have used not water but other substitutes for wine (such as juice) that might still have been seen as festal. There is, then, no real parallel between the bread-and-water tradition and the 'wineless kiddush' either in motivation or the actual form of modification of a festal cup. Further, a specifically Babylonian origin for the bread-and-water tradition seems unlikely, given the continued use of wine in the Palestinian Jewish sources, which ought to be closer to some or even most of the Christian texts discussed.

To summarize, the particular forms of dietary concern visible in the bread-and-water tradition have some resemblance to, and were also probably derived from, attested Jewish ones of the same period, but both need also to be related to earlier and continuing pagan dissident patterns of eating. Where concern about meat and wine as idolatrous food emerges, it is in the specific context of commensality with Gentiles. The bread-and-water tradition is largely attested for Christian commu-

[10] Felix Cirlot, *The Early Eucharist* (London: SPCK, 1939), 1–14, 232–5; Ismar Elbogen, 'Eingang und Ausgang des Sabbats nach talmudischen Quellen', in M. Brann and J. Elbogen (eds.), *Festschrift zu Israel Lewy's siebzigstem Geburtstag* (2 vols.; Breslau: M. & H. Marcus, 1911), i. 173–87, esp. 181–2; and *Der jüdische Gottesdienst in seiner geschichtlichen Entwicklung*, 4th edn. (Hildesheim: Georg Olms, 1962), 111–12. Elbogen linked the difficulty in obtaining wine to the transfer of the Sabbath *qidduš* from home to synagogue, where pooled resources made the purchase easier.

nities who seem to have avoided all commensality with non-members, and regarded all instances of these foods as to be avoided, not just some that were ritually problematic. In these ascetic Christian groups, biblical materials regarding some meat are used to bolster avoidance of all meat, and biblical materials supporting avoidance of wine by some are used to support avoidance of wine by all; but the sense that emerges is of a tradition that mines the Hebrew Bible, rather than one which stands firmly upon it and proceeds directly out of it.

The resort to Judaism as a form of explanation of these Christian dietary and ritual practices arguably has more to do with the assumption that dietary oddness and Judaism go hand in hand than with solid evidence of a self-definition based on Jewish identity among the groups assembled here as the bread-and-water tradition. It is only one form of 'peculiar' diet that can be linked to Judaism; all cultures have their exclusions and fetishes. The issues which are of most concern to the early Christian ascetics of the bread-and-water tradition are also related to Gentile culture and religion; and while we might expect opposition to those to be real in Jewish circles, the models of opposition seem ultimately to owe more to earlier Graeco-Roman forms of asceticism than to Jewish ones. The logic of avoidance of the cuisine of sacrifice has already been discussed, but these specific models deserve some further consideration.

A Cynic Mystery[11]

The issues for the Christians (and Jews) who avoided meat and wine ultimately came largely, it has been argued, from Graeco-Roman sacrifice as the constitutive ritual of the city and of the Empire, and the continuation of the classical Greek view of animal, human, and divine worlds recognized and re-established by the offering of one by the other to the third. It remains to be seen just how important the earlier forms of dietary dissent, such as the Pythagorean and Cynic tendencies to avoid meat, were in the construction of an ascetic Christian self-understanding, or to what extent the similarities and differences are otherwise illuminating.

The question of a relationship between at least some of the ascetic Christians of the bread-and-water tradition and Cynicism was raised in antiquity by heresiologists anxious to label the dissenting groups as deviant, as well as more recently by scholars with an interest in the

---

[11] Filastrius, *Div. Haer. Lib.* 49.

possible use of Cynic tradition by Jesus and/or early Christians. Some assessment will have to be made of these Cynic-hypothesis suggestions, at least as they apply to the second- and third-century evidence, but this discussion will not proceed on the basis that Cynicism or any other movement or tradition is likely to explain the ritual and ascetic practices being discussed. This does not mean that there are no connections, whether those of genesis (i.e. that some aspect of the bread-and-water use was taken over from models linked with Cynicism) or for that matter of structural similarity (i.e. that Cynics and Christians responded similarly to dominant ritual and meal practice by avoiding similar food and drink). But the relevant question is not 'Is this a Cynic practice?', but 'What light do comparisons with Cynic practice shed?'[12]

Two ancient authors noted above accused those who refused wine in the eucharistic cup of being Cynics rather than Christians. Hippolytus used this as a term of reproach for Encratites, and rather later Filastrius applied the same label to Montanists. In both cases this accusation was made in specific connection with the use of bread and water in the eucharist. Hippolytus gives a brief description of the Encratites in his *Refutation of all Heresies* (8. 13) where they are distinguished from other Christians mainly in their asceticism: 'They suppose that by meats they magnify themselves, while abstaining from animal food, being water-drinkers, and forbidding to marry, and devoting themselves during the remainder of life to habits of asceticism. But persons of this description are estimated Cynics rather than Christians . . .' Apparently Hippolytus thinks that any or all of these things are Cynic; in fact none of them are quite a perfect fit for what we could say was typical of Cynics, despite the difficulty in establishing just what that might have been! Yet the Cynic concern for autonomy and freedom has already been noted as having led to an ascetic, rather than a luxurious or debauched, lifestyle. Meat was often rejected or avoided, and water-drinking was certainly a feature used before then to distinguish Cynics from others.[13] Hippolytus drew a reasonable comparison between Encratite practice and Cynic ideals, but

---

[12] In this respect I have no quarrel at all with the method of comparison (and avoidance of the question of origins as an all-consuming end) suggested by Leif Vaage in *Galilean Upstarts: Jesus' First Followers According to Q* (Valley Forge, Pa.: Trinity Press International, 1994), 10–15. While I have no intention to assess here the Cynic hypothesis in terms of the Q document or the historical Jesus, it will be evident from the discussion below that I think Vaage and its other exponents exaggerate the coherence and self-consciousness of the Cynic tradition.

[13] Water: Diogenes Laertius, *Lives*, 6. 2. 31 (Diogenes); 6. 5. 90 (Crates); cf. 6. 9. 104; Lucian, *Fugitivi*, 14; Ps.-Lucian, *The Cynic*, 5. The Cynic might also feel called to forsake conventional marital relations: see Downing, *Cynics and Christian Origins*, 140 n. 119.

important differences must still be accounted for in just how the different ascetics reached their goals.

Filastrius' use of the label 'Cynic' for Montanist eucharistic meals ('mysterium cynicon') should probably be understood in the same terms, and especially with reference to the distinctive use of water. His report is accompanied by the accusation of ritual infanticide, another possible link with Cynics, although the association can and has been exaggerated.[14] In any case, Filastrius certainly presents the two charges as quite different things.

But these instances of the more accommodating heresiologists calling ascetic Christians 'Cynics' reflect on more than just diet. The Cynic label is appropriate, not merely because the objects of the taunt might resemble certain philosophically minded pagans in dress, speech, or conduct, but because it was a term of abuse. Just as at one point Christians had been called cannibals by pagans and then began to trade the insult among themselves, so too now 'Cynic' became a way for those Christians who were working hard to assimilate themselves to the wider society to distinguish themselves from those who sought, by means including use of foods, to mark themselves off more clearly. This designation is therefore to be understood as an exercise in labelling or ritual insult as much or more than as an accurate descriptive term.[15]

Unlike the cannibal accusations perhaps, the Cynic comparison has a more helpful or suggestive side as well. There probably were some instances where aspects of Christian identity were related, directly or indirectly, to Cynic tradition. The attempts of F. Gerald Downing and others to pursue the nexus between Cynic and Christian into the second and third centuries are not without interest here. The Christian philosopher could at times perhaps have been taken for a Cynic, whether in terms of teaching or of lifestyle, emphasizing simplicity of dress and diet.[16] Yet the use of commonplace attacks on other philosophical schools is a passing resemblance rather than a matter of substance; if Christians used arguments also used by Cynics, this identifies common enemies rather than common ground.[17]

Among the candidates Downing introduces as possible indicators of

---

[14] See the discussion in Ch. 2 above.

[15] See Bruce J. Malina and Jerome H. Neyrey, 'Conflict in Luke-Acts: Labelling and Deviance Theory', in Neyrey (ed.), *The Social World of Luke-Acts: Models for Interpretation*, 97–122.

[16] Justin suggests that his attacker Crescens is trying to make the differences between them clearer (*2 Apol.* 3). See Downing, *Cynics and Christian Origins*, 170–1, 179–80.

[17] Downing, *Cynics and Christian Origins*, 175–94, makes rather more of such similarities.

ongoing Cynic influence, the rather conformist positions of the anonymous *Letter to Diognetus* or the *Shepherd* of Hermas do not seem promising for identifying Cynic lifestyle, whatever rhetorical influences may be identified. Tatian, and perhaps Justin, are better contenders for positive comparison because we know in these cases that their ascetic practice, as well as their rhetoric, was not dissimilar to that of Cynics.[18] Tatian is also happy to depict Christianity in terms of rejection of social norms (*Orat.* 11; 32–4). The Pseudo-Clementines have Peter adopting a diet and mode of dress that could well have been those of a Cynic (*Hom.* 12. 6; *Recog.* 7. 6. 4). The apostolic heroes of the apocryphal *Acts* also dress and eat in ways that could owe something to Cynic tradition (*Acts of Thomas*, 20). Tertullian, too, uses arguments reminiscent of Cynicism (*De Pallio*).[19]

The bread-and-water tradition is certainly well represented among the Christians who have been assembled in the attempt to pursue the Cynic hypothesis into the third century. Yet one might wonder whether the persistence of these ideas, or even of a Cynic stereotype, really suggests a clear ongoing Cynic identity and tradition so much as the reuse of these practices in different contexts, such as for the construction of the identity of the sophist or as general expressions of social dissent.

Further, as soon as we begin to acknowledge some similarity of diet among the possible evidence of Cynic influence, a most important difference has to be acknowledged: we know of no clear case where the use of bread and water in the Christian meal is presented as part of a lifestyle free from constraint. The picture is always one of a more restrained diet than the norm, imposed by the community's rejection of idolatry and dissipation, rather than of freedom to ignore the social norms of sacrificial cuisine. Peregrinus' strife with the Christians (Lucian, *De Morte Pereg.* 16) is a neat vignette that illustrates the difference; he was acceptable to them for a while, observing the same dietary ascesis as they did, but was ultimately not willing or able to accept the prohibition of some forbidden food (probably meat, one must say, after the evidence already presented). In eating rather than refusing, Lucian's Peregrinus did act as a Cynic ought to have done; and by rejecting him for this reason, the Christians of the story certainly showed themselves something other than Cynic in inspiration.

The similarity, then, is real but ultimately superficial.[20] There may be

---

[18] Ibid. 179–90.   [19] Barnes, *Tertullian*, 229–31.

[20] In this matter at least Clement of Alexandria sees the point, comparing the diet of Christian and Cynic; the Christian ought to eat the way Diogenes did, and is equally free to eat anything within the constraints of moderation (*Paed.* 2. 1. 16. 3).

some elements derived from Cynic tradition in use in the lifestyle and theological argument of various Christian groups, but they are not overwhelming and do not explain the 'Cynic mystery' of bread and water in the eucharist. More generally, the quest for a substantial and specific Cynic influence in Christianity is probably misconceived. In many of the cases discussed, the conflation of various traditions in sophistry is more than enough to account for the use of Cynic-sounding arguments.[21] The resemblances between Cynic and radical Christian diet derive from the similar structure of sacrificial ritual and diet that they reject; this structure suggests its own opposition, and some similarity of practice between dissenters of different kinds is to be expected.

Pythagoras' Theory

There is a case for some consideration of similarities between the bread-and-water tradition and Pythagorean practices or ideals. Claude Rambaux has argued that Tertullian in particular was under the influence of Neo-Pythagorean, rather than Cynic, models of philosophical ascesis.[22] Tertullian refers explicitly to a recent Pythagorean revival in attempting to distinguish the practice of the New Prophecy from that of others so rigorist as to exclude meat, not only on particular occasions, but altogether (*De Ieiun.* 15. 1). It has also been tempting for some to see the dietary aspect of later Christian asceticism, such as that of the desert monks, as Pythagorean in inspiration.[23]

In his own emphasis on fasting, Tertullian does at times seem to warrant comparison with Porphyry and those who regarded the elimination not merely of animal food but of all food (!) from the diet as desirable, if rather unlikely (Porphyry, *De Abst.* 1. 38). This is a somewhat different form of asceticism, more conscious of the individual body and of the effects of food on it than of the wider society and the importance of food therein. The mere fact of the existence in Christianity, prior to Tertullian, of the tradition that uses bread and water in

[21] See Barnes, *Tertullian*, 211–32.
[22] See Claude Rambaux, *Tertullien face aux morales des trois premiers siècles* (Paris: Belles-Lettres, 1979), 198–9, 202–3; criticized by Downing on behalf of the Cynic-seekers, *Cynics and Christian Origins*, 209–10.
[23] See Anthony Meredith, 'Asceticism—Christian and Greek', *JTS* NS 27 (1976), 313–32, which gives a useful comparative account of these forms of asceticism but perhaps puts the food issue too simply when discussing Antony's diet: 'We seem to be here in the presence of some form of fairly identifiable Pythagorean taboo about wine and meat' (p. 318).

the eucharistic meal is probably a better explanation for his own practices than any supposed philosophical influence; but the existence of similar concerns among philosophers is not to be ignored.

Nevertheless, in the ascetic Christian meal tradition as a whole, one does not have a sense of the individual philosopher using bread and water as the means of edification, so much as one of the exclusion by whole communities of what is seen as polluting. The notion of transmigration of souls or any related idea that would suggest concern for the well-being of the animal is certainly not apparent.[24] The dynamic of exclusion (or of 'strong group' characteristics, in Mary Douglas's terms) found in the bread-and-water tradition is, at least in this social aspect, more like that of Pythagoras himself and of the carnivorous but selective followers of his, than it is like the musings of later armchair Pythagoreans such as Plutarch, Seneca (*Ep.* 108. 22), or Porphyry.[25] This means that in looking at the relation between Pythagoreanism and these Christian communities, comparison of structures may be again more useful than attempts to look for direct influence.

In the discussion of Pythagoras and Pythagoreanism in Ch. 2 I drew attention to the controversy in ancient times over whether Pythagoras really did refuse all meat. The conflicting traditions concerning the sage himself and his early followers such as the people at Croton suggest that this philosophical tradition was, in its early stages at least, one of careful sacrifice rather than rejection of sacrifice. This care, expressed in some instances by refusal of meat, in others by choice of specific victims and elsewhere by special vegetable offerings, seems to have been joined to concern both for individual self-discipline and community self-definition.

The Christians of the bread-and-water tradition are generally like the old Pythagoreans not only in the actual exclusion of meat, but in the association of such an exclusion with a religious community that was, in many cases at least, itself highly exclusive and disciplined. This discipline is very evident in the Pseudo-Clementines and suggested by the sectarian aspects of the lives of many other groups. I have argued that the level of concern over food and meals in the apocryphal *Acts* is connected to the degree of opposition to sacrifice and other aspects of the life of

---

[24] I acknowledge the odd appearances of rather anthropomorphic animals such as those in the apocryphal *Acts*. These seem to fit rather well with the suggestion of the sacrificial structure as ordering animal, human, and divine, and it makes sense that the rejection of animal sacrifice gives rise to the parade of talking and even believing beasts who represent a sort of restored paradise in Judaeo-Christian terms.

[25] See Ch. 2 above.

'normal' society. In both cases the strong emphasis on group and anxiety about the porousness of the social body is mirrored by concern for diet, and for control over what enters the individual body. To this extent the similarity is a matter of social dynamics that might even be predictable across different cultures; yet the fact that Pythagorean and ascetic Christian exclusions both centre on meat has to do with the presence of both groups in that culture of the cuisine of sacrifice.

It would therefore be unhelpful and inaccurate to see this (or other Christian dietary ascesis such as that of the desert monks) as somehow Pythagorean simply because of the exclusion of meat. While the teaching and example of Pythagoras himself seem to have made an impact across the world of Graeco-Roman antiquity, the specific connections are vague and shed little light on the Christian ascetic and ritual meal tradition.

Certain Cynics, Pythagoreans, and Christians all took steps that had the effect of removing meat from diet. What they had in common was participation in a culture where sacrifice was the constitutive ritual, and meat its dietary correlate. Beyond this the specific connections are, if not impossible, then at least difficult to establish. It is more important to acknowledge the differences in the various responses to participation in that society and its ritual. The basic pattern of the dissenting response to the cuisine of sacrifice could possibly be traced through Jewish, Pythagorean, and Cynic manifestations, if we had sufficient evidence to do so, but we do not. It may have to be enough to say that these things were in the air.

Meal of the Poor

While at the outset I emphasized the fact that questions of food and meals must be regarded as necessarily part of structures of economy and power, as well as of culture and religion, most of the discussion of the bread-and-water tradition here has been undertaken from a cultural perspective rather than an economic one. This is partly because there is relatively little information about the social placement of the participants in the bread-and-water tradition, and that which we do have suggests that they had choices in the realm of food, and otherwise. All the ascetics refused wine, we are told, and this implies it was available. While wine was probably not hard to come by, this leaves us dealing not with the poorest of the poor in any case. In the Pseudo-Clementines and apocryphal *Acts* the rich and noble are enticed to give up their wealth in favour of the gospel; despite the novelistic aspect of this focus on the rich and famous, an ethic of renunciation seems to lie behind these depictions. Cyprian's opponents were conscious enough of good social form to quibble about the right time to drink wine. While these indications of wealth or power could also be due to the fact that we have literary evidence, which by its very nature must tend to come from the higher end of the social scale, the fact remains that choice plays a large part in all these examples and the others. Both meat and wine are excluded by those who could otherwise have used them.

Nevertheless the diet common to some Christians, as well as to many Cynics, had an economic as well as a ritual aspect to it. Bread, salt, and perhaps some herbs and vegetables, with water to drink, would have been recognizable not merely as pure or natural food but as frugal, as the food of the poor. While wine of some sort was probably accessible to most, clearly water was cheaper, and the poorest would have had to drink it. Meat was a luxury food, and if even the urban poor could obtain it under some circumstances it was relatively rare and expensive. The argument already presented that the bread-and-water tradition is best comprehended in terms of an asceticism that responds to sacrificial cuisine ought not to be seen to exclude some sense of invoking poverty as a symbol of protest or disengagement.

The impact on the sacrificial system itself of refusal to eat meat is attested by Pliny the Younger, who writes to Trajan on the subject of the provision of victims and the activity of the temples as a matter of state importance (*Ep.* 10. 96). This correspondence apparently combines what we would see as economic, religious, and political aspects, although these might not have been as easily separable to the ancients. We have plentiful examples of the use of the same foods in the same way by pagans of various sorts; Cynics are prominent but hardly unique among them. Cato used this sort of diet (Plutarch, *Life of Cato*, 1. 13) as an act of solidarity with his troops, obviously not as a permanent lifestyle change but by way of delay of gratification, expecting conquest and booty to follow. Plutarch uses it as a sign of true friendship, believing that some bonds were not weakened but rather had their strength demonstrated by poor food (*Quaest. Conv.* 684 E–F).

Cynics originally took the quest for a natural and simple diet which would do the body good to mean a frugal one in which bread and water were the most common elements; eventually these foods became a sort of badge by which, along with the philosopher's cloak and staff, the sage ought to be recognizable. Other philosophers sought to practice an ascesis of self-improvement by removing or restricting luxurious foods.

The tradition of Nazirite abstinence, although of quite a different religious origin, may deserve mention here also; the Nazirite, understood as holy, defined by an allegiance which requires a diet that differentiates that person from the wider community, was not only another example of this sort of abstinence but one of which some use was made in the bread-and-water tradition. Thus there was not one way but a whole variety of ways in which a diet expressing voluntary poverty might be used: to have an effect on the self or others, as a choice for a season or for a lifetime, to indicate stern self-control or benign indifference. These are all, however, choices made by those who had the resources to have lived otherwise had they wished.

The fact that the bread-and-water tradition also signals poverty in what often seems a deliberate fashion need not lead us to conclude that the ascetic meal pattern in early Christianity has an entirely élite social origin. While daily use of meat as well as wine may have been rare, few had no access to them whatsoever.[26] Christians such as those represented in the literature of the bread-and-water tradition may have been presented with the dilemma of ritually slaughtered meat because they were less well-off and only had the opportunity to eat it when attending the meetings of *collegia*, or on other occasions when it was all but certain to have been offered to idols; but this would merely place them somewhere in the middle of society, rather than at the poorest end.[27] The sources do not contain much by way of a polemic against the rich and powerful *per se*. Even the romances of the apostolic heroes in which wives of wealthy magistrates are converted from participation in the lives of their husbands, food, sex, wealth, and all, do not emphasize the economic aspect of renunciation beyond the others.

It may also be worth emphasizing that while economic or similar factors have sometimes been allowed in previous scholarly discussion of these meals, they have tended to be used as the explanation for a deviation from the normal bread-and-wine eucharist; protests against economic and sexual engagement have typically been taken as evidence of a late influence often labelled as encratism. The logic of choice might seem to support at least the possibility of a deviation in ritual practice, but only if we were to assume that every primitive tradition included wine in the communal meal. As we have seen, there is probably evidence for a more ascetic meal tradition as far back as the New Testament itself.

The economic aspect of the bread-and-water tradition seems therefore

---

[26] See Ch. 2 above.   [27] See Goody, *Cooking, Cuisine and Class*, 97–127.

to be one of voluntary poverty rather than of enforced adaptation of a normative bread-and-wine tradition; it is, in other words, not so much a matter of economic circumstance as one of deliberate asceticism.

'Normal' Meal?

The fact that bread and water are not merely food and drink of the poor but ordinary and unremarkable foods, has also been used in attempts to contribute to the question of origins.[28] The similarity between the bread-and-water meal (as well as those involving additional foods such as cheese) and the typical diet of many inhabitants of the ancient Mediterranean led Harnack and Lietzmann to suggest these meals might indicate indifference to the content of the cup (or plate) in the eucharist.[29]

Reasons have already been given for not favouring that explanation, except where 'ordinary diet' is taken to mean the very specific and rigidly observed ascetic diet observed by the communities in question. In fact the meals of the bread-and-water tradition seem, in some important senses at least, to be self-consciously odd rather than ordinary; and the use of water is far from being a matter of indifference. The hypothesis that the water eucharist and the instances of 'additional' foods being employed were both indicators of a tradition in which (or of a point in time at which) the eucharistic meal was a version of typical eating seems to have arisen in part as a result of polemics about order in early Christianity. Even a hundred years after the event, the vehemence with which the conservative critics of Harnack's original suggestion about the use of water in the eucharistic cup responded to the idea of this somewhat romanticized picture of early Christian eating is striking, but so is the original naïveté of the proposal.

ASCETICISM AND THE CUISINE OF SACRIFICE

Interpreting Asceticism

The bread-and-water tradition suggests an understanding of both the bread-and-water elements of the eucharistic meal as symbols taken and eaten in ascetic opposition to the pagan sacrificial system of meat and

---

[28] Lietzmann, *Mass and Lord's Supper*, 204–5.
[29] Harnack, 'Brod und Wasser', 136–43; Lietzmann, *Mass and Lord's Supper*, 195–203.

wine. But as discussion of Pythagorean and Cynic attitudes to food and meals indicated, the tendency to conceive of asceticism as a one-dimensional scale extending from moderation to extreme self-denial (with self-indulgence or luxury the other implied pole) is inadequate to deal with the ways in which ancient Greeks and Romans used food and drink as creators of, and expressions of, self-identity and sociability. So too, accounts of asceticism that work largely or wholly in terms of the desired impact of practice upon the individual are not sufficient to deal with the kinds of use of foods under discussion.

Asceticism should be understood not as an ahistorical tendency to self-discipline through reduction of dietary or sexual activity, but as a type of action that involves a conscious response to the normal patterns of such activities in a given situation or society. This response is usually or perhaps always related to quantity in some sense, but does not necessarily begin and end there. Consideration of asceticism in a given context should be related to the familiar and prevalent patterns. Removal or specific regulation of a particular activity takes on its significance in relation to what is normal; to exclude pork from diet means nothing where there are no pigs. The traditional Greek and Jewish responses to the predominant eating patterns of classical antiquity seem to be arranged in ways which are concerned not only (and sometimes not much) with references to questions of 'more or less' but rather more with questions of 'what, when, and how'. More specifically, the use of meat and the practice of sacrifice which Pythagoreans, Cynics, and some Jews and Christians rejected in different ways, seem to be the most fundamental issues of participation in 'normal' eating for Graeco-Roman society.

The response of the Christians of the bread-and-water tradition to the normal eating habits of their society is, not surprisingly, couched in terms of the most ritually and socially significant foods of that society, as were those of Cynics, Pythagoreans, and of some Jewish dissidents. The similarity does not, therefore, lead immediately and exclusively to questions of influence and dependence with those traditions, but merely identifies the various groups as participants in ascetic responses to the dominant culture and cuisine. The conjunction of vegetarian and teetotal practice, as it were, attested in the bread-and-water tradition is not merely personal but profoundly social in nature; it represents not merely (if at all) a concern for the effects of particular foods on the bodies of individuals, but a concern to avoid a particular form of sociability that was religiously unacceptable.

Sacrifice, it has been argued, had a fundamental religious as well as social significance throughout the Graeco-Roman world. While recent studies have pursued these issues in the rituals of archaic and classical Greek cities, the logic of sacrifice seems to continue into later antiquity, just as do other elements of religious and political life. The evidence from the Pauline discussions of food and drink in Romans and 1 Corinthians makes it clear enough that the questions of meat and wine as sacrificial foods were of fundamental religious importance in the first century. In the next century and more, the importance of sacrifice as the test of the staunch martyr on the one hand, or apostate on the other, indicates that sacrifice and food continued to be seen as socially constitutive in late antiquity as well.

There were, of course, changes in the practice and meaning of the cuisine of sacrifice as well, and the emergence of the Roman Empire and the principate at its head are not without significance for the meaning of these patterns of avoidance in the second and third centuries. Often we find that the sacrifices Christians were called upon to make in times of persecution were to the Emperor; the emergence of this person as the embodiment of the whole *oikoumene* and its well-being could only serve to sharpen the focus of the role of sacrifice as a political event. The Pseudo-Clementines provide the clearest political interpretation of the dissident diet: 'Those who have determined to accept the blessings of the future reign have no right to regard as their own the things that are here, since they belong to a foreign king, with the exception only of water and bread, and those things procured with sweat to maintain life . . . and also one garment' (*Hom.* 15. 7. 6).

The use of both meat and wine as the key elements of pagan sacrificial cuisine meant that Christians (as well as Jews and others) had to take up a stance towards the use of these foods, not simply as signs or symbols of religion, but actually *as* religion. To eat and drink from the table of demons was to be a participant in demons, as Paul says not only on his own behalf, but also on behalf of the 'weak' who avoided these tables and all that they reeked of (1 Cor. 10: 20–1); to eat and drink thus was to internalize that world-view and to become embedded in it. The meal cannot be reduced to some other aspect of social life regarded as more real or fundamental, which we would be doing if we regarded it merely as a metaphor of concern for group boundaries. To eat and drink is sociability and community, not just a sign of it.

The New Testament already witnesses to a number of different responses to sacrifice among the fledgling Christian communities; the full accommodation of the 'strong', the rigorous opposition of the 'weak', and the critical engagement of Paul himself. Paul's own response to the challenge of the cuisine of sacrifice could be characterized as the creation of a parallel meal-universe based on the tradition of the Lord's Supper as a sacrificial meal. Without accepting the suggestions that the story and the ritual of the Last Supper are a Pauline invention, we can see nevertheless that his contribution is nearly as radical as an invention would be, in that he constructs the Christian meal as one comprehensible in terms of the logic of pagan sacrifice. To participate in the Christian meal is, for Paul, to renounce the table of demons, but it is also to create another table whose logic is actually quite similar to that which he attacks (1 Cor. 10: 16–21).

The bread-and-water tradition, on the other hand, tends to be anti-sacrificial generally. When this opposition is not made explicit in texts, this argument must rest on silence to some extent, although the meal elements themselves are not wholly inarticulate when carefully examined. Where sacrifice is not mentioned, the logic of sacrifice can be assumed to be rejected, at least where the meal elements of bread and water are present to suggest that. But there are important exceptions where silence turns into polemical speech. This is particularly evident in the Pseudo-Clementines and apocryphal *Acts*, where the opposed practices of offering sacrifices to demons and prayer to God are understood very concretely as acts empowering the spiritual forces aligned on each side. A similar opposition is evident in the *Martyrdom of Pionius*, where meat was very much in evidence as the test of fidelity to the faith, and where water is the logical form of ritual drink. So too, in the *Martyrdom of Perpetua and Felicitas*, which is not actually a witness to the bread-and-water tradition but is not far removed from some of the texts discussed both in world-view and otherwise, the peaceable realm of God is starkly contrasted with the bloodshed of the arena.

The absence or at least lack of emphasis in the texts discussed on the sacrificial or body and blood language associated with the more sacrificial and eventually normative bread-and-wine tradition, at least from Paul onwards, may also be more than accidental. Justin is, as has been noted, an exception to this correlation between silence about the Last Supper traditions and other indications of non- or anti-sacrificial thought, but he is an exception which makes the rule itself look no less strong overall. While Justin knows and makes use of the language of Jesus' Last Supper as a sacrificial memorial, his apologetic account of the eucharist is addressed to the *princeps*, the personal embodiment of the cosmos that was kept in place by sacrifice, and his task is to try to depict the ritual life of Christians as in keeping with the pious and patriotic practices of other citizens.

Ritual and Asceticism

While the usual liturgical approaches have, as I have already argued, tended to see the eucharistic meals of the early Christian communities as *sui generis*, or as actions comprehensible in terms of cultic procedure or understanding but not of other meals, the specific evidence suggests that this distinction is problematic, at least for the bread-and-water tradition. In fact at this point in time at least, it is arguable that all Christian eucharistic meals figure the structure of the other meals known to the participants, and are in fact understood to do so.[30] Rather than a hard and fast distinction between liturgy and life there is, as we might expect from the suggestions of more anthropological models, at least an analogy, and perhaps a more substantial connection, between the different meals in the culture or subcultures being discussed.

The specifically eucharistic meals (when they can be identified as such) of the ascetically minded Christians of the bread-and-water tradition certainly reflected the same concerns that seem to have been prevalent for their other meals. In the cases discussed it is often very difficult to decide that one form of meal should be understood as 'ritual' or 'sacral' while another is not. In fact we would be better off to jettison the sacred/secular distinctions that underlie this sort of analysis as largely anachronistic, or at least inappropriate to the ordering of the sacral in some of these communities. The ordering of the sacral is not structured in the same way in all times and places. While there are distinctions to be drawn between different meals in antiquity, and even between different meals within the bread-and-water tradition, the supposedly universal division between the sacred and the profane seems unhelpful here. The varieties of meal suggest that a 'field' or 'grid', over which the meal evidence can be seen as spread according not only to level but also to type of concern, would be more analytically and interpretatively helpful than a single axis or dimension such as apparent presence or absence of religious emphasis. Only with a more subtle set of

---

[30] This is the sense one has, for instance, from the discussions of eating by Clement of Alexandria; see Leyerle, 'Clement of Alexandria on the Importance of Table Etiquette', 123–41. See also the *Letter to Diognetus*, 5. 1–10, which seeks to depict communal Christian eating in terms of typical diet and behaviour.

categories could we really do justice to the picture presented by the literary treatments such as the apocryphal *Acts* and Pseudo-Clementines in particular.

For these examples at least, what Mary Douglas suggests about the character and relation of various meals in the life of a given community seems to hold true, i.e. that different meals are as much linked by common structure as they are distinguished by differences of importance, festivity, and other factors. In fact for the bread-and-water tradition this seems to hold true to a rather greater extent than for the normative Christian tradition. For other groups which seem to have been more integrated into the life of the wider society (or willing to become so), a eucharistic meal may have been more clearly distinguished from other normal meals of that community than was the case at least in the Pseudo-Clementines and apocryphal *Acts*. For the radical ascetics of the pseudepigraphic works, the character of the eucharist and of all other meals is markedly different from the meal-understanding of other members of society, primarily in the rejection of meat and wine.

The strange conjunction of the additional eucharistic foods discussed in Ch. 3 and the bread-and-water tradition begins to make sense in these terms. It was more likely for the other elements of a radical ascetic diet, milk, cheese, fruit, vegetables, oil, and salt, to be present in a eucharistic meal in these communities, because there were only relatively soft distinctions between the most important communal meals of those groups and the least important acts of eating by individuals and households. In Douglas's own terms we would seem to be dealing, in some of these cases at least, with a 'strong group' and 'low grid' situation, i.e. one in which there is great concern for self-definition and demarcation of the group relative to the rest of society, but relatively little anxiety about internal divisions and distinctions: 'The smallest, meanest meal metonymically figures the structure of the grandest . . .'[31]

Thus a larger distance seems to be established between all meals of the community and all meals of others in these cases, whereas in the other more accommodating communities, everyday food seems to have been much the same as for other people, but the eucharistic meal was increasingly odd. The different placement of the most important distinctions between meals in these two different forms of Christianity has its logical expression in the different uses of food in the eucharists of the respective communities.

[31] Douglas, 'Deciphering a Meal', 257.

Summary

The bread-and-water tradition has a meaning, therefore, which can in some sense at least be deciphered. It is the dietary self-expression of a dissident group or groups embedded in ancient Graeco-Roman society and confronted with its cuisine of sacrifice. The significance of this meal is as much negative as it is positive; there is, at least, no essence to be discovered in this set of practices, but rather part of a set of oppositions. Hence it is possible for the different practitioners of the bread-and-water eucharistic meal to differ greatly in theology and other aspects of social practice.

The theological differences are self-evident. Practical differences include the various positions that seem to be reflected on the role and placement of women in the Christian communities. Rejection of the wider society and its cuisine might, or might not, involve rejection of particular institutions and roles. Thus while it is instructive that the rejection of sacrifice seems in certain cases to have involved rejection of the social ordering of gender relations, as the theory of Nancy Jay would have suggested, there are instances where this is not the case. What does seem to be true in each case is that a space for the construction of a different community self-definition was involved.[32] Discussion of the specific uses of this space in different cases belongs to more specific studies of these communities and their lives.

CONCLUSION

I began with a critique of the approaches to eucharistic meals which have been characteristic of most liturgical scholarship until quite recently. It may then seem only fair to end by indicating briefly what the implications of the foregoing discussion are for the reconstruction of a history of eucharistic meals.

Although I have both assumed and found diversity, I have also indicated that the differences between early Christian meals of one pattern and another are not merely random or a matter of ancient whim. The diversity of early eucharistic practice is real, but limited. Although attention has here been given to traditions whose liturgical future turned out to be limited, and whose days were in fact numbered

[32] See Stowers, 'Greeks Who Sacrifice and Those Who Do Not', 293–333.

when Christianity found mass appeal, the tasks not only of reconstructing a more complete picture but of interpreting the eventually normative tradition may now be seen in a somewhat different light.

Just as the bread-and-water tradition was comprehensible in terms of present meaning in context rather than merely of origins, so too the surviving pattern of eucharistic meals of bread and wine may be better understood in context as a synthesis of sacrificial and non-sacrificial tendencies, or perhaps as a compromise between them, rather than merely as the repetition of an inherited tradition. Paul's role as an innovator or interpreter has been suggested before, but that of Cyprian has perhaps been underestimated, nor has the potential for reflection on what he achieved or represented been exhausted here. If Cyprian did not actually establish the eucharist as a sacrifice in a more than metaphorical sense, the tendency to see this as an early and universal understanding has masked his originality. Hence the theological question of the meaning of sacrifice might also benefit from some consideration of these issues, at least to supplement the thorough (or exaggerated) ways in which scholars have tried to show the continuity and dependence of early Christian thought on earlier Jewish, and sometimes Greek, ideas of sacrifice.[33] Resistance to sacrifice was arguably as important to many Christians as was the quest for a rational or bloodless sacrifice.

Food alone does not make a meal. There are also quite different possibilities for describing and interpreting early eucharistic practice offered by pursuing different aspects of ancient meal practice in addition to the well-travelled paths of analysing prayer texts. Words are indeed important, but so is their relationship to practice, and the significance of prayers and issues such as nomenclature may well be taken further. Order has long been recognized as an important area for the history of the eucharist, but there are further questions to explore in the proceedings of the meal as well. So too, participation, presidency, and other matters to do with the eaters, as well as the eaten, need to be considered in the light of different presuppositions in order to construct a fuller picture of early Christian eating. Recent as well as ancient experience suggests that the questions of persons, those who eat and those who do not, those who preside and those who may not, are as important as any other issue in the practice of Christian meals.

The emergence of a more diverse picture of early Christian practice in this and other respects may seem a threat to those who wish to maintain

[33] See Daly, *Christian Sacrifice*, and Young, *Sacrificial Ideas*.

and appreciate tradition, but the threat is not so much to tradition as to ideology based on myths of immutable custom. Now as in the past, there are certain choices which the Christian communities have had to face, not simply on the basis of what had previously been done, but of what had still to be done.

Select Bibliography

PRIMARY TEXTS AND TRANSLATIONS

The following collections of texts and/or translations have been used where no other is specified:

The Bible: New Revised Standard Version (NRSV) Anglicized.
Early Christian texts: Ante-Nicene Fathers (ANF), Nicene and Post-Nicene Fathers (NPNF).
Classical texts: Loeb Classical Library (LCL).

Acta Andreae, ed. Jean-Marc Prieur, CCSA 5, 6 (Turnhout: Brepols, 1989).
Acta Apostolorum Apocrypha, ed. Richard Lipsius and Max Bonnet (Hildesheim: Georg Olms, 1959).
Acta Iohannis, ed. Eric Junod and Jean-Daniel Kaestli, CCSA 1, 2 (Turnhout: Brepols, 1983).
The Acts of Andrew and the Acts of Andrew and Matthias in the City of the Cannibals, ed. and trans. Dennis R. Macdonald, SBLTT 33 (Atlanta: Scholars Press, 1990).
The Acts of the Christian Martyrs: Introduction, Texts and Translations, ed. Herbert Musurillo (Oxford: Clarendon, 1972).
The Apocryphal New Testament: A Collection of Apocryphal Christian Literature in an English Translation, ed. J. K. Elliot (Oxford: Clarendon, 1993).
Die Apostolischen Väter, ed. and trans. Karl Bihlmeyer *et al.* (Tübingen: J. C. B. Mohr (Paul Siebeck), 1992).
(Ps.-) CLEMENT OF ROME, *Ad Virgines*, PG 1. 350–452.
——*Die Pseudoklementinen I: Homilien*, ed. Bernhard Rehm and Georg Strecker, GCS 42/1 (Berlin: Akademie-Verlag, 1992).
——*Die Pseudoklementinen II: Rekognitionen*, ed. Bernard Rehm, GCS 42/2 (Berlin: Akademie-Verlag, 1953).
Concilia Africae a. 345–a. 525, ed. Charles Munier, CCL 149 (Turnhout: Brepols, 1974).
CYPRIAN, *S. Thasci Caecili Cypriani Opera Omnia*, ed. G. Hartel, CSEL 3 (Vienna: F. Tempsky, 1868–71).
——*The Letters of St Cyprian of Carthage*, trans. G. W. Clarke, ACW 43–4, 46–7 (New York: Newman, 1986).
EPHRAEM SYRUS, *Des heiligen Ephraem des Syrers Hymnen contra haereses*, ed. and trans. Edmund Beck, CSCO 169–70 (Louvain: L. Durbecq, 1957).
EPIPHANIUS OF SALAMIS, *Epiphanius*, ed. Karl Holl and Jurgen Dummer, 2nd edn., GCS 25, 31, 37 (Berlin: Akademie-Verlag, 1980).

EPIPHANIUS OF SALAMIS, *The Panarion of St. Epiphanius, Bishop of Salamis: Selected Passages*, trans. Philip R. Amidon (New York: Oxford University Press, 1990).

EUSEBIUS OF CAESAREA, *Eusebius Werke*, ed. E. Schwarz, GCS 9/1–3 (Leipzig: J. C. Hinrichs, 1903–9).

EZNIK OF KOLB, *De Deo*, ed. and trans. Louis Maries and Ch. Mercier, PO 28/3–4 (Paris: Firmin-Didot, 1959).

FILASTRIUS OF BRESCIA, *Filastrii Episcopi Brixiensis Diversarum Hereseon Liber*, ed. F. Heylen, CCL 9/2 (Turnhout: Brepols, 1957).

GREGORY OF TOURS, *Gregorii Episcopi Turonensis miracula et opera minora*, ed. M. Bonnet, MGH Scriptores Rerum Merovingicarum, 1/1 (Hanover: Hahn, 1885).

HIPPOLYTUS, *Refutatio Omnium Haeresium*, ed. P. Wendland, GCS 3 (Leipzig: J. C. Hinrichs, 1897).

—— (attr.), *La Tradition apostolique de saint Hippolyte: Essai de reconstruction*, ed. and trans. Bernard Botte, Liturgiewissenschaftliche Quellen und Forschungen, 39 (Münster: Aschendorff, 1963).

—— *The Treatise on the Apostolic Tradition of St. Hippolytus*, ed. and trans. Gregory Dix, 2nd edn., rev. with preface and corrections by Henry Chadwick (London: SPCK, 1968).

IAMBLICHUS, *On the Pythagorean Way of Life*, ed. John Dillon and Jackson Herschbell, SBLTT 29 (Atlanta: Scholars Press, 1991).

IBN AL-NADIM, MUHAMMAD IBN ISHAQ, *The Fihrist of al-Nadim: A Tenth-Century Survey of Muslim Culture*, trans. B. Dodge (New York: Columbia University Press, 1970).

IRENAEUS, *Contre les hérésies*, ed. Alain Rousseau and Louis Doutreleau, SC 263, 264 (Paris: Éditions du Cerf, 1979).

JUSTIN MARTYR, *Apologies*, ed. André Wartelle (Paris: Études augustiniennes, 1987).

Der Kölner Mani-Kodex: Über das Werden seines Leibes, ed. and trans. L. Koenen and C. Römer, Papyrologica Coloniensia, 14 (Opladen: Westdeutscher, 1988).

The Mishnah: A New Translation, ed. and trans. Jacob Neusner (New Haven: Yale University Press, 1988).

The Montanist Oracles and Testimonia, ed. Ronald E. Heine, Patristic Monograph Series, 14 (Macon, Ga.: Mercer University Press, 1989).

The Old Testament Pseudepigrapha, ed. J. H. Charlesworth (2 vols; New York: Doubleday, 1983).

Patristic Evidence for Jewish-Christian Sects, ed. A. F. J. Klijn and G. J. Reinink, NovTSup 36 (Leiden: E. J. Brill, 1973).

PERPETUA, *The Passion of S. Perpetua*, ed. J. Armitage Robinson, TextsS 1/2 (Cambridge: Cambridge University Press, 1891).

Les Sources de l'histoire du Montanisme, ed. P. de Labriolle (Fribourg: Librairie de l'Université, 1913).

TATIAN, *Oratio ad Graecos and Fragments*, ed. and trans. Molly Whittaker (Oxford: Clarendon, 1982).

——*Diatessaron Persiano*, ed. G. Messina, Biblica et Orientalia, 14 (Rome: Pontifical Biblical Institute, 1951).

——*Diatessaron de Tatian: Texte arabe établi, traduit en français, collationne avec les anciennes versions syriaques, suivi d'un evangeliaire diatessarique syriaque*, ed. and trans. A.-S. Marmardji (Beirut: Imprimerie catholique, 1935).

TERTULLIAN, *Quinti Septimi Florentis Tertulliani Opera*, ed. E. Dekkers *et al.*, CCL 1, 2 (Turnhout: Brepols, 1964).

THEODOTUS, *Clément d'Alexandrie: Extraits de Théodote*, ed. and trans. F. Sagnard, SC 23 (Paris: Éditions du Cerf, 1970).

SECONDARY SOURCES

ANDRÉ, J., *L'Alimentation et la cuisine à Rome* (Paris: C. Klincksieck, 1961).

ATTRIDGE, HAROLD W., *First-Century Cynicism in the Epistles of Heraclitus*, HTS 29 (Missoula, Mont.: Scholars Press, 1976).

AUDET, J.-P., *La Didachè: Instructions des Apôtres* (Paris: Lecoffre, 1958).

AUNE, DAVID E., 'Septem Sapientium Convivium', *Plutarch's Ethical Writings and Early Christian Literature*, ed. H. D. Betz (Leiden: E. J. Brill, 1978), 51–105.

BAHR, GORDON J., 'The Seder of Passover and the Eucharistic Words', *NovT* 12 (1970), 181–202.

BARNARD, LESLIE W., 'The Heresy of Tatian—Once Again', *JEH* 19 (1968), 1–10.

——*Justin Martyr: His Life and Thought* (Cambridge: Cambridge University Press, 1967).

BARNES, TIMOTHY D., *Tertullian: A Historical and Literary Study*, rev. edn. (Oxford: Clarendon, 1985).

BARRETT, C. K., *A Commentary on the Epistle to the Romans*, 2nd edn. (London: A. & C. Black, 1962).

——*A Commentary on the First Epistle to the Corinthians*, 2nd edn. (London: A. & C. Black, 1971).

BAUER, J. B., 'Die Fruchtesegnung in Hippolyts Kirchenordnung', *ZTK* 74 (1952), 71–5.

BAUER, WALTER, *Orthodoxy and Heresy in Earliest Christianity*, ed. and trans. Robert Kraft *et al.* (Philadelphia: Fortress, 1971).

BAZELL, DIANNE M., 'Strife Among the Table-Fellows: Conflicting Attitudes of Early and Medieval Christians toward the Eating of Meat', *JAAR* 65 (1997), 73–99.

BECKWITH, R. T., 'The Vegetarianism of the Therapeutae, and the Motives for Vegetarianism in Early Jewish and Christian Circles', *RevQ* 13/49–52 (1988), 407–10.

BERTHIAUME, GUY, *Les Rôles du mágeiros: Étude sur la boucherie, la cuisine et la sacrifice dans la Grèce ancienne*, Mnemosyne Supplementum, 70 (Leiden: E. J. Brill, 1982).

BETZ, JOHANNES, 'Der Abendmahlskelch im Judenchristentum', in M. Reding (ed.), *Abhandlungen über Theologie und Kirche: Festschrift für Karl Adam* (Düsseldorf: Patmos, 1952).

——*Die Eucharistie in der Zeit der griechischen Väter* (2 vols.; Freiburg: Herder, 1955).

BIANCHI, UGO (ed.), *La Tradizione dell'Enkrateia: Motivazioni ontologiche e protologiche* (Rome: Edizioni dell'Ateneo, 1985).

BISHOP, EDMUND, 'Observations on the Liturgy of Narsai', in R. H. Connolly (ed.), *The Liturgical Homilies of Narsai*, TextsS 8/1 (Cambridge: Cambridge University Press, 1909), 85–163.

BLACK, MATTHEW, *The Scrolls and Christian Origins: Studies in the Jewish Background of the New Testament* (London: Nelson, 1961).

BOBERTZ, CHARLES A., 'The Role of the Patron in the *Cena Dominica* of Hippolytus' *Apostolic Tradition*', *JTS* NS 44 (1993), 170–84.

BOKSER, BARUCH, 'Philo's Description of Jewish Practices', *Center for Hermeneutical Studies: Protocol of the Thirtieth Colloquy* (Berkeley: Center for Hermeneutical Studies, 1977), 1–11.

BRADSHAW, PAUL F., *The Search for the Origins of Christian Worship* (New York: Oxford University Press, 1992).

——'*Zebah Todah* and the Origins of the Eucharist', *Ecclesia Orans*, 8 (1991), 255–60.

——and HOFFMAN, LAWRENCE A. (eds.), *The Making of Jewish and Christian Worship* (Notre Dame, Ind.: University of Notre Dame Press, 1991).

BROCK, SEBASTIAN, 'The Baptist's Diet in Syriac Sources', *OrChr* 54 (1970), 113–24.

——'Early Syrian Asceticism', *Numen*, 20 (1973), 1–19.

BROSHI, MAGEN, 'The Diet of Roman Palestine in the Roman Period: Introductory Notes', *Israel Museum Journal*, 5 (1986), 41–56.

BROTHWELL, DON, 'Food, Cooking and Drugs', in Michael Grant and Rachel Kitzinger (eds.), *Civilization of the Ancient Mediterranean: Greece and Rome* (New York: Scribner, 1988), 247–61.

BROTHWELL, DON and PATRICIA, *Food in Antiquity: A Survey of the Diet of Early Peoples* (New York: Frederick A. Praeger, 1969).

BROWN, PETER, *The Body and Society: Men, Women, and Sexual Renunciation in Early Christianity* (New York: Columbia University Press, 1988).

BROWN, RAYMOND, *The Gospel According to John*, AB 29–29A (2 vols.; Garden City, N.Y.: Doubleday, 1966–70).

——and MEIER, JOHN H., *Antioch and Rome: New Testament Cradles of Catholic Christianity* (New York: Paulist Press, 1983).

BUCKLEY, JORUNN JACOBSEN, 'Libertines or Not: Fruit, Bread, Semen and Other Bodily Fluids in Gnosticism', *JECS* 2 (1994), 15–31.

BURKERT, WALTER, *Homo Necans: Interpretationen altgriechischer Opferriten und Mythen* (Berlin: De Gruyter, 1972).

—— 'Oriental Symposia: Contrasts and Parallels', in W. J. Slater (ed.), *Dining in a Classical Context* (Ann Arbor: University of Michigan Press, 1991), 7–24.

BURRUS, VIRGINIA, 'Chastity as Autonomy: Women in the Stories of the Apocryphal Acts', *Semeia*, 38 (1986), 101–17.

—— *Chastity as Autonomy: Women in the Stories of Apocryphal Acts*, Studies in Women and Religion, 23 (Lewiston: Edwin Mellen, 1987).

—— *The Making of a Heretic: Gender, Authority and the Priscillianist Controversy* (Berkeley: University of California Press, 1995).

BURTCHAELL, JAMES T., *From Synagogue to Church: Public Service and Office in the Earliest Church Communities* (Cambridge: Cambridge University Press, 1992).

BYNUM, CAROLINE WALKER, *Holy Feast and Holy Fast: The Religious Significance of Food to Medieval Women* (Berkeley: University of California Press, 1987).

CHILTON, BRUCE, *A Feast of Meanings: Eucharistic Theologies from Jesus through Johannine Circles*, NovTSup 72 (Leiden: E. J. Brill, 1994).

CIRLOT, FELIX, *The Early Eucharist* (London: SPCK, 1939).

CONNOLLY, R. H., 'Agape and Eucharist in the Didache', *Downside Review*, 55 (1937), 477–89.

CONZELMANN, HANS, *1 Corinthians: A Commentary on the First Epistle to the Corinthians*, Hermeneia (Philadelphia: Fortress, 1975).

CORBIER, MIREILLE, 'The Ambiguous Status of Meat in Ancient Rome', *Food and Foodways*, 3 (1989), 223–64.

CORLEY, KATHLEEN, *Private Women, Public Meals: Social Conflict in the Synoptic Tradition* (Peabody, Mass.: Hendrickson, 1993).

CRANFIELD, C. E. B., 'Some Observations on the Interpretation of Romans 14,1–15,13', *Communio Viatorum*, 17 (1974), 193–204.

CROSSAN, JOHN DOMINIC, *The Historical Jesus: The Life of a Galilean Peasant* (San Francisco: HarperSanFrancisco, 1991).

CULLMANN, OSCAR, *Le Problème littéraire et historique du roman Pseudo-Clémentin: Étude sur le rapport entre le Gnosticisme et le Judéo-Christianisme* (Paris: Félix Alcan, 1930).

—— 'La Signification de la Sainte-Cène dans le christianisme primitif', *RHPR* 16 (1936), 1–22.

DALBY, ANDREW, *Siren Feasts: A History of Food and Gastronomy in Greece* (London: Routledge, 1996).

DALY, ROBERT J., *Christian Sacrifice: The Judaeo-Christian Background Before Origen* (Washington: Catholic University of America Press, 1978).

D'ARMS, JOHN H., 'Control, Companionship, and *Clientela*: Some Social Functions of the Roman Communal Meal', *Echos du monde classique / Classical Views*, NS 3 (1984), 327–48.

—— 'The Roman *Convivium* and the Idea of Equality', in O. Murray (ed.), *Sympotica: A Symposium on the 'Symposion'*, 308–20.

DAVIDSON, JAMES, '*Opsophagia*: Revolutionary Eating at Athens', in John Wilkins *et al.* (ed.), *Food in Antiquity* (Exeter: Exeter University Press, 1995), 204–13.

DAVIES, STEVAN L., 'Ascetic Madness', in Robert C. Smith and John Lounibos (eds.), *Pagan and Christian Anxiety: A Response to E.R. Dodds* (Lanham, NY: University Press of America, 1984), 13–26.

—— *The Revolt of the Widows: The Social World of the Apocryphal Acts* (Carbondale, Ill.: Southern Illinois University Press, 1980).

DENTZER, JEAN-MARIE, 'Aux origines de l'iconographie du banquet couché', *Revue archéologique*, 2 (1971), 215–58.

—— *Le Motif du banquet couché dans le proche-orient et le monde grec du VIIe au IVe siècle avant J.-C.* (Rome: École française de Rome, 1982).

DETIENNE, MARCEL, 'Between Beasts and Gods', in R. L. Gordon (ed.), *Myth, Religion and Society* (Cambridge: Cambridge University Press, 1981), 215–28.

—— 'La Cuisine de Pythagore', *Archives de Sociologie des Religions*, 29 (1970), 141–62.

—— 'Culinary Practices and the Spirit of Sacrifice', in M. Detienne and J.-P. Vernant (eds.), *The Cuisine of Sacrifice among the Greeks*, 1–20. French original: M. Detienne and J.-P. Vernant (eds.), *La Cuisine du sacrifice en pays grec* (Paris: Gallimard, 1979).

—— and VERNANT JEAN-PIERRE, (eds.) *The Cuisine of Sacrifice among the Greeks* (Chicago: University of Chicago Press, 1989).

DIBELIUS, MARTIN, and CONZELMANN, HANS, *The Pastoral Epistles*, Hermeneia (Philadelphia: Fortress, 1972).

DIX, GREGORY, *The Shape of the Liturgy* (London: SPCK, 1937; repr. New York: Seabury, 1982).

DODDS, E. R., *Pagan and Christian in an Age of Anxiety* (Cambridge: Cambridge University Press, 1965).

DÖLGER, FRANZ J., *ΙΧΘΥΣ: Das Fischsymbol in frühchristlicher Zeit* i: *Religionsgeschichtliche und epigraphische Untersuchungen* (Rome: Spithöver, 1910).

—— *ΙΧΘΥΣ: Das Fischsymbol in frühchristlicher Zeit* ii–v. *Der heilige Fisch in den antiken Religionen und im Christentum* (4 vols.; Münster: Aschendorff, 1922–43).

DOMBROWSKI, DANIEL A., *The Philosophy of Vegetarianism* (Amherst, Mass.: University of Massachusetts Press, 1984).

DORNIER, P., *Les Épitres pastorales*, SB (Paris: Lecoffre, 1969).

DOUGLAS, MARY, 'Deciphering a Meal', *Implicit Meanings* (London: Routledge & Kegan Paul, 1975), 249–75.

—— 'Food as a System of Communication', *In the Active Voice* (London: Routledge & Kegan Paul, 1982), 82–124.

—— *Purity and Danger: An Analysis of Concepts of Pollution and Taboo*, rev. edn. (London: Routledge & Kegan Paul, 1976).

DOWNING, F. GERALD, *Cynics and Christian Origins* (Edinburgh: T. & T. Clark, 1992).

——'Cynics and Christians, Oedipus and Thyestes', *JEH* 44 (1993), 1–10.

DREWS, PAUL, 'Untersuchungen zur Didache', *ZNW* 5 (1904), 74–9.

DROWER, E. S., *Water into Wine: A Study of Ritual Idiom in the Middle East* (London: John Murray, 1956).

DUCHESNE, LOUIS, *Origines du culte chrétien: Étude sur la liturgie latine avant Charlemagne*, 5th edn. (Paris: E. de Boccard, 1925).

DURAND, JEAN-LOUIS, 'Greek Animals: Toward a Topology of Edible Bodies', in M. Detienne and J.-P. Vernant (eds.), *The Cuisine of Sacrifice Among the Greeks*, 87–118.

——'Ritual as Instrumentality', in M. Detienne and J.-P. Vernant (eds.), *The Cuisine of Sacrifice Among the Greeks*, 119–28.

ELBOGEN, ISMAR, 'Eingang und Ausgang des Sabbats nach talmudischen Quellen', in M. Brann and J. Elbogen (eds.), *Festschrift zu Israel Lewy's siebzigstem Geburtstag* (2 vols.; Breslau: M. & H. Marcus, 1911), i. 173–87.

——*Der jüdische Gottesdienst in seiner geschichtlichen Entwicklung*, 4th edn. (Hildesheim: Georg Olms, 1962).

FEELEY-HARNIK, GILLIAN, *The Lord's Table: Eucharist and Passover in Early Christianity* (Philadelphia: University of Pennsylvania Press, 1981).

FERGUSON, W. S., 'The Attic Orgeones', *HTR* 37 (1944), 61–140.

FITZMYER, JOSEPH, *The Gospel According to Luke*, AB 28, 28A (2 vols.; New York: Doubleday, 1981–5).

——*Romans: A New Translation with Introduction and Commentary*, AB 33 (New York: Doubleday, 1992).

FOX, ROBIN LANE, *Pagans and Christians* (New York: Alfred A. Knopf, 1987).

FRAYN, JOAN, 'The Roman Meat Trade', in J. Wilkins, D. Harvey, and M. Dobson (eds.), *Food in Antiquity*, 107–14.

FUNK, F. X., 'Die Abendmahlselemente bei Justin', *Kirchengeschichtliche Abhandlungen und Untersuchungen* (2 vols.; Paderborn: Schöningh, 1897), i. 278–92.

GARNSEY, PETER, 'Mass Diet and Nutrition in the City of Rome', *Nourir la plèbe: Actes du colloque tenu a Genève les 28 et 29 IX 1989 en hommage à Denis van Berchem*, Schweizerische Beiträge zur Altertumswissenschaft, 22 (Basle: F. Reinhardt, 1991), 67–99.

GEERTZ, CLIFFORD, 'Thick Description: Toward an Interpretive Theory of Culture', *The Interpretation of Cultures: Selected Essays* (New York: Basic Books, 1973), 3–30.

GOGUEL, MAURICE, *L'Eucharistie des origines à Justin Martyr* (Paris: Fischbacher, 1910).

GOOCH, PETER D., *Dangerous Food: 1 Corinthians 8–10 in Its Context*, Studies in Christianity and Judaism, 5 (Waterloo, Ont.: Wilfred Laurier, 1993).

GOODY, JACK, *Cooking, Cuisine and Class: A Study in Comparative Sociology* (Cambridge: Cambridge University Press, 1982).

GORDON, R. L. (ed.), *Myth, Religion and Society: Structuralist Essays by M. Detienne, L. Gernet, J.-P. Vernant and P. Vidal-Naquet* (Cambridge: Cambridge University Press, 1981).

GRAF, F., 'Milch, Honig und Wein: Zum Verständnis der Libation im griechischen Ritual', *Perennitas: Studi in onore di Angelo Brelich* (Rome: Edizioni dell'Ateneo, 1980), 209–21.

GRANT, ROBERT M., 'The Heresy of Tatian', *JTS* NS 7 (1956), 246–8.

GREIFF, A., 'Brot, Wasser und Mischwein die Elemente der Taufmesse', *TQ* 113 (1932), 11–34.

GRIMM, VERONIKA, *From Feasting to Fasting, the Evolution of a Sin: Attitudes to Food in Late Antiquity* (London: Routledge, 1996).

HAMEL, GILDAS, *Poverty and Charity in Roman Palestine, First Three Centuries C.E.* (Berkeley: University of California Press, 1990).

HAMMAN, ADALBERT, 'Pour une lecture concrète des textes', in F. Paschke (ed.), *Überlieferungsgeschichtliche Untersuchungen*, TU 125 (Berlin: Akademie-Verlag, 1981), 285–92.

—— *Vie liturgique et vie sociale* (Paris: Desclée, 1968).

HANSSENS, J. M., *La Liturgie d'Hippolyte: Documents et études* (Rome: Gregorian University, 1970).

—— *La Liturgie d'Hippolyte: Ses documents, son titulaire, ses origines et son caractère*, Orientalia Christiana Analecta, 155 (Rome: Pontifical Institute of Oriental Studies, 1959).

HARNACK, ADOLF VON, 'Brod und Wasser: Die eucharistischen Elemente bei Justin', *Über das gnostische Buch Pistis-Sophia; Brod und Wasser, die eucharistischen Elemente bei Justin: Zwei Untersuchungen*, TU 7 (Leipzig: J. C. Hinrichs, 1891), 115–44.

—— *Marcion: Das Evangelium vom fremden Gott: Eine Monographie zur Geschichte der Grundlegung der Katholischen Kirche*, 2nd edn. (Leipzig: J. C. Hinrichs, 1924). Eng. trans. John E. Steely and Lyle D. Bierma, *Marcion: The Gospel of The Alien God* (Durham, NC: Labyrinth, 1990).

HAUSSLEITER, JOHANNES, *Der Vegetarismus in der Antike* (Berlin: Alfred Töpelmann, 1935).

HAY, DAVID, 'Things Philo Said and Did Not Say About the Therapeutae', *SBLSP* 31 (1992), 673–83.

HEFFERNAN, THOMAS J., *Sacred Biography: Saints and their Biographers in the Middle Ages* (New York: Oxford University Press, 1988).

HIERS, RICHARD H., and KENNEDY, CHARLES A., 'The Bread and Fish Eucharist in the Gospels and Early Christian Art', *Perspectives in Religious Studies*, 3 (1976), 20–47.

HIGGINS, A. J. B., *The Lord's Supper in the New Testament*, SBT 6 (London: SCM, 1952).

HOFFMAN, LAWRENCE A., 'A Symbol of Salvation in the Passover Haggadah', *Worship*, 53 (1979), 519–37.

—— *Beyond the Text: A Holistic Approach to Liturgy* (Bloomington, Ind.: Indiana University Press, 1987).

—— 'Reconstructing Ritual as Identity and Culture', in P. F. Bradshaw and L. A. Hoffman (eds.), *The Making of Jewish and Christian Worship*, 22–41.

HOFFMANN, R. JOSEPH, *Marcion: On the Restitution of Christianity: An Essay on the Development of Radical Paulinist Theology in the Second Century* (Chico, Calif.: Scholars Press, 1984).

ISENBERG, M., 'The Sale of Sacrificial Meat', *Classical Philology*, 70 (1975), 271–3.

JACKSON, MICHAEL, 'Knowledge of the Body', *Man*, NS 18 (1983), 327–45.

JASTRZEBOWSKA, E., 'Les Scènes de banquet dans les peintures et sculptures chrétiennes des IIIe et IVe siècles', *Recherches Augustiniennes*, 14 (1979), 3–90.

JAY, NANCY, *Throughout Your Generations Forever: Sacrifice, Religion and Paternity* (Chicago: University of Chicago Press, 1992).

JEREMIAS, JOACHIM, *The Eucharistic Words of Jesus* (New York: Scribner, 1966). German original: *Die Abendmahlsworte Jesu*, 3rd edn. (Göttingen: Vandenhoeck & Ruprecht, 1960).

JONES, F. STANLEY, 'The Pseudo-Clementines: A History of Research', *SecCent* 2 (1982), 1–33, 63–96.

JOURDAN, G. V., 'Agape or Lord's Supper: A Study of Certain Passages in the Canons of Hippolytus', *Hermathena*, 64 (1944), 32–43.

JÜLICHER, A., 'Zur Geschichte der Abendmahlsfeier in der ältesten Kirche', *Theologische Abhandlungen: Carl von Weizsäcker zu seinem siebzigsten Geburtstage* (Freiburg: J. C. B. Mohr (Paul Siebeck), 1892), 217–50.

JUNGMANN, JOSEF A., *The Early Liturgy to the Time of Gregory the Great* (Notre Dame, Ind.: University of Notre Dame Press, 1959).

KANE, J. P., 'The Mithraic Cult Meal in its Greek and Roman Environment', in John R. Hinnells (ed.), *Mithraic Studies: Proceedings of the First International Congress of Mithraic Studies* (2 vols.; Manchester: Manchester University Press, 1975), ii. 313–51.

KARRIS, ROBERT J., 'Romans 14:1–15:13 and the Occasion of Romans', in Karl Donfried (ed.), *The Romans Debate*, 2nd edn. (Peabody, Mass.: Hendrickson, 1991), 65–84.

KÄSEMANN, ERNST, 'The Canon of the New Testament and the Unity of the Church', *Essays on New Testament Themes*, SBT 41 (London: SCM, 1964), 95–107.

—— *Commentary on Romans*, ed. and trans. Geoffrey W. Bromiley (Grand Rapids, Mich.: Eerdmans, 1980).

KEATING, J. F., *The Agape and the Eucharist in the Early Church* (New York: AMS, 1969).

KENNEDY, CHARLES, 'The Cult of the Dead in Corinth', *Love and Death in the Ancient Near East: Essays in Honor of Marvin H. Pope* (Guilford, Conn.: Four Quarters, 1987), 227–36.

KILMARTIN, EDWARD J., 'A First Century Chalice Dispute', *ScEccl* 12 (1960), 403–8.

KOCH, GLENN A., 'A Critical Investigation of Epiphanius' Knowledge of the Ebionites: A Translation and Discussion of *Panarion* 30', Ph.D. dissertation, University of Pennsylvania, 1976.

KUHN, KARL GEORG, 'The Lord's Supper and the Communal Meal at Qumran', in K. Stendahl (ed.), *The Scrolls and the New Testament* (New York: Harper, 1957), 65–93.

LABRIOLLE, P. DE, *La Réaction paienne: Étude sur la polémique antichrétienne du Ier au VIe siècle* (Paris: Artisan du livre, 1938).

LATHAM, JAMES E., *The Religious Symbolism of Salt*, Théologie Historique, 64 (Paris: Éditions Beauchesne, 1982).

LATHROP, GORDON, *Holy Things: A Liturgical Theology* (Minneapolis: Fortress, 1993).

LEBEAU, PAUL, *Le Vin nouveau du Royaume: Étude exégétique et patristique sur la parole eschatologique de Jésus à la Cène* (Paris: Desclée de Brouwer, 1966).

LEON, HARRY J., *The Jews of Ancient Rome* (Philadelphia: Jewish Publication Society of America, 1960).

LÉON-DUFOUR, XAVIER, *Le Partage du pain eucharistique selon le Nouveau Testament* (Paris: Seuil, 1982).

LEYERLE, BLAKE, 'Clement of Alexandria on the Importance of Table Etiquette', *JECS* 3 (1995), 123–41.

—— 'Meal Customs in the Graeco-Roman World', in P. F. Bradshaw and L. A. Hoffman (eds.), *Passover and Easter: The Liturgical Structuring of a Sacred Season* (Notre Dame, Ind.: University of Notre Dame Press, forthcoming).

LIETZMANN, HANS, *Mass and Lord's Supper* (Leiden: E. J. Brill, 1979). German original: *Messe und Herrenmahl: Eine Studie zur Geschichte der Liturgie*, Arbeiten zur Kirchengeschichte, 8 (Bonn: A. Marcus and E. Weber's Verlag, 1926).

LIEU, SAMUEL N. C., *Manichaeism in the Late Roman Empire and Medieval China*, 2nd edn., WUNT 63 (Tübingen: J. C. B. Mohr (Paul Siebeck), 1992).

LOHSE, EDUARD, *Colossians and Philemon*, Hermeneia (Philadelphia: Fortress, 1971).

MCGOWAN, ANDREW, 'Eating People: Accusations of Cannibalism against Christians in the Second Century', *JECS* 2 (1994), 413–42.

—— '"First Regarding the Cup": Papias and the Diversity of Early Eucharistic Practice', *JTS* NS 46 (1995), 551–5.

—— 'Naming the Feast: The *Agape* and the Diversity of Early Christian Meals', in Elizabeth A. Livingstone (ed.), *Studia Patristica XXX* (Leuven: Peeters, 1997), 314–18.

MCHUGH, JOHN, 'Num solus panis triticeus sit materia valida SS. Eucharistae?' *Verbum Domini*, 39 (1961), 229–39.

MACK, BURTON L., *A Myth of Innocence: Mark and Christian Origins* (Philadelphia: Fortress, 1988).

MCLEAN, BRADLEY H., 'The Agrippinilla Inscription: Religious Associations and

Early Church Formation', in B. McLean (ed.), *Origins and Method: Towards a New Understanding in Judaism and Christianity*, JSNTSup 86 (Sheffield: Sheffield Academic Press, 1993), 239–70.

MAGNE, JEAN, 'Pour en finir avec la "Tradition d'Hippolyte"', *Bulletin de litterature ecclésiastique*, 89 (1988), 5–22.

MARTIN, DALE, *The Corinthian Body* (New Haven: Yale University Press, 1995).

MARTIN, JOSEF, *Symposion: Die Geschichte einer literarischen Form* (Paderborn: F. Schöningh, 1931).

MARX, ALFRED, *Les Offrandes végétales dans l'ancien Testament: Du tribut d'hommage au repas eschatologique*, VTSup 57 (Leiden: E. J. Brill, 1994).

MEEKS, WAYNE A., *The First Urban Christians: The Social World of the Apostle Paul* (New Haven: Yale University Press, 1983).

MEGGITT, JUSTIN J., 'Meat Consumption and Social Conflict in Corinth', *JTS* NS 45 (1994), 137–41.

METZGER, MARCEL, 'Enquêtes autour de la prétendue *Tradition Apostolique*', *Ecclesia Orans*, 9 (1992), 7–36.

——'Nouvelles perspectives pour la prétendue *Tradition Apostolique*', *Ecclesia Orans*, 5 (1988), 241–59.

MILBURN, R. L. P., *Early Christian Art and Architecture* (Berkeley: University of California Press, 1988).

MOXNES, HALVOR, 'Meals and the New Community in Luke', *SEÅ* 51 (1987), 158–67.

MURRAY, OSWYN (ed.), *Sympotica: A Symposium on the 'Symposion'* (Oxford: Clarendon, 1990).

NEUSNER, JACOB, 'Two Pictures of the Pharisees: Philosophical Circle or Eating Club', *ATR* 64 (1982), 525–38.

NEYREY, JEROME H., 'Ceremonies in Luke-Acts: The Case of Meals and Table Fellowship', in J. H. Neyrey (ed.), *The Social World of Luke-Acts: Models for Interpretation*, 361–87.

——*Paul, In Other Words: A Cultural Reading of His Letters* (Louisville, Ky.: Westminster/John Knox, 1990).

——(ed.), *The Social World of Luke-Acts: Models for Interpretation* (Peabody, Mass.: Hendrickson, 1991).

NIEDERWIMMER, KURT, *Die Didache*, Kommentar zu den Apostolischen Vätern, 1 (Göttingen: Vandenhoeck & Ruprecht, 1989).

OESTERLEY, W. O. E., *The Jewish Background of the Christian Liturgy* (Oxford: Oxford University Press, 1925; repr. Gloucester, Mass.: Peter Smith, 1965).

O'NEILL, J. C., 'Bread and Wine', *SJT* 48 (1995), 169–84.

OSBORNE, CATHERINE, 'Ancient Vegetarianism', in J. Wilkins, D. Harvey, and M. Dobson (eds.), *Food in Antiquity*, 214–24.

PEASE, A. S., 'Ölbaum', PW xvii. 1998–2022.

PERVO, RICHARD I., 'Wisdom and Power: Petronius' *Satyricon* and the Social World of Early Christianity', *ATR* 67 (1985), 307–25.

PETERSON, ERIK, 'Die Häretiker der Philippus-Akten', *ZNW* 31 (1932), 97–111.

PURCELL, NICHOLAS, 'Eating Fish: The Paradoxes of Seafood', in J. Wilkins, D. Harvey, and M. Dobson (eds.), *Food in Antiquity*, 132–49.

QUASTEN, JOHANNES, '"Vetus Superstitio et Nova Religio": The Problem of *Refrigerium* in the Ancient Church of North Africa', *HTR* 33 (1940), 253–66.

RAMBAUX, CLAUDE, *Tertullien face aux morales des trois premiers siècles* (Paris: Belles-Lettres, 1979).

RAUER, M., *Die 'Schwachen' in Korinth und Rom nach den Paulusbriefen*, BibS(F) 21 (Freiburg: Herder, 1923).

REICKE, BO, *Diakonie, Festfreude und Zelos in Verbindung mit der altchristlichen Agapenfeier*, Uppsala Universitets Årsskrift, 5 (1951) (Uppsala and Wiesbaden: Lundequistska, 1951).

RICHARDSON, R. D., 'A Further Inquiry into Eucharistic Origins', in H. Lietzmann, *Mass and Lord's Supper*, 219–702.

RIGGS, J. W., 'From Gracious Table to Sacramental Elements: The Tradition History of Didache 9 and 10', *SecCent* 4 (1984), 83–101.

——'The Sacred Food of *Didache 9–10* and Second Century Ecclesiologies', in Clayton N. Jefford (ed.), *The Didache in Context: Essays on Its Text, History and Transmission*, NovTSup 77 (Leiden: E. J. Brill, 1995), 256–83.

ROBINSON, JAMES M., and KOESTER, HELMUT, *Trajectories through Early Christianity* (Philadelphia: Fortress Press, 1971).

RORDORF, WILLY (ed.), *L'Eucharistie des premiers Chrétiens* (Paris: Éditions Beauchesne, 1976).

ROUSELLE, ALINE, *Porneia: On Desire and the Body in Antiquity*, trans. F. Pheasant (Oxford: Basil Blackwell, 1988).

RUCH, C., 'La Messe d'après les pères, jusqu'à St Cyprien', *DTC* x. 898–907.

SALDARINI, ANTHONY J., *Pharisees, Scribes and Sadducees in Palestinian Society: A Sociological Approach* (Wilmington, Del.: Michael Glazier, 1988).

SATRAN, DAVID, 'Daniel: Seer, Philosopher, Holy Man', in George W. E. Nickelsburg and John J. Collins (eds.), *Ideal Figures in Ancient Judaism*, SBLSCS 12 (Chico, Calif.: Scholars Press, 1980), 33–48.

SCHEIWILER, ALOYS, *Die Elemente der Eucharistie in den ersten drei Jahrhunderten* (Mainz: Franz Kirchheim, 1903).

SCHIFFMAN, LAWRENCE W., 'Communal Meals at Qumran', *RevQ* 10 (1979), 45–56.

SCHMITT-PANTEL, PAULINE, *La Cité au banquet: Histoire des repas publics dans les cités grecques* (Rome: École française de Rome, 1992).

——'Sacrificial Meal and *Symposion*: Two Models of Civic Institutions in the Archaic City?', in O. Murray (ed.), *Sympotica: A Symposium on the 'Symposion'*, 14–33.

SCHNEEMELCHER, WILHELM (ed.), *New Testament Apocrypha* (2 vols.; Cambridge: James Clarke & Co.; Louisville, Ky.: Westminster/John Knox, 1992).

SCHOEDEL, WILLIAM R., *Ignatius of Antioch: A Commentary on the Letters of Ignatius of Antioch*, Hermeneia (Philadelphia: Fortress, 1985).

SCHÜRMANN, HEINZ, 'Das apostolische Interesse am eucharistischen Kelch', *MTZ* 4 (1953), 223–31.

SCHWEIZER, EDUARD, *Der Brief an die Kolosser*, EKKNT (Zurich: Benziger, 1976).

——*The Lord's Supper According to the New Testament* (Philadelphia: Fortress, 1967).

SEGAL, ALAN F., *Paul the Convert: The Apostolate and Apostasy of Saul the Pharisee* (New Haven: Yale University Press, 1990).

SEGELBERG, ERIC, 'The Benedictio Olei in the Apostolic Tradition of Hippolytus', *OrChr* 48 (1964), 268–81.

SHERWIN-WHITE, A. N., *The Letters of Pliny: A Historical and Social Commentary* (Oxford: Clarendon, 1966).

SIMON, MARCEL, 'L'Ascéticisme dans les sectes juives', in Ugo Bianchi (ed.), *La tradizione dell'Enkrateia: Motivazione ontologiche e protologiche*, ed. U. Bianchi (Rome: Edizioni dell'Ateneo, 1985), 393–426.

SMITH, DENNIS E., 'The Historical Jesus at Table', *SBLSP* (1989), 466–86.

——'Social Obligation in the Context of Communal Meals: A Study of the Christian Meal in 1 Corinthians in Comparison with Graeco-Roman Communal Meals', Th.D. dissertation, Harvard Divinity School, 1980.

——'Table Fellowship as a Literary Motif in the Gospel of Luke', *JBL* 106 (1987), 613–38.

——and TAUSSIG HAL, *Many Tables: The Eucharist in the New Testament and Liturgy Today* (London: SCM, 1990).

SMITH, JONATHAN Z., *Drudgery Divine: On the Comparison of Early Christianities and the Religions of Late Antiquity* (Chicago: University of Chicago Press, 1990).

SNYDER, GRAYDON, *Ante Pacem: Archaeological Evidence of Church Life before Constantine* (Atlanta: Mercer University Press, 1985).

SPARKES, BRIAN, 'A Pretty Kettle of Fish', in J. Wilkins, D. Harvey, and M. Dobson (eds.), *Food in Antiquity*, 150–61.

SPITTA, FRIEDRICH, *Zur Geschichte und Litteratur des Urchristentums* (3 vols.; Göttingen: Vandenhoeck & Ruprecht, 1893–1907).

STEIN, S., 'The Influence of Symposia Literature on the Literary Form of the Pesah Haggadah', *JJS* 8 (1957), 13–44.

STOWERS, STANLEY, 'Greeks Who Sacrifice and Those Who Do Not: Toward an Anthropology of Greek Religion', in L. Michael White and O. Larry Yarborough (eds.), *The Social World of the First Christians: Essays in Honor of Wayne A. Meeks* (Minneapolis: Augsburg Fortress, 1995), 293–333.

STRECKER, GEORG, *Das Judenchristentum in den Pseudoklementinen*, 2nd edn., TU 70 (Berlin: Akademie-Verlag, 1981).

STROBEL, A., *Das heilige Land der Montanisten*, Religionsgeschichtliche Versuche und Vorarbeiten, 37 (Berlin: De Gruyter, 1980).

STUIBER, A., *Refrigerium Interim: Die Vorstellungen vom Zwischenzustand und die frühchristliche Grabeskunst*, Theophaneia, 11 (Bonn: Peter Hanstein, 1957).

TALLEY, THOMAS, 'From *Berakah* to *Eucharistia*: A Reopening Question', *Worship*, 50 (1976), 115–37.

THEISSEN, GERD, 'The Strong and the Weak in Corinth: A Sociological Analysis of a Theological Quarrel', in John H. Schütz (ed. and trans.), *The Social Setting of Pauline Christianity: Essays on Corinth* (Philadelphia: Fortress, 1982), 121–43.

TROUT, DENNIS, 'Christianizing the Nolan Countryside: Animal Sacrifice at the Tomb of St Felix', *JECS* 3 (1995), 281–98.

TYSON, J. B., 'Acts 6:1–7 and Dietary Regulations in Early Christianity', *Perspectives in Religious Studies*, 10 (1983), 145–61.

USENER, H., 'Milch und Honig', *Rheinisches Museum*, 57 (1902), 177–95.

VERNANT, J.-P., 'At Man's Table: Hesiod's Foundation Myth of Sacrifice', in M. Detienne and J.-P. Vernant (eds.), *The Cuisine of Sacrifice Among the Greeks*, 21–86.

VOGEL, CYRILLE, 'Le Repas sacré au poisson chez les chrétiens', *RevScRel* 40 (1966), 1–26.

——'Symboles cultuels chrétiens: Les Aliments sacrés, Poisson et Refrigeria', *Simboli e Simbologia nell'alto Medioevo* (2 vols.; Spoleto: Presso la Sede del Centro, 1976), i. 197–252.

——'Symbols in Christian Worship: Food and Drink', *Concilium*, 132 (1980), 67–73.

VÖÖBUS, ARTHUR, *History of Asceticism in the Syrian Orient: A Contribution to the History of Culture in the Near East* i. *The Origin of Asceticism: Early Monasticism in Persia*, CSCO 184 (Louvain: Secrétariat du CorpusSCO, 1958).

——*Liturgical Traditions in the Didache* (Stockholm: Este, 1968).

WALTZING, J. P., *Étude historique sur les corporations professionnelles chez les Romains depuis les origines jusqu'à la chute de l'Empire d'Occident* (4 vols.; Louvain: C. Peeters, 1895–1900).

WARD, ROY B., 'James of Jerusalem in the First Two Centuries', *ANRW* 26/1 (1987), 779–812.

WATSON, FRANCIS, 'The Two Roman Congregations: Romans 14:1–15:13', in Karl Donfried (ed.), *The Romans Debate*, 2nd edn. (Peabody, Mass.: Hendrickson, 1991), 203–15.

WILKEN, ROBERT L., 'Collegia, Philosophical Schools, and Theology', *The Catacombs and the Colosseum: The Roman Empire as the Setting of Primitive Christianity* (Valley Forge, Pa.: Judson, 1971), 268–91.

WILKINS, JOHN, HARVEY, DAVID, and DOBSON, MIKE (eds.), *Food in Antiquity* (Exeter: University of Exeter Press, 1995).

WILLIS, G. G., 'St Cyprian and the Mixed Chalice', *Downside Review*, 100 (1982), 110–15.

WILLIS, WENDELL LEE, *Idol Meat in Corinth: The Pauline Argument in 1 Corinthians 8 and 10*, SBLDS 68 (Chico, Calif.: Scholars Press, 1985).

WINKLER, GABRIELE, 'The Origins and Idiosyncrasies of the Earliest Form of

Asceticism', in W. Skudlarek (ed.), *The Continuing Quest for God: Monastic Spirituality in Tradition and Transition* (Collegeville, Minn.: Liturgical Press, 1982), 9–43.

WOOD, ROY C., *The Sociology of the Meal* (Edinburgh: Edinburgh University Press, 1995).

YOUNG, FRANCES, *The Use of Sacrificial Ideas in Greek Christian Writers from the New Testament to John Chrysostom*, Patristic Monograph Series, 5 (Philadelphia: Philadelphia Patristic Foundation, 1979).

ZAHAVY, TZVEE, *The Mishnaic Law of Blessings and Prayers: Tractate Berakhot*, BJS 88 (Atlanta: Scholars Press, 1987).

ZAHN, TH., *Brot und Wein im Abendmahl der alten Kirche* (Leipzig: A. Deichert, 1892).

ZUCHSCHWERDT, ERNST, 'Das Naziräat des Herrenbruders Jakobus nach Hegesipp (Euseb, h.e. II 23, 5–6)', *ZNW* 68 (1977), 276–87.

Index Locorum

Note: English titles of works have been given where these are are well-known and used in the text.

BIBLICAL LITERATURE

Hebrew Bible

Genesis
  4: 3–4 95
  6: 1–4 154, 180
  9: 1–5 181
  9: 3–4 81
  9: 4 180
  9: 20–1 205
  14: 18 205
  49: 8–12 152
  49: 11 205
Exodus
  29: 40 83 n. 174
  33: 3 107
Leviticus
  3: 17 81, 82
  11: 34 81 n. 167
  11: 37–8 81 n. 167
  16: 4 150
  16: 32 150
  23: 13 83 n. 174
Numbers
  6 150
  11: 5 126
  13: 24 126
  15: 5 83 n. 174
  15: 7 83 n. 174
  15: 10 83 n. 174
  18: 19 124
  28: 14 83 n. 174
Deuteronomy
  8: 8 126
Judges
  13 149
1 Samuel
  1 149
Esther
  3: 15 202
Job
  6: 6 41

Psalms
  21: 17 189
  105: 28 201
Proverbs
  9: 1–5 205
Isaiah
  33: 16
  43: 18–21 205
  48: 21 205
  63 205
Ezekiel
  3: 3 112 n. 73
Daniel
  1: 8–16 85
  10: 3 85, 235, 248
Amos
  2: 13 156

New Testament

Matthew
  26: 17 148, 241
  26: 28–9 205
  26: 29 157
Mark
  5: 11–14 42
  6: 30–44 127
  6: 40–4 129
  6: 41 247
  7: 19 52 n. 77
  8: 1–10 127
  8: 8 132
  14: 22 247
  14: 25 92, 157
Luke
  1 149
  1: 15 234 n. 44
  5: 37–9 234 n. 44
  7: 34 234 n. 44
  20: 27–40 156
  22: 8 242
  22: 15 242

Luke (*cont.*)
  22: 16 241
  22: 17–20 234
  22: 18 157, 234, 241
  23: 36 234 n. 44
  24: 25 233
  24: 30 128 n. 117, 247
  24: 35 185, 233
  24: 41–3 127, 128
John
  2: 1–11 236
  4 236
  6 95, 236
  6: 5–8 129
  6: 9 95
  6: 11–15 128
  6: 13 95
  6: 53–6 236
  10: 12 189
  19: 34 237
  21 132
  21: 9–13 127, 128
  24: 41–3 128
Acts
  1: 4 119 n. 92
  2: 13 23
  2: 42 185, 233
  2: 46 185, 233
  10: 1–16 52 n. 77
  11: 1–18 52 n. 77
  15: 1–29 52 n. 77
  15: 20 234
  15: 29 234
  20: 7–11 233, 234
  20: 7 185, 233
  20: 11 185, 233
  27: 35 185, 233
  32: 15 208 n.
Romans
  14 220, 226–7
  14: 1–3 226–7
  14: 1 230
  14: 2–6 230
  14: 3 230
  14: 5–6 229, 235
  14: 6 247
  14: 10 230
  14: 11 230
  14: 16 230
  14: 20–1 226–7
  14: 23–15: 2 230
1 Corinthians
  1: 1 227 n. 24

1: 26–9 224
1: 26 222
1: 27
3: 2 108
3: 9 107
4: 10 221
5: 7 92
8 62 n. 112, 66, 220, 224, 230 n.34
8: 1–7 223
8: 7–12 221
8: 7–10 221
8: 9–13 223
8: 10 223
10 62 n. 112, 66, 220, 224, 230 n.34
10: 14–33 223
10: 16–21 226
10: 16 240, 247
11 221
11: 21 240
11: 23–9 92
11: 23–7 21 n. 43
11: 23–6 205
11: 23 240
Galatians
  2: 11–14 52 n. 77
Colossians
  2: 16 235
  2: 21 235
1 Thessalonians
  5: 7–8 208 n.
1 Timothy
  2: 1–4 232
  2: 8–15 232
  3: 3 232
  3: 9 232
  4: 3 232, 247
  4: 8 232
  5: 23 231
Hebrews
  5: 12–16: 2 236
  5: 12–13 107
  9: 10 236
  13: 9 236
James
  5: 14–15 115 n. 80
1 Peter
  2: 2 107
1 John
  5: 5–8 236
  5: 6–8 237
Revelation
  1: 4–3: 22 237
  7: 17 237

8: 10 237
10: 9–10 112 n. 73
14: 8–20 237
17: 2 237
17: 16 237
18: 3 237

19: 3 237
19: 18–21 237
21: 6 237
21: 22 237
22: 17 237

RABBINIC AND EARLY JEWISH LITERATURE

Mishna
  m. 'Abot.
    6: 4 120
  m. 'Abod. Zar.
    2: 3 86
    2: 5 86 n. 184
  m. B. Qam.
    7: 7 86 n. 185
  m. Ber.
    6: 4 126 n. 108
    6: 6 55
    8 55 n. 91
  m. Bik
    1: 3 126 n. 108
    3: 9 126 n. 108
  m. 'Erub.
    6: 2 84 n. 178
  m. Ketub.
    5:8–9 37
    5:8 38
  m. Ma'aś
    3. 1–3 39 n. 16
  m. Pesah
    10. 1–9 54 n. 82
  m. Sota
    3: 4 84 n. 178
  m. Ta'an.
    1: 4–7 168
Talmud
  b. B. Bat.
    60b 83, 84 n. 175, 247
  b. Ber.
    38a-b 94
    43a 54
  b. Ḥul.
    16b 82
  b. Ketub.
    8b 84 n. 176
  b. Šabb.
    118b 137 n. 160
    119a 137 n. 160
  b. Sanh.
    70a 84 n. 176

  b. Yoma
    74a 82
Tosefta
  t. 'Arak
    4. 27. 548 39 n. 15
  t. Ber.
    3: 25 84 n. 178
    4 54
    4: 1–7 54
    4: 8 55 n. 90
    6: 1–4 54
    6: 5–6 55
    7 55 n. 90
    7. 3 55 n. 90
    7. 5 55 n. 90
    8 54
    9 54
  t. Makš.
    81 n. 167
  t. Sota
    15: 11–12 83
Midrash
  Genesis Rabba
    15. 7 94
    34 82
  Midrash on the Psalms
    137: 6 83
  Mekilta
    Amalek 4 86
Targums
  Targum Neofiti
    Deut 1: 1 82 n. 171
  Targum Ps.-Jonathan
    82 n. 171
Apocrypha and Pseudepigrapha
  2 Apocalypse of Baruch
    29 137 n. 159
  1 Enoch
    60: 7 137 n. 159
  4 Ezra
    6: 49–52 137 n. 159
  Joseph and Aseneth
    58 n. 101, 112

Apocrypha and Pseudepigrapha (*cont.*)
　8. 9 112 n. 74
　15. 5 112 n. 74
　16. 16 112 n. 74
　Sibylline Oracles
　8. 217–50 136 n. 155
　Testament of Reuben
　1. 10 86
Josephus
　Antiquities
　10. 190–4 85
　Jewish War
　2 § 123 150 n. 16
　2 § 130 81
　2 § 131 58
　2 § 133 81
　Life
　14 85
Philo
　De Vita Contemplativa
　37 56, 79, 120
　58–64 69
　64–89 56

67–9 59
73–4 79
81 79
82 80
Hypothetica 8
11. 11 80
11. 13 59
Quod Omnis Probus Liber Sit
75–87 80
75 80
81 59
84 80
Dead Sea Scrolls
1QS
6 59
6: 4–5 58, 81
6: 13–23 81
1QSa
59
2 58 n. 101
2: 11–22 58, 81
CD
12. 15–17 150 n. 16

GREEK AND ROMAN LITERATURE

Aeschylus
　Eumenides
　107 65
Apuleius
　Apology
　32 43
　41 43, 137 n. 157
　57 208 n.
Aristotle
　On the Soul
　2. 3. 414 A–415 A 72
　Politics
　1. 1. 9 72
Artemidorus
　Oneirocriticon
　1. 65 35 n. 1
　1. 66 44 n. 42, 75
　1. 69 38, 126 n. 109
　1. 70 42
　1. 73 126 n. 109
Athenaeus
　Deipnosophistae
　2. 36 B–C 51 nn. 71, 74, 110 n. 64
　4. 149 E 51 n. 73

5. 149 47
5. 179 D 51 n. 73
5. 209 43 n. 34
6. 274–5 42 n. 33
6. 275 43 n. 34
7. 297 64 n. 118
7. 303 64 n. 118
10. 419 51 n. 76
14. 628 A–B 51 n. 74
15. 675 B–C 47
Aulus Gellius
　Noctes Atticae (Attic Nights)
　4. 11 70
Cassius Dio
　Roman History
　60. 6. 7 222
　62. 14. 2 222
Cato
　De Agricultura
　25 44
　56–8 37
　56 39 n. 16
　58 40
　104 44
　117–19 40 n. 21

Cicero
  Ad Familiares
    9. 24. 3 48
  De Natura Deorum
    2. 67 51 n. 72
  De Officiis
    2. 52 66
  Philippics
    2. 34. 87 208 n.
Columella
  De Re Rustica
    4. 2 42
    12. 15. 5 39 n. 18
    12. 49 40 n. 21
Cornelius Nepos
  Lives
    pr. 6–7 50 n. 66
Diodorus Siculus
    4. 3 51 n. 69, 54 n. 83
Diogenes Laertius
  Lives
    6. 1. 9 75
    6. 2. 25–6 74
    6. 2. 28 74, 75
    6. 2. 31 75
    6. 2. 34 74
    6. 2. 35 74, 75
    6. 2. 46 74
    6. 2. 48 74
    6. 2. 49 74
    6. 2. 54 75
    6. 2. 55–6 75
    6. 2. 57 74
    6. 2. 58 74
    6. 2. 59 74
    6. 2. 61 73, 74
    6. 2. 64 75
    6. 2. 69 74
    6. 2. 73–4 74
    6. 2. 76 74
    6. 5. 85 75
    6. 5. 90 75
    6. 7. 97 73
    6. 9. 104 75
    8. 12 70
    20 70
    34 70
Empedocles
    fr. 128 71 n. 140
    fr. 130 71 n. 140
Euripides
  Bacchae
    142 112 n. 71

Orestes
    115 110
Hesiod
  Theogony
    535–616 63
  Works and Days
    45–105 63
Hippocrates
  De Medicina Antiqua
    13 231
Homer
  Iliad
    9. 214 41
  Odyssey
    10. 519 65, 110
  Homeric Hymn to Hestia
    1. 5 51 n. 72
Horace
  Satires
    2. 2. 17–18 41
    2. 6. 63–4 40
Iamblichus
  De Mysteriis
    14. 5 154, 180, 191
  De Vita Pythagorica
    18. 85 70
    97–8 70
    107 70
Inscriptions
  CIL
    iii. 801–41 42 n. 33
    xiv. 2112 47 n. 54, 49 n. 61, 133 n.
      140
    xiv. 2112 col. 2. 29–30 64 n. 120
  IG
    ii^2. 334 49 n. 61
    ii^2. 1301 63 n. 116, 224 n. 18
    ii^2. 1368 64 n. 121
Juvenal
  Satires
    5 49 n. 63
    6. 32 154 n. 34
    8. 167–78 224
Livy
    34. 1 62 n. 110
Lucian
  De Morte Peregrini
    12–13 169 n., 201
    16 143
  Demonax
    5 75 n. 153
  Fugitivi
    14 41, 43, 44, 120

Zeus Catechized
  5 75
Pseudo-Lucian
  The Cynic
    5 74 n. 152, 75
    11 76
Martial
  Epigrams
    3. 60 49 n. 63
    7. 61 224
    10. 48. 6 132 n. 136
    10. 48. 16 40
Menander
  Dyskolos
    430–9 42
Oribasius
  Libri Incerti
    2. 68. 6 62
    20 113 n. 76
Ovid
  Fasti
    3. 736 112 n. 71
Philemon
  fr. 98 40
Philostratus
  Vita Apollonii
    1. 8 77
    1. 10–11 77
    2. 6–7 65, 77
    2. 35–7 77
    3. 41 77
Plato
  Leges
    6. 782C 232
  Politicus
    271 D-272 B 71
  Republic
    404 B-C 43
  Symposium
    176 A 51 n. 73
    176 E 48 n. 57
    197 D 57 n. 95
Plautus
  Mostellaria
    48 40 n. 24
  Poenulus
    4. 2. 1–13 224
Pliny the Elder
  Naturalis Historia
    13. 45 39 n. 19
    14. 14. 91 49 n. 63
    14. 28. 143 51 n. 69
    14. 89 45 n. 44

    14. 143 54 n. 83
    15. 16 40 n. 21
    15. 24–32 40
    15. 83 39 n. 18
    18. 27–8 38
    18. 27 38
    18. 30 40
    18. 68 41
    18. 90 38 n. 9
    19. 79 40
    31. 89 41
Pliny the Younger
  Letters
    2. 6 49
    10. 96 63 n. 113, 64
Plutarch
  Cato the Elder
    1. 13 44
  Cato the Younger
    12 49 n. 64
  Moralia
    132 E 65
    464 C 65
  De Esu Carnium
    993 B 97 n. 22
    994 F 97 n. 22
    996 C 97 n. 22
  De San. Praec.
    19 231
  Quaest. Conv.
    612 F 50 n. 66
    629 D 51 n. 68
    642 F 48 n. 59
    643 A 48 n. 59
    667 C-669 E 43, 137 n. 161
    668 A 40
    668 B 42 n. 33, 137 n. 157
    668 E-669 E 41
    669 B 40 n. 24
    669 D-E 71, 138
    684 E-F 41
    684 F-685 D 41
    692 B-93 E 51 n. 70
    697 C 45
    729 C-D 64
    729 C 223
  Septem Sapientium Convivium
    149 A-B 50
    150 D-155 E 50 n. 66
Polybius
  Histories
    31 42 n. 33

Porphyry
De Abstinentia
2. 4. 3 222
2. 6 77
2. 19 77
2. 20 65
2. 36 154
2. 42 191
4. 4 77
De Antro Nympharum
15–16 112
Vita Pythagorae
34–6 71 n. 139
Soranus
Gynaeceia
2. 11. 17 113 n. 76
Strabo
3. 4. 2 43 n. 34
Suetonius
Domitian
5 49 n. 62
Nero

16
Tacitus
Annales
12. 63 43 n. 34
Theophrastus
fr. 12 65
fr. 13 97 n. 22
Thucydides
1. 138. 5 35 n. 1
Varro
De Re Rustica
2. 4. 10 42
Ps-Virgil
Moretum
40–51 39 n. 13
119 39 n. 13
Xenophon
Cyropaedia
1. 4. 17 62
Symposium
9. 7 48 n. 57

EARLY CHRISTIAN AND RELATED LITERATURE

Acta Sanctorum
Febr. III 63 A–B 110, 111 n. 67
Acts of Andrew
5 189
13 190
20 190, 245
25 190
27 190
28 193
46 186 n., 190
53 190
54 190
126 193
Acts of Andrew and Matthias
1 191 n. 34
Acts of John
38–45 187
46 186
48–54 187
63–86 187
72 125, 185, 186
84 125 n. 105
85–6 187
86 125, 185
92–4 186
109 187, 187 n. 27, 194, 245
Acts of Paul

4 185
5 185
7 185, 186
Acts of Paul and Thecla
5 185
8 186
13 186
23 186
25 125, 185
27–8 185
Acts of Peter
Codex Berol. 8502 187
2 187
5 188
6 188
7 189
8 188, 189
9 189
12 189
17 188
18 188
22 188
25 188
28 188
29 188
30 188
34 186 n.

Acts of Philip
  8–15 122
  8 122
Acts of (Judas) Thomas
  6–9 193
  20 191
  27 115 n. 81, 191
  29 115 n. 81, 120, 122, 191, 192
  49–51 115 n. 81, 191
  49–50 192
  49 245 n.
  50 192
  51 192
  76–7 193
  90 193
  95–8 193
  121 115 n. 81, 199
  133 115 n. 81, 191
  152 116, 191
  158 115 n. 81, 191, 192, 194, 244
Apostolic Constitutions
  5. 18 217
  6. 30 135 n. 147
Athanasius
  Life of Anthony
    7 215
Augustine
  Confessions
    1. 11. 7 123 n. 102
    3. 10 172 n. 88
    6. 2 135
  De Baptismo contra Donatistas
    3. 15 166 n. 70
  De Catechizandis Rudibus
    26. 50 123 n. 102
  De Haeresibus
    26 167 n. 75
    28 95
  Letters
    222. 2 96 n. 20
Epistle of Barnabas
  6 107
Basil of Caesarea
  Letters
    188 215
    188, can. 1 161, 212
Clement of Alexandria
  Excerpta ex Theodoto
    76–7 162 n. 60
    82. 1 116, 162
    82. 2 162, 163
  Paedagogus
    1. 6. 34. 3–35. 1 108

  1. 6. 39. 1–50. 2 108
  1. 6. 42. 2 108
  1. 6. 46. 2–3 108
  1. 6. 47. 1 108
  1. 6. 50. 3 108
  1. 6. 51. 1 108
  1. 6. 51. 3 108
  2. 1. 16. 1 150 n. 18
  2. 2 93 n. 12, 160
  2. 2. 32 160
  Stromateis
    1. 19. 96
    3. 12 81 155
Pseudo-Clementine Literature
  Homilies
  Ep. Pet. 2 197
  Cont. 1. 2 118, 177, 182
  Cont. 2. 1 177
  Cont 4. 3 118, 119 n. 92, 177
  Ep. Clem. 9. 1–2 119, 178
  Ep. Clem. 9. 2 119 n. 92
  1. 22 118
  1. 22. 3 119 n. 92
  1. 22. 5 121, 178
  2. 43 219
  7. 3. 1 179, 180
  7. 4. 2 179, 180
  8. 15–16 97 n. 22, 180
  8. 19. 1 179
  9. 3–23 181
  10. 26. 2 121, 177 n. 7
  11. 15. 6 179
  11. 34. 1 119 n. 92
  12. 6 179
  12. 25. 1 121, 177 n. 7
  13. 4 118, 121, 178, 246
  14. 1. 4 118, 119 n. 92, 177, 246
  15. 7. 6 179
  Recognitions
  1. 19. 3 121, 178
  1. 27–71 180
  1. 29–30 179
  2. 72. 6 121, 177 n. 7
  4. 13–36 181
  4. 14–20 181 n. 15
  7. 6. 4 179
  7. 29 178
  7. 38. 2 119
  8. 48. 5 179
  9. 6. 6 179
  10. 27. 4 179

Epistulae ad Virgines
  1. 10 183
  2. 2 183
  2. 3–5 183
  2. 6 183
Cologne Mani Codex
  5 171
  6 172
  80–1 172
  91–4 172
Councils
  Breviarum Hipponense
    23 89
  Canons of the Synod of Gangra
    1 214
    2 214
    4 214
    5 214
    11 215
    13 215
    17 215
  Concilium Carthaginense
    III. 5 123
    III. 24 89 n. 1, 110
Cyprian
  Letter 63
    1. 1 204, 207
    3–7 205
    3 205
    8. 1–2 205
    8. 1 205
    9–10 205
    10. 2 205
    12–13 205
    15 210, 244
    15. 2 206
    16 208, 210
    34 135 n. 147
    73. 4 166 n. 70
(Ps-?)Cyril of Jerusalem
  Mystagogic Catecheses
    18. 26 100
  Didache
    9. 2 92
    9. 4 94
  Didascalia Apostolorum
    prol. 148 n. 12
Ephraem the Syrian
  Hymni contra Haereses
    47. 1 99 n. 30
    47. 2 99
    47. 6 98
    47. 6. 5–6 99

Epiphanius
  Panarion
    Prol. 4. 4 161 n. 57
    Anac. 46 161 n. 57
    18 148
    18. 1. 4 148
    18. 3. 3–4 148
    19. 1. 6 177 n. 6
    19. 3. 6 171
    19. 3. 7 171
    19. 6. 4 177 n. 6
    25–6 90 n. 4
    6. 5. 6 91 n. 4
    30. 1. 8–9 147 n. 11
    30. 2. 3–5 146
    30. 3. 7 147
    30. 4–12 147 n. 11
    30. 13. 2 147
    30. 13. 4–5 146
    30. 13. 4 148
    30. 14. 2 147
    30. 14. 3 147
    30. 15. 1 146
    30. 15. 3–4 146
    30. 15. 3 146
    30. 16. 1 146
    30. 16. 4 148
    30. 18. 7 147
    30. 22. 3–5 146
    30. 22. 4 148, 241
    42. 3. 3 164
    42. 11. 6 241
    45. 1. 6–8 158
    46 161 n. 57
    46. 1–4 156
    47. 1. 1 161
    47. 1. 2–3 161
    47. 1. 5 161
    48–9 167
    49. 1. 1 95
    49. 2. 6 95
    53. 1. 4 171
    53. 1. 7 171
    61 161
    61. 1. 2 161 n. 57
Eusebius
  HE
    2. 23. 4–6 149
    4. 29 158
    4. 30 219
    5. 3. 2–3 169, 203
    5. 3. 4 170
    6. 38 170 n.

Eznik of Kolb
De Deo
  407 99, 139, 165
  409 166 n. 72
Filastrius of Brescia
Diversarum Haereseon Liber
  49 167
  74 95
  77 211
Firmicus Maternus
De Errore Profanarum Religionum
  3 96 n. 21, 100 n. 34
Gospel of Philip
  91 106 n. 55
Gospel of Thomas
  7 193 n., 237
  8 137 n. 157
  12 237
  13 237
  28 237
  40 237
  60 237
Gregory of Tours
Liber de Miraculis Beati Andreae Apostoli
  20 194
Hippolytus
Refutatio Omnium Haeresium
  8. 9 155
  8. 19 167, 168
  8. 19. 2 127 n. 110
  8. 20 160, 167 n. 77
  9. 13. 1 171
  9. 14. 1 160 n.
  9. 15. 2 171
  10. 25–6 168
Hippolytus (attr.)
'Apostolic Tradition'
  5 104 n. 50, 117
  6 104, 104 n. 50, 105, 105 n. 51
  10–11 117 n. 85
  21 117 n. 86
  23. 1–11 93 n. 9, 109
  23. 2 112
  26. 1–12 234
  28. 6 126
Ignatius of Antioch
Letter to the Ephesians
  20. 2 117
Letter to the Romans
  2. 2 207 n.
  7. 3 93 n. 10
Letter to the Smyrnaeans
  7. 1 2038. 1 203

Irenaeus
Adversus Haereses
  1 Prol. 2 163 n. 64
  1. 13. 2 92, 93 n. 9, 110 n. 65
  1. 24 158
  1. 26. 2 144
  1. 28 166
  1. 28. 1 155, 160
  3. 21. 1 145
  4. 33. 4 145
  5. 1. 3 92, 93 n. 12, 145
  5. 33. 3–4 94
  5. 33. 3 92
Jerome
Adversus Jovinianum
  1. 3 156
Adversus Luciferianos
  8 111 n. 68
Commentarii in Isaiam Prophetam
  15. 55. 1–2 111 n. 68
Commentariorum in Amos
  1. 2. 11–12 156
Commentariorum in Epistolam ad Galatas
  2. 3 95 n. 17
  2. 3. 2 97 n. 25
Commentariorum in Epistolam ad Titum
  Praef. 233
Letters
  22. 8 216
  41. 4 167 n. 75
Ps.-Jerome
Indiculus de Haeresibus
  20 95
John Chrysostom
Homilia in Matthaeum
  82. 2 211
John the Deacon
Ad Senarium
  3 123
Justin Martyr
Acta Iustini
  3. 3 155
  4. 7–8 154
1 Apology
  26 219
  32 152
  54 151, 152
  65–7 151, 152
  65 152, 153
  65. 3–4 243
  66 151, 152, 242
  66. 1 243
  66. 3 243

66. 4 243
67 153
2 Apology
5. 3–4 154, 180
Dialogue with Trypho
41 152
47–8 144 n. 2
52–4 152
63 152
69 151, 152
70 151, 152
76 152
Leo the Great
Sermons
42. 5 172 n. 89
Martyrdom of Montanus and Lucius
8. 3–5 103
Martyrdom of Perpetua and Felicitas
2. 2 102
3. 5 102 n. 44
3. 8–9 102
4. 3–4 102
4. 9–10 100
4. 10 112
6. 2–3 103
6. 7–8 102
10. 7 103
10. 8–9 103
15. 1–7 102 n. 43
18. 3 102 n. 43
18. 4–5
19–21 103
20 103
20. 1 102 n. 43
21. 8–11 103
Martyrium Pionii
3. 1 200, 201
4. 11 201
4. 19 201
4. 21–4 201
7. 1 202
9. 1–2 200 n. 2
10. 7 202
11. 2 200
11. 3 202
12. 6–7 202
12. 7 202 n. 6
18. 13 202
21. 5 200
Martyrium Polycarpi
14 207 n.
15.2 202 n. 7
18 135 n. 147

Origen
Commentarii in Matthaeum
11. 12 145
16. 12 145
Commentarius in Evangelium Johannis
2. 12 145 n.
Contra Celsum
5. 61 145
8. 29–31 61 n. 108
8: 30–1 191
8. 68 62
De Principiis
2. 7. 3 167
Homiliae in Jeremiam
15. 4 145 n.
In Epistolam ad Titum
fr. 167
In Matthaeum Commentariorum Series
79 94, 145
Pamphilus
Apologia Pro Origene
167
Polycarp
Letter to the Philippians
7. 202 n. 7
11 202 n. 7
'Praedestinatus'
Praedestinatorum Haeresis
1. 26 167 n. 75
1. 28 95, 96
Priscillian of Avila
Tractatus
1. 27–8
Sozomen
Ecclesiastical History
6. 33 216
Sulpicius Severus
Dialogues
3. 2 117 n. 87
Tatian
Diatessaron (Arabic)
45. 16 242
Oratio ad Graecos
23 155
Tertullian
Adversus Marcionem
1. 14. 3 99, 100, 109, 109 n. 62,
136, 139, 164, 203
1. 14. 5 166
4. 40 164, 165 n. 69, 241, 242 n. 65
5. 4 139 n. 164
5. 21 233 n. 22

306 *Index Locorum*

Apologia
14. 1 42
39 164
40. 14 168 n.
De Baptismo
1 136
De Corona
3. 3 104 n. 46, 109, 136
De Ieiunio contra psychicos
1. 4 165
9. 8 165
12 169 n.
12. 3 201
14. 1 165
15 166

15. 1 155, 165, 210
15. 3 155
Theodoret
Ecclesiastical History
1. 2 216 n. 35
Haereticorum Fabularum Compendium
1. 20 156, 161, 211
1. 21 158
3. 2 167
Timothy of Constantinople
De Receptione Haereticorum
97
Ex Niconis Pandecte
2 97 n. 26

Subject Index

Abel 95
Abercius 131
Acta Justini 154–5
Acts of Andrew 161, 184, 189–91
Acts of the Apostles 25, 185
Acts of John 163, 184, 186–7
Acts of (Judas) Thomas, see *Acts of Thomas*
Acts of Paul (and Thecla) 125, 127, 184, 185–6, 187
Acts of Peter 184, 187–9, 198
Acts of Philip 122–3
Acts of Susanna 110–11
Acts of Thomas 115–16, 117, 125, 161, 163, 184, 191–3, 238, 244–5
Aelia Secundula, mensa of 135
Africa 35, 39, 42, 89, 100–4, 107, 109, 110, 123, 124, 135, 140, 164, 204–11
agape 11, 22, 26, 30, 125, 143, 185, 186, 191–2, 200–1, 214–15
Alcibiades (martyr of Lyons) 169–70, 203, 253
Alcibiades of Apamea (Elkesaite) 171
Ambrose 136
Anthony 215–16
Antisthenes 73
Apelles 158
'Apicius', *De Re Coquinaria* 36, 42
apocryphal *Acts* 118, 120, 122, 135, 140–1, 161, 175, 181, 183–98, 199, 210–11, 214, 233, 244–5, 247, 252–3, 266, 267, 275
see also individual names
Apollonius of Tyana 76–7
Apostolic Constitutions 217
'*Apostolic Tradition*' 25, 28, 104–7, 109–10, 111, 117, 118, 125–7, 141, 217, 253
Apostolics ('Renouncers') 161–2
Apuleius 43
Aquarians 211–12, 252–3
see also *Hydroparastatai*
Aristotle 71–2, 78
Artotyritai 95–8, 99, 101, 102, 103, 105, 106, 140, 167, 253
asceticism 34, 67–88, 140, 143, 156, 158, 159–60, 173–4, 178–9, 193, 209, 216–

17, 218–19, 231–2, 235, 270–6 and *passim*
Asia (minor), Asians 131, 144, 155, 161, 162, 163–4, 166, 168, 169–70, 173, 198, 202, 214, 215, 232–3, 237, 254–5
Athenaeus, *Deipnosophistae* 36
Attalus (martyr of Lyons) 169–70, 203
Augustine of Hippo 95–6, 106, 123, 135, 172, 211, 216

banquets 34, 45–60, 74, 77, 133–6
baptism 21, 25, 31, 98–100, 101, 104, 107–15, 116, 118–21, 123–4, 136, 153, 162, 164, 165–6, 171, 182, 188, 191
barley 37, 38, 95, 126
see also bread
Basil of Caesarea 161, 212, 215
Bauer, Walter 28
Baur, F. C. 26, 28
beer 43
blood 180, 206–7, 209, 210, 236–7
Bradshaw, Paul F. 29
bread 38–9, 63, 64, 66, 75, 79, 80, 81, 83, 93–4, 95, 104, 105, 109, 110, 115, 116, 118, 122, 132, 138, 162, 164, 177, 179, 182, 185, 187, 188, 190–2, 215–17, 253–4, 258, 268
'breaking of the bread' 122, 185, 187, 207, 220, 233–5, 240–1, 245–6, 247, 253
ration 201–2; *see also* grain dole
unleavened 94–5, 146
Brown, Peter 159

Caecilius, bishop of Biltha 204–5
Cain 95
cake 148
see also honey-cake
cannibalism 73, 74, 75, 167, 263
Canons of Hippolytus 127
Carthage, Council of (397) 89, 107, 111, 123
catacombs 132–6
of Callistus 134
Cataphrygians 167
see also Montanists

catechumenate 123–5, 141
Cathars 161, 212
Cato the Elder 268
  De Agri Cultura 36–45
Celsus 62
cheese 91, 95–107, 125, 140, 247, 253, 275
Church Order literature 18, 21, 104–7, 111, 127
  see also *'Apostolic Tradition'*
Cilicia 161
Cirlot, Felix 260
Clement of Alexandria 21, 93, 107–8, 109, 116, 155, 160, 162–3, 213, 216
Clement of Rome, *see* Pseudo-Clementines
Clementine novels, *see* Pseudo-Clementines
clubs, see *collegia*
Codex Ottobianus 152–3
collegia 46, 55, 63, 64, 65, 269
Cologne Mani Codex 171–2
Contestatio see Pseudo-Clementines
'cook-shops' 222–4
Councils, *see individual names*
Crates 75
Cullmann, Oscar 245
Cynics 43, 44, 73–7, 78, 79, 116, 120, 160, 167–8, 179, 225, 229, 261–5, 268, 271
Cyprian 23, 204–11, 212, 213, 244, 254, 277
  Letter 63 23, 204–11
(Ps-?)Cyril of Jerusalem, *Mystagogic Catecheses* 100

Damis 77
Daniel 85, 248, 257, 258, 259
dates 39
  wine 77
De Morte Peregrini 143
Decius 204
Demetrius of Phalerum 75
demons 154, 158–9, 180, 184, 190–1, 192–3, 273
Desert Fathers 216
  see also Anthony
Detienne, Marcel 60
deutero-Pauline letters, *see* Paul
Diatessaron 155–7, 242
Didache (Teaching of the Twelve Apostles) 21–4, 25, 92, 94, 248, 255
dietary law, Jewish 87–8 see also *kašrut*
Diogenes (Cynic) 73–5

Diogenes Laertius, *Lives of the Famous Philosophers* 73, 75
Dionysus, cult of 13, 112, 151
Dix, Dom Gregory 19–23, 25, 27, 30, 54, 151
docetists 203
Douglas, Mary 3, 6, 7, 8, 12, 78, 266, 275
Downing, F. Gerald 73, 263–4
Durkheim, Emile 3, 13

Ebionites 84, 94, 144–8, 159, 176, 252–3, 254
  see also *Gospel of the Ebionites*; Jewish-Christians
Ecclesiastical History (Eusebius) 149, 169
Egypt 40, 105
Egyptian Church Order, see *'Apostolic Tradition'*
Elbogen, Ismar 260
Elkesaites 170–2
Empedocles 71
Encratites 157, 160–2, 211, 212, 215, 252–3, 254, 262
Ephesus 155, 232
Ephraem (the Syrian) 98–100, 111
Epiphanius of Salamis 95–6, 146–8, 155, 158, 161–2, 164, 166, 171, 241–2
Epistle of Barnabas 107
Epistles of Heraclitus 76
Epistula Apostolorum 94
Epistula Clementis, see Pseudo-Clementines
Epistula Petri, see Pseudo-Clementines
Epistulae ad Virgines, see Pseudo-Clementines
eschatology 247–8
Essenes 56, 58–9, 79, 80–1, 151, 257
eucharist *passim*
  of bread alone 93, 115, 125, 177–8, 181–2, 189–90, 192, 194, 233–5, 245–6, 253
  of bread and water 22–3, 26, 31, 93, 115, 116–17, 125, 142, 143–278 *and passim*
  of bread and wine 66, 91–5, 104–5, 109–10, 128–9, 136, 143, 213–14, 252, 277
  with cheese 95–107
  eucharistia 245–7
  with fish 127–40
  with milk and honey 107–15
  with salt 118–25, 176–7
  theory of dual origins 25–7, 255
Eusebius 149, 158, 169–70

Eustathius, Eustathians 214–15
Excerpta ex Theodoto 116–17, 162–4
Eznik of Kolb 99, 139

fasting 4, 141–2, 165–6, 168, 186, 188, 191, 192, 210, 217
Felicitas 102, 103
figs 37, 38, 39, 75, 85–6, 126, 258
Fihrist of al-Nadim 171–2
Filastrius 95–6, 167, 211, 262–3
first-fruits 125–6
fish 41, 42–3, 63, 64, 75, 91, 99, 127–40, 166, 189
 pickle/sauce 37, 43
Flood 81
flour 75
 see also barley; bread; wheat
Foucault, Michel 68
Frazer, James 13
fruit 39, 83, 91, 125–7, 141, 214, 275
 see also individual names
Galatia 161
Galen 36, 79
ganeae, see cook-shops
Gangra, Synod of 214–15
garlic 40, 75, 126
gender, gender roles 8, 61–2, 72, 76, 103, 197, 198, 214–15, 232
Genesis Rabbah 82
gnostics 107–8, 162–4, 186, 232, 254
 see also Marcus; Theodotus; Valentinians
Goody, Jack 5, 7
Gospel of the Ebionites 147, 148–9, 241
'Gospel of the Hebrews' 146–7
 see also *Gospel of the Ebionites*
Gospel of Thomas 237–8
Gospels 46, 52, 58, 92, 94, 115–16, 127–30, 136, 138, 147, 148–9, 194, 195, 220, 240–5
 see also John, Gospel of; Luke, Gospel of; Mark, Gospel of; Matthew, Gospel of
grain dole 38
grapes 39, 77, 126
Gregory of Tours 189–90, 196
guilds, see *collegia*

haburah 25, 52, 54–6
 see also *collegia*
Harnack, Adolf von 151–3, 159, 241, 251–2, 270
Hebrews, Letter to the 220, 236

Hegesippus 149–50
Heraclitus (Ps-), see *Epistles of Heraclitus*
herbs 192, 268
 see also thyme, vegetables
Hermas, see *Shepherd*
Hiers, Richard 129–30
Hippo, Council of (393) 89, 111
Hippolytus of Rome, 25, 96, 145, 155, 160, 167, 171, 234, 262
 see also *'Apostolic Tradition'*; *Canons of Hippolytus*
Hoffman, Lawrence A. 15
Holy Week 217
Homilies, Pseudo-Clementine
 see Pseudo-Clementines
honey 65, 89, 91, 98, 126, 136, 156; see *also* milk
honey-cake 128
Hydroparastatai 160–2, 211–12
hyssop 79

Iamblichus 180
Ignatius of Antioch 93, 117, 203, 255
 Letter to the Smyrnaeans 203
institution narrative 205–6, 240–5
 see also Last Supper
Irenaeus 21, 92, 144–6, 155, 157, 160, 169, 202–3
Isauria 161

James the Just 149–50
Jay, Nancy 61, 76, 276
Jerome 111, 156, 216
Jesus 11, 18, 21, 23, 25, 29, 30, 59, 92, 121, 128, 130, 131, 139, 141, 145, 148, 151, 152, 157, 160, 177, 192, 205, 213, 220–1, 233, 262
 vow of abstinence from wine 157, 206, 234, 241, 242, 248
 see also Gospels; Last Supper
Jewish-Christians 84, 94, 144–51, 158–60, 170–1, 180
Jews, *see* Judaism
John, Gospel of 128, 129–30, 188, 220, 236–7
John, Revelation to 237
John the Baptist 149, 156, 258
John Chrysostom 211
John the Deacon 123
John the Evangelist, *see Acts of John*; John, Gospel of; John, Revelation to
Joseph and Aseneth 112
Josephus 58, 85

Joshua ben Hananiah 83
Journeyings of Peter 146
Judaism 201
    asceticism 79–87, 225, 227–9, 257–61
    liturgy 15
    meals 52–60, 90, 137, 140, 260
    mysticism 235
    Sabbath 137, 140, 200, 235, 260
    see also Jewish-Christians; *kašrut*;
        Temple, Jerusalem
Jude, Letter of 30
Jungmann, Josef 24, 29
Justin Martyr 21, 93, 118, 151–5, 157–60,
    180, 199, 213, 242–4, 252–3, 273–4

kašrut 79, 80, 145–51, 228, 257–61
Kennedy, Charles 129–30
Kerygmata Petrou 120
kosher, see *kašrut*

Last Supper 11, 18, 21, 23, 29, 30, 46,
    52, 54, 58, 59, 90, 91, 121, 128, 157,
    177, 190, 207, 210, 234, 239, 240–5,
    252, 273
legumes (beans, lentils, pulse) 37, 38, 40
lentils, *see* legumes
Leo the Great 172
Letter, see *Epistle*
Letter to Diognetus 264
Letter of Ptolemy to Flora 163
Lévi-Strauss, Claude 3, 5, 6
Leviathan 137
Licinia Amias 131
Lietzmann, Hans 25–7, 30, 54, 233–4,
    245–6, 249, 251–2, 255, 270
Lieu, Samuel 172
locusts 148, 156, 241
love-feast, see *agape*
Lucian 43, 44, 75, 143, 264
Luke, Gospel of; Luke-Acts 127, 220,
    233–5, 241, 245–6

Mani 171–2
Manichaeism 171–2, 214
Manual of Discipline (1QS) 81
Marcion, Marcionites 97–100, 106, 109,
    111, 113, 114, 139, 155, 158, 164–7,
    169, 200, 210, 212, 233, 241–2, 252–
    3, 254
Marcus (Gnostic) 92
Mariamne 122
Mark, Gospel of 58, 130, 157
marriage 156–7, 161, 233

Martha 122
Martyrdom of Montanus and Lucius 103–4
Martyrdom of Perpetua and Felicitas 100–
    3, 186, 273
Matthew, Gospel of 58, 144, 147, 157,
    205
Mauss, Marcel 13
meat 41–2, 60–4, 77, 81, 82, 86, 216,
    221–31
    avoidance/prohibition 69–79, 83, 85,
    86, 97, 99, 116, 122, 139, 140, 143,
    146–8, 149–50, 160, 166, 171, 173–4,
    175, 179–81, 184, 235, 237, 257, 259,
    261, 275
    see also sacrifice
medicine 117, 231–2
Meeks, Wayne A. 31
Mekilta 86
Messalians 214–15
metempsychosis, *see* transmigration of
    souls
Midrash on Psalms 83
    see also *Genesis Rabbah*
milk 43–4, 65, 89, 91, 97–9, 100, 106,
    140, 189, 275
    and honey 98–101, 107–15, 141, 156,
    164
Mishna 36, 53, 59
    'Aboda Zara 86, 258
    Berakot 53, 54
Mithras, cult of 13, 88, 112, 114, 152, 243
monasticism 68, 190, 215–17
Monica 135
Montanists 95–98, 101–2, 105, 113, 140,
    164–9, 170, 200, 209–10, 212, 252–3,
    254, 262, 262
myrrh 189

Nasareans 148
nazirite vow, nazirites 83, 149–50, 165,
    167, 257, 269
Neo-Pythagoreans 76–7, 265–7
Nero 85
Noah, covenant with 82, 97, 148, 180–1,
    205
nuts 85–6, 258

oil 37, 38, 40, 65, 83, 91, 104–5, 115–17,
    126, 140, 162, 164, 171, 191, 253,
    275
olives 37, 39–40, 104–6, 125, 126, 179
onions 40, 126
    see also vegetables

Origen 94, 145–6, 167
Orphism 69
'Osseans' 170–1

Palestine 36, 39, 42, 44, 144, 168, 201, 260
Pamphylia 161
Papias 92
Passover 30, 52–4, 82–3, 92, 94, 145, 148, 150, 241
Pastoral Epistles 233, 239
  see also Paul
Paul 11, 18, 20, 25, 30, 59, 66, 131, 213, 219, 223–4, 228–30, 232, 233, 258, 273, 277
  Colossians 220, 235, 237
  Romans 226–31
  1 Corinthians 18, 51, 66–7, 68–9, 92, 207, 221–6, 240
  1 Timothy 220, 231–3, 239
  see also *Acts of Paul*
Pectorius 131
Pentateuch, *see* Torah
Pepuzians 95, 167
  see also Artotyritai, Montanists
Peregrinus Proteus 143, 264
Perpetua 100–3, 108, 207
Persephone 134
pērushim 83–4, 85, 151, 247–8, 258–9
Peter the apostle 118, 176–80
  see also *Acts of Peter*
Pharisees 84
  see also *pērushim*
Philip 122
Philo of Alexandria 56–7, 69, 79, 120, 144, 257
philosophy, Graeco-Roman 69–79
  see also Cynics; Pythagoreans
Philostratus 77
Phrygia 161, 168, 169, 170, 255
  'burnt' 161
Pionius of Smyrna 199–204, 206, 207, 209, 254, 273
Pisidia 161
Pliny the Elder, *Natural History* 36, 41
Pliny the Younger 268
Plotinus 71
Plutarch 41, 42, 45, 71, 137, 266
Pluto 134
Polycarp 199–200, 202, 233
popinae, *see* cook-shops
Porphyry 71, 76, 77, 180, 222, 265, 266
poverty 267–70

'Praedestinatus' 95
Priscillian of Avila, Priscillianists 214
Priscillians (Montanist group) 95, 167
  see also Artotyritai; Montanists
Pseudo-Clementines 118–25, 140–1, 146–7, 175–83, 195–8, 199, 200, 210–11, 235, 246, 253, 266, 267, 275
  Epistulae ad Virgines 183
pulse, *see* legumes
Pythagoras 69–70, 78
Pythagoreans 69–71, 73, 77, 78, 116, 165, 225, 257, 261, 265–7, 271
  see also Neo-Pythagoreans

qidduš 52, 56, 260
Quintillians 95, 167
  see also Artotyritai; Montanists
Qumran 52, 56, 58–9, 81, 151, 257

Rambaux, Claude 265
Rechabites 83, 86, 151, 257
Recognitions, see Pseudo-Clementines
refrigerium 133, 135–6, 188
'Renouncers', *see* Apostolics
Revelation to John, *see* John, Revelation to
Roman Christians 66
Rome, Romans 35, 36, 38, 39, 41, 42, 44–5, 48, 49, 54, 66, 85–6, 105, 123, 124, 132–4, 144, 154, 159, 161, 171, 175, 188, 226–31, 257

Sabbath, *see* Judaism
sacrifice 60–7, 69–73, 188, 190–1, 207–8, 213, 236
  criticism/avoidance of 70–9, 103, 139, 148–50, 154, 179–81, 187, 190–1, 197, 241, 249–50, 272–4, 276, 277
  cuisine of 34, 60–7, 77, 84, 98–9, 138, 141, 150, 182, 191, 193, 201–2, 226, 228, 238, 267, 272–4 *and passim*
Sadducees 84
salt 37, 40–1, 79, 80, 91, 115, 116, 118–25, 140, 141, 171, 176, 178, 179, 191, 192, 215, 217, 253, 268, 275
Sampseans 171
Samson 149
Samuel 149
Saragossa, Council of (380) 214
Sarapion, liturgy of 25
Saturninus 155, 158, 159
Seder, *see* Passover
Seneca 266
'seven kinds' 126

Severus 158–9
sexuality, sexual abstinence 3–4, 97, 160–
    1, 183, 184, 186, 187, 188, 190, 193,
    194, 196–7, 216, 233, 262, 269
Shepherd of Hermas 264
sigma tables 132
Simon Magus 180, 188
spices 189
Strecker, Georg 119–20, 121
'strong' 66, 221–31
Structuralism 5, 8
symposium 46, 48, 50–1, 57, 58, 69, 110
Syria, Syrians 35, 105, 111, 144, 154–5,
    158–62, 163–4, 168–9, 171, 173, 183,
    196, 198, 199, 216, 233, 254–5

Talmud 82, 83, 84, 259
Targums 82
Tatian 155–60, 161, 165, 172, 182, 200,
    210, 233, 242, 248, 252–3, 258
'Tatianites' 161
Temple, Jerusalem 80, 82–4, 148–50, 237
Tertullian 21, 93, 99, 100, 101, 102, 109,
    136, 139, 145, 155, 164–9, 182, 203,
    209–10, 213, 216, 241, 265
    Against Marcion 165, 241
    Apology 164
    De Ieiunio contra Psychicos 165
Theissen, Gerd 65–6, 221–6
Theodoret 156, 161, 167–8, 211, 216
    History of the Monks in Syria 216
Theodotus 116–17, 162–4, 252–3
Theophrastus 65, 71
Therapeutae 56–7, 79–80, 144, 151, 257
thyme 75
    see also herbs; vegetables
time of day 208–9
Timothy of Constantinople 97–8, 99, 106
tiroš 81
    see also wine
todah 52, 56

Torah 120, 144, 145, 257
Tosefta 83
Trajan 268
transmigration of souls 69–70

Valentinians 92, 116–7, 157, 162–4
    see also gnostics; Marcus; Theodotus
Varro, M. Terentius 41, 42
vegetables 38, 40, 75, 91, 106, 115, 116,
    122, 125–17, 140, 179, 185, 190, 216–
    7, 253, 258, 268, 275
    see also individual names
Vibia 134
Vienne and Lyons, martyrs of 169–70
vinegar 37, 44, 86, 192
    see also wine
Vogel, Cyrille 128–9

water 44, 64–5, 75, 79, 80, 83, 109–10,
    115, 142, 164, 171, 179, 188, 191,
    215–17, 231–3, 236, 252–4, 255, 258,
    268
'weak' 65, 221–31
wheat 37, 38, 126
    see also bread, grain dole
widows 184, 196
wine 37, 44–5, 51, 53–4, 75, 81, 86, 92–3,
    104, 105, 106, 109, 110, 111, 132,
    152–3, 189, 216, 233–4, 268
    avoidance/prohibition 75–6, 77, 83, 85,
    86, 98, 116, 122, 139, 149, 156, 158–
    9, 162, 166, 172, 173–4, 179–81, 184,
    226–31, 231–3, 235, 257, 261, 275
    and sacrifice 64–5, 66, 77
words of institution, *see* institution narrat-
    ive

zebaḥ todah, see *todah*
Zoroastrianism 172
Zuchschwerdt, Ernst 150